Contents

Student Edition Answers

Workbook Answers

Math in Focus
Student Edition Answers
Grade 1

1 Numbers to 10

One, two, three, four,
Hear the mighty ocean roar!
Five, six, seven, eight,
Time to play, so don't be late!
What's next? Nine and ten.
Let's start all over again!

Lesson 1 Counting to 10
Lesson 2 Comparing Numbers
Lesson 3 Making Number Patterns

BIG IDEA Count and compare numbers to 10.

1

Recall Prior Knowledge

Counting

The toys are matched to show the same number.

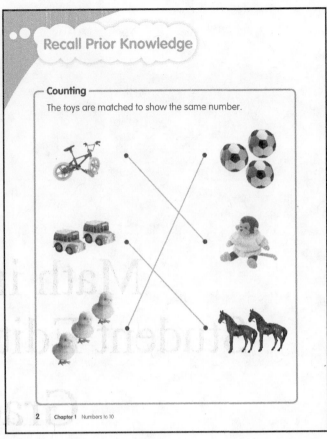

2   Chapter 1   Numbers to 10

✔ Quick Check

Match the ▲ to the ⬭ to show the same number.

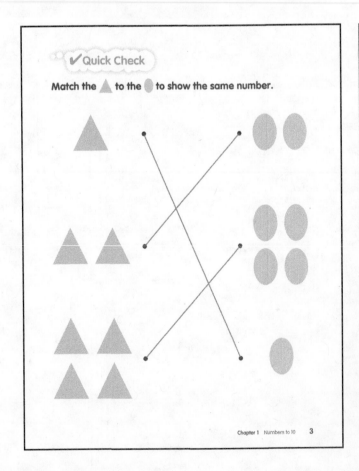

Chapter 1   Numbers to 10   3

LESSON 1 Counting to 10

Lesson Objectives
- Count from 0 to 10 objects.
- Read and write 0–10 in numbers and words.

Vocabulary

zero	one	two
three	four	five
six	seven	eight
nine	ten	

Learn Point with your finger and count.

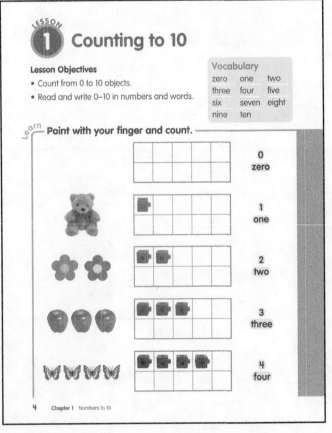

4   Chapter 1   Numbers to 10

Student Edition Answers: Chapter 1
Math in Focus Homeschool Answer Key, Grade 1

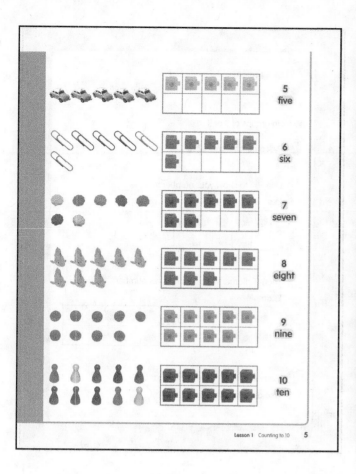

5 five
6 six
7 seven
8 eight
9 nine
10 ten

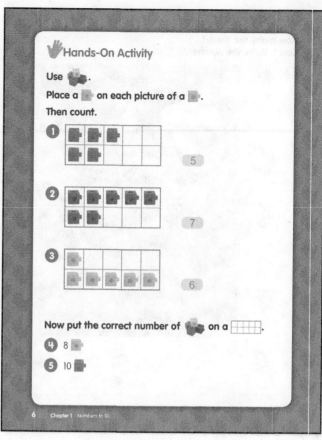

Hands-On Activity

Use 🚗.

Place a 🟦 on each picture of a 🚗.

Then count.

1   5

2   7

3   6

Now put the correct number of 🧊 on a ▭▭▭▭.

4 8 🟦

5 10 🟦

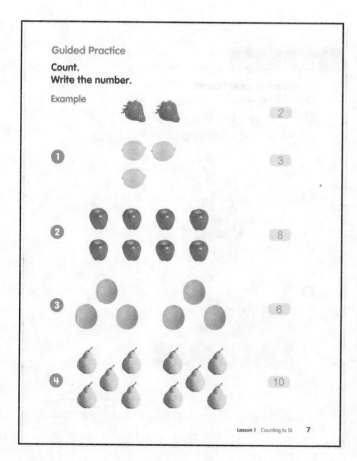

Guided Practice

Count.
Write the number.

Example   2

1   3

2   8

3   6

4   10

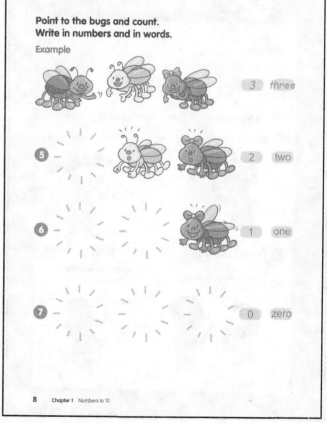

Point to the bugs and count.
Write in numbers and in words.

Example

3 three

5   2 two

6   1 one

7   0 zero

3

How many are there?
Count. Write the number.

8 🍄 0
❀ 10
🐰 3
🐝 6

🧚 5   🦆 2   🐢 4   🦋 7

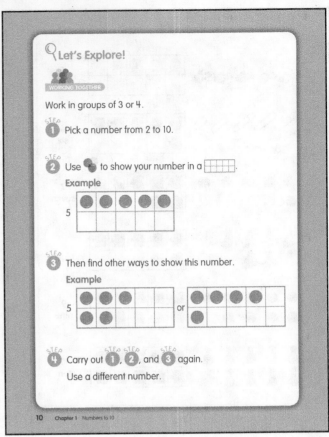

🔍 **Let's Explore!**

WORKING TOGETHER

Work in groups of 3 or 4.

1 Pick a number from 2 to 10.

2 Use ● to show your number in a ▭▭▭▭▭.
Example
5

3 Then find other ways to show this number.
Example
5   or

4 Carry out 1, 2, and 3 again.
Use a different number.

WORKING TOGETHER Game

Land on 10!

Players: 3

How to play: Use only 1, 2, or 3 fingers to count.

1 Player 1 starts counting from 1.   2 Player 2 counts on.

1, 2   3, 4, 5

3 Player 3 counts on.

End
The player who lands on 10 wins!

6, 7, 8, 9
Oops! 6, 7, 8

9, 10.
I win!

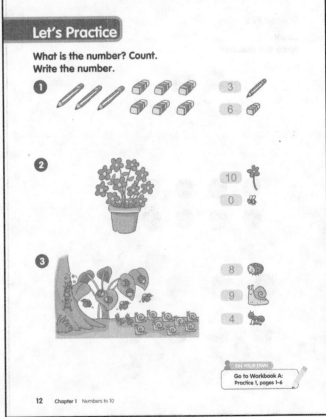

Let's Practice

What is the number? Count.
Write the number.

1 ✏️✏️✏️ 🟦🟦🟦
🟦🟦🟦   3 ✏️
                6 🟦

2   🌼(flower pot)   10 🌸
                            0 🐝

3   (plant with snails)   8 🐛
                                9 🐌
                                4 🐜

ON YOUR OWN
Go to Workbook A:
Practice 1, pages 1–6

4

Student Edition Answers: Chapter 1
Math in Focus Homeschool Answer Key, Grade 1

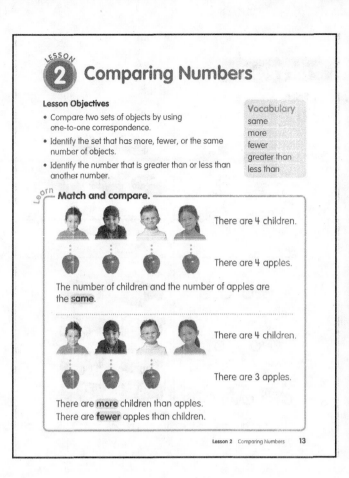

LESSON 2 Comparing Numbers

Lesson Objectives

- Compare two sets of objects by using one-to-one correspondence.
- Identify the set that has more, fewer, or the same number of objects.
- Identify the number that is greater than or less than another number.

Vocabulary
same
more
fewer
greater than
less than

Learn Match and compare.

There are 4 children.

There are 4 apples.

The number of children and the number of apples are the **same**.

There are 4 children.

There are 3 apples.

There are **more** children than apples.
There are **fewer** apples than children.

Lesson 2 Comparing Numbers **13**

✋ **Hands-On Activity**

Use a copy of these socks and shoes.

STEP 1 Cut the 👟 and 🧦 out.

STEP 2 Use two ▭▭▭▭▭.
Paste all the 👟 in one ▭▭▭▭▭.
Paste all the 🧦 in the other ▭▭▭▭▭.

STEP 3 Match and compare the number of 👟 and 🧦.
Write **more** or **fewer**.
There are more 🧦 than 👟.
There are fewer 👟 than 🧦.

STEP 4 Carry out STEP 1, STEP 2, and STEP 3 again.
Use a different number of 👟 and 🧦.

14 Chapter 1 Numbers to 10

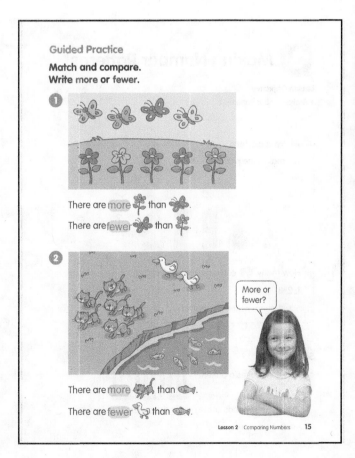

Guided Practice

Match and compare.
Write **more** or **fewer**.

1

There are more 🌸 than 🦋.
There are fewer 🦋 than 🌸.

2

More or fewer?

There are more 🐱 than 🐟.
There are fewer 🦆 than 🐟.

Lesson 2 Comparing Numbers **15**

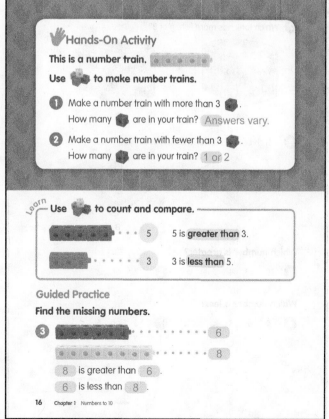

✋ **Hands-On Activity**

This is a number train.
Use 🧊 **to make number trains.**

1 Make a number train with more than 3 🔷.
How many 🔷 are in your train? Answers vary.

2 Make a number train with fewer than 3 🔷.
How many 🔷 are in your train? 1 or 2

Learn Use 🧊 **to count and compare.**

5 · · · · 5 is **greater than** 3.

3 · · · · 3 is **less than** 5.

Guided Practice

Find the missing numbers.

3

· · · · 6

· · · · 8

8 is greater than 6.

6 is less than 8.

16 Chapter 1 Numbers to 10

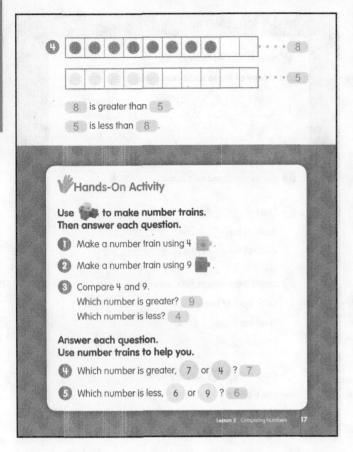

8 is greater than 5.

5 is less than 8.

✋ **Hands-On Activity**

Use 🧊 to make number trains.
Then answer each question.

1. Make a number train using 4 🧊.

2. Make a number train using 9 🧊.

3. Compare 4 and 9.
   Which number is greater? 9
   Which number is less? 4

Answer each question.
Use number trains to help you.

4. Which number is greater, 7 or 4 ? 7

5. Which number is less, 6 or 9 ? 6

Lesson 2 Comparing Numbers   17

Solve.

1. Point to the two groups that show the same number.

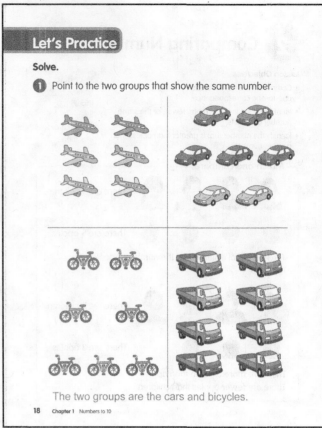

The two groups are the cars and bicycles.

18   Chapter 1 Numbers to 10

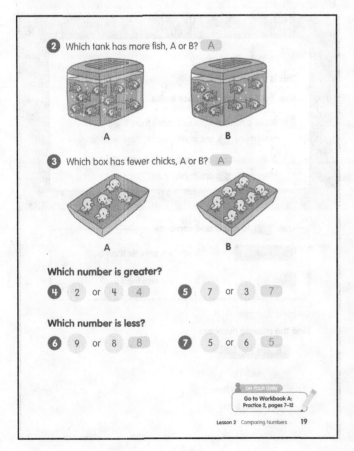

2. Which tank has more fish, A or B? A

3. Which box has fewer chicks, A or B? A

Which number is greater?

4. 2 or 4 4   5. 7 or 3 7

Which number is less?

6. 9 or 8 8   7. 5 or 6 5

ON YOUR OWN
Go to Workbook A:
Practice 2, pages 7–12

Lesson 2 Comparing Numbers   19

LESSON

3 Making Number Patterns

Lesson Objective
• Make number patterns.

Vocabulary
pattern
more than
less than

Learn **Make a pattern.**

Joe makes the **pattern** below using 🧊.

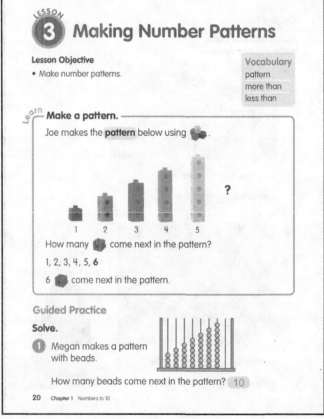

How many 🧊 come next in the pattern?

1, 2, 3, 4, 5, **6**

6 🧊 come next in the pattern.

Guided Practice

Solve.

1. Megan makes a pattern
   with beads.

   How many beads come next in the pattern? 10

20   Chapter 1 Numbers to 10

---

2 John makes a pattern.

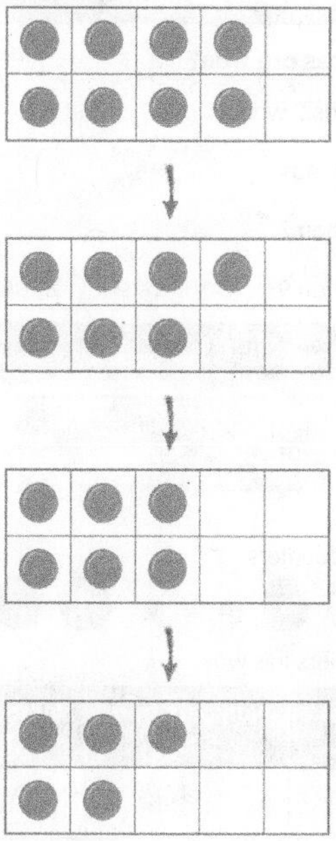

How many ● are there in the next ▭? 4

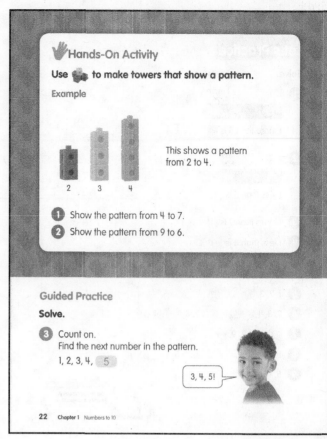

Hands-On Activity

Use [cubes] to make towers that show a pattern.

Example

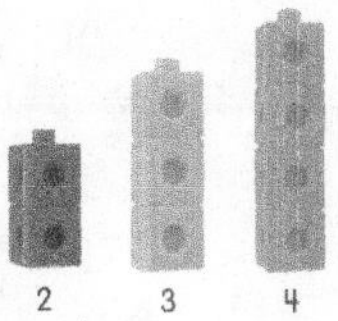

This shows a pattern from 2 to 4.

1 Show the pattern from 4 to 7.

2 Show the pattern from 9 to 6.

Guided Practice

Solve.

3 Count on.
Find the next number in the pattern.
1, 2, 3, 4, 5

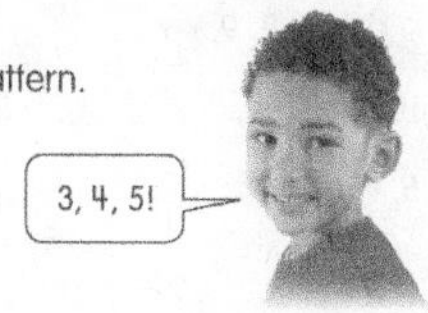

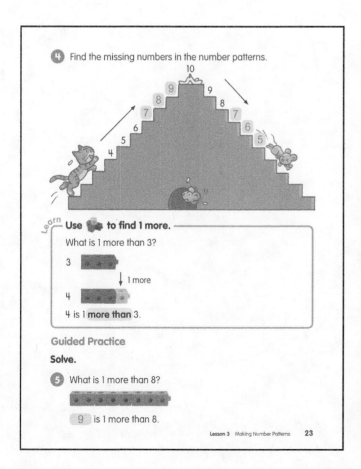

4 Find the missing numbers in the number patterns.

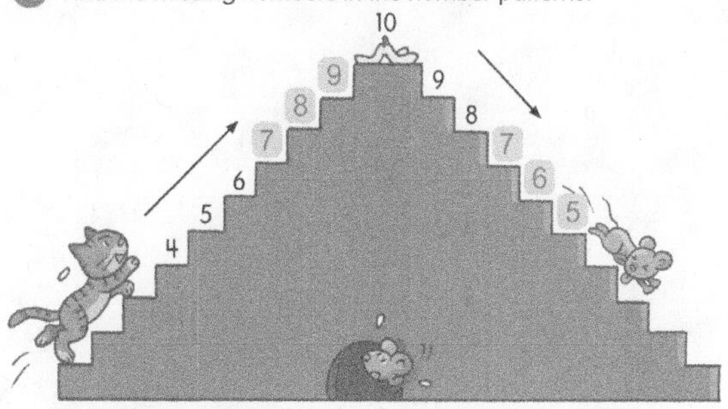

Learn **Use [cubes] to find 1 more.**

What is 1 more than 3?

3

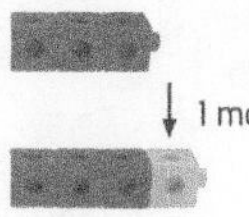

1 more

4

4 is 1 **more than** 3.

Guided Practice

Solve.

5 What is 1 more than 8?

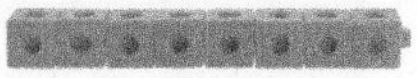

9 is 1 more than 8.

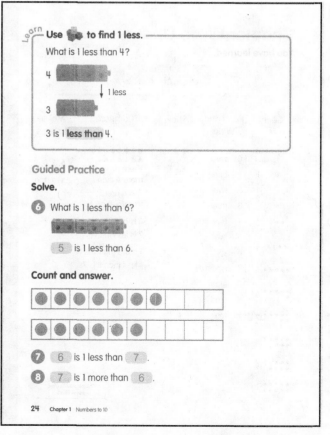

Learn **Use [cubes] to find 1 less.**

What is 1 less than 4?

4

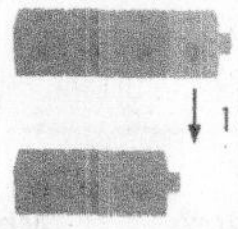

1 less

3

3 is 1 **less than** 4.

Guided Practice

Solve.

6 What is 1 less than 6?

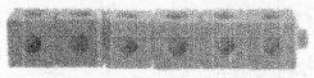

5 is 1 less than 6.

Count and answer.

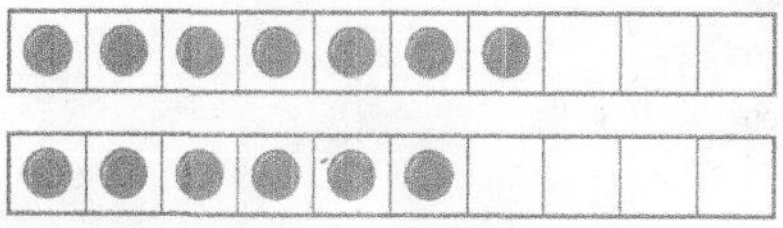

7 6 is 1 less than 7.

8 7 is 1 more than 6.

Let's Practice

Solve.

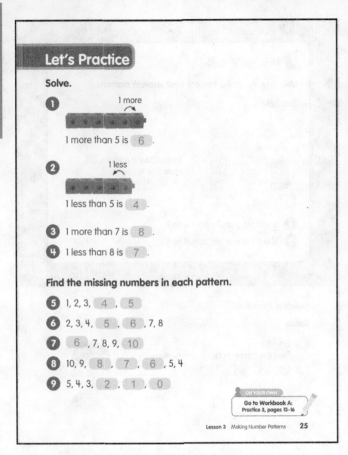

1 more than 5 is (6).

1 less than 5 is (4).

3 1 more than 7 is (8).

4 1 less than 8 is (7).

Find the missing numbers in each pattern.

5 1, 2, 3, (4), (5)

6 2, 3, 4, (5), (6), 7, 8

7 (6), 7, 8, 9, (10)

8 10, 9, (8), (7), (6), 5, 4

9 5, 4, 3, (2), (1), (0)

ON YOUR OWN
Go to Workbook A:
Practice 3, pages 13–16

Lesson 3   Making Number Patterns   **25**

READING AND WRITING MATH
Math Journal

Which sentences are true?

1 A bicycle has 2 wheels.

2 A cat has 4 legs.

3 5 is more than 7.

4 8 is 1 less than 9.   Sentences 1, 2, and 4 are true.

CRITICAL THINKING SKILLS
Put On Your Thinking Cap!

PROBLEM SOLVING
Here are some counters.

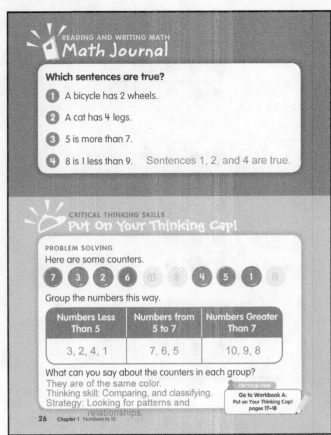

Group the numbers this way.

Numbers Less Than 5	Numbers from 5 to 7	Numbers Greater Than 7
3, 2, 4, 1	7, 6, 5	10, 9, 8

What can you say about the counters in each group?
They are of the same color.
Thinking skill: Comparing, and classifying.
Strategy: Looking for patterns and relationships.

ON YOUR OWN
Go to Workbook A:
Put on Your Thinking Cap!
pages 17–18

26   Chapter 1   Numbers to 10

Chapter Wrap Up

BIG IDEA
Count and compare numbers to 10.

You have learned...

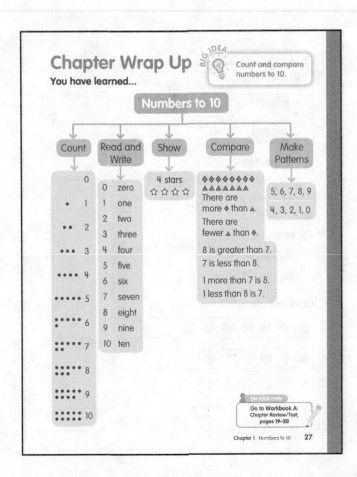

Numbers to 10

Count | Read and Write | Show | Compare | Make Patterns

Count:
0
• 1
•• 2
••• 3
•••• 4
••••• 5
•••••• 6
••• •••• 7
•••• •••• 8
••••• •••• 9
••••• ••••• 10

Read and Write:
0 zero
1 one
2 two
3 three
4 four
5 five
6 six
7 seven
8 eight
9 nine
10 ten

Show:
4 stars
◇◇◇◇

Compare:
◆◆◆◆◆◆◆
▲▲▲▲▲▲
There are more ◆ than ▲.
There are fewer ▲ than ◆.

8 is greater than 7.
7 is less than 8.

1 more than 7 is 8.
1 less than 8 is 7.

Make Patterns:
5, 6, 7, 8, 9
4, 3, 2, 1, 0

ON YOUR OWN
Go to Workbook A:
Chapter Review/Test,
pages 19–20

Chapter 1   Numbers to 10   **27**

CHAPTER 2 Number Bonds

Kittens, kittens, cute little kittens,
How I love them so!
Seven on the inside,
Three on the outside,
Each dressed up in a bow!

How many kittens are there?

BIG IDEA Number bonds can be used to show parts and whole.

Lesson 1 Making Number Bonds

28

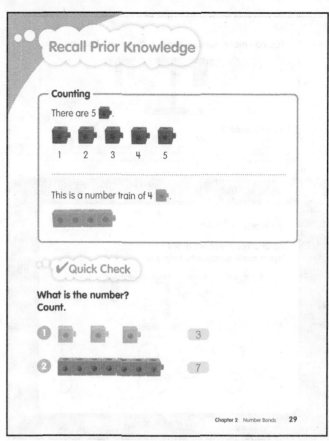

Recall Prior Knowledge

Counting

There are 5.

1 2 3 4 5

This is a number train of 4.

✔ Quick Check

What is the number?
Count.

1   3

2   7

Chapter 2 Number Bonds   29

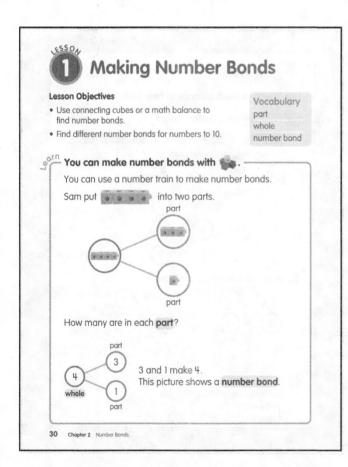

LESSON 1 Making Number Bonds

Lesson Objectives

- Use connecting cubes or a math balance to find number bonds.
- Find different number bonds for numbers to 10.

Vocabulary
part
whole
number bond

Learn You can make number bonds with 🟦.

You can use a number train to make number bonds.

Sam put 🟦🟦🟦🟦 into two parts.

part

part

How many are in each **part**?

part
4 — 3
whole — 1
part

3 and 1 make 4.
This picture shows a **number bond**.

30   Chapter 2 Number Bonds

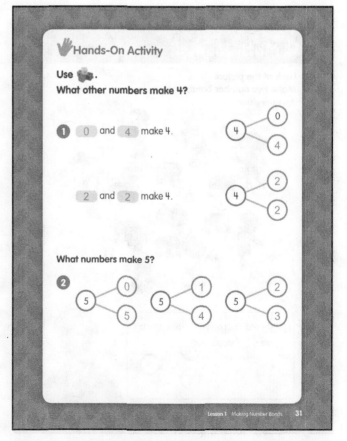

✋ Hands-On Activity

Use 🟦.
What other numbers make 4?

1   0 and 4 make 4.

4 — 0
4 — 4

2 and 2 make 4.

4 — 2
4 — 2

What numbers make 5?

2   5 — 0
5 — 5

5 — 1
5 — 4

5 — 2
5 — 3

Lesson 1 Making Number Bonds   31

9

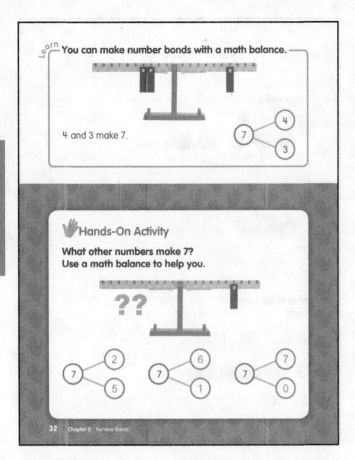

Learn **You can make number bonds with a math balance.**

4 and 3 make 7.

7 — 4
7 — 3

✋ **Hands-On Activity**

What other numbers make 7?
Use a math balance to help you.

??

7 — 2, 5
7 — 6, 1
7 — 7, 0

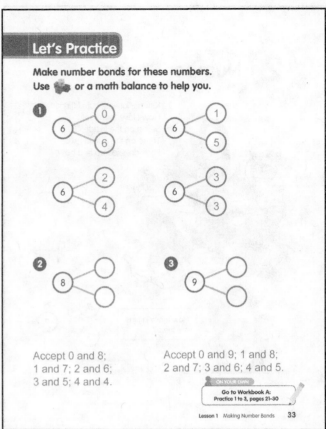

Let's Practice

Make number bonds for these numbers.
Use 🧩 or a math balance to help you.

1

6 — 0, 6
6 — 1, 5
6 — 2, 4
6 — 3, 3

2

8 — ◯, ◯

3

9 — ◯, ◯

Accept 0 and 8;
1 and 7; 2 and 6;
3 and 5; 4 and 4.

Accept 0 and 9; 1 and 8;
2 and 7; 3 and 6; 4 and 5.

ON YOUR OWN
Go to Workbook A:
Practice 1 to 3, pages 21–30

READING AND WRITING MATH
Math Journal

Look at the picture.
Make two number bonds.
Answers vary.

1 red stool and 5 blue stools
make 6 stools.

1 — 6
5 — 6

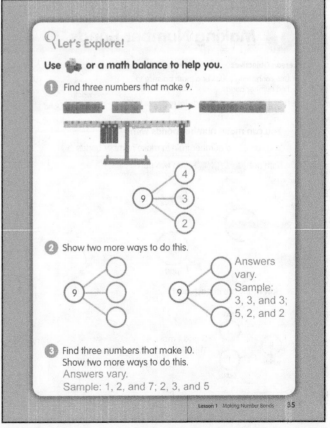

🔍 **Let's Explore!**

Use 🧩 or a math balance to help you.

1 Find three numbers that make 9.

9 — 4, 3, 2

2 Show two more ways to do this.

9 — ◯, ◯, ◯

9 — ◯, ◯, ◯ Answers
vary.
Sample:
3, 3, and 3;
5, 2, and 2

3 Find three numbers that make 10.
Show two more ways to do this.
Answers vary.
Sample: 1, 2, and 7; 2, 3, and 5

10

Let's Explore!

Use 🔲.

1 Put some 🔲 and 🔳 together to make a number train.
Now add some 🔳 to your number train.
Make sure your number train has 10 or less 🔲.

2 Count the total number of 🔲 and 🔳. Answers vary.
Count the number of 🔳. Answers vary.
Add the total number of 🔲 and 🔳 to the number of 🔳.
What number do you get? Answers vary.

3 Count the total number of 🔳 and 🔳. Answers vary.
Count the number of 🔲. Answers vary.
Add the number of 🔲 to the total number of 🔳 and 🔳.
What number do you get? Answers vary.

Did you get the same number for **2** and **3**? Yes.
Choose different numbers of 🔲, 🔳, and 🔳.
Carry out **1**, **2**, and **3** again.
What do you notice?
The number I get in **3** is always the same as what I get in **2**.

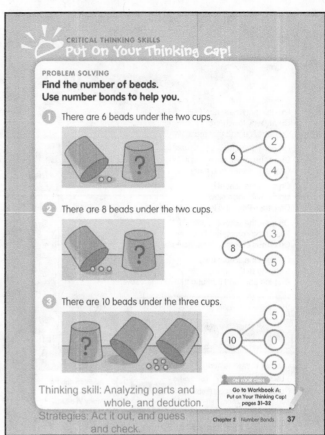

CRITICAL THINKING SKILLS
Put On Your Thinking Cap!

PROBLEM SOLVING
Find the number of beads.
Use number bonds to help you.

1 There are 6 beads under the two cups.

2 There are 8 beads under the two cups.

3 There are 10 beads under the three cups.

Thinking skill: Analyzing parts and whole, and deduction.
Strategies: Act it out, and guess and check.

ON YOUR OWN
Go to Workbook A:
Put on Your Thinking Cap!
pages 31–32

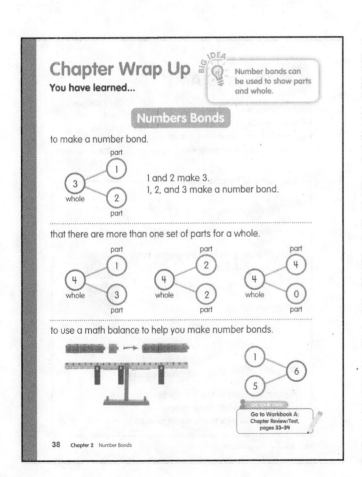

Chapter Wrap Up

BIG IDEA Number bonds can be used to show parts and whole.

You have learned...

Numbers Bonds

to make a number bond.

1 and 2 make 3.
1, 2, and 3 make a number bond.

that there are more than one set of parts for a whole.

to use a math balance to help you make number bonds.

ON YOUR OWN
Go to Workbook A:
Chapter Review/Test,
pages 33–34

3 Addition Facts to 10

I'm riding on the school bus,
On my way to school,
On hops Lou and that makes two.

On goes the school bus,
Down the street, not too fast,
On leaps Sheree and that makes three!

On goes the school bus,
Up the hill, oh so slow!
On jumps Paul and then there are four!

On goes the school bus,
Round the corner, hold on tight!
On climbs Clive and then there are five!

On goes the school bus,
Stopping at the lights,
On plod Sam and Ben and that makes... seven!

Chapter 3

Lesson 1 Ways to Add
Lesson 2 Making Addition Stories
Lesson 3 Real-World Problems:
Addition

BIG IDEA
Addition can be
used to find how
many in all.

39

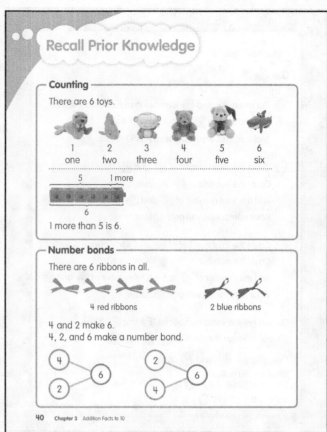

Recall Prior Knowledge

Counting

There are 6 toys.

| 1 | 2 | 3 | 4 | 5 | 6 |
| one | two | three | four | five | six |

5   1 more

6

1 more than 5 is 6.

Number bonds

There are 6 ribbons in all.

4 red ribbons   2 blue ribbons

4 and 2 make 6.
4, 2, and 6 make a number bond.

40   Chapter 3 Addition Facts to 10

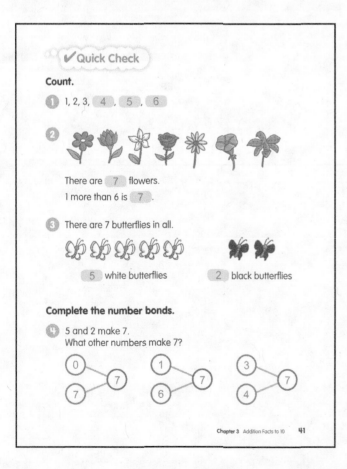

✔ Quick Check

Count.

① 1, 2, 3, 4 , 5 , 6

②

There are 7 flowers.
1 more than 6 is 7 .

③ There are 7 butterflies in all.

5 white butterflies   2 black butterflies

Complete the number bonds.

④ 5 and 2 make 7.
What other numbers make 7?

Chapter 3 Addition Facts to 10   41

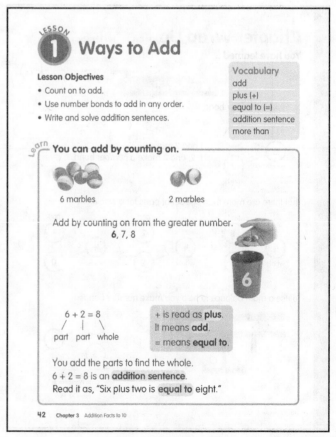

LESSON

1 Ways to Add

Lesson Objectives
• Count on to add.
• Use number bonds to add in any order.
• Write and solve addition sentences.

Vocabulary
add
plus (+)
equal to (=)
addition sentence
more than

Learn **You can add by counting on.**

6 marbles   2 marbles

Add by counting on from the greater number.
6, 7, 8

6

6 + 2 = 8
part part whole

+ is read as **plus**.
It means **add**.
= means **equal to**.

You add the parts to find the whole.
6 + 2 = 8 is an **addition sentence**.
Read it as, "Six plus two is **equal to** eight."

42   Chapter 3 Addition Facts to 10

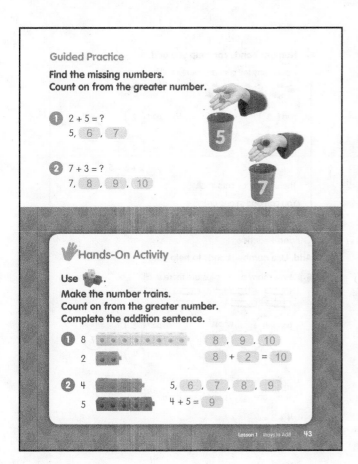

Guided Practice

Find the missing numbers.
Count on from the greater number.

1. $2 + 5 = ?$
   5, **6**, **7**

2. $7 + 3 = ?$
   7, **8**, **9**, **10**

✋ Hands-On Activity

Use 🧊.
Make the number trains.
Count on from the greater number.
Complete the addition sentence.

1. 8
   2
   8, **9**, **10**
   8 + 2 = **10**

2. 4
   5
   5, **6**, **7**, **8**, **9**
   $4 + 5 = $ **9**

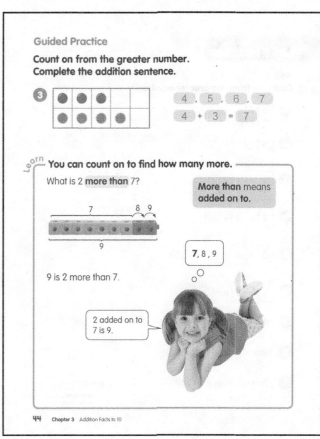

Guided Practice

Count on from the greater number.
Complete the addition sentence.

3. **4**, **5**, **6**, **7**
   4 + **3** = **7**

Learn — You can count on to find how many more.

What is 2 **more than** 7?

> **More than** means added on to.

7 → 8 9

9

9 is 2 more than 7.

7, 8, 9

2 added on to 7 is 9.

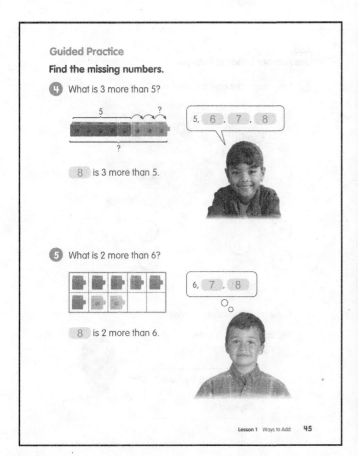

Guided Practice

Find the missing numbers.

4. What is 3 more than 5?

   5 → ? ?
   ?

   5, **6**, **7**, **8**

   8 is 3 more than 5.

5. What is 2 more than 6?

   6, **7**, **8**

   8 is 2 more than 6.

👥 WORKING TOGETHER Game

Card Fun!

How to play:

> Players: 3
> You need:
> • 2 packs of cards

STEP 1 Make two packs of cards.

Pack X: 1 2 3 0 / 1 2 3

Pack Y: 1 2 3 4 5 / 6 7

STEP 2 Player 1 picks a card from Pack X.

STEP 3 Player 2 picks a card from Pack Y.

STEP 4 Player 3 adds the numbers on the cards, then says the answer.

STEP 5 Players 1 and 2 check the answer.

$5 + 3 = 8$ Correct!

STEP 6 Player 3 gets one point if the answer is correct. Take turns to pick cards and add.

After six rounds, the player with the most points wins!

Let's Practice

Add.
Count on from the greater number.

1. $\boxed{4} + \boxed{2} = 6$

2. $\boxed{6} + \boxed{1} = 7$

3. $\boxed{2} + \boxed{3} = 5$

4. $\boxed{7} + \boxed{3} = 10$

5. $\boxed{3} + \boxed{5} = 8$

6. $\boxed{2} + \boxed{8} = 10$

7. What is 4 more than 5? 9

8. What is 3 more than 6? 9

9. What is 2 more than 7? 9

ON YOUR OWN
Go to Workbook A:
Practice 1, pages 41-44

Learn Number bonds can help you add.

How many toy cars are there in all?

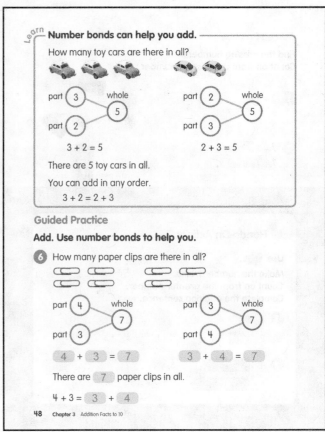

part 3 whole 5 part 2

3 + 2 = 5

part 2 whole 5 part 3

2 + 3 = 5

There are 5 toy cars in all.

You can add in any order.

3 + 2 = 2 + 3

Guided Practice

Add. Use number bonds to help you.

6. How many paper clips are there in all?

part 4 whole 7 part 3

$4 + 3 = 7$

part 3 whole 7 part 4

$3 + 4 = 7$

There are 7 paper clips in all.

$4 + 3 = \boxed{3} + \boxed{4}$

Learn Number bonds can help you add.

How many lemons are there in all?

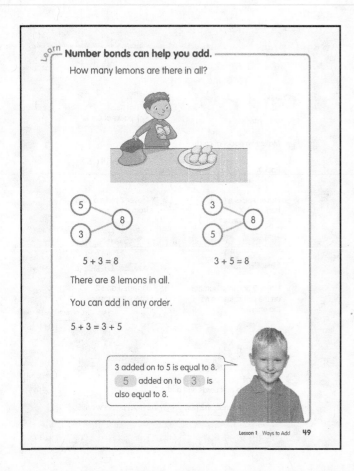

5 3 8

5 + 3 = 8

3 5 8

3 + 5 = 8

There are 8 lemons in all.

You can add in any order.

5 + 3 = 3 + 5

3 added on to 5 is equal to 8.
5 added on to 3 is also equal to 8.

Add.
Use number bonds to help you.

7. How many monkeys are there in all?

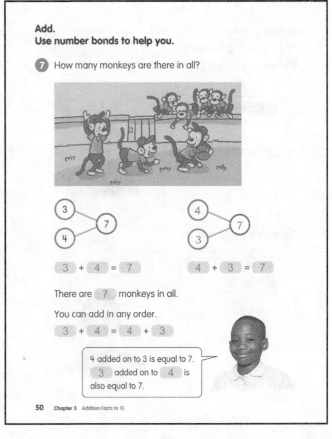

3 4 7

$3 + 4 = 7$

4 3 7

$4 + 3 = 7$

There are 7 monkeys in all.

You can add in any order.

$3 + 4 = 4 + 3$

4 added on to 3 is equal to 7.
3 added on to 4 is also equal to 7.

14

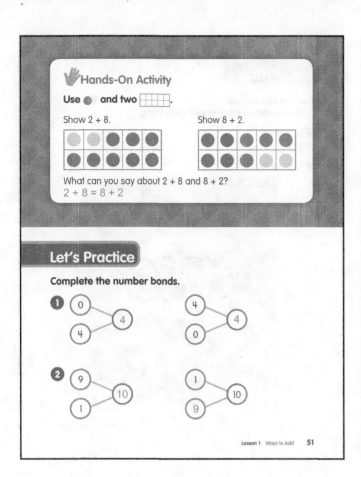

Hands-On Activity

Use ● and two ▭.

Show 2 + 8.

Show 8 + 2.

What can you say about 2 + 8 and 8 + 2?

2 + 8 = 8 + 2

Let's Practice

Complete the number bonds.

❶ 0, 4 → 4

4, 0 → 4

❷ 9, 1 → 10

1, 9 → 10

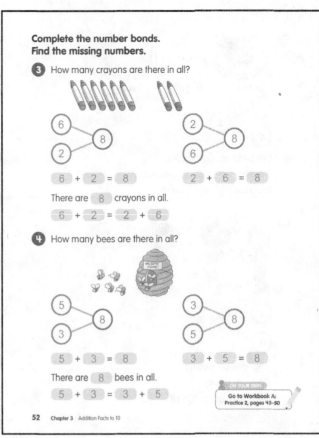

Complete the number bonds.
Find the missing numbers.

❸ How many crayons are there in all?

6, 2 → 8   2, 6 → 8

6 + 2 = 8   2 + 6 = 8

There are 8 crayons in all.

6 + 2 = 2 + 6

❹ How many bees are there in all?

5, 3 → 8   3, 5 → 8

5 + 3 = 8   3 + 5 = 8

There are 8 bees in all.

5 + 3 = 3 + 5

ON YOUR OWN
Go to Workbook A:
Practice 2, pages 45–50

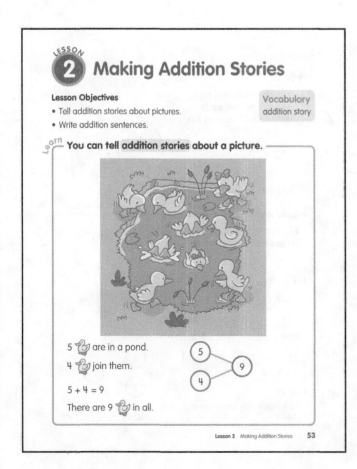

LESSON 2 Making Addition Stories

Lesson Objectives
- Tell addition stories about pictures.
- Write addition sentences.

Vocabulary
addition story

You can tell addition stories about a picture.

5 🐤 are in a pond.

4 🐤 join them.

5, 4 → 9

5 + 4 = 9

There are 9 🐤 in all.

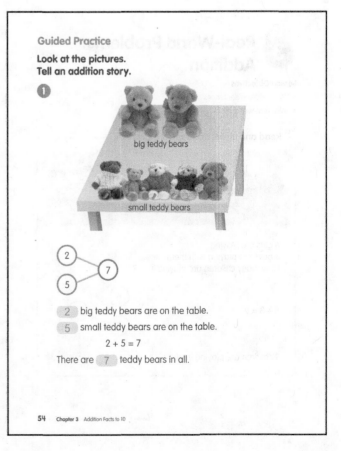

Guided Practice

Look at the pictures.
Tell an addition story.

❶

big teddy bears

small teddy bears

2, 5 → 7

2 big teddy bears are on the table.

5 small teddy bears are on the table.

2 + 5 = 7

There are 7 teddy bears in all.

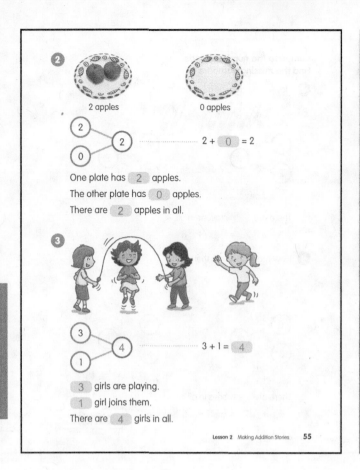

2

2 apples   0 apples

2
0 → 2   2 + 0 = 2

One plate has 2 apples.
The other plate has 0 apples.
There are 2 apples in all.

3

3
1 → 4   3 + 1 = 4

3 girls are playing.
1 girl joins them.
There are 4 girls in all.

Lesson 2   Making Addition Stories   55

Look at the picture.
Tell an addition story about each thing.

1 the birds
2 the bicycles   Answers vary.
3 the turtles

ON YOUR OWN
Go to Workbook A:
Practice 3, pages 51–54

56   Chapter 3   Addition Facts to 10

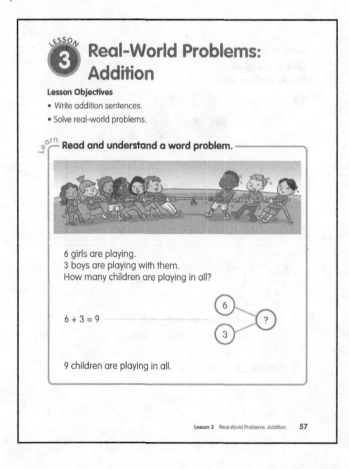

LESSON 3

Real-World Problems: Addition

Lesson Objectives
• Write addition sentences.
• Solve real-world problems.

Learn Read and understand a word problem.

6 girls are playing.
3 boys are playing with them.
How many children are playing in all?

6 + 3 = 9   6
3 → ?

9 children are playing in all.

Lesson 3   Real-World Problems: Addition   57

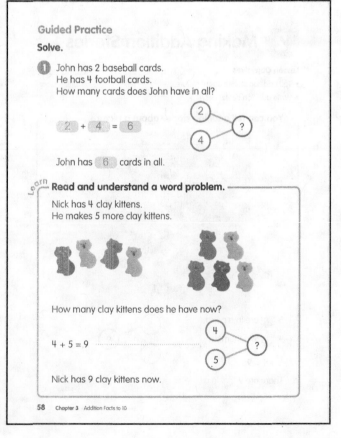

Guided Practice

Solve.

1 John has 2 baseball cards.
He has 4 football cards.
How many cards does John have in all?

2 + 4 = 6   2
4 → ?

John has 6 cards in all.

Learn Read and understand a word problem.

Nick has 4 clay kittens.
He makes 5 more clay kittens.

How many clay kittens does he have now?

4 + 5 = 9   4
5 → ?

Nick has 9 clay kittens now.

58   Chapter 3   Addition Facts to 10

Student Edition Answers: Chapter 3
Math in Focus Homeschool Answer Key, Grade 1

Guided Practice

Solve.

2

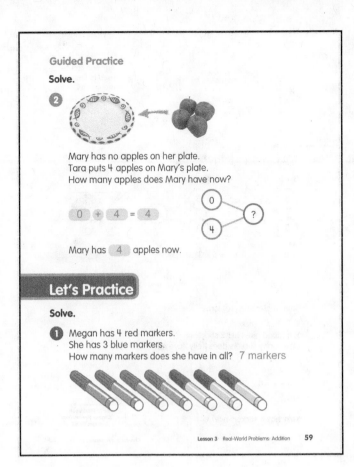

Mary has no apples on her plate.
Tara puts 4 apples on Mary's plate.
How many apples does Mary have now?

$$0 + 4 = 4$$

Mary has 4 apples now.

Let's Practice

Solve.

1 Megan has 4 red markers.
She has 3 blue markers.
How many markers does she have in all? 7 markers

2 2 children are dancing.
7 children join them.
How many children are dancing now? 9 children

3

Jar A   Jar B

Jar A has 5 marbles.
Jar B has 0 marbles.
How many marbles are there in all? 5 marbles

ON YOUR OWN
Go to Workbook A:
Practice 4, pages 55–56

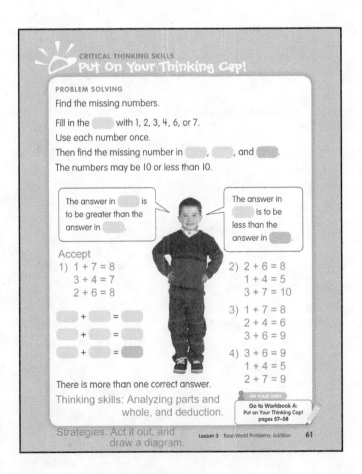

CRITICAL THINKING SKILLS
Put On Your Thinking Cap!

PROBLEM SOLVING

Find the missing numbers.

Fill in the ⬜ with 1, 2, 3, 4, 6, or 7.
Use each number once.
Then find the missing number in ⬜, ⬜, and ⬜.
The numbers may be 10 or less than 10.

The answer in ⬜ is to be greater than the answer in ⬜.

The answer in ⬜ is to be less than the answer in ⬜.

Accept
1) $1 + 7 = 8$
   $3 + 4 = 7$
   $2 + 6 = 8$

   ⬜ + ⬜ = ⬜
   ⬜ + ⬜ = ⬜
   ⬜ + ⬜ = ⬜

2) $2 + 6 = 8$
   $1 + 4 = 5$
   $3 + 7 = 10$

3) $1 + 7 = 8$
   $2 + 4 = 6$
   $3 + 6 = 9$

4) $3 + 6 = 9$
   $1 + 4 = 5$
   $2 + 7 = 9$

There is more than one correct answer.

Thinking skills: Analyzing parts and whole, and deduction.

Strategies: Act it out, and draw a diagram.

ON YOUR OWN
Go to Workbook A:
Put on Your Thinking Cap!
pages 57–58

Chapter Wrap Up

You have learned...

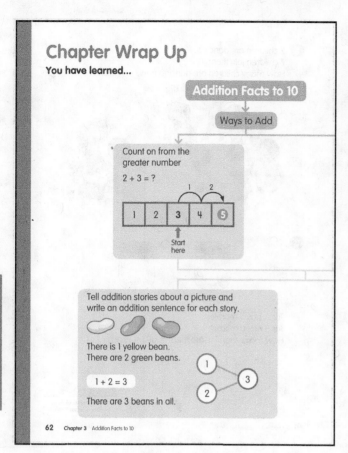

Addition Facts to 10

Ways to Add

Count on from the greater number

2 + 3 = ?

| 1 | 2 | 3 | 4 | 5 |

Start here

Tell addition stories about a picture and write an addition sentence for each story.

There is 1 yellow bean.
There are 2 green beans.

1 + 2 = 3

There are 3 beans in all.

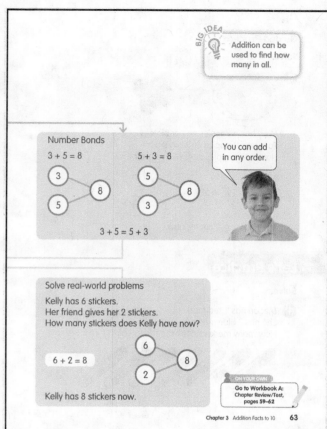

Number Bonds

3 + 5 = 8   5 + 3 = 8

3 + 5 = 5 + 3

You can add in any order.

Solve real-world problems

Kelly has 6 stickers.
Her friend gives her 2 stickers.
How many stickers does Kelly have now?

6 + 2 = 8

Kelly has 8 stickers now.

BIG IDEA
Addition can be used to find how many in all.

ON YOUR OWN
Go to Workbook A:
Chapter Review/Test,
pages 59–62

62   Chapter 3 Addition Facts to 10

Chapter 3 Addition Facts to 10   63

CHAPTER 4 Subtraction Facts to 10

Lesson 1 Ways to Subtract
Lesson 2 Making Subtraction Stories
Lesson 3 Real-World Problems: Subtraction
Lesson 4 Making Fact Families

BIG IDEA
Subtraction can be used to find how many are left.

64

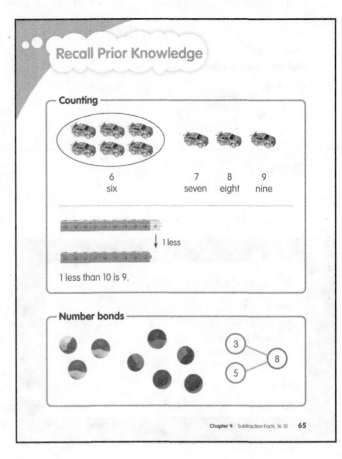

Counting

6 six   7 seven   8 eight   9 nine

↓ 1 less

1 less than 10 is 9.

Number bonds

3
8
5

Chapter 4   Subtraction Facts to 10   65

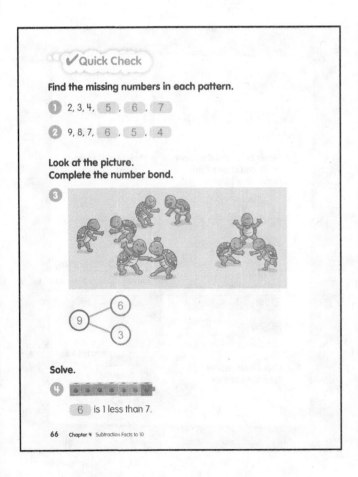

✔ **Quick Check**

Find the missing numbers in each pattern.

1 2, 3, 4, **5**, **6**, **7**

2 9, 8, 7, **6**, **5**, **4**

Look at the picture.
Complete the number bond.

3

9
6
3

Solve.

4 **6** is 1 less than 7.

66   Chapter 4   Subtraction Facts to 10

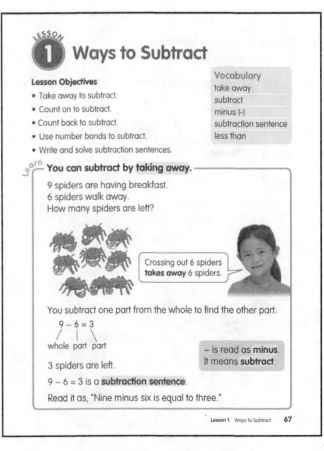

LESSON
1 Ways to Subtract

Lesson Objectives
- Take away to subtract.
- Count on to subtract.
- Count back to subtract.
- Use number bonds to subtract.
- Write and solve subtraction sentences.

Vocabulary
take away
subtract
minus (–)
subtraction sentence
less than

Learn **You can subtract by taking away.**

9 spiders are having breakfast.
6 spiders walk away.
How many spiders are left?

Crossing out 6 spiders **takes away** 6 spiders.

You subtract one part from the whole to find the other part.

9 – 6 = 3
whole part part

3 spiders are left.

9 – 6 = 3 is a **subtraction sentence**.

Read it as, "Nine minus six is equal to three."

– is read as **minus**. It means **subtract**.

Lesson 1   Ways to Subtract   67

Guided Practice

Find how many are left.

1

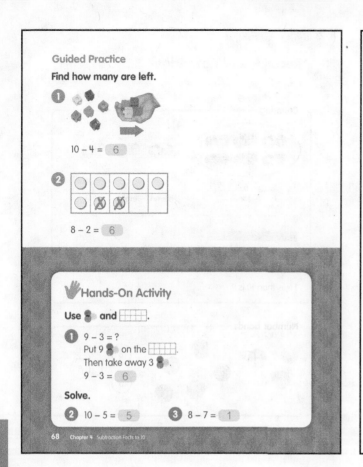

$10 - 4 = \boxed{6}$

2

○ ○ ○ ○ ○
○ ⊘ ⊘

$8 - 2 = \boxed{6}$

✋ Hands-On Activity

Use 🔵 **and** ▭ .

1 $9 - 3 = ?$
Put 9 🔵 on the ▭ .
Then take away 3 🔵 .
$9 - 3 = \boxed{6}$

Solve.

2 $10 - 5 = \boxed{5}$ **3** $8 - 7 = \boxed{1}$

Learn   You can take away to find how many less.

What is 2 less than 6?

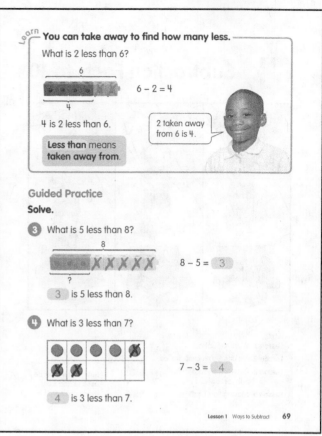

$6 - 2 = 4$

4 is 2 less than 6.

Less than means **taken away from.**

2 taken away from 6 is 4.

Guided Practice

Solve.

3 What is 5 less than 8?

8

[▭ X X X X X]

?

$8 - 5 = \boxed{3}$

$\boxed{3}$ is 5 less than 8.

4 What is 3 less than 7?

● ● ● ● ⊘
⊘ ⊘

$7 - 3 = \boxed{4}$

$\boxed{4}$ is 3 less than 7.

Learn   You can count on to subtract.

9 birds are on a wire.
6 birds fly away.
How many birds are still on the wire?

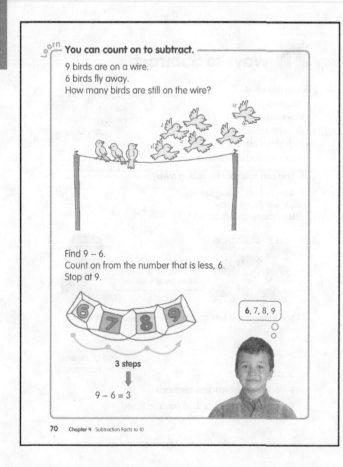

Find $9 - 6$.
Count on from the number that is less, 6.
Stop at 9.

6, 7, 8, 9

3 steps

$9 - 6 = 3$

WORKING TOGETHER Game

What's Hidden?

Players: 3-4
You need.

How to play:

STEP 1 Player 1 chooses a number of 🔵 and shows them to the other players.

STEP 2 Player 1 hides some of them.

STEP 3 The other players must tell the number of 🔵 Player 1 hid. Count on to find out.

There were 8.   Now there are 5.

5, 6, 7, 8
You hid 3 🔵!

STEP 4 Check their answer. Take turns to play!

Correct!

20

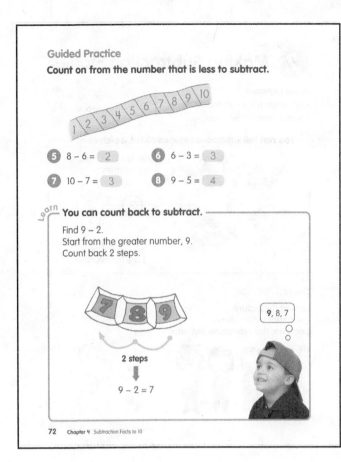

Guided Practice

Count on from the number that is less to subtract.

5 8 – 6 = 2   **6** 6 – 3 = 3

7 10 – 7 = 3   **8** 9 – 5 = 4

Learn **You can count back to subtract.**

Find 9 – 2.
Start from the greater number, 9.
Count back 2 steps.

9, 8, 7

2 steps

9 – 2 = 7

72   Chapter 4   Subtraction Facts to 10

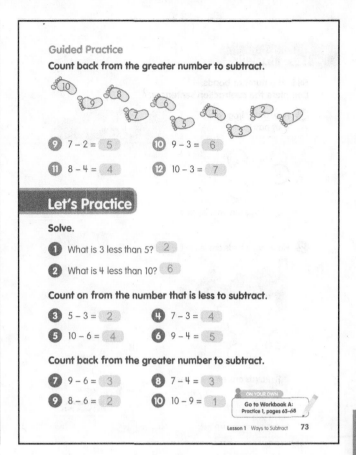

Guided Practice

Count back from the greater number to subtract.

9 7 – 2 = 5   **10** 9 – 3 = 6

11 8 – 4 = 4   **12** 10 – 3 = 7

Let's Practice

Solve.

1 What is 3 less than 5? 2

2 What is 4 less than 10? 6

Count on from the number that is less to subtract.

3 5 – 3 = 2   **4** 7 – 3 = 4

5 10 – 6 = 4   **6** 9 – 4 = 5

Count back from the greater number to subtract.

7 9 – 6 = 3   **8** 7 – 4 = 3

9 8 – 6 = 2   **10** 10 – 9 = 1

ON YOUR OWN
Go to Workbook A:
Practice 1, pages 63–68

Lesson 1   Ways to Subtract   73

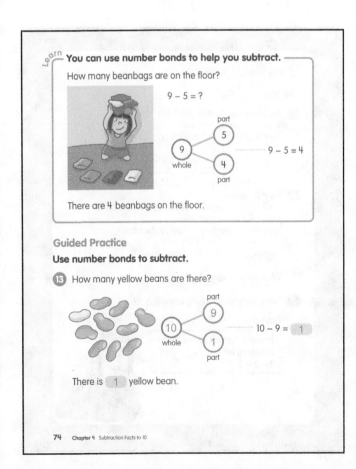

Learn **You can use number bonds to help you subtract.**

How many beanbags are on the floor?

9 – 5 = ?

part
5
9
whole
4
part

9 – 5 = 4

There are 4 beanbags on the floor.

Guided Practice

Use number bonds to subtract.

13 How many yellow beans are there?

part
9
10
whole
1
part

10 – 9 = 1

There is 1 yellow bean.

74   Chapter 4   Subtraction Facts to 10

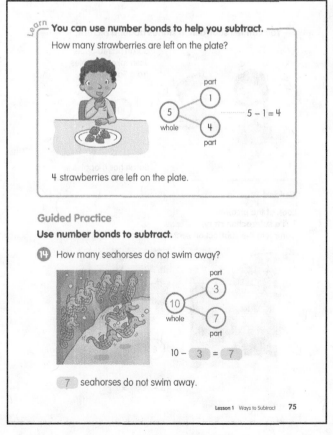

Learn **You can use number bonds to help you subtract.**

How many strawberries are left on the plate?

part
1
5
whole
4
part

5 – 1 = 4

4 strawberries are left on the plate.

Guided Practice

Use number bonds to subtract.

14 How many seahorses do not swim away?

part
3
10
whole
7
part

10 – 3 = 7

7 seahorses do not swim away.

Lesson 1   Ways to Subtract   75

Student Edition Answers: Chapter 4
Math in Focus Homeschool Answer Key, Grade 1

Let's Practice

Fill in the number bonds.
Complete the subtraction sentences.

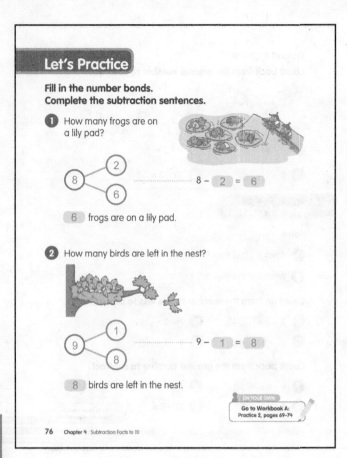

1 How many frogs are on a lily pad?

8 — 2 = 6

6 frogs are on a lily pad.

2 How many birds are left in the nest?

9 — 1 = 8

8 birds are left in the nest.

ON YOUR OWN
Go to Workbook A:
Practice 2, pages 69–74

---

2 Making Subtraction Stories

Lesson Objectives

• Tell subtraction stories about pictures.

• Write subtraction sentences.

Vocabulary
subtraction story

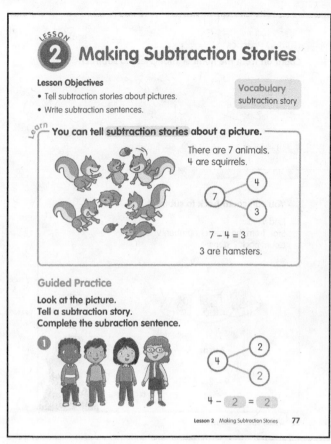

Learn You can tell subtraction stories about a picture.

There are 7 animals.
4 are squirrels.

7 — 4 = 3

3 are hamsters.

Guided Practice

Look at the picture.
Tell a subtraction story.
Complete the subtraction sentence.

1

4 — 2 = 2

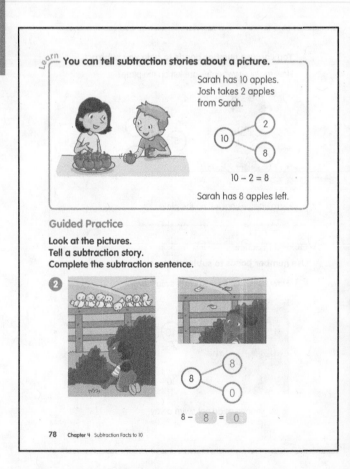

Learn You can tell subtraction stories about a picture.

Sarah has 10 apples.
Josh takes 2 apples from Sarah.

10 — 2 = 8

Sarah has 8 apples left.

Guided Practice

Look at the pictures.
Tell a subtraction story.
Complete the subtraction sentence.

2

8 — 8 = 0

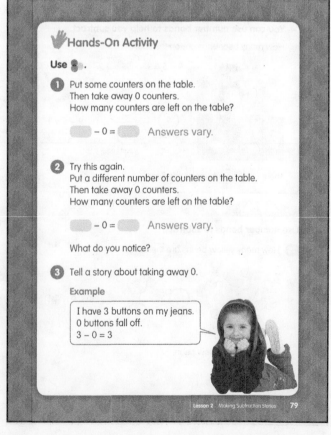

✋ **Hands-On Activity**

Use 🔴.

1 Put some counters on the table.
Then take away 0 counters.
How many counters are left on the table?

⬜ — 0 = ⬜   Answers vary.

2 Try this again.
Put a different number of counters on the table.
Then take away 0 counters.
How many counters are left on the table?

⬜ — 0 = ⬜   Answers vary.

What do you notice?

3 Tell a story about taking away 0.

Example

I have 3 buttons on my jeans.
0 buttons fall off.
3 — 0 = 3

Let's Practice

Make a subtraction sentence for each picture.

1

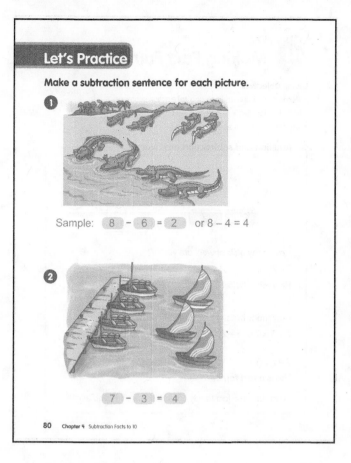

Sample: $8 - 6 = 2$ or $8 - 4 = 4$

2

$7 - 3 = 4$

Look at the picture.
Tell subtraction stories about it.
Make a subtraction sentence for each story.

3

ON YOUR OWN
Go to Workbook A:
Practice 3, pages 75–78

LESSON 3 Real-World Problems: Subtraction

Lesson Objectives

- Write subtraction sentences.
- Solve real-world word problems.

Learn Read and understand a word problem.

Nora and Keisha have 9 oranges.
Nora has 7 oranges.
How many oranges does Keisha have?

$9 - 7 = 2$

Keisha has 2 oranges.

Guided Practice

Solve.

1 There are 8 ants.
3 ants are black.
How many ants are red?

$8 - 3 = 5$

5 ants are red.

Learn Subtract to solve word problems by taking away.

There are 10 biscuits on a plate.
Luis takes some.
6 biscuits are left.
How many biscuits does he take?

$10 - 6 = 4$

Luis takes 4 biscuits.

Guided Practice

Solve.

2 Jackie has 9 balloons.
2 balloons burst.
How many balloons does Jackie have left?

$9 - 2 = 7$

Jackie has 7 balloons left.

23

Solve.

①

A tree has 7 lemons.
2 of the lemons are yellow.
How many lemons are green? 5 lemons

②

There are 10 muffins.
Hector takes some.
3 muffins are left.
How many muffins does Hector take?
7 muffins

ON YOUR OWN
Go to Workbook A:
Practice 4, pages 79–80

84   Chapter 4 Subtraction Facts to 10

---

^{LESSON} **4 Making Fact Families**

Lesson Objectives
• Recognize related addition and subtraction sentences.
• Write fact families.
• Use fact families to solve real-world problems.

Vocabulary
fact family

^{Learn} **Addition and subtraction are related.**

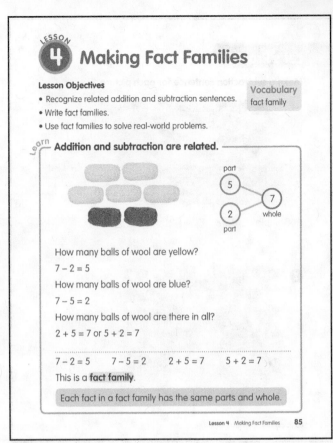

How many balls of wool are yellow?
7 − 2 = 5
How many balls of wool are blue?
7 − 5 = 2
How many balls of wool are there in all?
2 + 5 = 7 or 5 + 2 = 7

7 − 2 = 5   7 − 5 = 2   2 + 5 = 7   5 + 2 = 7

This is a **fact family**.

Each fact in a fact family has the same parts and whole.

Lesson 4 Making Fact Families   85

Guided Practice

Look at the picture.
Find the missing numbers in the fact family.

①

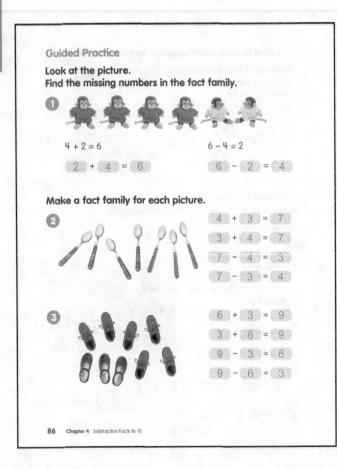

4 + 2 = 6   6 − 4 = 2
2 + 4 = 6   6 − 2 = 4

Make a fact family for each picture.

②

4 + 3 = 7
3 + 4 = 7
7 − 4 = 3
7 − 3 = 4

③

6 + 3 = 9
3 + 6 = 9
9 − 3 = 6
9 − 6 = 3

86   Chapter 4 Subtraction Facts to 10

---

^{Learn} **You can use related addition facts to solve subtraction sentences.**

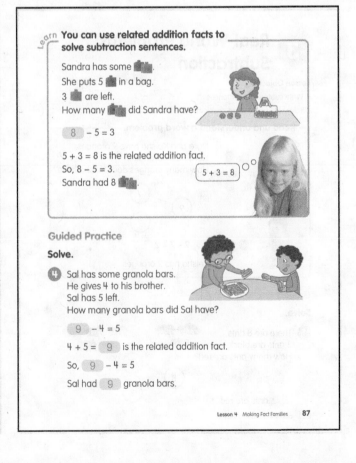

Sandra has some 🎒.
She puts 5 🎒 in a bag.
3 🎒 are left.
How many 🎒 did Sandra have?

8 − 5 = 3

5 + 3 = 8 is the related addition fact.
So, 8 − 5 = 3.
Sandra had 8 🎒.

5 + 3 = 8

Guided Practice

Solve.

④ Sal has some granola bars.
He gives 4 to his brother.
Sal has 5 left.
How many granola bars did Sal have?

9 − 4 = 5

4 + 5 = 9 is the related addition fact.

So, 9 − 4 = 5

Sal had 9 granola bars.

Lesson 4 Making Fact Families   87

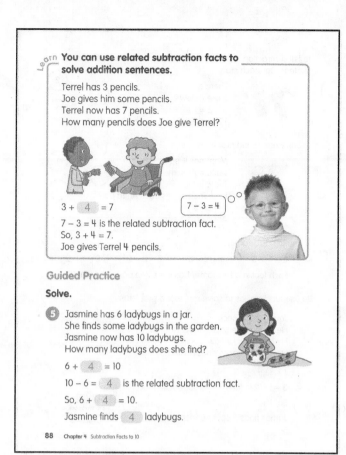

Learn You can use related subtraction facts to solve addition sentences.

Terrel has 3 pencils.
Joe gives him some pencils.
Terrel now has 7 pencils.
How many pencils does Joe give Terrel?

$3 + \boxed{4} = 7$

$7 - 3 = 4$

$7 - 3 = 4$ is the related subtraction fact.
So, $3 + 4 = 7$.
Joe gives Terrel 4 pencils.

Guided Practice

Solve.

5 Jasmine has 6 ladybugs in a jar.
She finds some ladybugs in the garden.
Jasmine now has 10 ladybugs.
How many ladybugs does she find?

$6 + \boxed{4} = 10$

$10 - 6 = \boxed{4}$ is the related subtraction fact.

So, $6 + \boxed{4} = 10$.

Jasmine finds $\boxed{4}$ ladybugs.

Use the pictures to write a fact family.

1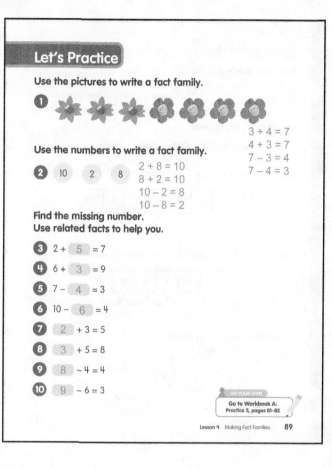

$3 + 4 = 7$
$4 + 3 = 7$
$7 - 3 = 4$
$7 - 4 = 3$

Use the numbers to write a fact family.

2 10   2   8

$2 + 8 = 10$
$8 + 2 = 10$
$10 - 2 = 8$
$10 - 8 = 2$

Find the missing number.
Use related facts to help you.

3 $2 + \boxed{5} = 7$

4 $6 + \boxed{3} = 9$

5 $7 - \boxed{4} = 3$

6 $10 - \boxed{6} = 4$

7 $\boxed{2} + 3 = 5$

8 $\boxed{3} + 5 = 8$

9 $\boxed{8} - 4 = 4$

10 $\boxed{9} - 6 = 3$

ON YOUR OWN
Go to Workbook A:
Practice 5, pages 81–82

Chapter 4

Let's Explore!

Use these cards.

2 3 6 8 9 10 + − =

Use the cards to make number sentences.
Use each card once in each number sentence.
Write all the number sentences you make.

$2 + 6 = 8$ $2 + 8 = 10$
$6 + 2 = 8$ $8 + 2 = 10$
$8 - 2 = 6$ $10 - 2 = 8$
$8 - 6 = 2$ $10 - 8 = 2$

$3 + 6 = 9$
$6 + 3 = 9$
$9 - 3 = 6$
$9 - 6 = 3$

CRITICAL THINKING SKILLS
Put On Your Thinking Cap!

PROBLEM SOLVING

1 Fill in the ⚪ with these numbers.

1 2 3 5 6 8 9

➔ and ⬇ mean =.
Use each number once.

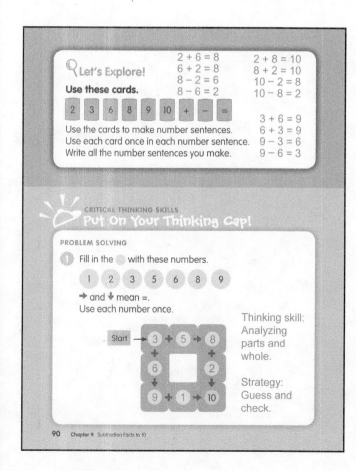

Thinking skill:
Analyzing parts and whole.

Strategy:
Guess and check.

CRITICAL THINKING SKILLS
Put On Your Thinking Cap!

PROBLEM SOLVING

2 Fill in the ⚪ with these numbers.

2 3 4 5 6 7 8

➔ and ⬇ mean =.
Use each number once.

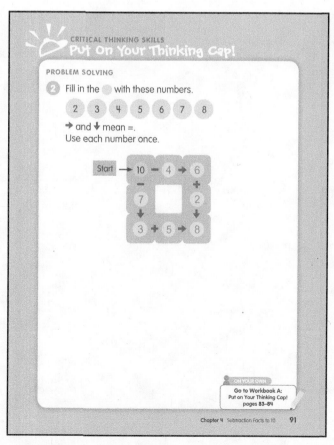

ON YOUR OWN
Go to Workbook A:
Put on Your Thinking Cap!
pages 83–84

25

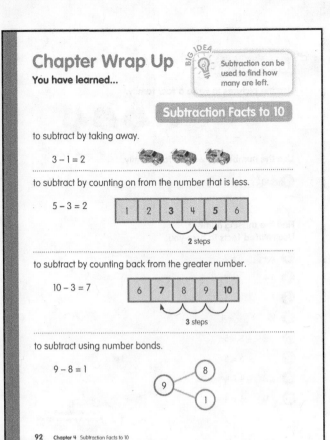

Chapter Wrap Up

You have learned...

BIG IDEA Subtraction can be used to find how many are left.

Subtraction Facts to 10

to subtract by taking away.

$3 - 1 = 2$

to subtract by counting on from the number that is less.

$5 - 3 = 2$

| 1 | 2 | 3 | 4 | 5 | 6 |

2 steps

to subtract by counting back from the greater number.

$10 - 3 = 7$

| 6 | 7 | 8 | 9 | 10 |

3 steps

to subtract using number bonds.

$9 - 8 = 1$

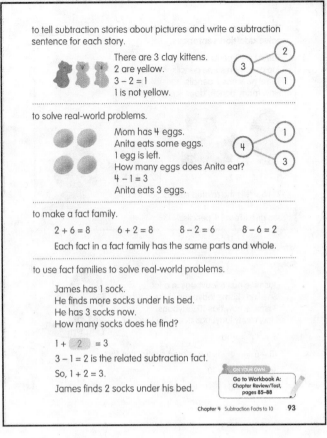

to tell subtraction stories about pictures and write a subtraction sentence for each story.

There are 3 clay kittens.
2 are yellow.
$3 - 2 = 1$
1 is not yellow.

to solve real-world problems.

Mom has 4 eggs.
Anita eats some eggs.
1 egg is left.
How many eggs does Anita eat?
$4 - 1 = 3$
Anita eats 3 eggs.

to make a fact family.

$2 + 6 = 8$ $6 + 2 = 8$ $8 - 2 = 6$ $8 - 6 = 2$

Each fact in a fact family has the same parts and whole.

to use fact families to solve real-world problems.

James has 1 sock.
He finds more socks under his bed.
He has 3 socks now.
How many socks does he find?

$1 + \boxed{2} = 3$
$3 - 1 = 2$ is the related subtraction fact.
So, $1 + 2 = 3$.
James finds 2 socks under his bed.

ON YOUR OWN
Go to Workbook A:
Chapter Review/Test,
pages 85–88

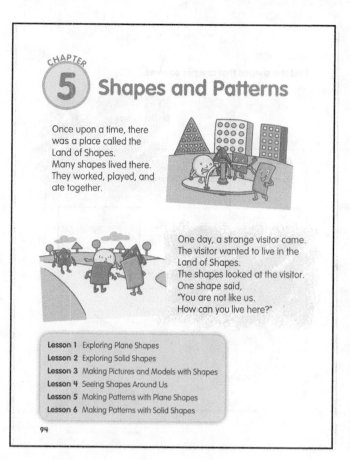

5 Shapes and Patterns

CHAPTER

Once upon a time, there was a place called the Land of Shapes. Many shapes lived there. They worked, played, and ate together.

One day, a strange visitor came. The visitor wanted to live in the Land of Shapes. The shapes looked at the visitor. One shape said, "You are not like us. How can you live here?"

Lesson 1 Exploring Plane Shapes
Lesson 2 Exploring Solid Shapes
Lesson 3 Making Pictures and Models with Shapes
Lesson 4 Seeing Shapes Around Us
Lesson 5 Making Patterns with Plane Shapes
Lesson 6 Making Patterns with Solid Shapes

94

The visitor smiled.
He said, "I am not only one shape, I can be any shape!"
He then turned himself into the different shapes.

The shapes thought this was great! They decided to let the visitor stay. So the visitor stayed and they all lived happily ever after.

BIG IDEA
Explore, identify, and compare plane and solid shapes in patterns and in the real world.

95

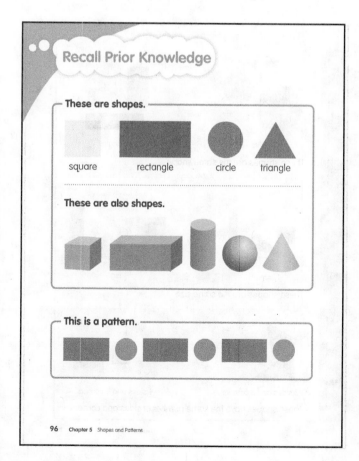

Recall Prior Knowledge

These are shapes.

square   rectangle   circle   triangle

These are also shapes.

This is a pattern.

96   Chapter 5   Shapes and Patterns

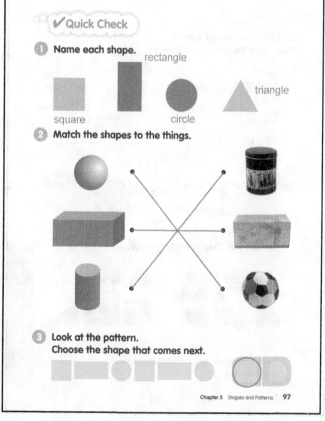

✔ Quick Check

1 Name each shape.

rectangle

square   circle   triangle

2 Match the shapes to the things.

3 Look at the pattern.
Choose the shape that comes next.

Chapter 5   Shapes and Patterns   97

Chapter 5

Student Edition Answers: Chapter 5
Math in Focus Homeschool Answer Key, Grade 1

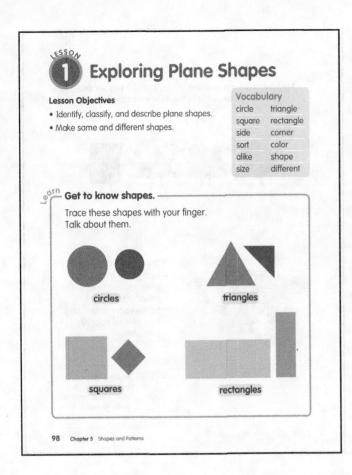

LESSON 1 Exploring Plane Shapes

Lesson Objectives
- Identify, classify, and describe plane shapes.
- Make same and different shapes.

Vocabulary
circle	triangle
square	rectangle
side	corner
sort	color
alike	shape
size	different

Learn **Get to know shapes.**

Trace these shapes with your finger.
Talk about them.

circles

triangles

squares

rectangles

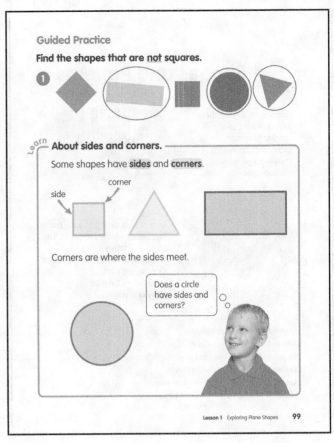

Find the shapes that are not squares.

1

Learn **About sides and corners.**

Some shapes have **sides** and **corners**.

side

corner

Corners are where the sides meet.

Does a circle have sides and corners?

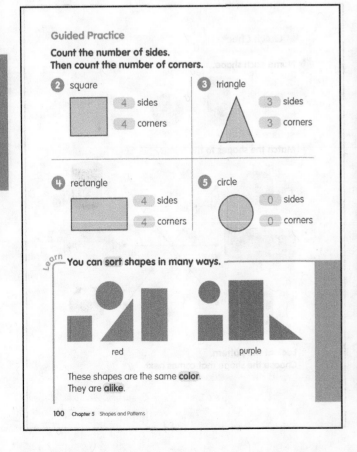

Guided Practice

Count the number of sides.
Then count the number of corners.

2 square
4 sides
4 corners

3 triangle
3 sides
3 corners

4 rectangle
4 sides
4 corners

5 circle
0 sides
0 corners

Learn **You can sort shapes in many ways.**

red

purple

These shapes are the same **color**.
They are **alike**.

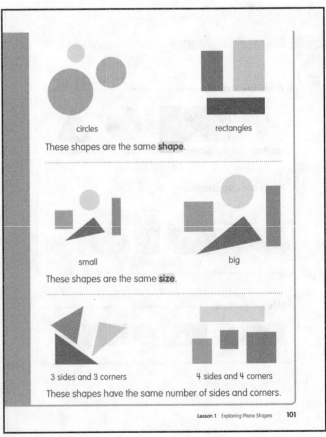

circles

rectangles

These shapes are the same **shape**.

small

big

These shapes are the same **size**.

3 sides and 3 corners

4 sides and 4 corners

These shapes have the same number of sides and corners.

28

Tell how these shapes are alike.

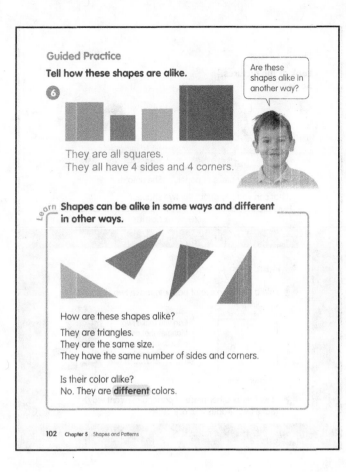

⑥

> Are these shapes alike in another way?

They are all squares.
They all have 4 sides and 4 corners.

Learn **Shapes can be alike in some ways and different in other ways.**

How are these shapes alike?

They are triangles.
They are the same size.
They have the same number of sides and corners.

Is their color alike?
No. They are **different** colors.

102   Chapter 5   Shapes and Patterns

Tell how these shapes are different.

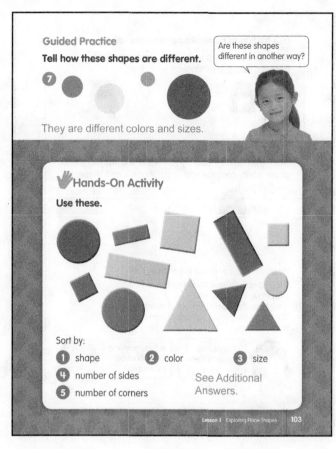

⑦

> Are these shapes different in another way?

They are different colors and sizes.

✋ **Hands-On Activity**

Use these.

Sort by:

1 shape   2 color   3 size

4 number of sides   See Additional
5 number of corners   Answers.

Lesson 1   Exploring Plane Shapes   103

Let's Practice

Find the answers.

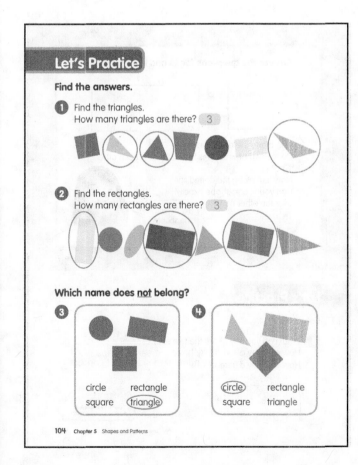

1 Find the triangles.
How many triangles are there? 3

2 Find the rectangles.
How many rectangles are there? 3

Which name does not belong?

3
circle   rectangle
square   (triangle)

4
(circle)   rectangle
square   triangle

104   Chapter 5   Shapes and Patterns

Find the answers.

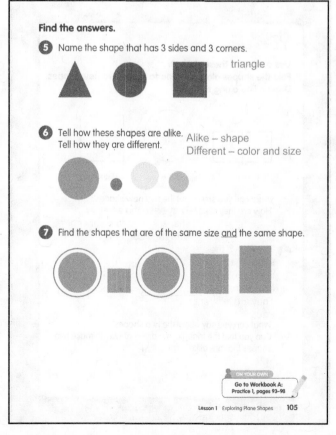

5 Name the shape that has 3 sides and 3 corners.
triangle

6 Tell how these shapes are alike.   Alike – shape
Tell how they are different.   Different – color and size

7 Find the shapes that are of the same size and the same shape.

> ON YOUR OWN
> Go to Workbook A:
> Practice 1, pages 93–98

Lesson 1   Exploring Plane Shapes   105

Chapter 5

Student Edition Answers: Chapter 5
Math in Focus Homeschool Answer Key, Grade 1

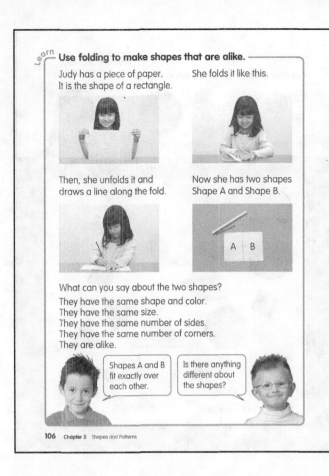

Use folding to make shapes that are alike.

Judy has a piece of paper. It is the shape of a rectangle.

She folds it like this.

Then, she unfolds it and draws a line along the fold.

Now she has two shapes Shape A and Shape B.

What can you say about the two shapes?
They have the same shape and color.
They have the same size.
They have the same number of sides.
They have the same number of corners.
They are alike.

Shapes A and B fit exactly over each other.

Is there anything different about the shapes?

106 Chapter 5 Shapes and Patterns

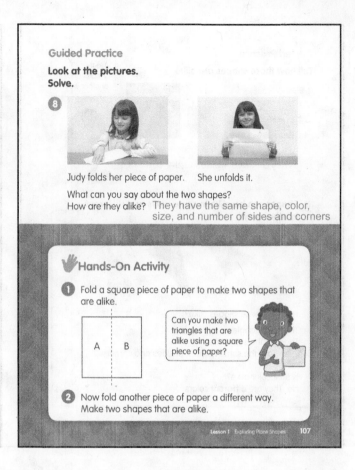

**Look at the pictures.
Solve.**

8

Judy folds her piece of paper.

She unfolds it.

What can you say about the two shapes?
How are they alike? They have the same shape, color, size, and number of sides and corners

Hands-On Activity

1 Fold a square piece of paper to make two shapes that are alike.

A B

Can you make two triangles that are alike using a square piece of paper?

2 Now fold another piece of paper a different way. Make two shapes that are alike.

Lesson 1 Exploring Plane Shapes 107

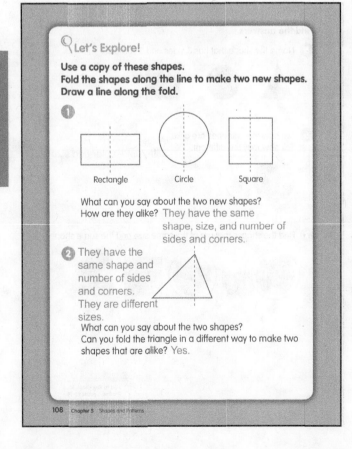

Let's Explore!

**Use a copy of these shapes.
Fold the shapes along the line to make two new shapes.
Draw a line along the fold.**

1

Rectangle   Circle   Square

What can you say about the two new shapes?
How are they alike? They have the same shape, size, and number of sides and corners.

2 They have the same shape and number of sides and corners.
They are different sizes.
What can you say about the two shapes?
Can you fold the triangle in a different way to make two shapes that are alike? Yes.

108 Chapter 5 Shapes and Patterns

Chapter 5

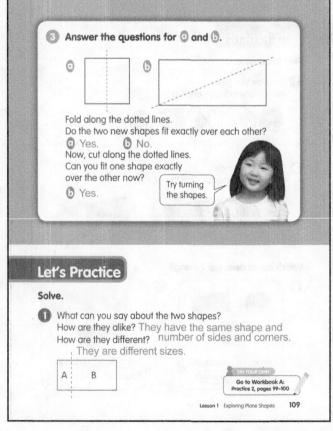

3 Answer the questions for ⓐ and ⓑ.

ⓐ   ⓑ

Fold along the dotted lines.
Do the two new shapes fit exactly over each other?
ⓐ Yes.   ⓑ No.
Now, cut along the dotted lines.
Can you fit one shape exactly over the other now?
ⓑ Yes.

Try turning the shapes.

Let's Practice

Solve.

1 What can you say about the two shapes?
How are they alike? They have the same shape and
How are they different? number of sides and corners.
They are different sizes.

A B

ON YOUR OWN
Go to Workbook A: Practice 2, pages 99–100

Lesson 1 Exploring Plane Shapes 109

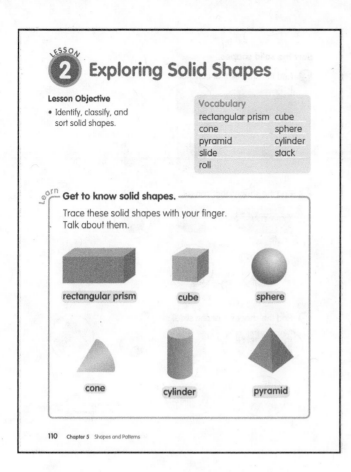

LESSON 2 Exploring Solid Shapes

Lesson Objective
- Identify, classify, and sort solid shapes.

Vocabulary
rectangular prism	cube
cone	sphere
pyramid	cylinder
slide	stack
roll	

Get to know solid shapes.

Trace these solid shapes with your finger.
Talk about them.

rectangular prism   cube   sphere

cone   cylinder   pyramid

110   Chapter 5   Shapes and Patterns

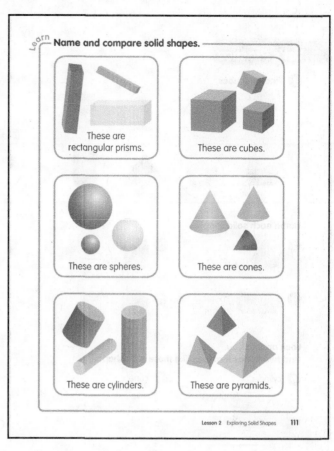

Name and compare solid shapes.

These are rectangular prisms.

These are cubes.

These are spheres.

These are cones.

These are cylinders.

These are pyramids.

Lesson 2   Exploring Solid Shapes   111

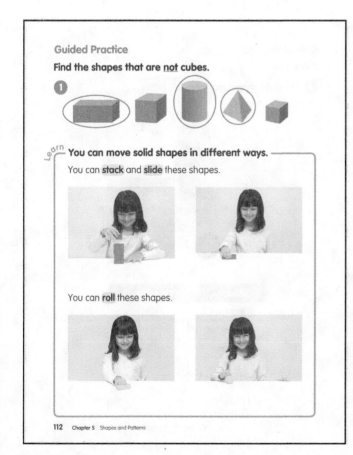

Guided Practice

Find the shapes that are not cubes.

1

You can move solid shapes in different ways.

You can **stack** and **slide** these shapes.

You can **roll** these shapes.

112   Chapter 5   Shapes and Patterns

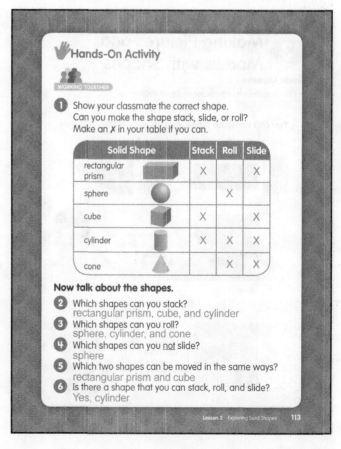

Hands-On Activity

WORKING TOGETHER

1 Show your classmate the correct shape.
Can you make the shape stack, slide, or roll?
Make an ✗ in your table if you can.

Solid Shape		Stack	Roll	Slide
rectangular prism		X		X
sphere			X	
cube		X		X
cylinder		X	X	X
cone			X	X

Now talk about the shapes.

2 Which shapes can you stack?
rectangular prism, cube, and cylinder
3 Which shapes can you roll?
sphere, cylinder, and cone
4 Which shapes can you not slide?
sphere
5 Which two shapes can be moved in the same ways?
rectangular prism and cube
6 Is there a shape that you can stack, roll, and slide?
Yes, cylinder

Lesson 2   Exploring Solid Shapes   113

Chapter 5

Student Edition Answers: Chapter 5
Math in Focus Homeschool Answer Key, Grade 1

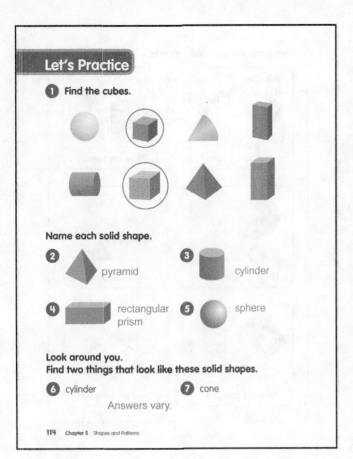

Let's Practice

1 Find the cubes.

Name each solid shape.

2 pyramid

3 cylinder

4 rectangular prism

5 sphere

Look around you.
Find two things that look like these solid shapes.

6 cylinder

7 cone

Answers vary.

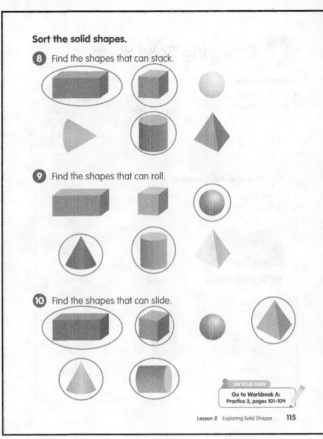

Sort the solid shapes.

8 Find the shapes that can stack.

9 Find the shapes that can roll.

10 Find the shapes that can slide.

ON YOUR OWN
Go to Workbook A:
Practice 3, pages 101-104

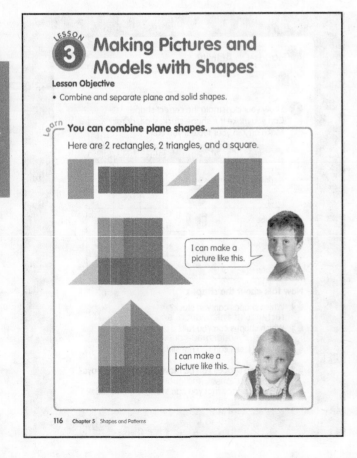

LESSON 3

Making Pictures and Models with Shapes

Lesson Objective
• Combine and separate plane and solid shapes.

Learn You can combine plane shapes.

Here are 2 rectangles, 2 triangles, and a square.

I can make a picture like this.

I can make a picture like this.

Guided Practice

Solve.

1 Name the shapes that make this picture.

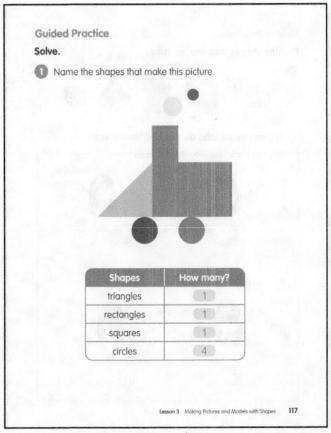

Shapes	How many?
triangles	1
rectangles	1
squares	1
circles	4

Chapter 5

Hands-On Activity

1. Make a picture with these shapes.
How many of each shape are there? Answers vary.

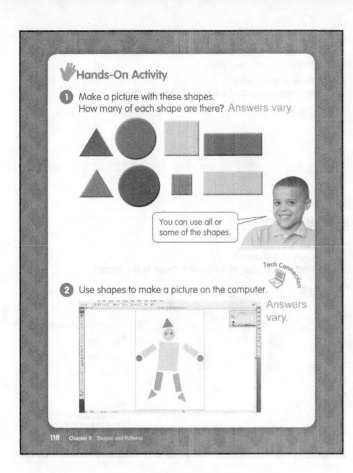

You can use all or some of the shapes.

Tech Connection

2. Use shapes to make a picture on the computer.

Answers vary.

Hands-On Activity

3. Cut a copy of these shapes.

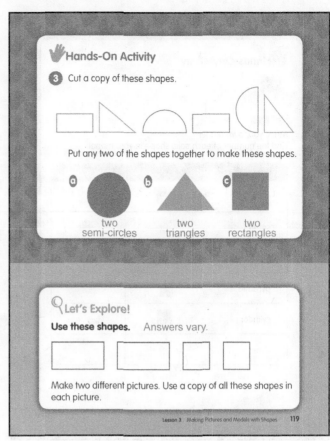

Put any two of the shapes together to make these shapes.

a. two semi-circles
b. two triangles
c. two rectangles

Let's Explore!

Use these shapes. Answers vary.

Make two different pictures. Use a copy of all these shapes in each picture.

Let's Practice

**Count.
Look at the picture.**

1. This picture is made of many shapes.

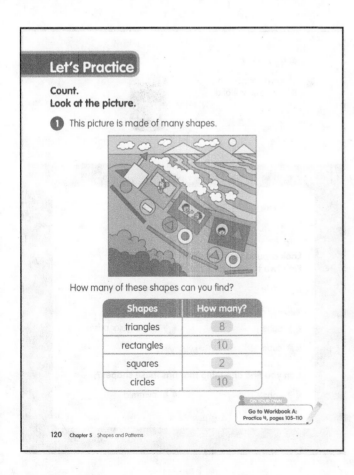

How many of these shapes can you find?

Shapes	How many?
triangles	8
rectangles	10
squares	2
circles	10

ON YOUR OWN
Go to Workbook A:
Practice 4, pages 105–110

Learn You can build models with solid shapes.

Here is 1 sphere, 2 pyramids, 4 cylinders, 2 cubes, 1 cone, and 1 rectangular prism.

I can make a model like this.

I can make a model like this.

Chapter 5

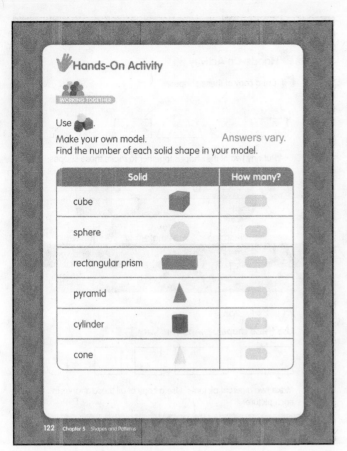

Hands-On Activity

WORKING TOGETHER

Use ▪▪.

Make your own model.   Answers vary.
Find the number of each solid shape in your model.

Solid		How many?
cube		
sphere		
rectangular prism		
pyramid		
cylinder		
cone		

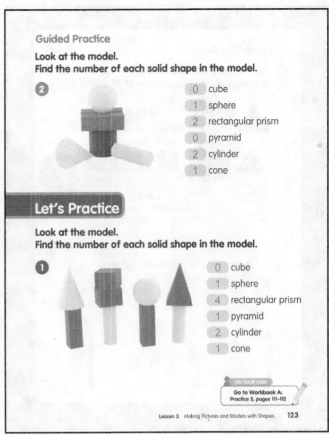

Guided Practice

Look at the model.
Find the number of each solid shape in the model.

2

0	cube
1	sphere
2	rectangular prism
0	pyramid
2	cylinder
1	cone

Let's Practice

Look at the model.
Find the number of each solid shape in the model.

1

0	cube
1	sphere
4	rectangular prism
1	pyramid
2	cylinder
1	cone

ON YOUR OWN!
Go to Workbook A:
Practice 5, pages 111–112

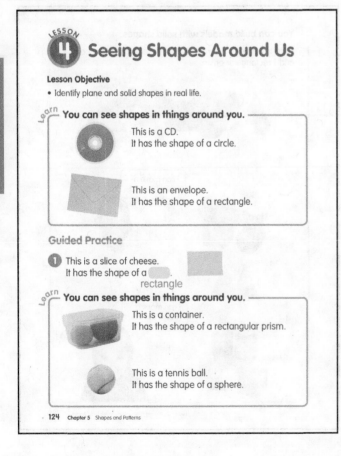

LESSON 4

Seeing Shapes Around Us

Lesson Objective
• Identify plane and solid shapes in real life.

Learn You can see shapes in things around you.

This is a CD.
It has the shape of a circle.

This is an envelope.
It has the shape of a rectangle.

Guided Practice

1 This is a slice of cheese.
It has the shape of a _rectangle_.

Learn You can see shapes in things around you.

This is a container.
It has the shape of a rectangular prism.

This is a tennis ball.
It has the shape of a sphere.

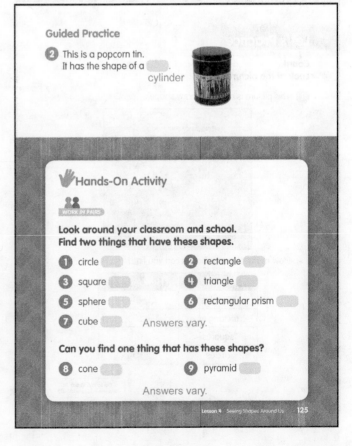

Guided Practice

2 This is a popcorn tin.
It has the shape of a ____.
cylinder

Hands-On Activity

WORK IN PAIRS

Look around your classroom and school.
Find two things that have these shapes.

1 circle ▭   2 rectangle ▭

3 square ▭   4 triangle ▭

5 sphere ▭   6 rectangular prism ▭

7 cube ▭   _Answers vary._

Can you find one thing that has these shapes?

8 cone ▭   9 pyramid ▭

Answers vary.

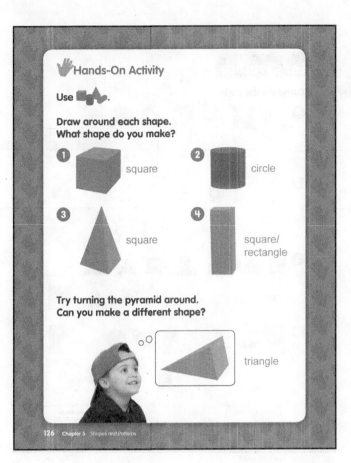

Hands-On Activity

Use [blocks].

Draw around each shape.
What shape do you make?

1 square

2 circle

3 square

4 square/rectangle

Try turning the pyramid around.
Can you make a different shape?

triangle

Look at the pictures.
Name the shapes you see.

1 circles
rectangles
triangles

2 circles
rectangles
triangles

3 rectangles
circles
cylinders   rectangular
prism

4 circles
cylinder

Answer the questions.

5 This is a sponge.
What shape does it have? rectangular prism
What other shapes do you see? rectangles

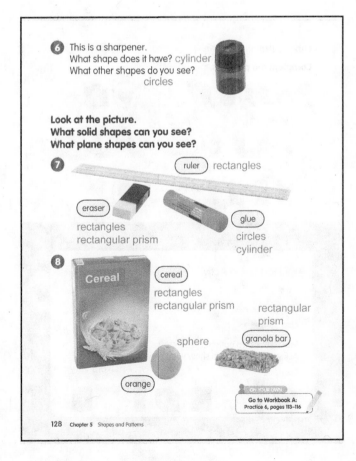

6 This is a sharpener.
What shape does it have? cylinder
What other shapes do you see?
circles

Look at the picture.
What solid shapes can you see?
What plane shapes can you see?

7 ruler   rectangles

eraser
rectangles
rectangular prism

glue
circles
cylinder

8 cereal
rectangles
rectangular prism

rectangular
prism

sphere

granola bar

orange

ON YOUR OWN
Go to Workbook A:
Practice 6, pages 113–116

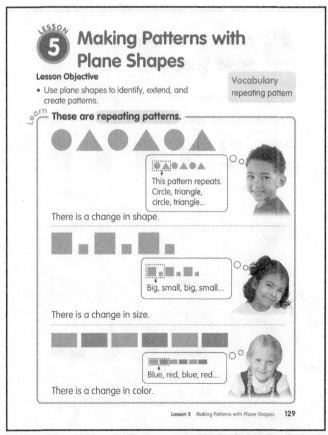

LESSON 5
Making Patterns with Plane Shapes

Lesson Objective
• Use plane shapes to identify, extend, and create patterns.

Vocabulary
repeating pattern

Learn These are repeating patterns.

This pattern repeats.
Circle, triangle,
circle, triangle...

There is a change in shape.

Big, small, big, small...

There is a change in size.

Blue, red, blue, red...

There is a change in color.

Chapter 5

35

Guided Practice

Complete the patterns.

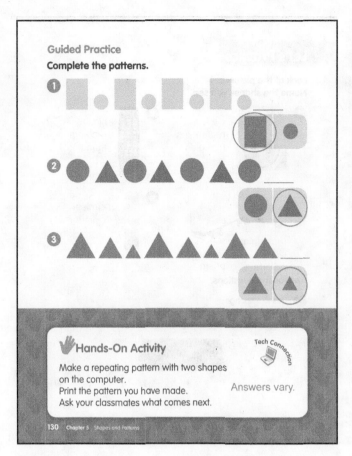

Hands-On Activity

Make a repeating pattern with two shapes on the computer.
Print the pattern you have made.
Ask your classmates what comes next.

Tech Connection

Answers vary.

130 Chapter 5 Shapes and Patterns

Let's Practice

Complete the patterns.

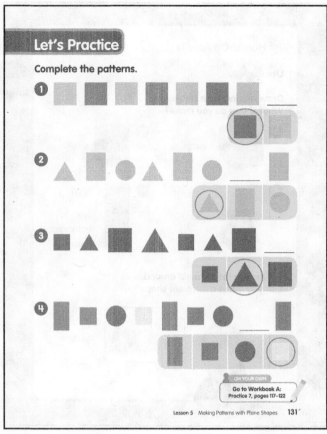

ON YOUR OWN
Go to Workbook A:
Practice 7, pages 117–122

Lesson 5 Making Patterns with Plane Shapes 131

LESSON 6 Making Patterns with Solid Shapes

Lesson Objective

• Use solid shapes to identify, extend, and create patterns.

Learn These are more repeating patterns.

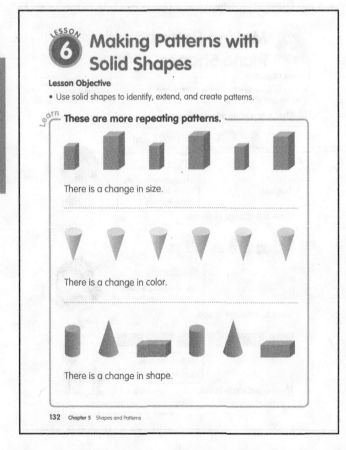

There is a change in size.

There is a change in color.

There is a change in shape.

132 Chapter 5 Shapes and Patterns

Guided Practice

Complete the patterns.

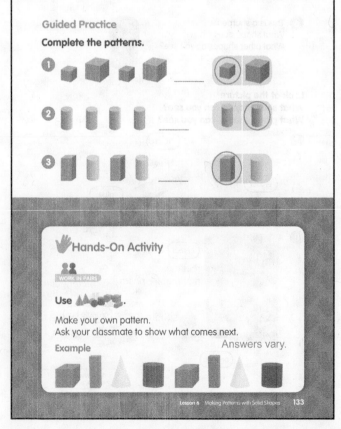

Hands-On Activity

WORK IN PAIRS

Use

Make your own pattern.
Ask your classmate to show what comes next.

Example

Answers vary.

Lesson 6 Making Patterns with Solid Shapes 133

Student Edition Answers: Chapter 5
Math in Focus Homeschool Answer Key, Grade 1

Let's Practice

Complete the patterns.

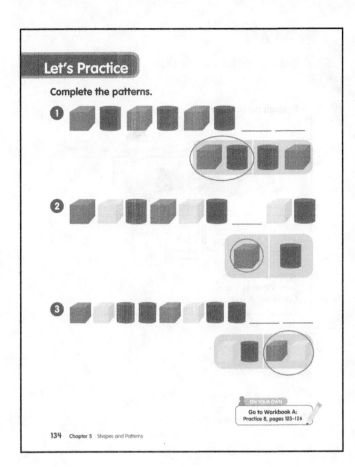

ON YOUR OWN
Go to Workbook A:
Practice 8, pages 123–126

134 Chapter 5 Shapes and Patterns

PROBLEM SOLVING

1 How are these shapes sorted?

Answers vary.
Shapes in Group A are pink.
The shapes in Group B are not pink.

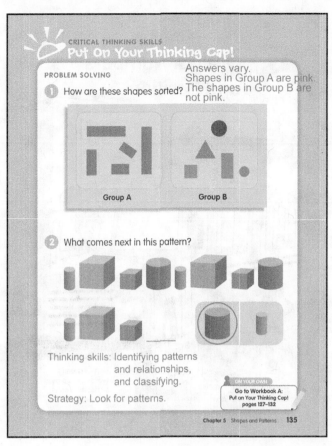

Group A   Group B

2 What comes next in this pattern?

Thinking skills: Identifying patterns and relationships, and classifying.

Strategy: Look for patterns.

ON YOUR OWN
Go to Workbook A:
Put on Your Thinking Cap!
pages 127–132

Chapter 5 Shapes and Patterns 135

Chapter Wrap Up

You have learned...

Shapes and Patterns

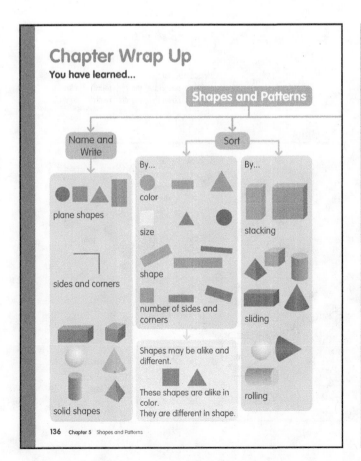

Name and Write — plane shapes — sides and corners — solid shapes

Sort — By... color, size, shape, number of sides and corners. Shapes may be alike and different. These shapes are alike in color. They are different in shape.

By... stacking, sliding, rolling

136 Chapter 5 Shapes and Patterns

BIG IDEA
Explore, identify, and compare plane and solid shapes in patterns and in the real world.

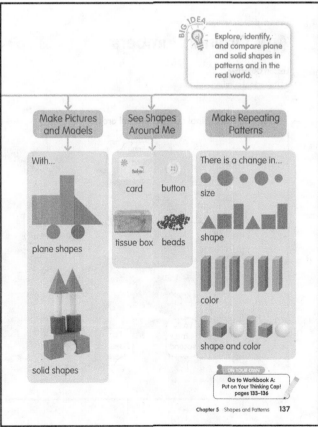

Make Pictures and Models — With... plane shapes — solid shapes

See Shapes Around Me — card, button, tissue box, beads

Make Repeating Patterns — There is a change in... size, shape, color, shape and color

ON YOUR OWN
Go to Workbook A:
Put on Your Thinking Cap!
pages 133–136

Chapter 5 Shapes and Patterns 137

Chapter 5

CHAPTER 6 Ordinal Numbers and Position

Stand In Line

BIG IDEA
Numbers and words can be used to describe order and position.

Lesson 1 Ordinal Numbers
Lesson 2 Position Words

138

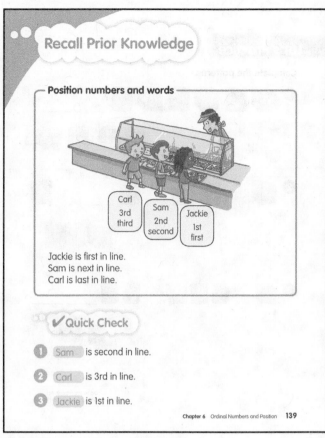

Recall Prior Knowledge

Position numbers and words

Carl
3rd
third

Sam
2nd
second

Jackie
1st
first

Jackie is first in line.
Sam is next in line.
Carl is last in line.

✔ Quick Check

1 Sam is second in line.

2 Carl is 3rd in line.

3 Jackie is 1st in line.

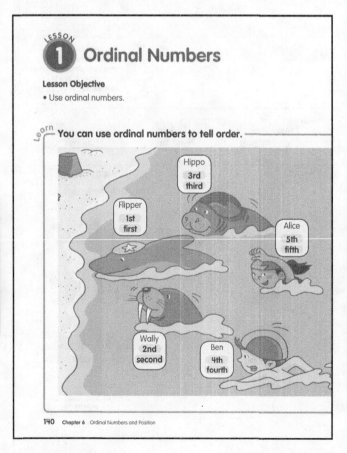

LESSON 1 Ordinal Numbers

Lesson Objective
• Use ordinal numbers.

Learn You can use ordinal numbers to tell order.

Hippo
3rd
third

Flipper
1st
first

Alice
5th
fifth

Wally
2nd
second

Ben
4th
fourth

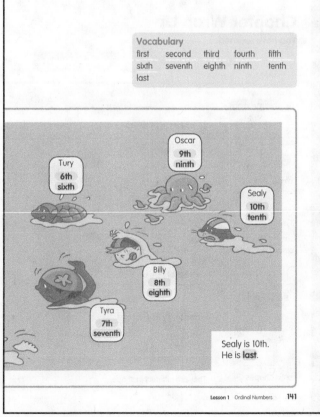

Vocabulary

first	second	third	fourth	fifth
sixth	seventh	eighth	ninth	tenth
last				

Tury
6th
sixth

Oscar
9th
ninth

Sealy
10th
tenth

Billy
8th
eighth

Tyra
7th
seventh

Sealy is 10th.
He is **last**.

Guided Practice

Look at the picture.
Answer the questions.

1. How many children are climbing the wall? 6
2. Who is 1st? Greg
3. Who is 2nd? Kyle
4. Who is 6th? Lionel

142 Chapter 6 Ordinal Numbers and Position

5. Who is 4th? Jason
6. In which position is Ally? 5th
7. In which position is Zack? 3rd
8. Who is last? Lionel

Lesson 1 Ordinal Numbers 143

Let's Practice

Look at the picture.
Answer the questions.

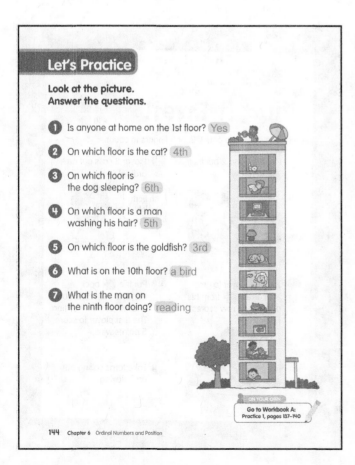

1. Is anyone at home on the 1st floor? Yes
2. On which floor is the cat? 4th
3. On which floor is the dog sleeping? 6th
4. On which floor is a man washing his hair? 5th
5. On which floor is the goldfish? 3rd
6. What is on the 10th floor? a bird
7. What is the man on the ninth floor doing? reading

ON YOUR OWN
Go to Workbook A:
Practice 1, pages 137–140

144 Chapter 6 Ordinal Numbers and Position

LESSON 2 Position Words

Lesson Objective
- Use position words to name relative positions.

Vocabulary

before	after	between
left	right	next to
under	above	below
behind	in front of	up
down	near	far

Learn You can use position words to tell order and position.

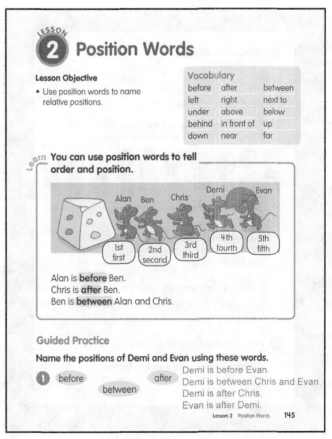

Alan is **before** Ben.
Chris is **after** Ben.
Ben is **between** Alan and Chris.

Guided Practice

Name the positions of Demi and Evan using these words.

1. before   after   between

Demi is before Evan.
Demi is between Chris and Evan.
Demi is after Chris.
Evan is after Demi.

Lesson 2 Position Words 145

Chapter 6

Learn **You can use left, right, and next to to tell where things are in relation to each other.**

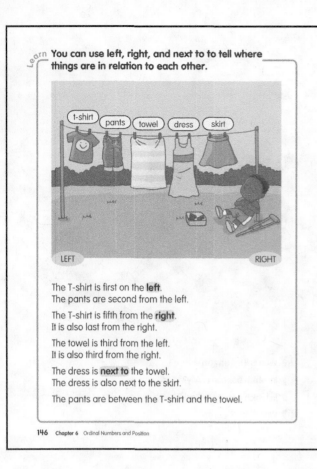

The T-shirt is first on the **left**.
The pants are second from the left.

The T-shirt is fifth from the **right**.
It is also last from the right.

The towel is third from the left.
It is also third from the right.

The dress is **next to** the towel.
The dress is also next to the skirt.

The pants are between the T-shirt and the towel.

Guided Practice

Answer the questions.

2 Who is first on the right? Jorge

3 Who is second from the left? Megan

4 Who is last from the left? Jorge

5 Who is next to Mr. Smith? Dylan and Jorge

Who is between Dylan and Jorge?

Hands-On Activity

WORKING TOGETHER

Carry out these activities.

1 Your teacher will choose ten children.
They should stand in a row facing the class.

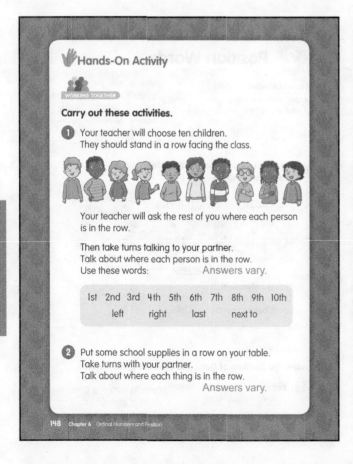

Your teacher will ask the rest of you where each person is in the row.

Then take turns talking to your partner.
Talk about where each person is in the row.
Use these words: Answers vary.

1st	2nd	3rd	4th	5th	6th	7th	8th	9th	10th
left		right		last		next to			

2 Put some school supplies in a row on your table.
Take turns with your partner.
Talk about where each thing is in the row.
          Answers vary.

WORKING TOGETHER **Game**

Players: 3
You need:
• 10
• 10

Find it First!

How to play: Use only 1, 2, or 3 fingers to count.

1 Players 1 and 2 put their ■ in a row.

2 Player 3 calls out an ordinal position.

9th from the left!

3 The first player to grab the correct ■ from his or her own row scores 1 point.

4 Put the ■ back. Player 3 then calls out another ordinal position. The first player to score 5 points wins.

5 Take turns calling out and playing.

Let's Practice

**Look at the picture.
Complete the sentences.**

1. The black mouse is before the brown mouse.
   The white mouse is after the brown mouse.

2. The brown mouse is between the black mouse and the white mouse.

3. The peanut butter is second from the left.

4. The cheese is first on the right.

5. The apple is next to the peanut butter.

6. The potato is third from the left and the right.

ON YOUR OWN
Go to Workbook A:
Practice 2, pages 141–144

Learn You can use the picture to learn more position words.

Jasmine is **under** the table.

Shenice is **above** Pedro.
Pedro is **below** Shenice.

Danny is **behind** the curtains.
Jacob is **in front of** the curtains.

Guided Practice

**Look at the picture.
Find the missing position words.**

| under | above | below | behind | in front of |

6. Tom is in front of Sue.
7. Sue is behind Tom.
8. The toys are above the books.
9. The books are below the toys.
10. The ball is under the shelf.

Learn You can use the picture to learn more position words.

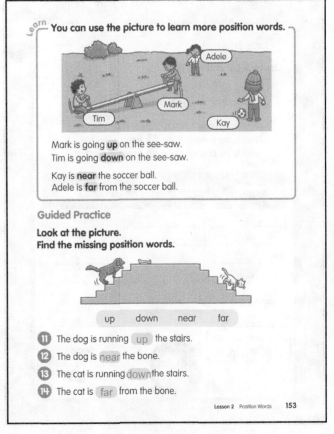

Mark is going **up** on the see-saw.
Tim is going **down** on the see-saw.

Kay is **near** the soccer ball.
Adele is **far** from the soccer ball.

Guided Practice

**Look at the picture.
Find the missing position words.**

| up | down | near | far |

11. The dog is running up the stairs.
12. The dog is near the bone.
13. The cat is running down the stairs.
14. The cat is far from the bone.

Let's Practice

Short Sally

Quick Quentin

Tall Tom

Funny Fred

Tiny Tim

LEFT

Mini Monkey

Hairy Harry

Tapping Tina

Bashful Betty

Sleeping Sam

RIGHT

Look at the picture.
Answer the questions.

1. Who is below Short Sally? Tall Tom
2. Who is in front of Tapping Tina? Sleeping Sam
3. Who is above Tall Tom? Short Sally
4. Who is under Bashful Betty's hat? Mini Monkey

5. Who is behind Sleeping Sam? Tapping Tina
6. Who is sliding down the pole? Hairy Harry
7. Who is climbing up the ladder? Quick Quentin
8. Who is near the ball? Tall Tom

ON YOUR OWN
Go to Workbook A:
Practice 3, pages 145–146

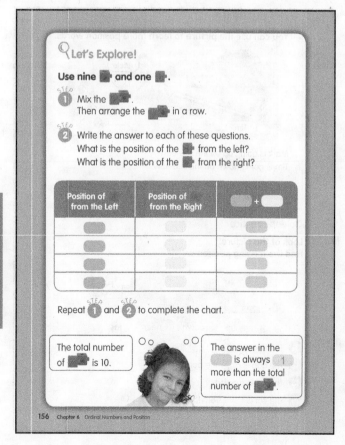

Let's Explore!

Use nine 🟥 and one ⬜.

STEP 1. Mix the 🟥.
Then arrange the 🟥 in a row.

STEP 2. Write the answer to each of these questions.
What is the position of the 🟥 from the left?
What is the position of the 🟥 from the right?

Position of 🟥 from the Left	Position of 🟥 from the Right	⬜ + ⬜

Repeat STEP 1 and STEP 2 to complete the chart.

The total number of 🟥 is 10.

The answer in the ⬜ is always 1 more than the total number of 🟥.

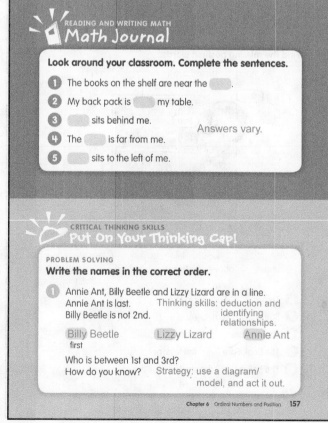

READING AND WRITING MATH
Math Journal

Look around your classroom. Complete the sentences.

1. The books on the shelf are near the ___.
2. My back pack is ___ my table.
3. ___ sits behind me.
4. The ___ is far from me.
5. ___ sits to the left of me.

Answers vary.

CRITICAL THINKING SKILLS
Put On Your Thinking Cap!

PROBLEM SOLVING
Write the names in the correct order.

1. Annie Ant, Billy Beetle and Lizzy Lizard are in a line.
Annie Ant is last.
Billy Beetle is not 2nd.

Thinking skills: deduction and identifying relationships.

Billy Beetle — first   Lizzy Lizard   Annie Ant

Who is between 1st and 3rd?
How do you know?   Strategy: use a diagram/model, and act it out.

Chapter 6

2 Tanya plants 4 flowers in a row.
The orchid is not 2nd from the left.
The daisy is between the rose and the sunflower.
The sunflower is 1st on the right.

Thinking skills: deduction and identifying relationships.

orchid   rose   daisy   sunflower
LEFT   RIGHT

Which flower is 3rd from the right?
How do you know? Strategy: use a diagram/model and act it out.

3 Joshua counts the number of children in his group.
Nick is the 4th person from the right.
He is also the 2nd person from the left.
How many people are there in his group?

Thinking skills: deduction, sequencing and identifying relationships.

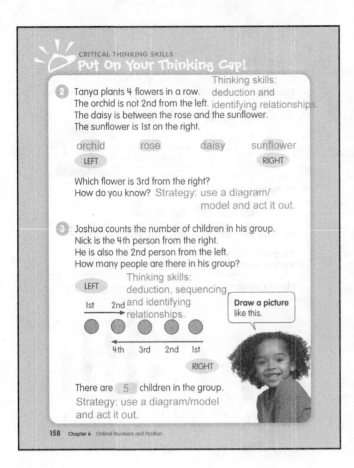

LEFT
1st   2nd
→

Draw a picture like this.

● ● ● ● ●
    ←
    4th   3rd   2nd   1st
RIGHT

There are 5 children in the group.
Strategy: use a diagram/model and act it out.

4 Beth arranges 10 beads in a row.
There is only one red bead.
The red bead is placed 6th from the right.
If Beth counts from the left, in what position is the red bead? 5

Thinking skills: deduction and identifying relationships.

Draw a picture or act it out.

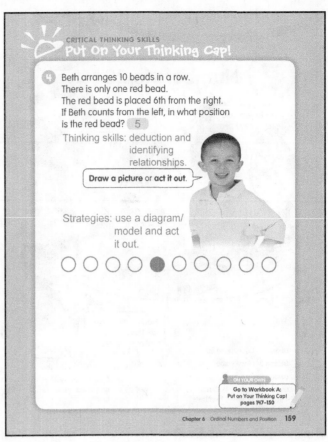

Strategies: use a diagram/model and act it out.

○ ○ ○ ○ ○ ● ○ ○ ○ ○

ON YOUR OWN
Go to Workbook A:
Put on Your Thinking Cap!
pages 147–150

Chapter Wrap Up
You have learned...

Ordinal Numbers and Position

↓

Use ordinal and position words to talk about where things are

↓

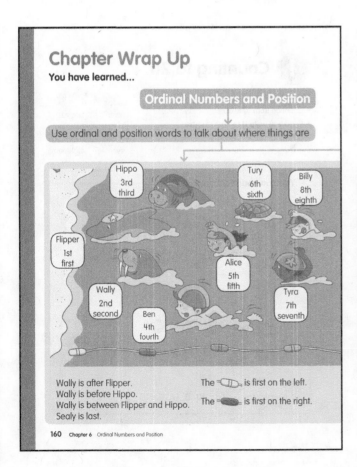

Hippo 3rd third
Tury 6th sixth
Billy 8th eighth
Flipper 1st first
Alice 5th fifth
Tyra 7th seventh
Wally 2nd second
Ben 4th fourth

Wally is after Flipper.
Wally is before Hippo.
Wally is between Flipper and Hippo.
Sealy is last.

The 🐟 is first on the left.
The 🐟 is first on the right.

BIG IDEA
Numbers and words can be used to describe order and position.

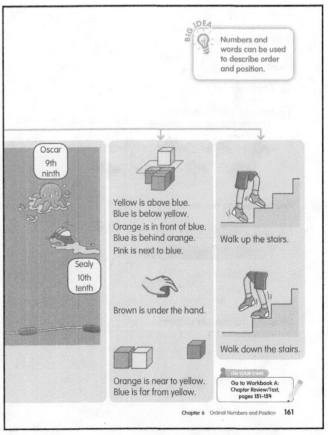

Oscar 9th ninth
Sealy 10th tenth

Yellow is above blue.
Blue is below yellow.
Orange is in front of blue.
Blue is behind orange.
Pink is next to blue.

Walk up the stairs.

Brown is under the hand.

Walk down the stairs.

Orange is near to yellow.
Blue is far from yellow.

ON YOUR OWN
Go to Workbook A:
Chapter Review/Test,
pages 151–154

Chapter 6

CHAPTER 7 Numbers to 20

I'm 10 years old!

I'm 3 years old!

How many candles are there in all?

Lesson 1 Counting to 20
Lesson 2 Place Value
Lesson 3 Comparing Numbers
Lesson 4 Making Patterns and Ordering Numbers

BIG IDEA Count, compare, and order numbers to 20.

162

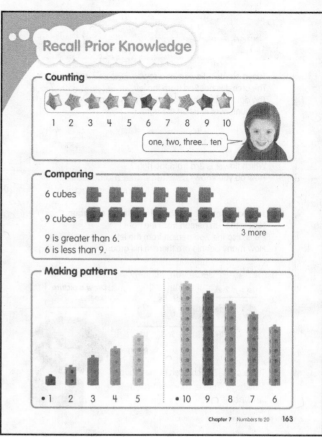

Recall Prior Knowledge

Counting

1 2 3 4 5 6 7 8 9 10

one, two, three... ten

Comparing

6 cubes

9 cubes

3 more

9 is greater than 6.
6 is less than 9.

Making patterns

1 2 3 4 5   10 9 8 7 6

Chapter 7 Numbers to 20 **163**

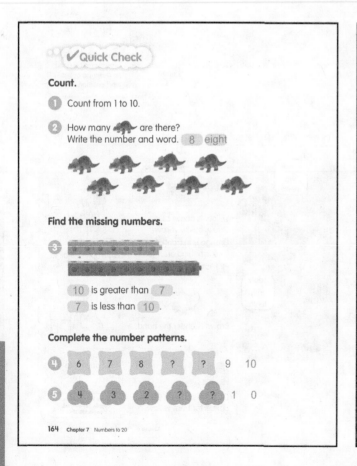

✔ Quick Check

Count.

1 Count from 1 to 10.

2 How many 🦕 are there?
Write the number and word. **8 eight**

Find the missing numbers.

3
10 is greater than **7**.
7 is less than **10**.

Complete the number patterns.

4 **6 7 8 ? ? 9 10**

5 **4 3 2 ? ? 1 0**

164 Chapter 7 Numbers to 20

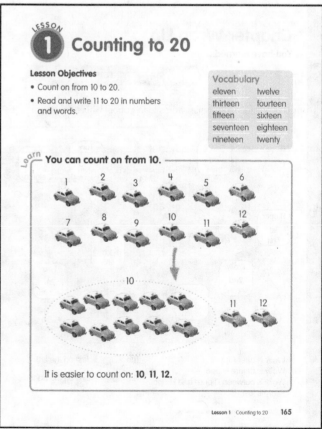

LESSON 1 Counting to 20

Lesson Objectives
• Count on from 10 to 20.
• Read and write 11 to 20 in numbers and words.

Vocabulary
eleven   twelve
thirteen fourteen
fifteen   sixteen
seventeen eighteen
nineteen twenty

Learn You can count on from 10.

1 2 3 4 5 6
7 8 9 10 11 12

10

11 12

It is easier to count on: **10, 11, 12.**

Lesson 1 Counting to 20 **165**

Chapter 7

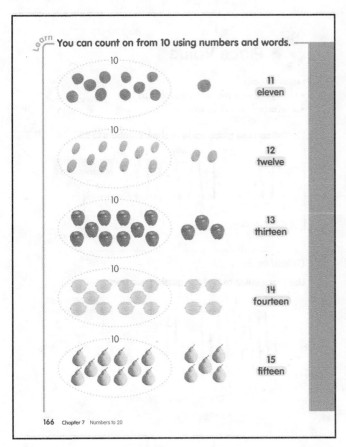

You can count on from 10 using numbers and words.

10 · · · · · · · · · · | ·   11 eleven

10 · · · · · · · · · · | · ·   12 twelve

10 · · · · · · · · · · | · · ·   13 thirteen

10 · · · · · · · · · · | · · · ·   14 fourteen

10 · · · · · · · · · · | · · · · ·   15 fifteen

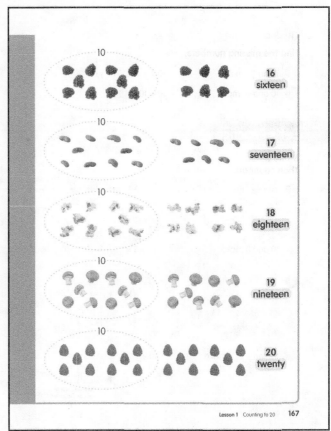

10 · · · · · · · · · · | · · · · · ·   16 sixteen

10 · · · · · · · · · · | · · · · · · ·   17 seventeen

10 · · · · · · · · · · | · · · · · · · ·   18 eighteen

10 · · · · · · · · · · | · · · · · · · · ·   19 nineteen

10 · · · · · · · · · · | · · · · · · · · · ·   20 twenty

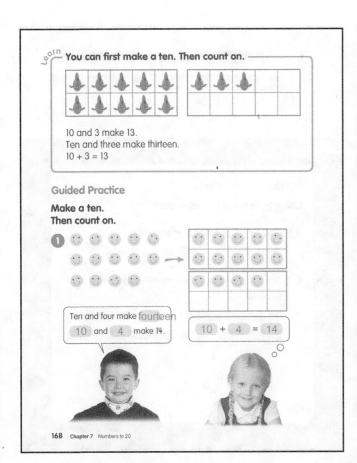

You can first make a ten. Then count on.

10 and 3 make 13.
Ten and three make thirteen.
10 + 3 = 13

Guided Practice

**Make a ten.
Then count on.**

1

Ten and four make fourteen
10 and 4 make 14.

10 + 4 = 14

WORKING TOGETHER **Game**

Players: 4
You need:
• one number cube
• base ten blocks

Roll the Number Cube!

STEP 1 Roll the number cube.
Then take this number of ·.

6!

STEP 2 Each player take turns to roll the number cube and take ·.

STEP 3 On your next turn, roll the number cube again.
Then take this number of ·.
If you have 10 ·, trade them for one _____.

6 + 4 = 10!

The first player to get 2 _____ wins!

Guided Practice

Find the missing numbers.

2 10 and 7 make 17 .   10 + 7 = 17

3 10 and 10 make 20 .   10 + 10 = 20

Let's Practice

Make a ten.
Then count on.

1
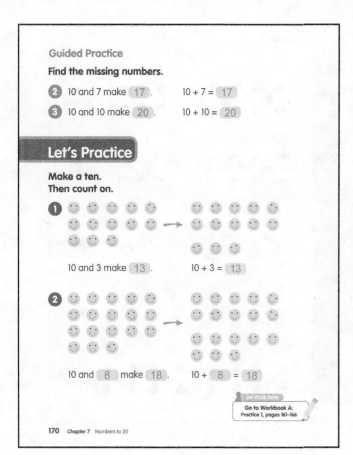

10 and 3 make 13 .   10 + 3 = 13

2

10 and 8 make 18 .   10 + 8 = 18

> **ON YOUR OWN**
> Go to Workbook A:
> Practice 1, pages 161–166

LESSON
2 Place Value

Lesson Objectives
- Use a place-value chart to show numbers up to 20.
- Show objects up to 20 as tens and ones.

> **Vocabulary**
> place-value chart

Learn You can use place value to show numbers to 20.

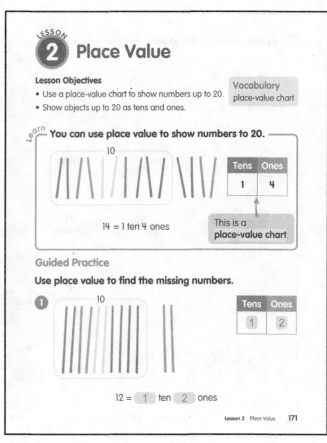

14 = 1 ten 4 ones

This is a **place-value chart**.

Guided Practice

Use place value to find the missing numbers.

1

Tens	Ones
1	2

12 = 1 ten 2 ones

2
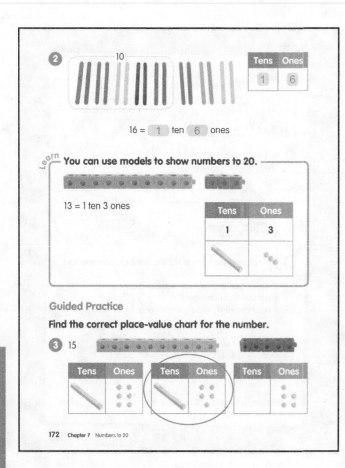

Tens	Ones
1	6

16 = 1 ten 6 ones

Learn You can use models to show numbers to 20.

13 = 1 ten 3 ones

Tens	Ones
1	3

Guided Practice

Find the correct place-value chart for the number.

3 15

Tens	Ones		Tens	Ones		Tens	Ones

---

4 17
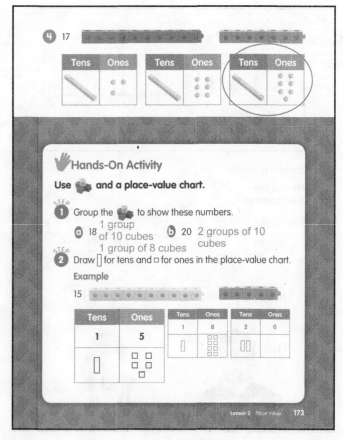

Tens	Ones		Tens	Ones		Tens	Ones

Hands-On Activity

Use 🧩 and a place-value chart.

STEP 1 Group the 🧩 to show these numbers.

a 18 1 group of 10 cubes
         1 group of 8 cubes

b 20 2 groups of 10 cubes

STEP 2 Draw ▯ for tens and ▢ for ones in the place-value chart.

Example

15

Tens	Ones		Tens	Ones		Tens	Ones
1	5		1	8		2	0

Look at each place-value chart.
What is the number shown?

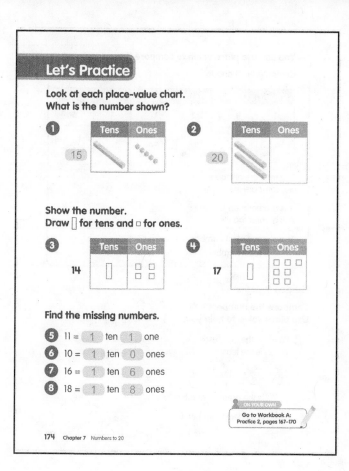

1 15

Tens	Ones

2 20

Tens	Ones

Show the number.
Draw ⊡ for tens and □ for ones.

3 14

Tens	Ones

4 17

Tens	Ones

Find the missing numbers.

5 11 = **1** ten **1** one

6 10 = **1** ten **0** ones

7 16 = **1** ten **6** ones

8 18 = **1** ten **8** ones

ON YOUR OWN
Go to Workbook A:
Practice 2, pages 167–170

174 Chapter 7 Numbers to 20

LESSON
3 Comparing Numbers

Lesson Objective
• Compare numbers to 20.

Vocabulary
greatest
least

Learn **Compare sets and numbers.**

Set A   12

Set B   10

Set A has 2 more than Set B.

Set B has 2 fewer than Set A.

12 is greater than 10.

10 is less than 12.

Lesson 3 Comparing Numbers 175

Guided Practice

Count.
Then answer the questions.

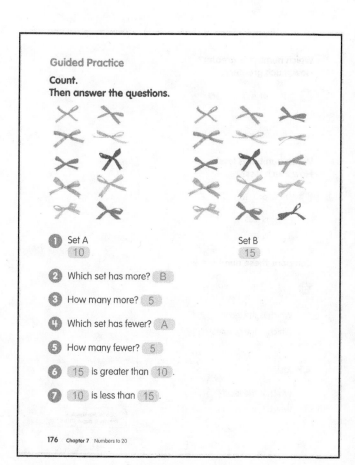

1 Set A
10

Set B
15

2 Which set has more? B

3 How many more? 5

4 Which set has fewer? A

5 How many fewer? 5

6 **15** is greater than **10**.

7 **10** is less than **15**.

176 Chapter 7 Numbers to 20

Learn **You can use place value to find how much greater or how much less.**

Compare 13 and 15.
Which number is greater?
How much greater is the number?

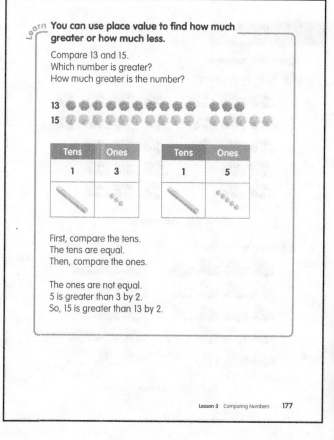

13

15

Tens	Ones
1	3

Tens	Ones
1	5

First, compare the tens.
The tens are equal.
Then, compare the ones.

The ones are not equal.
5 is greater than 3 by 2.
So, 15 is greater than 13 by 2.

Lesson 3 Comparing Numbers 177

Chapter 7

Guided Practice

**Compare the numbers.
Use place value to help you.**

8 Which number is greater?
How much greater?

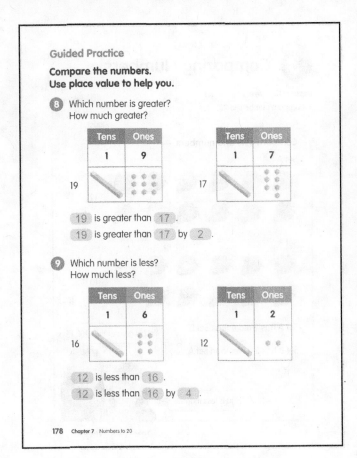

Tens	Ones
1	9

19

Tens	Ones
1	7

17

19 is greater than 17 .

19 is greater than 17 by 2 .

9 Which number is less?
How much less?

Tens	Ones
1	6

16

Tens	Ones
1	2

12

12 is less than 16 .

12 is less than 16 by 4 .

Learn You can use place value to compare three numbers.

Compare 14, 11 and 16.

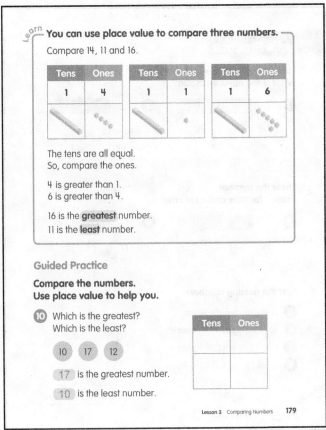

Tens	Ones
1	4

Tens	Ones
1	1

Tens	Ones
1	6

The tens are all equal.
So, compare the ones.

4 is greater than 1.
6 is greater than 4.

16 is the **greatest** number.
11 is the **least** number.

Guided Practice

**Compare the numbers.
Use place value to help you.**

10 Which is the greatest?
Which is the least?

10   17   12

Tens	Ones

17 is the greatest number.

10 is the least number.

Let's Practice

Count and compare.

1 Which set has more?

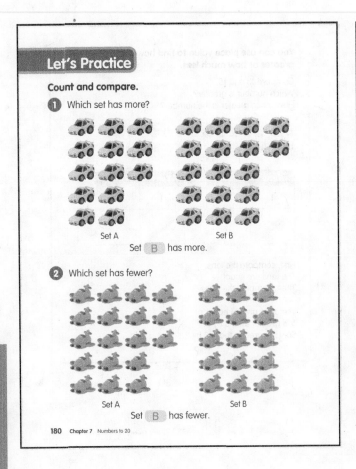

Set A   Set B

Set B has more.

2 Which set has fewer?

Set A   Set B

Set B has fewer.

**Which number is greater?
How much greater?**

3 9 or 5

9 is greater.

It is greater by 4 .

**Which number is less?
How much less?**

4 19 or 10

10 is less.

It is less by 9 .

Compare these numbers.

5 12   18   14

Which is the least? 12

Which is the greatest? 18

6 11   20   10

Which is the least? 10

Which is the greatest? 20

ON YOUR OWN
Go to Workbook A:
Practice 3, pages 171–178

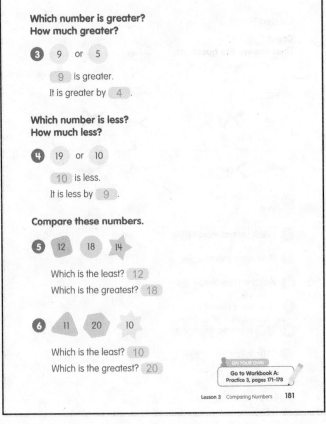

Chapter 7

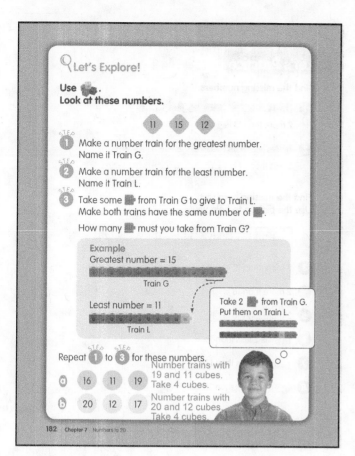

Let's Explore!

Use ![cube].
Look at these numbers.

11   15   12

STEP 1 Make a number train for the greatest number. Name it Train G.

STEP 2 Make a number train for the least number. Name it Train L.

STEP 3 Take some ![cube] from Train G to give to Train L. Make both trains have the same number of ![cube].

How many ![cube] must you take from Train G?

Example
Greatest number = 15

Train G

Least number = 11

Train L

Take 2 ![cube] from Train G. Put them on Train L.

Repeat **STEP 1** to **STEP 3** for these numbers.

ⓐ 16   11   19   Number trains with 19 and 11 cubes. Take 4 cubes.

ⓑ 20   12   17   Number trains with 20 and 12 cubes. Take 4 cubes.

182 Chapter 7 Numbers to 20

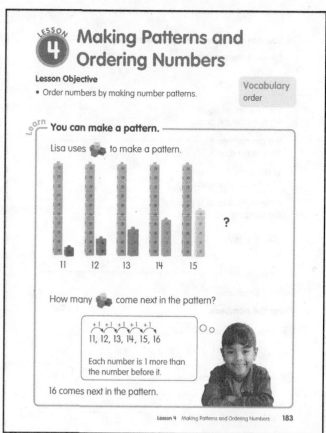

Making Patterns and Ordering Numbers

Lesson Objective
• Order numbers by making number patterns.

Vocabulary
order

You can make a pattern.

Lisa uses ![cubes] to make a pattern.

11   12   13   14   15   ?

How many ![cubes] come next in the pattern?

+1 +1 +1 +1 +1
11, 12, 13, 14, 15, 16

Each number is 1 more than the number before it.

16 comes next in the pattern.

Lesson 4 Making Patterns and Ordering Numbers 183

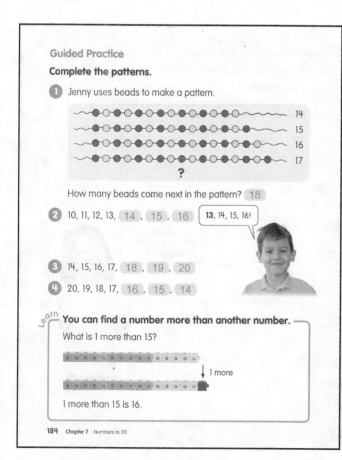

Guided Practice

Complete the patterns.

① Jenny uses beads to make a pattern.

14
15
16
17
?

How many beads come next in the pattern? 18

② 10, 11, 12, 13, 14 , 15 , 16   *13, 14, 15, 16!*

③ 14, 15, 16, 17, 18 , 19 , 20

④ 20, 19, 18, 17, 16 , 15 , 14

You can find a number more than another number.

What is 1 more than 15?

1 more

1 more than 15 is 16.

184 Chapter 7 Numbers to 20

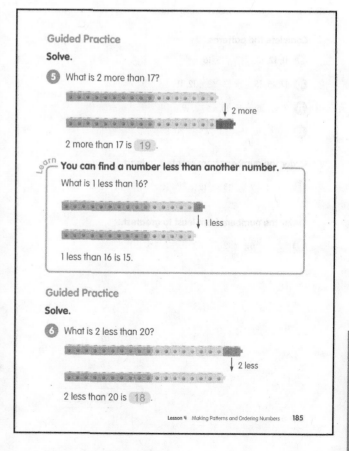

Guided Practice

Solve.

⑤ What is 2 more than 17?

2 more

2 more than 17 is 19 .

You can find a number less than another number.

What is 1 less than 16?

1 less

1 less than 16 is 15.

Guided Practice

Solve.

⑥ What is 2 less than 20?

2 less

2 less than 20 is 18 .

Lesson 4 Making Patterns and Ordering Numbers 185

Chapter 7

Student Edition Answers: Chapter 7
Math in Focus Homeschool Answer Key, Grade 1

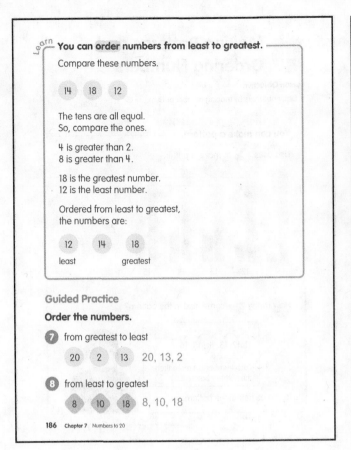

Learn You can order numbers from least to greatest.

Compare these numbers.

14 18 12

The tens are all equal.
So, compare the ones.

4 is greater than 2.
8 is greater than 4.

18 is the greatest number.
12 is the least number.

Ordered from least to greatest,
the numbers are:

12 14 18
least   greatest

Guided Practice

Order the numbers.

7 from greatest to least

20 2 13   20, 13, 2

8 from least to greatest

8 10 18   8, 10, 18

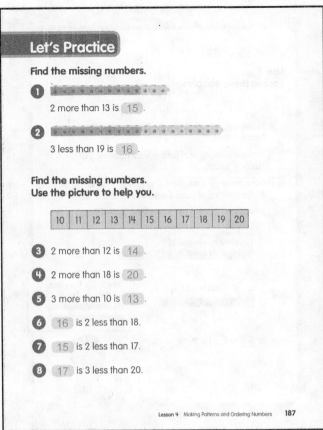

Let's Practice

Find the missing numbers.

1 ████████████████
2 more than 13 is 15 .

2 ████████████████
3 less than 19 is 16 .

**Find the missing numbers.
Use the picture to help you.**

| 10 | 11 | 12 | 13 | 14 | 15 | 16 | 17 | 18 | 19 | 20 |

3 2 more than 12 is 14 .

4 2 more than 18 is 20 .

5 3 more than 10 is 13 .

6 16 is 2 less than 18.

7 15 is 2 less than 17.

8 17 is 3 less than 20.

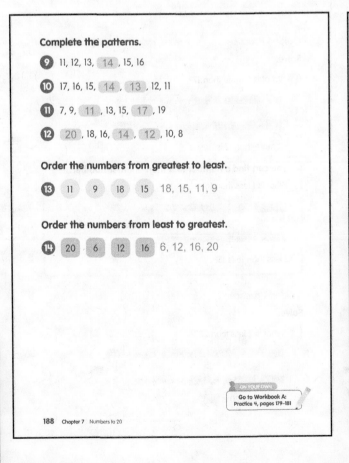

Complete the patterns.

9 11, 12, 13, 14 , 15, 16

10 17, 16, 15, 14 , 13 , 12, 11

11 7, 9, 11 , 13, 15, 17 , 19

12 20 , 18, 16, 14 , 12 , 10, 8

Order the numbers from greatest to least.

13 11   9   18   15   18, 15, 11, 9

Order the numbers from least to greatest.

14 20   6   12   16   6, 12, 16, 20

ON YOUR OWN
Go to Workbook A:
Practice 4, pages 179–181

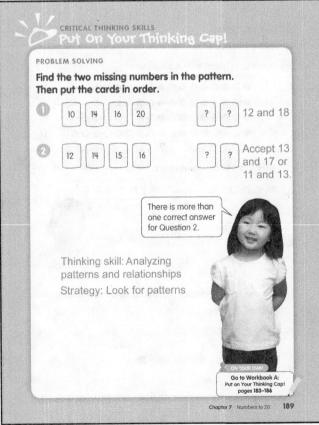

CRITICAL THINKING SKILLS
Put On Your Thinking Cap!

PROBLEM SOLVING

**Find the two missing numbers in the pattern.
Then put the cards in order.**

1 | 10 | 14 | 16 | 20 | | ? | ? | 12 and 18

2 | 12 | 14 | 15 | 16 | | ? | ? | Accept 13 and 17 or 11 and 13.

There is more than
one correct answer
for Question 2.

Thinking skill: Analyzing
patterns and relationships
Strategy: Look for patterns

ON YOUR OWN
Go to Workbook A:
Put on Your Thinking Cap!
pages 183–186

Chapter Wrap Up

You have learned...

Numbers to 20

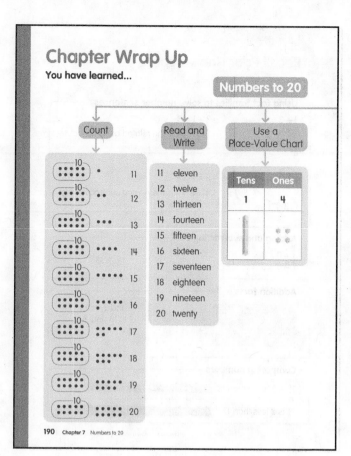

Count

10 •	•	11
10 •	••	12
10 •	•••	13
10 •	••••	14
10 •	•••••	15
10 •	••••••	16
10 •	•••••••	17
10 •	••••••••	18
10 •	•••••••••	19
10 •	••••••••••	20

Read and Write

11	eleven
12	twelve
13	thirteen
14	fourteen
15	fifteen
16	sixteen
17	seventeen
18	eighteen
19	nineteen
20	twenty

Use a Place-Value Chart

Tens	Ones
1	4
│	•• ••

BIG IDEA Count, compare, and order numbers to 20.

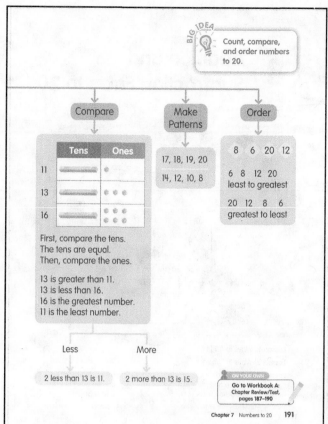

Compare

	Tens	Ones
11	▬	•
13	▬	•••
16	▬	••• •••

First, compare the tens.
The tens are equal.
Then, compare the ones.

13 is greater than 11.
13 is less than 16.
16 is the greatest number.
11 is the least number.

Less → 2 less than 13 is 11.

More → 2 more than 13 is 15.

Make Patterns

17, 18, 19, 20

14, 12, 10, 8

Order

8   6   20   12

6   8   12   20
least to greatest

20   12   8   6
greatest to least

ON YOUR OWN
Go to Workbook A:
Chapter Review/Test,
pages 187–190

51

CHAPTER 8 Addition and Subtraction Facts to 20

Lesson 1 Ways to Add
Lesson 2 Ways to Subtract
Lesson 3 Real-World Problems: Addition and Subtraction Facts

BIG IDEA
Different strategies can be used to add and subtract.

192

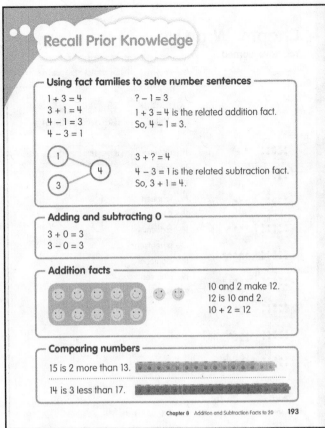

Recall Prior Knowledge

Using fact families to solve number sentences

$1 + 3 = 4$
$3 + 1 = 4$
$4 - 1 = 3$
$4 - 3 = 1$

$? - 1 = 3$
$1 + 3 = 4$ is the related addition fact.
So, $4 - 1 = 3$.

$3 + ? = 4$
$4 - 3 = 1$ is the related subtraction fact.
So, $3 + 1 = 4$.

Adding and subtracting 0

$3 + 0 = 3$
$3 - 0 = 3$

Addition facts

10 and 2 make 12.
12 is 10 and 2.
$10 + 2 = 12$

Comparing numbers

15 is 2 more than 13.

14 is 3 less than 17.

Chapter 8 Addition and Subtraction Facts to 20   **193**

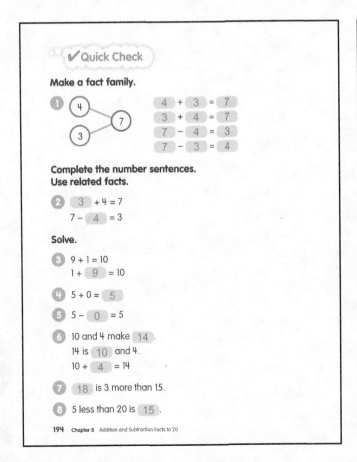

✔ Quick Check

Make a fact family.

1

$4 + 3 = 7$
$3 + 4 = 7$
$7 - 4 = 3$
$7 - 3 = 4$

Complete the number sentences. Use related facts.

2   $3 + 4 = 7$
    $7 - 4 = 3$

Solve.

3   $9 + 1 = 10$
    $1 + 9 = 10$

4   $5 + 0 = 5$

5   $5 - 0 = 5$

6   10 and 4 make 14.
    14 is 10 and 4.
    $10 + 4 = 14$

7   18 is 3 more than 15.

8   5 less than 20 is 15.

194   Chapter 8 Addition and Subtraction Facts to 20

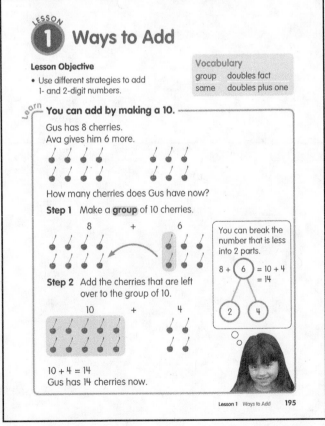

LESSON 1 Ways to Add

Lesson Objective
• Use different strategies to add 1- and 2-digit numbers.

Vocabulary
group   doubles fact
same   doubles plus one

learn You can add by making a 10.

Gus has 8 cherries.
Ava gives him 6 more.

How many cherries does Gus have now?

Step 1 Make a **group** of 10 cherries.

8   +   6

Step 2 Add the cherries that are left over to the group of 10.

10   +   4

You can break the number that is less into 2 parts.

$8 + 6 = 10 + 4$
$= 14$

2   4

$10 + 4 = 14$
Gus has 14 cherries now.

Lesson 1 Ways to Add   **195**

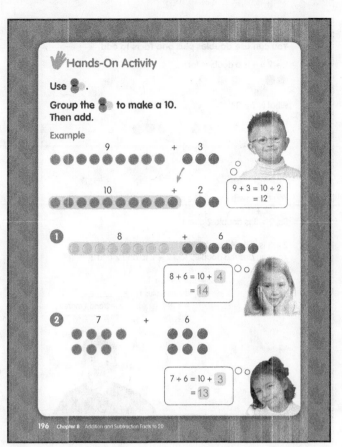

Hands-On Activity

Use 🔵.

Group the 🔵 to make a 10.
Then add.

Example

9 + 3

10 + 2

9 + 3 = 10 + 2
= 12

1 8 + 6

8 + 6 = 10 + 4
= 14

2 7 + 6

7 + 6 = 10 + 3
= 13

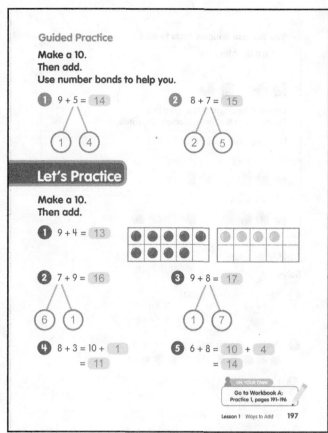

Guided Practice

Make a 10.
Then add.
Use number bonds to help you.

1 9 + 5 = 14

1   4

2 8 + 7 = 15

2   5

Let's Practice

Make a 10.
Then add.

1 9 + 4 = 13

2 7 + 9 = 16

6   1

3 9 + 8 = 17

1   7

4 8 + 3 = 10 + 1
= 11

5 6 + 8 = 10 + 4
= 14

ON YOUR OWN
Go to Workbook A:
Practice 1, pages 191–196

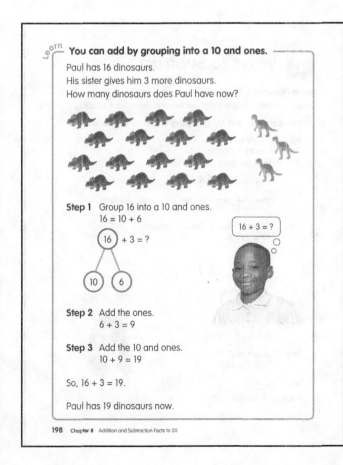

You can add by grouping into a 10 and ones.

Paul has 16 dinosaurs.
His sister gives him 3 more dinosaurs.
How many dinosaurs does Paul have now?

16 + 3 = ?

Step 1 Group 16 into a 10 and ones.
16 = 10 + 6

16 + 3 = ?

10   6

Step 2 Add the ones.
6 + 3 = 9

Step 3 Add the 10 and ones.
10 + 9 = 19

So, 16 + 3 = 19.

Paul has 19 dinosaurs now.

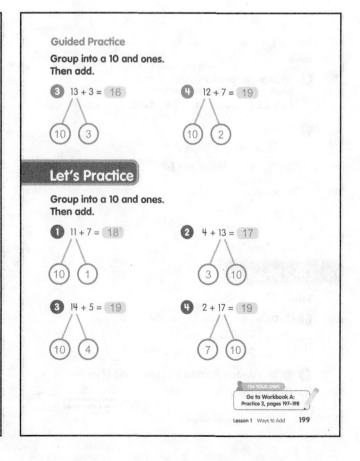

Guided Practice

Group into a 10 and ones.
Then add.

3 13 + 3 = 16

10   3

4 12 + 7 = 19

10   2

Let's Practice

Group into a 10 and ones.
Then add.

1 11 + 7 = 18

10   1

2 4 + 13 = 17

3   10

3 14 + 5 = 19

10   4

4 2 + 17 = 19

7   10

ON YOUR OWN
Go to Workbook A:
Practice 2, pages 197–198

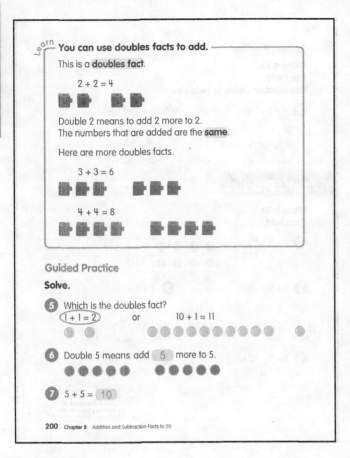

You can use doubles facts to add.

This is a **doubles fact**.

$2 + 2 = 4$

Double 2 means to add 2 more to 2.
The numbers that are added are the **same**.

Here are more doubles facts.

$3 + 3 = 6$

$4 + 4 = 8$

Guided Practice

Solve.

5) Which is the doubles fact?
(1 + 1 = 2)   or $10 + 1 = 11$

6) Double 5 means add ⟨5⟩ more to 5.

7) $5 + 5 = $ ⟨10⟩

200   Chapter 8   Addition and Subtraction Facts to 20

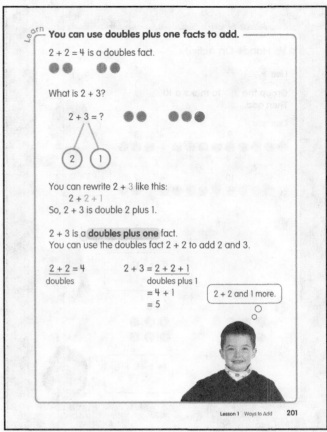

You can use doubles plus one facts to add.

$2 + 2 = 4$ is a doubles fact.

What is $2 + 3$?

$2 + 3 = ?$

You can rewrite $2 + 3$ like this:
$2 + 2 + 1$
So, $2 + 3$ is double 2 plus 1.

$2 + 3$ is a **doubles plus one** fact.
You can use the doubles fact $2 + 2$ to add 2 and 3.

$2 + 2 = 4$ $2 + 3 = 2 + 2 + 1$
doubles   doubles plus 1
                        $= 4 + 1$ 2 + 2 and 1 more.
                        $= 5$

Lesson 1   Ways to Add   201

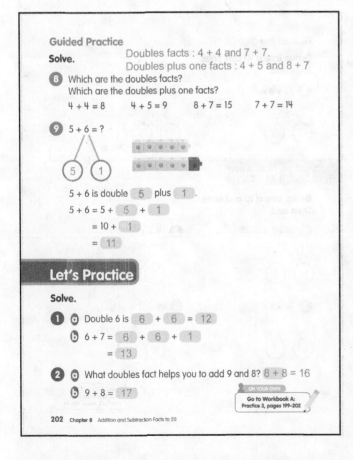

Guided Practice

Solve.   Doubles facts : $4 + 4$ and $7 + 7$.
                        Doubles plus one facts : $4 + 5$ and $8 + 7$

8) Which are the doubles facts?
Which are the doubles plus one facts?
$4 + 4 = 8$ $4 + 5 = 9$ $8 + 7 = 15$ $7 + 7 = 14$

9) $5 + 6 = ?$

$5 + 6$ is double ⟨5⟩ plus ⟨1⟩.
$5 + 6 = 5 +$ ⟨5⟩ $+$ ⟨1⟩
$= 10 +$ ⟨1⟩
$=$ ⟨11⟩

Let's Practice

Solve.

1) a) Double 6 is ⟨6⟩ $+$ ⟨6⟩ $=$ ⟨12⟩
   b) $6 + 7 = $ ⟨6⟩ $+$ ⟨6⟩ $+$ ⟨1⟩
      $=$ ⟨13⟩

2) a) What doubles fact helps you to add 9 and 8? $8 + 8 = 16$
   b) $9 + 8 = $ ⟨17⟩

ON YOUR OWN
Go to Workbook A:
Practice 3, pages 199–202

202   Chapter 8   Addition and Subtraction Facts to 20

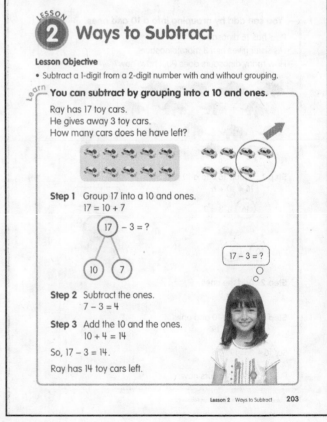

LESSON
2) Ways to Subtract

Lesson Objective
• Subtract a 1-digit from a 2-digit number with and without grouping.

You can subtract by grouping into a 10 and ones.

Ray has 17 toy cars.
He gives away 3 toy cars.
How many cars does he have left?

Step 1   Group 17 into a 10 and ones.
$17 = 10 + 7$

$17 - 3 = ?$ $17 - 3 = ?$

Step 2   Subtract the ones.
$7 - 3 = 4$

Step 3   Add the 10 and the ones.
$10 + 4 = 14$

So, $17 - 3 = 14$.

Ray has 14 toy cars left.

Lesson 2   Ways to Subtract   203

Guided Practice

**Group the numbers into a 10 and ones.
Then subtract.**

1 17 − 5 = 12
10   7

2 18 − 3 = 15
10   8

**Solve the riddle.
Subtract, then write the letter on the correct line.**

3

13 − 3 = 10 **T**   17 − 6 = 11 **S**

15 − 3 = 12 **H**   18 − 5 = 13 **W**

16 − 1 = 15 **E**   19 − 3 = 16 **I**

17 − 0 = 17 **U**   18 − 4 = 14 **O**

Where does the President of the United States live?

THE W   H   I   T   E
     13 12 16 10 15

     H   O   U   S   E
     12 14 17 11 15

 You can subtract by grouping into a 10 and ones.

Shawn makes 12 stars.
He gives 7 to Gina.
How many stars does Shawn have left?

Step 1 Group 12 into a 10 and ones.
12 = 10 + 2

12 − 7 = ?
2   10

Step 2 You cannot subtract 7 from 2.
So, subtract 7 from 10.
10 − 7 = 3

Step 3 Add the ones.
2 + 3 = 5

So, 12 − 7 = 5.

Shawn has 5 stars left.

Guided Practice

**Group the numbers into a 10 and ones.
Then subtract.**

4 11 − 3 = 8
1   10

5 13 − 6 = 7
3   10

 **You can use doubles facts of addition to
help you subtract.**

Joe buys 12 eggs.
He uses 6 eggs to bake a cake.

6 + 6 = 12
So, 12 − 6 = 6

12 − 6 = 6
Joe has 6 eggs left.

Guided Practice

Solve.

6 10 − 5 = 5

7 14 − 7 = 7

WORKING TOGETHER Game

Spin and Subtract!

Players: **3**

You need:
• 2 spinners (A and B)

How to play:

Spinner A   Spinner B

STEP 1 Player 1 uses Spinner A to get a number.

STEP 2 Player 1 then uses Spinner B to get a another number.

STEP 3 Player 2 and Player 3 subtract the two numbers.

12

7

STEP 4 The player who gets the right subtraction sentence first gets 1 point. Take turns spinning the spinner.

The player who gets the most points after six turns wins!

12 − 7 = 5

55

Let's Practice

Subtract.
You can use number bonds to help you.

1 16 – 3 = 13

(10) (6)

2 17 – 4 = 13

(10) (7)

3 18 – 7 = 11

4 19 – 5 = 14

5 15 – 6 = 9

(5) (10)

6 12 – 5 = 7

(2) (10)

7 11 – 4 = 7

8 14 – 8 = 6

9 20 – 9 = 11

10 18 – 9 = 9

ON YOUR OWN
Go to Workbook A:
Practice 4, pages 203–210

208 Chapter 8 Addition and Subtraction Facts to 20

LESSON 3

Real-World Problems: Addition and Subtraction Facts

Lesson Objective
• Solve real-world problems.

Learn Add to solve this word problem.

Ramon has 9 .
Ana gives him 6 .

How many  does Ramon have in all?

9 + 6 = 15

Ramon has 15  in all.

Guided Practice

Solve.

1 Lin makes 6 pasta rings.
Kate makes 6 pasta rings.
How many pasta rings do they
make in all?

6 + 6 = 12

They make 12 pasta rings in all.

Lesson 3 Real-World Problems: Addition and Subtraction Facts 209

Learn Subtract to solve this word problem.

Ali has 16 clay shells.
He gives Mani 5 clay shells.
How many clay shells does Ali have left?

16 – 5 = 11

Ali has 11 clay shells left.

Guided Practice

Solve.

2 George has 11 paper clips.
3 paper clips are blue.
The rest are red.
How many paper clips are red?

11 – 3 = 8

8 paper clips are red.

Let's Practice

Solve.

1 Terry picks 8 tomatoes.
Nan picks 8 tomatoes.
How many tomatoes do Terry
and Nan have in all?

8 + 8 = 16

They have 16 tomatoes in all.

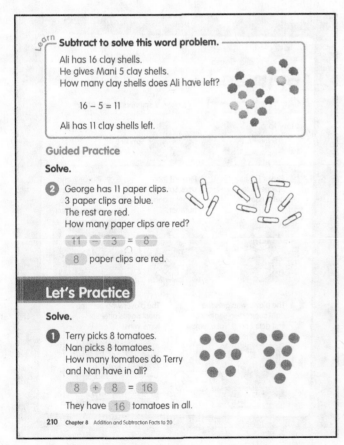

210 Chapter 8 Addition and Subtraction Facts to 20

---

2 Pam makes 14 paper flowers.
9 are blue.
How many are pink?

14 – 9 = 5

5 flowers are pink.

3 Walter finds 15 leaves.
His brother gives him 4 more leaves.
How many leaves does Walter have in all?

15 + 4 = 19

Walter has 19 leaves in all.

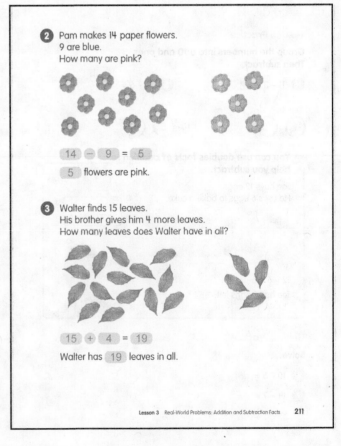

Lesson 3 Real-World Problems: Addition and Subtraction Facts 211

Student Edition Answers: Chapter 8
Math in Focus Homeschool Answer Key, Grade 1

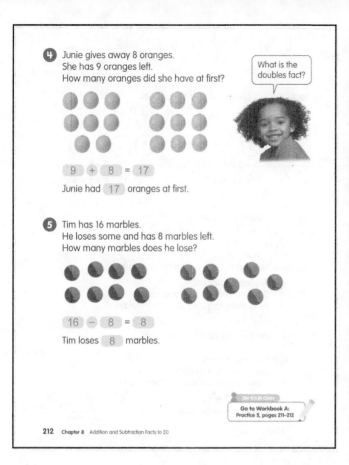

4 Junie gives away 8 oranges.
She has 9 oranges left.
How many oranges did she have at first?

What is the doubles fact?

9 + 8 = 17

Junie had 17 oranges at first.

5 Tim has 16 marbles.
He loses some and has 8 marbles left.
How many marbles does he lose?

16 − 8 = 8

Tim loses 8 marbles.

ON YOUR OWN
Go to Workbook A:
Practice 5, pages 211–212

212   Chapter 8   Addition and Subtraction Facts to 20

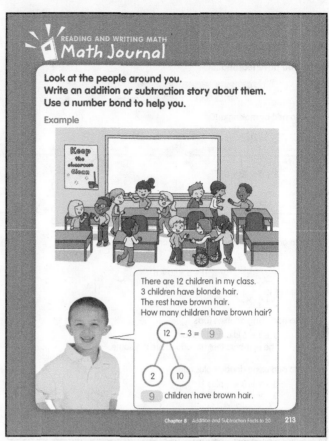

READING AND WRITING MATH
Math Journal

Look at the people around you.
Write an addition or subtraction story about them.
Use a number bond to help you.

Example

There are 12 children in my class.
3 children have blonde hair.
The rest have brown hair.
How many children have brown hair?

12 − 3 = 9

2   10

9 children have brown hair.

Chapter 8   Addition and Subtraction Facts to 20   213

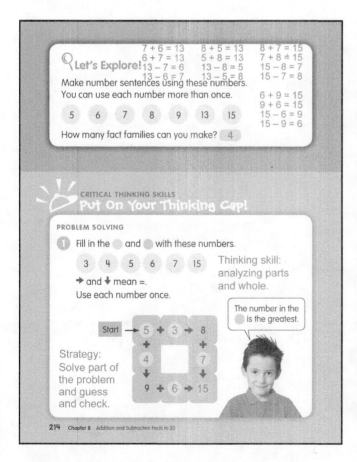

7 + 6 = 13   8 + 5 = 13   8 + 7 = 15
6 + 7 = 13   5 + 8 = 13   7 + 8 = 15
13 − 7 = 6   13 − 8 = 5   15 − 8 = 7
13 − 6 = 7   13 − 5 = 8   15 − 7 = 8

Let's Explore!
Make number sentences using these numbers.
You can use each number more than once.

5   6   7   8   9   13   15

6 + 9 = 15
9 + 6 = 15
15 − 6 = 9
15 − 9 = 6

How many fact families can you make?   4

CRITICAL THINKING SKILLS
Put On Your Thinking Cap!

PROBLEM SOLVING

1 Fill in the ⬭ and ⬤ with these numbers.

3   4   5   6   7   15

➜ and ⬇ mean =.
Use each number once.

Thinking skill:
analyzing parts
and whole.

The number in the ⬤ is the greatest.

Start ➜ 5 + 3 ➜ 8
+   +
4   7
⬇   ⬇
9 + 6 ➜ 15

Strategy:
Solve part of
the problem
and guess
and check.

214   Chapter 8   Addition and Subtraction Facts to 20

CRITICAL THINKING SKILLS
Put On Your Thinking Cap!

PROBLEM SOLVING

2 Fill in the ⬭ and ⬤ with these numbers.

3   4   6   7   8   17

➜ and ⬇ mean =.
Use each number once.

Start ➜ 17 − 7 ➜ 10
8   4
⬇   ⬇
9 − 3 ➜ 6

ON YOUR OWN
Go to Workbook A:
Put on Your Thinking Cap!
pages 213–216

Chapter 8   Addition and Subtraction Facts to 20   215

Student Edition Answers: Chapter 8
Math in Focus Homeschool Answer Key, Grade 1

Chapter Wrap Up

You have learned...

Addition and Subtraction Facts to 20

to add by making a 10.

$$8 + 5 = 10 + 3$$
$$= 13$$

8 + 5

$$8 + 2 = 10$$
$$8 + 5 = 10 + 3$$
$$= 13$$

to add by grouping into a 10 and ones.

11 + 5

$$5 + 1 = 6$$
$$11 + 5 = 10 + 6$$
$$= 16$$

to add using doubles facts.

3 + 3 = 6 is a doubles fact.
The numbers that are added are the same.

to add using doubles plus one.

$$3 + 4 \text{ is } 3 + 3 \text{ plus } 1$$
$$3 + 4 = 3 + 3 + 1$$
$$= 7$$

216 **Chapter 8** Addition and Subtraction Facts to 20

Different strategies can be used to add and subtract.

to subtract by grouping into a 10 and ones.

1 15 − 3

10   5

$$5 - 3 = 2$$
$$15 - 3 = 10 + 2$$
$$= 12$$

2 15 − 6

5   10

$$10 - 6 = 4$$
$$15 - 6 = 4 + 5$$
$$= 9$$

to subtract using doubles facts.

$$7 + 7 = 14$$
So, $14 - 7 = 7$.

to add or subtract to solve real-world problems.

1 Joy has 8 tadpoles.
Ben gives her 5 more tadpoles.
How many tadpoles does she have now?

$$8 + 5 = 13$$

Joy has 13 tadpoles now.

2 Con has 18 marbles.
He gives Pete 9 marbles.
How many marbles does Con have left?

$$18 - 9 = 9$$

Con has 9 marbles left.

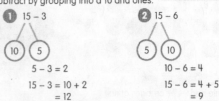

ON YOUR OWN

Go to Workbook A:
Chapter Review/Test,
pages 217–218

Chapter 8 Addition and Subtraction Facts to 20   217

Lesson 1 Comparing Two Things
Lesson 2 Comparing More Than Two Things
Lesson 3 Using a Start Line
Lesson 4 Measuring Things
Lesson 5 Finding Length in Units

BIG IDEA

Compare the height and length of things. Measure with non-standard units to find length.

218

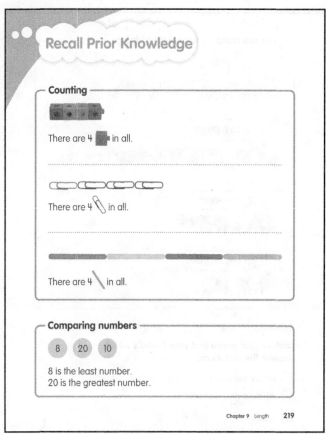

Recall Prior Knowledge

Counting

There are 4 in all.

There are 4 in all.

There are 4 in all.

Comparing numbers

8   20   10

8 is the least number.
20 is the greatest number.

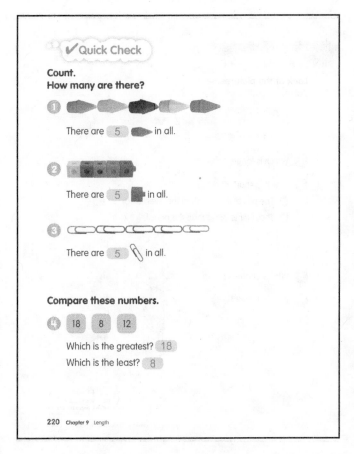

✔ **Quick Check**

**Count.
How many are there?**

1 There are 5 in all.

2 There are 5 in all.

3 There are 5 in all.

Compare these numbers.

4 18   8   12

Which is the greatest? 18

Which is the least? 8

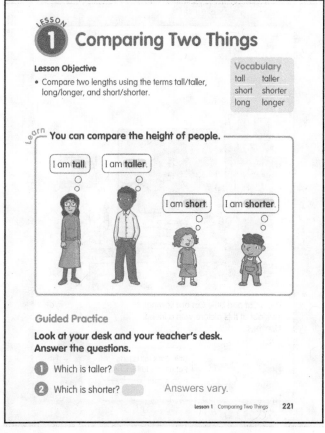

LESSON

1 Comparing Two Things

Lesson Objective
• Compare two lengths using the terms tall/taller, long/longer, and short/shorter.

Vocabulary
tall   taller
short   shorter
long   longer

Learn **You can compare the height of people.**

I am **tall**.   I am **taller**.   I am **short**.   I am **shorter**.

Guided Practice
**Look at your desk and your teacher's desk.
Answer the questions.**

1 Which is taller?

2 Which is shorter?   Answers vary.

Student Edition Answers: Chapter 9
Math in Focus Homeschool Answer Key, Grade 1

Learn You can compare the length of things.

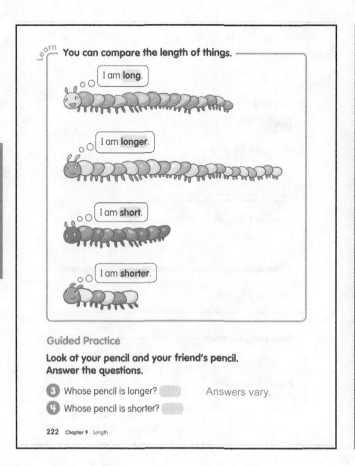

I am **long**.

I am **longer**.

I am **short**.

I am **shorter**.

Guided Practice

Look at your pencil and your friend's pencil.
Answer the questions.

3 Whose pencil is longer? Answers vary.

4 Whose pencil is shorter?

222 Chapter 9 Length

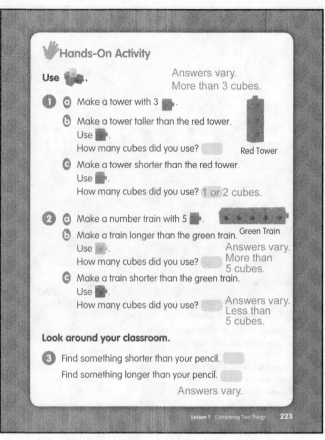

✋ Hands-On Activity

Use 🧊.

Answers vary.
More than 3 cubes.

1 ⓐ Make a tower with 3 🧊.

ⓑ Make a tower taller than the red tower.
Use 🧊.
How many cubes did you use? Red Tower

ⓒ Make a tower shorter than the red tower.
Use 🧊.
How many cubes did you use? 1 or 2 cubes.

2 ⓐ Make a number train with 5 🧊. Green Train

ⓑ Make a train longer than the green train.
Use 🧊.
How many cubes did you use? Answers vary.
More than 5 cubes.

ⓒ Make a train shorter than the green train.
Use 🧊.
How many cubes did you use? Answers vary.
Less than 5 cubes.

Look around your classroom.

3 Find something shorter than your pencil.

Find something longer than your pencil.

Answers vary.

Lesson 1 Comparing Two Things 223

🔍 Let's Explore!

WORK IN PAIRS

Papa Cat and Little Cat are sewing!
Talk about this picture with a friend.
Use these words.

Answers vary.

tall   taller

long   longer

short   shorter

Little Cat's tail is long.
Papa Cat's tail is longer.

224 Chapter 9 Length

Let's Practice

Look at the pictures.
Solve.

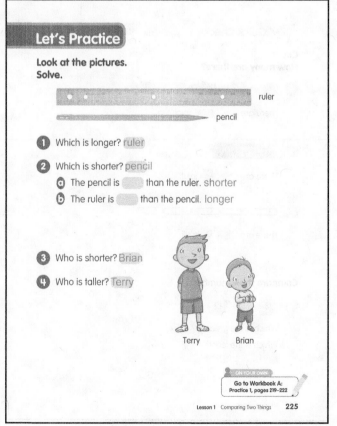

ruler

pencil

1 Which is longer? ruler

2 Which is shorter? pencil
ⓐ The pencil is than the ruler. shorter
ⓑ The ruler is than the pencil. longer

3 Who is shorter? Brian

4 Who is taller? Terry

Terry   Brian

ON YOUR OWN
Go to Workbook A:
Practice 1, pages 219–222

Lesson 1 Comparing Two Things 225

LESSON 2 Comparing More Than Two Things

Lesson Objectives
- Compare two lengths by comparing each with a third length.
- Compare more than two lengths using the terms tallest, longest, and shortest.

Vocabulary
tallest
shortest
longest

Learn **You can compare the height of more than two people.**

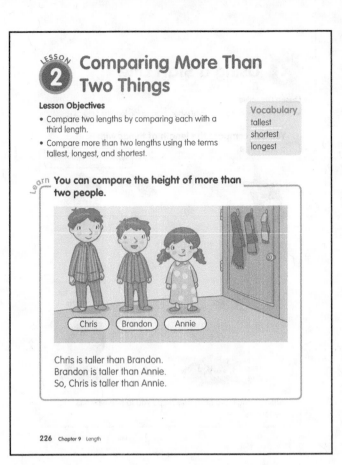

Chris   Brandon   Annie

Chris is taller than Brandon.
Brandon is taller than Annie.
So, Chris is taller than Annie.

226   Chapter 9   Length

Guided Practice

Fill in the blanks.

1.

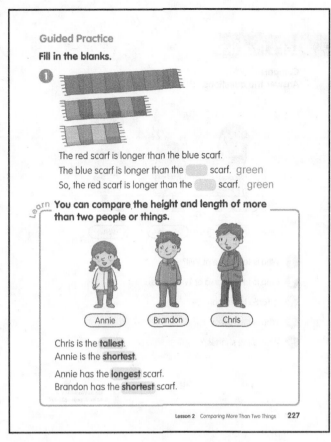

The red scarf is longer than the blue scarf.
The blue scarf is longer than the ___ scarf. green
So, the red scarf is longer than the ___ scarf. green

Learn **You can compare the height and length of more than two people or things.**

Annie   Brandon   Chris

Chris is the **tallest**.
Annie is the **shortest**.

Annie has the **longest** scarf.
Brandon has the **shortest** scarf.

Lesson 2   Comparing More Than Two Things   227

Guided Practice

Look at the picture.
Answer the questions.

Pablo and Erin see some animals in the zoo.

2. Which is the tallest animal? giraffe

3. Which is the shortest animal? zebra

4. Which is the longest animal? crocodile

5. Which is the shortest animal? turtle

228   Chapter 9   Length

Hands-On Activity

Use ▇.

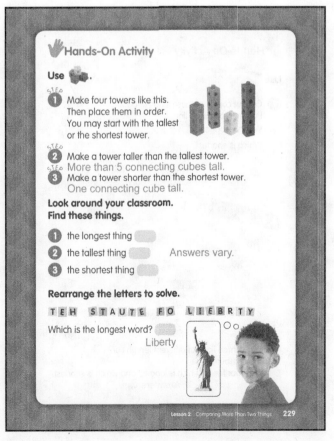

STEP 1. Make four towers like this.
Then place them in order.
You may start with the tallest or the shortest tower.

STEP 2. Make a tower taller than the tallest tower.
More than 5 connecting cubes tall.

STEP 3. Make a tower shorter than the shortest tower.
One connecting cube tall.

Look around your classroom.
Find these things.

1. the longest thing ___
2. the tallest thing ___   Answers vary.
3. the shortest thing ___

Rearrange the letters to solve.

TEH STAUTE FO LIEBRTY

Which is the longest word? ___
Liberty

Lesson 2   Comparing More Than Two Things   229

Let's Practice

Compare.
Answer the questions.

Lee   Tania   Will

1. Who is taller, Lee or Will? Will
2. Who is taller, Tania or Will? Tania
3. Is Tania taller than Lee? Yes
4. Who is the tallest? Tania
5. Who is the shortest? Lee

ON YOUR OWN
Go to Workbook A:
Practice 2, pages 223–227

230 Chapter 9 Length

---

3 Using a Start Line

Lesson Objective
• Use a common starting point when comparing lengths.

Vocabulary
start line

Learn You can compare the length of things with a start line.

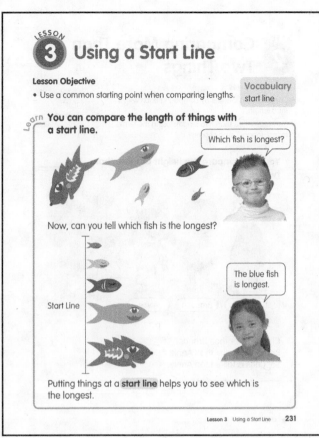

Which fish is longest?

Now, can you tell which fish is the longest?

The blue fish is longest.

Start Line

Putting things at a **start line** helps you to see which is the longest.

Lesson 3 Using a Start Line **231**

✋ Hands-On Activity

Use [image of paper strips].

1. Cut out copies of these strips of paper.
   Put them at a start line.
   Which is longest? A
   Which is shortest? F

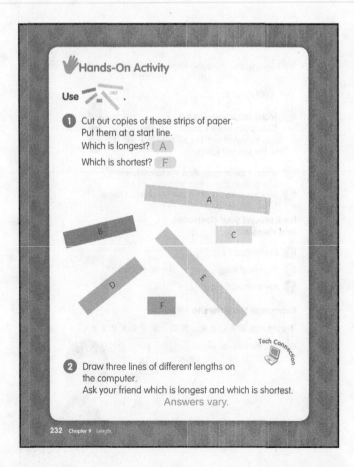

2. Draw three lines of different lengths on the computer.
   Ask your friend which is longest and which is shortest.
   Answers vary.

232 Chapter 9 Length

Let's Practice

Solve.

C
A
B

1. a Which ribbon is longer than Ribbon A?
      Name it Ribbon B.
   b Which ribbon is shorter than Ribbon A?
      Name it Ribbon C.
   c Which ribbon is the longest? B
      Which ribbon is the shortest? C

2. a Which is the tallest
      building? P
   b Which is the shortest
      building? R
   c Which building is as tall
      as Building Q? S

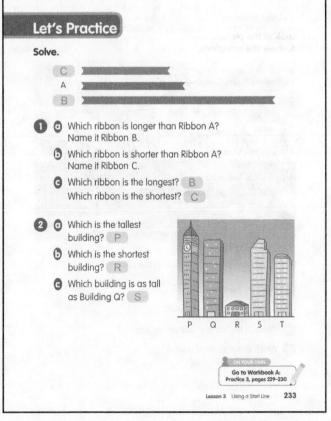

P   Q   R   S   T

ON YOUR OWN
Go to Workbook A:
Practice 3, pages 229–230

Lesson 3 Using a Start Line **233**

---

4 Measuring Things

Lesson Objectives
- Measure lengths using non-standard units.
- Understand that using different non-standard units may give different measurements for the same item.

Vocabulary
about

You can measure length with objects.

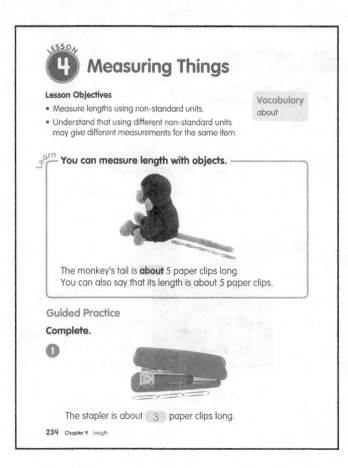

The monkey's tail is **about** 5 paper clips long.
You can also say that its length is about 5 paper clips.

Guided Practice

Complete.

1

The stapler is about **3** paper clips long.

2

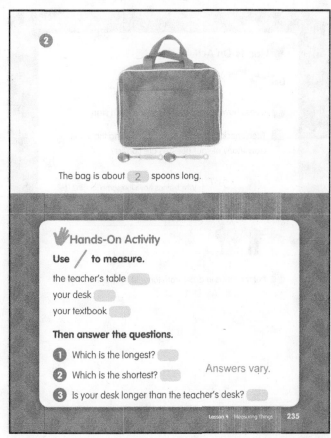

The bag is about **2** spoons long.

✋ Hands-On Activity

Use / to measure.

the teacher's table

your desk

your textbook

Then answer the questions.

1 Which is the longest?

2 Which is the shortest?   Answers vary.

3 Is your desk longer than the teacher's desk?

You can use different objects to measure the same thing.

The pencil is about 5 paper clips long.
It is about 1 craft stick long.

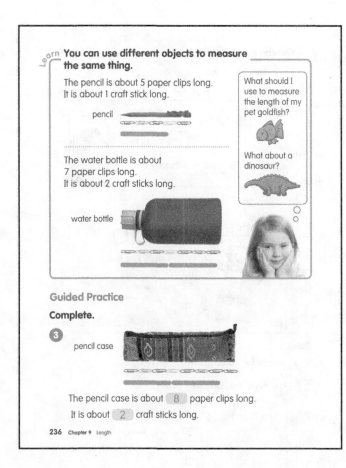

pencil

The water bottle is about
7 paper clips long.
It is about 2 craft sticks long.

water bottle

What should I use to measure the length of my pet goldfish?

What about a dinosaur?

Guided Practice

Complete.

3

pencil case

The pencil case is about **8** paper clips long.

It is about **2** craft sticks long.

✋ Hands-On Activity

WORK IN PAIRS

Use ☐ .

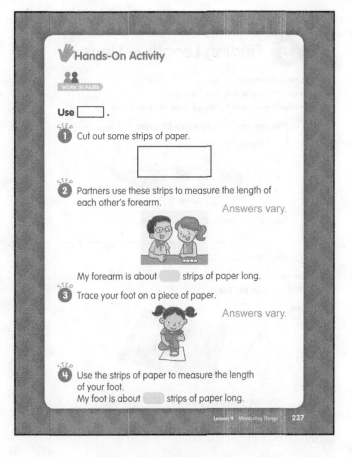

1 Cut out some strips of paper.

2 Partners use these strips to measure the length of each other's forearm.   Answers vary.

My forearm is about ___ strips of paper long.

3 Trace your foot on a piece of paper.   Answers vary.

4 Use the strips of paper to measure the length of your foot.
My foot is about ___ strips of paper long.

Hands-On Activity

Use 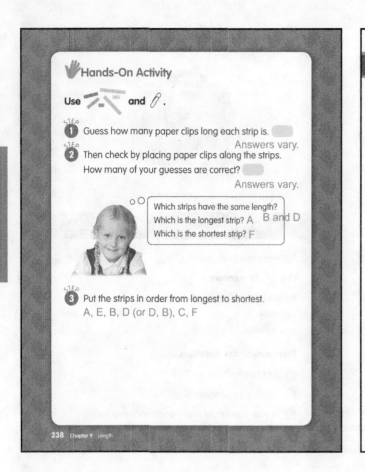 and ✏.

STEP 1 Guess how many paper clips long each strip is. ▢

Answers vary.

STEP 2 Then check by placing paper clips along the strips.
How many of your guesses are correct? ▢

Answers vary.

Which strips have the same length?
Which is the longest strip? A   B and D
Which is the shortest strip? F

STEP 3 Put the strips in order from longest to shortest.
A, E, B, D (or D, B), C, F

Let's Practice

Look at the picture.
Answer the questions.

1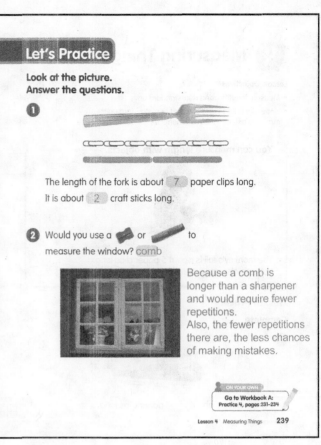

The length of the fork is about ▢ 7 paper clips long.
It is about ▢ 2 craft sticks long.

2 Would you use a 🪮 or 🖊 to
measure the window? comb

Because a comb is
longer than a sharpener
and would require fewer
repetitions.
Also, the fewer repetitions
there are, the less chances
of making mistakes.

ON YOUR OWN
Go to Workbook A:
Practice 4, pages 231–234

LESSON 5 Finding Length in Units

Lesson Objectives
- Use the term "unit" to describe length.
- Count measurement units in a group of ten and ones.

Vocabulary
unit

Learn You can measure length with units.

1 ╱ stands for 1 **unit**.

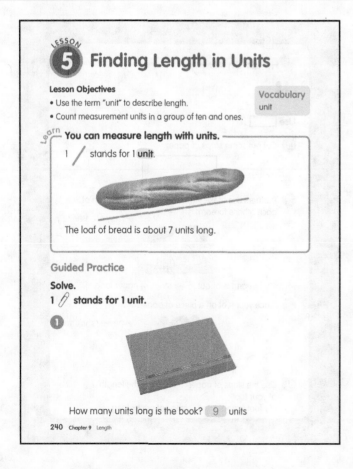

The loaf of bread is about 7 units long.

Guided Practice

Solve.
1 ✏ stands for 1 unit.

1

How many units long is the book? ▢ 9 units

Learn You can measure length with units.

1 ╱ stands for 1 unit.

    10 units   4 units

14 is 10 and 4.

The jump rope is about 14 units long.

Guided Practice

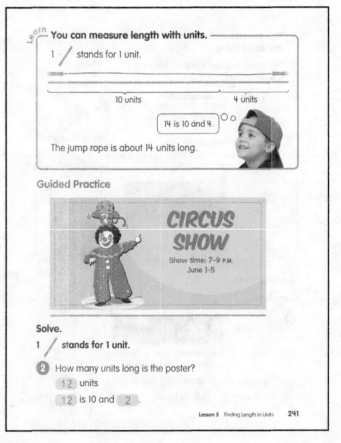

CIRCUS
SHOW

Show time: 7–9 P.M.
June 1–5

Solve.
1 ╱ stands for 1 unit.

2 How many units long is the poster?
▢ 12 units
▢ 12 is 10 and ▢ 2.

Look at the picture.
Then answer the questions.
Each ☐ stands for 1 unit.

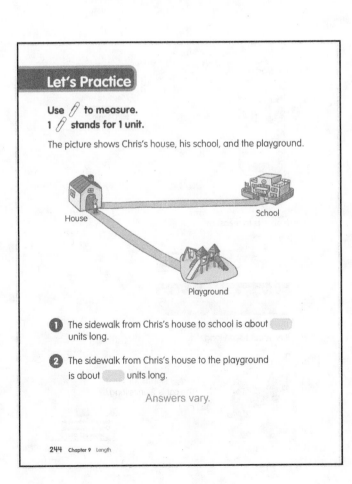

3 How long is the towel rack? **2** units

4 How tall is the shower? **14** units
14 is 10 and **4** .

5 How tall is the boy? **11** units
11 is **10** and **1** .

6 Is the brush longer than the mirror? **No** .

7 Which is shorter, the brush or the towel rack? **towel rack**

242 Chapter 9 Length

✋**Hands-On Activity**

Use ✏ and ╱ to measure these things in
your classroom.

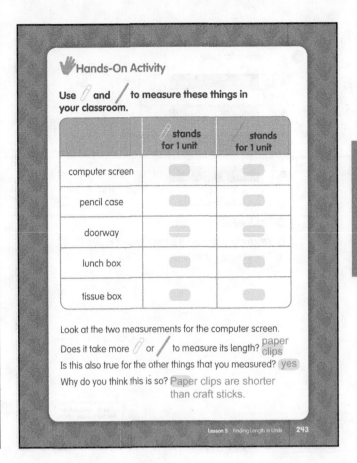

	✏ stands for 1 unit	╱ stands for 1 unit
computer screen		
pencil case		
doorway		
lunch box		
tissue box		

Look at the two measurements for the computer screen.

Does it take more ✏ or ╱ to measure its length? **paper clips**

Is this also true for the other things that you measured? **yes**

Why do you think this is so? **Paper clips are shorter
than craft sticks.**

Lesson 5 Finding Length in Units 243

Let's Practice

Use ✏ to measure.
1 ✏ stands for 1 unit.

The picture shows Chris's house, his school, and the playground.

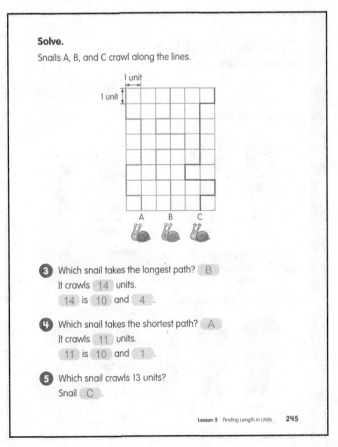

1 The sidewalk from Chris's house to school is about ☐
units long.

2 The sidewalk from Chris's house to the playground
is about ☐ units long.

Answers vary.

244 Chapter 9 Length

Solve.
Snails A, B, and C crawl along the lines.

3 Which snail takes the longest path? **B**
It crawls **14** units.
14 is **10** and **4** .

4 Which snail takes the shortest path? **A**
It crawls **11** units.
11 is **10** and **1** .

5 Which snail crawls 13 units?
Snail **C** .

Lesson 5 Finding Length in Units 245

---

6 1 ☐ stands for 1 unit.

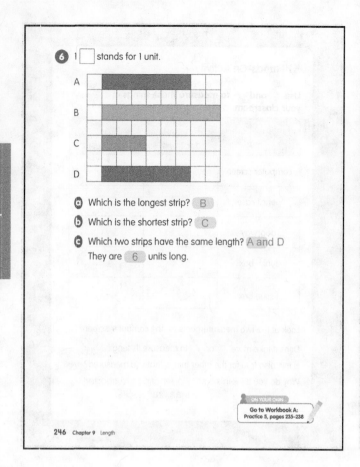

a Which is the longest strip? B

b Which is the shortest strip? C

c Which two strips have the same length? A and D
They are 6 units long.

ON YOUR OWN
Go to Workbook A:
Practice 5, pages 235–238

CRITICAL THINKING SKILLS
Put On Your Thinking Cap!

PROBLEM SOLVING

1 Look at the loaf of bread and the book.

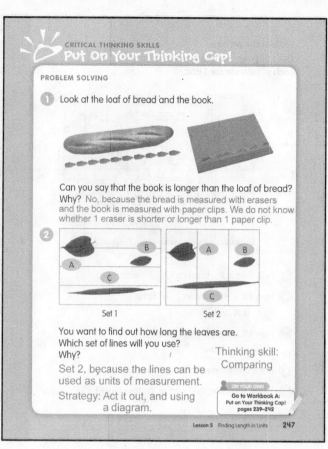

Can you say that the book is longer than the loaf of bread?
Why? No, because the bread is measured with erasers
and the book is measured with paper clips. We do not know
whether 1 eraser is shorter or longer than 1 paper clip.

2

Set 1   Set 2

You want to find out how long the leaves are.
Which set of lines will you use?
Why?

Thinking skill:
Comparing

Set 2, because the lines can be
used as units of measurement.

Strategy: Act it out, and using
a diagram.

ON YOUR OWN
Go to Workbook A:
Put on Your Thinking Cap!
pages 239–242

Chapter Wrap Up

You have learned...

Length

to compare two things.

tall   taller   short   shorter

long   longer

to compare more than two things.

Ally   Ben   Carlo

Ally is taller than Ben.
Ben is taller than Carlo.
So, Ally is also taller
than Carlo.

Ally is the tallest.
Carlo is the shortest.

---

to use a start line.

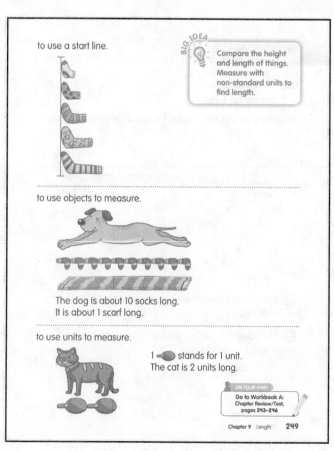

BIG IDEA
Compare the height
and length of things.
Measure with
non-standard units to
find length.

to use objects to measure.

The dog is about 10 socks long.
It is about 1 scarf long.

to use units to measure.

1 ◗ stands for 1 unit.
The cat is 2 units long.

ON YOUR OWN
Go to Workbook A:
Chapter Review/Test,
pages 243–246

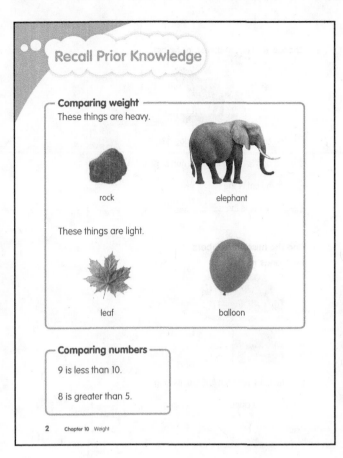

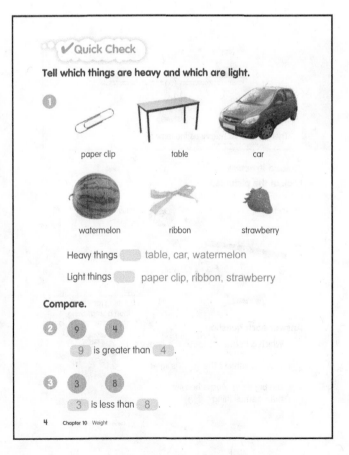

Choose shorter, shortest, or tallest.

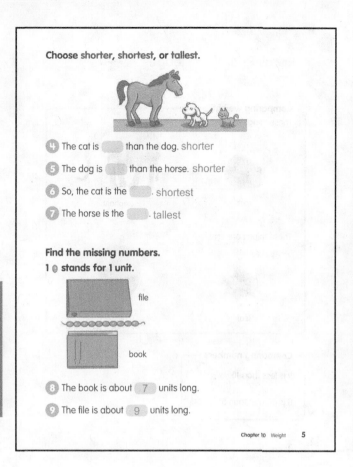

(4) The cat is ____ than the dog. shorter

(5) The dog is ____ than the horse. shorter

(6) So, the cat is the ____. shortest

(7) The horse is the ____. tallest

Find the missing numbers.
1 ⊚ stands for 1 unit.

file

book

(8) The book is about 7 units long.

(9) The file is about 9 units long.

Comparing Things

Lesson Objectives
- Compare the weight of two things using the terms 'heavy', 'heavier', 'light', 'lighter', and 'as heavy as'.
- Compare the weight of more than two things using the terms, 'lightest' and 'heaviest'.

Vocabulary

heavy	heavier	heaviest
light	lighter	lightest
weight	as heavy as	

You can compare the weight of things.

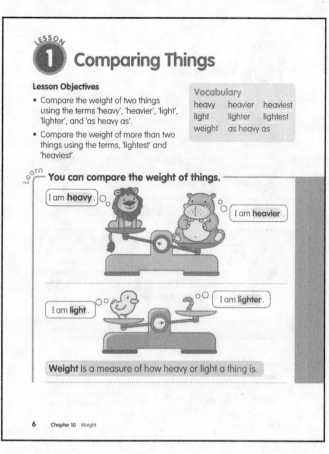

I am **heavy**.   I am **heavier**.

I am **light**.   I am **lighter**.

Weight is a measure of how heavy or light a thing is.

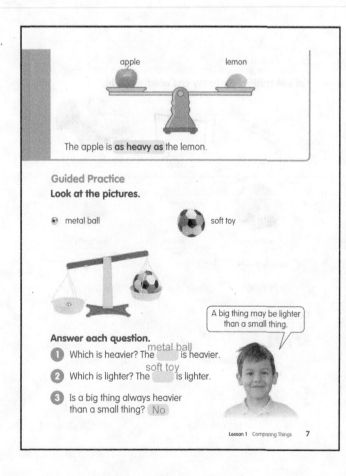

apple   lemon

The apple is **as heavy as** the lemon.

Guided Practice
Look at the pictures.

• metal ball   soft toy

Answer each question.

(1) Which is heavier? The ____ is heavier. metal ball

(2) Which is lighter? The ____ is lighter. soft toy

(3) Is a big thing always heavier than a small thing? No

A big thing may be lighter than a small thing.

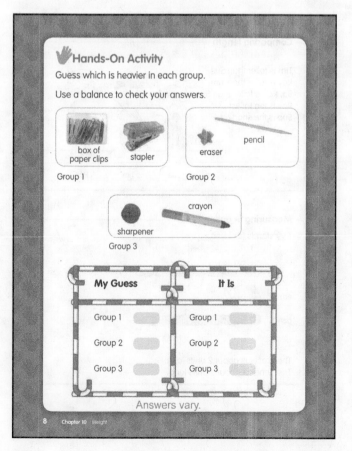

✋**Hands-On Activity**

Guess which is heavier in each group.

Use a balance to check your answers.

box of paper clips   stapler
Group 1

eraser   pencil
Group 2

sharpener   crayon
Group 3

My Guess	It Is
Group 1 ____	Group 1 ____
Group 2 ____	Group 2 ____
Group 3 ____	Group 3 ____

Answers vary.

68

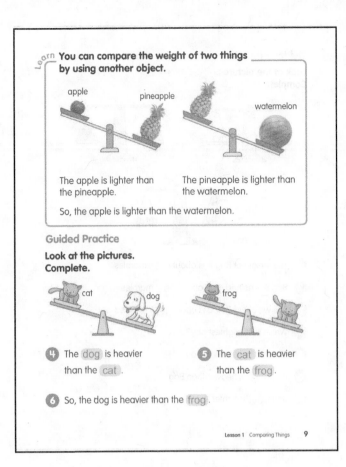

Learn You can compare the weight of two things by using another object.

apple — pineapple

pineapple — watermelon

The apple is lighter than the pineapple.

The pineapple is lighter than the watermelon.

So, the apple is lighter than the watermelon.

Guided Practice

Look at the pictures.
Complete.

cat — dog   frog — cat

4 The dog is heavier than the cat.

5 The cat is heavier than the frog.

6 So, the dog is heavier than the frog.

Lesson 1 Comparing Things **9**

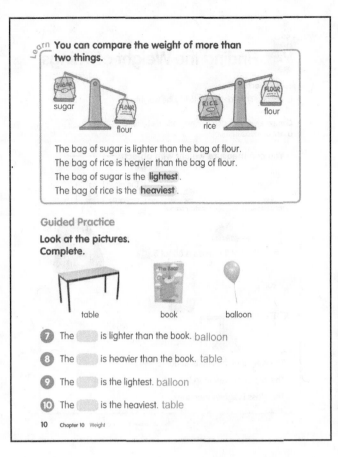

Learn You can compare the weight of more than two things.

sugar — flour   rice — flour

The bag of sugar is lighter than the bag of flour.
The bag of rice is heavier than the bag of flour.
The bag of sugar is the **lightest**.
The bag of rice is the **heaviest**.

Guided Practice

Look at the pictures.
Complete.

table   book   balloon

7 The ____ is lighter than the book. balloon

8 The ____ is heavier than the book. table

9 The ____ is the lightest. balloon

10 The ____ is the heaviest. table

10 Chapter 10 Weight

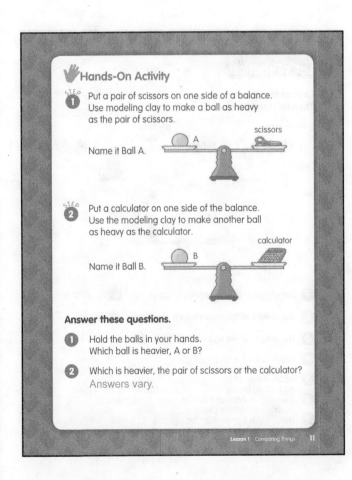

✋**Hands-On Activity**

STEP 1 Put a pair of scissors on one side of a balance. Use modeling clay to make a ball as heavy as the pair of scissors.

Name it Ball A.

A — scissors

STEP 2 Put a calculator on one side of the balance. Use the modeling clay to make another ball as heavy as the calculator.

Name it Ball B.

B — calculator

Answer these questions.

1 Hold the balls in your hands. Which ball is heavier, A or B?

2 Which is heavier, the pair of scissors or the calculator? Answers vary.

Lesson 1 Comparing Things **11**

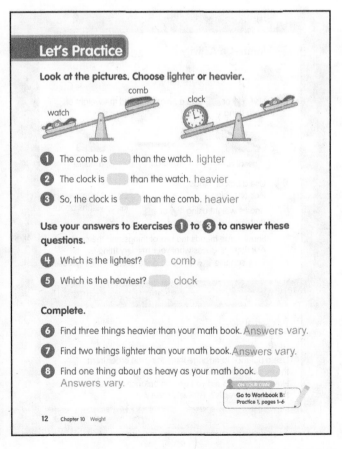

Let's Practice

Look at the pictures. Choose lighter or heavier.

watch — comb   clock

1 The comb is ____ than the watch. lighter

2 The clock is ____ than the watch. heavier

3 So, the clock is ____ than the comb. heavier

Use your answers to Exercises **1** to **3** to answer these questions.

4 Which is the lightest? ____ comb

5 Which is the heaviest? ____ clock

Complete.

6 Find three things heavier than your math book. Answers vary.

7 Find two things lighter than your math book. Answers vary.

8 Find one thing about as heavy as your math book. Answers vary.

Go to Workbook B:
Practice 1, pages 1–6

12 Chapter 10 Weight

Student Edition Answers: Chapter 10
Math in Focus Homeschool Answer Key, Grade 1

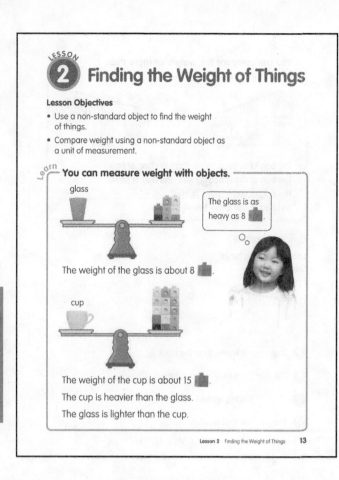

LESSON 2 Finding the Weight of Things

Lesson Objectives

- Use a non-standard object to find the weight of things.
- Compare weight using a non-standard object as a unit of measurement.

Learn You can measure weight with objects.

glass

The glass is as heavy as 8 🧊.

The weight of the glass is about 8 🧊.

cup

The weight of the cup is about 15 🧊.

The cup is heavier than the glass.
The glass is lighter than the cup.

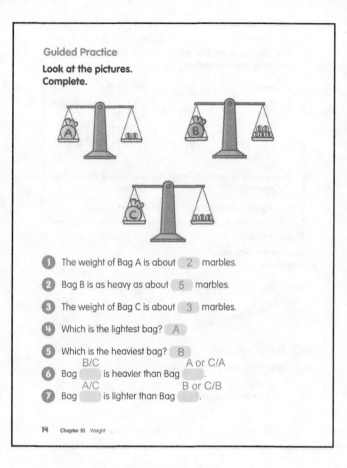

Guided Practice

Look at the pictures.
Complete.

1. The weight of Bag A is about 2 marbles.

2. Bag B is as heavy as about 5 marbles.

3. The weight of Bag C is about 3 marbles.

4. Which is the lightest bag? A

5. Which is the heaviest bag? B

   B/C   A or C/A
6. Bag ____ is heavier than Bag ____.

   A/C   B or C/B
7. Bag ____ is lighter than Bag ____.

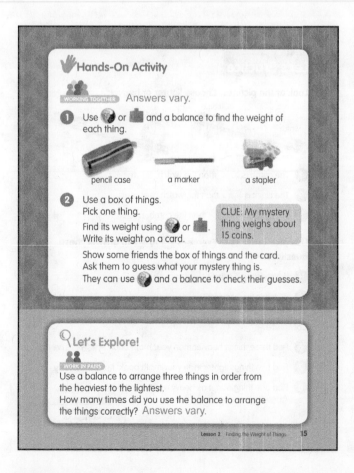

✋ Hands-On Activity

WORKING TOGETHER Answers vary.

1. Use 🪙 or 🧊 and a balance to find the weight of each thing.

   pencil case   a marker   a stapler

2. Use a box of things.
   Pick one thing.

   Find its weight using 🪙 or 🧊.
   Write its weight on a card.

   > **CLUE:** My mystery thing weighs about 15 coins.

   Show some friends the box of things and the card.
   Ask them to guess what your mystery thing is.
   They can use 🪙 and a balance to check their guesses.

🔍 Let's Explore!

WORK IN PAIRS

Use a balance to arrange three things in order from the heaviest to the lightest.
How many times did you use the balance to arrange the things correctly? Answers vary.

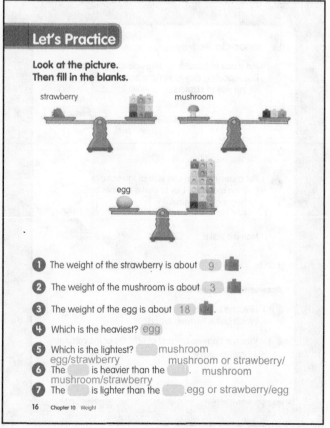

Let's Practice

Look at the picture.
Then fill in the blanks.

strawberry   mushroom

egg

1. The weight of the strawberry is about 9 🧊.

2. The weight of the mushroom is about 3 🧊.

3. The weight of the egg is about 18 🧊.

4. Which is the heaviest? egg

5. Which is the lightest? mushroom

   egg/strawberry   mushroom or strawberry/
6. The ____ is heavier than the ____. mushroom
   mushroom/strawberry
7. The ____ is lighter than the ____. egg or strawberry/egg

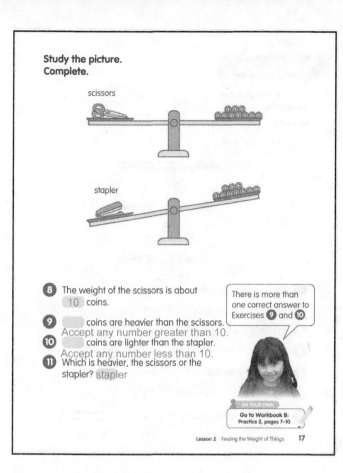

Study the picture.
Complete.

scissors

stapler

8 The weight of the scissors is about
   10 coins.

9 _____ coins are heavier than the scissors.
   Accept any number greater than 10.

10 _____ coins are lighter than the stapler.
   Accept any number less than 10.

11 Which is heavier, the scissors or the
   stapler? stapler

There is more than
one correct answer to
Exercises 9 and 10 .

ON YOUR OWN
Go to Workbook B:
Practice 2, pages 7–10

Lesson 2 Finding the Weight of Things 17

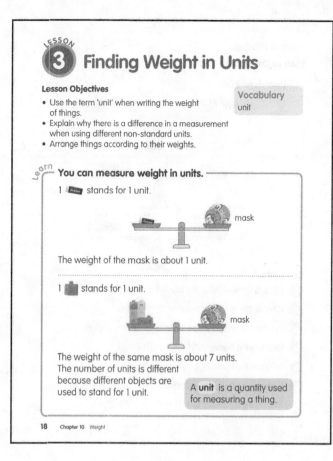

3 Finding Weight in Units

Lesson Objectives
- Use the term 'unit' when writing the weight of things.
- Explain why there is a difference in a measurement when using different non-standard units.
- Arrange things according to their weights.

Vocabulary
unit

Learn **You can measure weight in units.**

1 [eraser] stands for 1 unit.

mask

The weight of the mask is about 1 unit.

1 [bag] stands for 1 unit.

mask

The weight of the same mask is about 7 units.
The number of units is different
because different objects are
used to stand for 1 unit.

A **unit** is a quantity used
for measuring a thing.

18 Chapter 10 Weight

Chapter 10

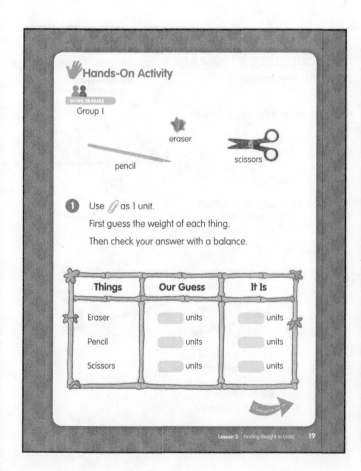

✋ **Hands-On Activity**

WORK IN PAIRS
Group 1

eraser

pencil

scissors

1 Use 📎 as 1 unit.
   First guess the weight of each thing.
   Then check your answer with a balance.

Things	Our Guess	It Is
Eraser	_____ units	_____ units
Pencil	_____ units	_____ units
Scissors	_____ units	_____ units

Continued on ▶

Lesson 3 Finding Weight in Units 19

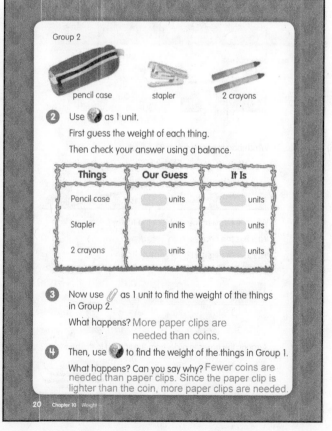

Group 2

pencil case   stapler   2 crayons

2 Use 🪙 as 1 unit.
   First guess the weight of each thing.
   Then check your answer using a balance.

Things	Our Guess	It Is
Pencil case	_____ units	_____ units
Stapler	_____ units	_____ units
2 crayons	_____ units	_____ units

3 Now use 📎 as 1 unit to find the weight of the things
   in Group 2.
   What happens? More paper clips are
                  needed than coins.

4 Then, use 🪙 to find the weight of the things in Group 1.
   What happens? Can you say why? Fewer coins are
   needed than paper clips. Since the paper clip is
   lighter than the coin, more paper clips are needed.

20 Chapter 10 Weight

Guided Practice

Look at the picture.

1 ▦ stands for 1 unit.

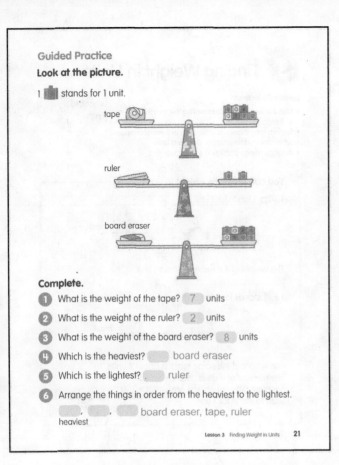

Complete.

1. What is the weight of the tape? **7** units

2. What is the weight of the ruler? **2** units

3. What is the weight of the board eraser? **8** units

4. Which is the heaviest? **board eraser**

5. Which is the lightest? **ruler**

6. Arrange the things in order from the heaviest to the lightest.

   board eraser, tape, ruler
   heaviest

Look at the pictures.
Complete.

Lesley has 1 watermelon slice, 1 apple, and a bunch of grapes.

1 🍊 stands for 1 unit.

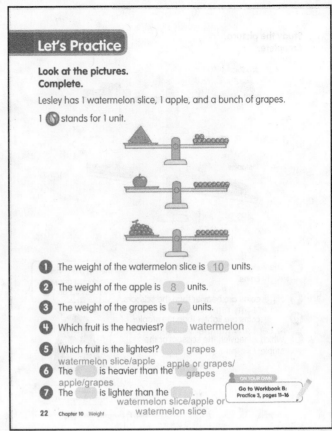

1. The weight of the watermelon slice is **10** units.

2. The weight of the apple is **8** units.

3. The weight of the grapes is **7** units.

4. Which fruit is the heaviest? **watermelon**

5. Which fruit is the lightest? **grapes**

6. The ▢ is heavier than the ▢.
   watermelon slice/apple   apple or grapes/
   apple/grapes   grapes

7. The ▢ is lighter than the ▢.
   watermelon slice/apple or
   watermelon slice

> ON YOUR OWN
> Go to Workbook B:
> Practice 3, pages 11–16

CRITICAL THINKING SKILLS
Put On Your Thinking Cap!

PROBLEM SOLVING

Thinking skills:
Comparing, Sequencing

Strategies:
Act it out,
Guess and check,
Simplify the problem

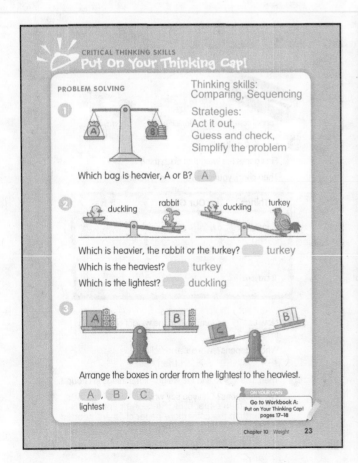

1. Which bag is heavier, A or B? **A**

2. Which is heavier, the rabbit or the turkey? **turkey**

   Which is the heaviest? **turkey**

   Which is the lightest? **duckling**

3. Arrange the boxes in order from the lightest to the heaviest.

   A , **B** , **C**
   lightest

> ON YOUR OWN
> Go to Workbook A:
> Put on Your Thinking Cap!
> pages 17–18

Chapter Wrap Up

You have learned...

> BIG IDEA
> The weight of things
> can be compared
> and measured with
> non-standard units.

to compare the weight of things.

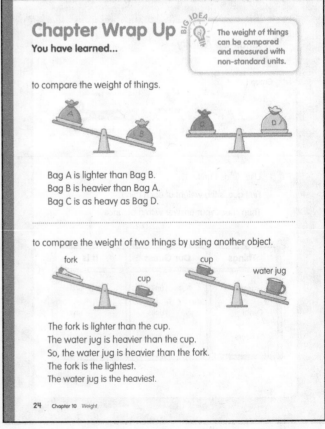

Bag A is lighter than Bag B.
Bag B is heavier than Bag A.
Bag C is as heavy as Bag D.

to compare the weight of two things by using another object.

fork   cup
cup   water jug

The fork is lighter than the cup.
The water jug is heavier than the cup.
So, the water jug is heavier than the fork.
The fork is the lightest.
The water jug is the heaviest.

---

to measure weight using non-standard units.

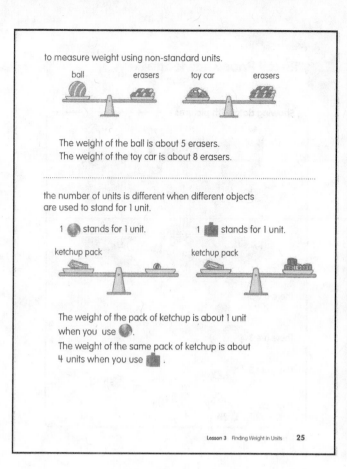

The weight of the ball is about 5 erasers.
The weight of the toy car is about 8 erasers.

the number of units is different when different objects
are used to stand for 1 unit.

The weight of the pack of ketchup is about 1 unit
when you use ⬤.
The weight of the same pack of ketchup is about
4 units when you use ⬛.

to tell the weight of a thing in units.
to arrange things in order from the heaviest or the lightest.

1 🐦 stands for 1 unit.

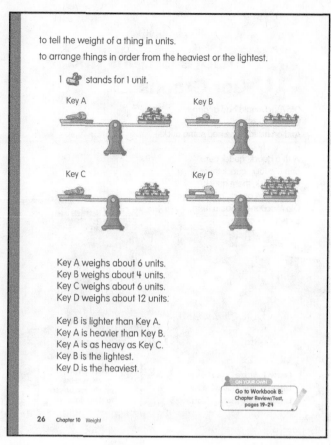

Key A weighs about 6 units.
Key B weighs about 4 units.
Key C weighs about 6 units.
Key D weighs about 12 units.

Key B is lighter than Key A.
Key A is heavier than Key B.
Key A is as heavy as Key C.
Key B is the lightest.
Key D is the heaviest.

ON YOUR OWN

Go to Workbook B:
Chapter Review/Test,
pages 19–24

CHAPTER 11 Picture Graphs and Bar Graphs

Old MacDonald had a farm,
E - i - e - i - o
And on his farm he had some ducks,
E - i - e - i - o
With a quack, quack here,
and a quack, quack there,
Here quack, there quack,
Everywhere quack, quack.
Old MacDonald had a farm,
E - i - e - i - o!

Lesson 1 Simple Picture Graphs
Lesson 2 More Picture Graphs
Lesson 3 Tally Charts and Bar Graphs

BIG IDEA Picture graphs, tally charts, and bar graphs can be used to show data.

27

Showing data with pictures

There are 5

There are 3

There are 3

There are 2

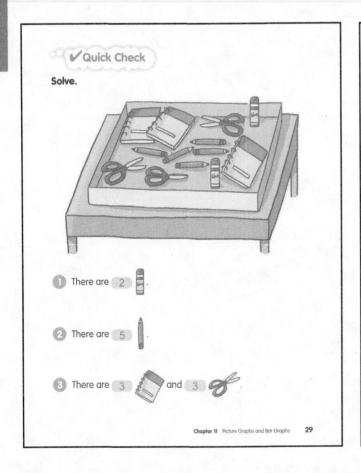

✔ Quick Check

Solve.

1 There are [2] .

2 There are [5] .

3 There are [3] and [3] .

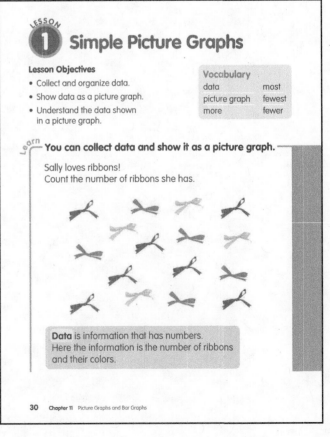

LESSON 1 Simple Picture Graphs

Lesson Objectives
- Collect and organize data.
- Show data as a picture graph.
- Understand the data shown in a picture graph.

Vocabulary

data	most
picture graph	fewest
more	fewer

Learn **You can collect data and show it as a picture graph.**

Sally loves ribbons!
Count the number of ribbons she has.

Data is information that has numbers.
Here the information is the number of ribbons and their colors.

74

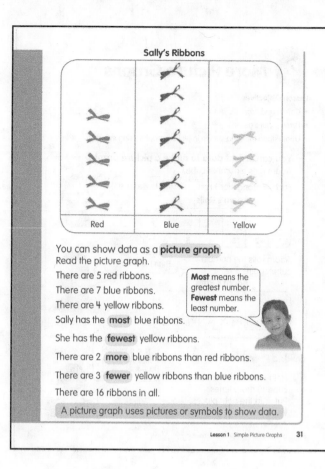

Sally's Ribbons

| | Red | Blue | Yellow |

You can show data as a **picture graph**.
Read the picture graph.

There are 5 red ribbons.

There are 7 blue ribbons.

There are 4 yellow ribbons.

Sally has the (most) blue ribbons.

She has the (fewest) yellow ribbons.

There are 2 (more) blue ribbons than red ribbons.

There are 3 (fewer) yellow ribbons than blue ribbons.

There are 16 ribbons in all.

> **Most** means the greatest number.
> **Fewest** means the least number.

A picture graph uses pictures or symbols to show data.

Lesson 1 Simple Picture Graphs **31**

**Look at the picture graph.
Then solve.**

There are three hens on Old Joe's farm.
The picture graph shows the number of eggs that each hen laid this week.

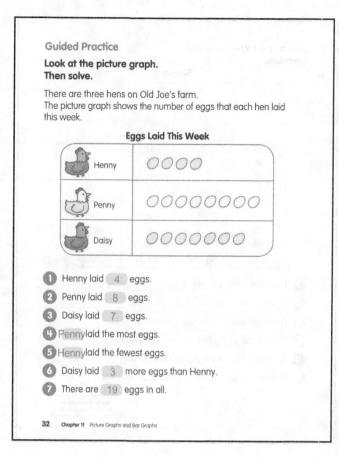

Eggs Laid This Week

1 Henny laid (4) eggs.

2 Penny laid (8) eggs.

3 Daisy laid (7) eggs.

4 Penny laid the most eggs.

5 Henny laid the fewest eggs.

6 Daisy laid (3) more eggs than Henny.

7 There are (19) eggs in all.

32 Chapter 11 Picture Graphs and Bar Graphs

Guided Practice

**Look at the picture graph.
Then answer the questions.**

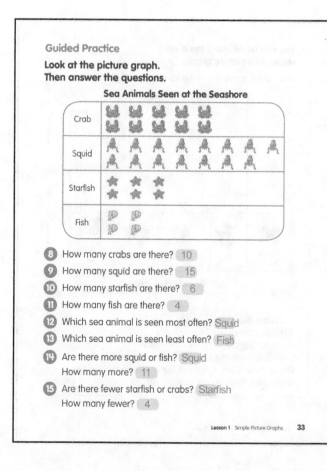

Sea Animals Seen at the Seashore

	Crab
	Squid
	Starfish
	Fish

8 How many crabs are there? (10)

9 How many squid are there? (15)

10 How many starfish are there? (6)

11 How many fish are there? (4)

12 Which sea animal is seen most often? Squid

13 Which sea animal is seen least often? Fish

14 Are there more squid or fish? Squid
How many more? (11)

15 Are there fewer starfish or crabs? Starfish
How many fewer? (4)

Lesson 1 Simple Picture Graphs **33**

Let's Practice

**Look at the picture graph.
Complete.**

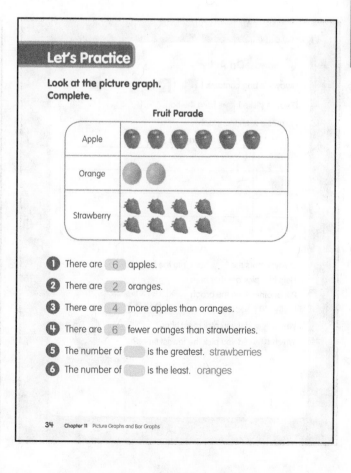

Fruit Parade

	Apple
	Orange
	Strawberry

1 There are (6) apples.

2 There are (2) oranges.

3 There are (4) more apples than oranges.

4 There are (6) fewer oranges than strawberries.

5 The number of ____ is the greatest. strawberries

6 The number of ____ is the least. oranges

34 Chapter 11 Picture Graphs and Bar Graphs

Student Edition Answers: Chapter 11
Math in Focus Homeschool Answer Key, Grade 1

Look at the picture graph. Complete.

Shapes

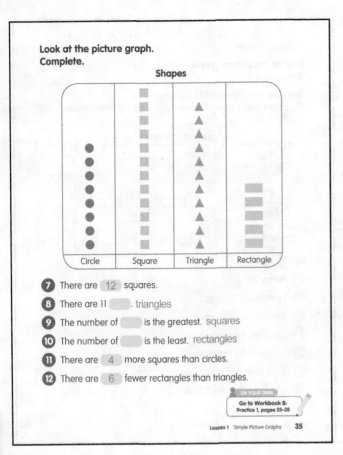

| Circle | Square | Triangle | Rectangle |

7 There are ⟨12⟩ squares.

8 There are 11 ⟨ ⟩. triangles

9 The number of ⟨ ⟩ is the greatest. squares

10 The number of ⟨ ⟩ is the least. rectangles

11 There are ⟨4⟩ more squares than circles.

12 There are ⟨6⟩ fewer rectangles than triangles.

ON YOUR OWN
Go to Workbook B:
Practice 1, pages 25–28

---

② More Picture Graphs

Lesson Objectives
- Collect and organize data.
- Draw picture graphs.
- Understand the data shown in picture graphs using symbols.

Learn You can collect data to make a picture graph.

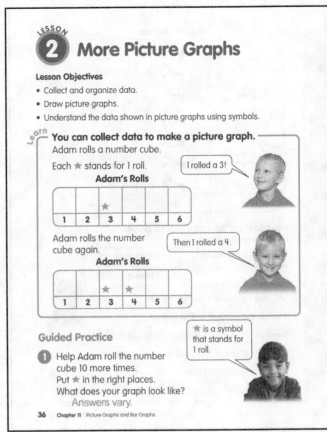

Adam rolls a number cube.

Each ★ stands for 1 roll.

I rolled a 3!

Adam's Rolls

| 1 | 2 | 3 | 4 | 5 | 6 |

Adam rolls the number cube again.

Then I rolled a 4.

Adam's Rolls

| 1 | 2 | 3 | 4 | 5 | 6 |

Guided Practice

① Help Adam roll the number cube 10 more times.
Put ★ in the right places.
What does your graph look like?
Answers vary.

★ is a symbol that stands for 1 roll.

Hands-On Activity

Dwayne's bag contains 1 ▣, 1 ▣, 1 ▣ and 1 ▣.

Dwayne picks 1 ▣ from the bag.

He puts a ✗ on the graph.

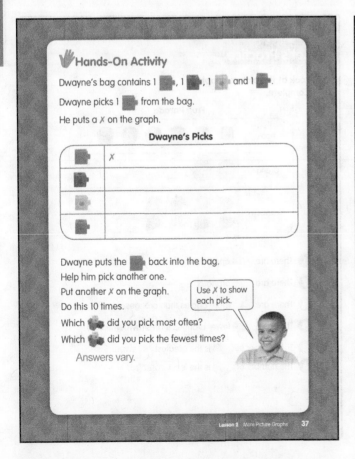

Dwayne's Picks

▣	✗
▣	
▣	
▣	

Dwayne puts the ▣ back into the bag.

Help him pick another one.

Put another ✗ on the graph.

Do this 10 times.

Which ▣ did you pick most often?

Which ▣ did you pick the fewest times?

Answers vary.

Use ✗ to show each pick.

Learn You can understand the data shown in a picture graph.

This picture graph shows the favorite toys of 18 children.

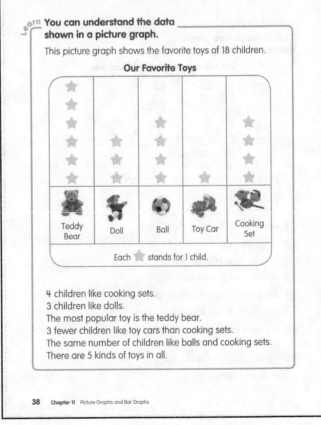

Our Favorite Toys

| Teddy Bear | Doll | Ball | Toy Car | Cooking Set |

Each ★ stands for 1 child.

4 children like cooking sets.
3 children like dolls.
The most popular toy is the teddy bear.
3 fewer children like toy cars than cooking sets.
The same number of children like balls and cooking sets.
There are 5 kinds of toys in all.

Chapter 11

Guided Practice

Look at the picture graph.
Then answer the questions.

This picture graph shows the favorite colors chosen by a first grade class.

Our Favorite Color

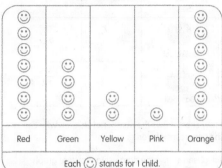

Each ☺ stands for 1 child.

2 How many children chose orange? 7
3 Which color did the children choose the least? pink
4 How many more children chose red than green? 3
5 How many fewer children chose yellow than orange? 5
6 How many children are there? 21

Look at the picture graph.
Then answer the questions.

This picture graph shows some cars in a parking lot.

Cars in a Parking Lot

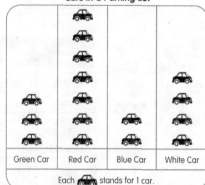

Each 🚗 stands for 1 car.

1 How many blue cars are there? 2
2 How many red cars and white cars are there in all? 11
3 How many more red cars than green cars are there? 4
4 How many cars are **not** green? 13

Look at the picture graph.
Then answer the questions.

This picture graph shows the favorite season of some children.

Favorite Seasons

Spring	● ● ●
Summer	● ● ● ●
Fall	● ●
Winter	● ● ● ● ● ●

Each ● stands for 1 child.

5 Winter is the favorite season of 6 children.
6 ___ is the favorite season of 4 children. Summer
7 How many children chose spring and fall as their favorite season? 5
8 Which is the most popular season? winter
9 Fall is the favorite season of the fewest children.

ON YOUR OWN
Go to Workbook B:
Practice 2, pages 29–34

LESSON
3 Tally Charts and Bar Graphs

Lesson Objectives
• Make a tally chart.
• Show data in a bar graph.
• Understand data shown in a bar graph.

Vocabulary
tally mark
tally chart
bar graph

Learn **You can collect data and organize it using a tally chart and bar graph.**

Mrs. Hanson has her class paste pictures of their favorite sport on a sheet of paper like this.

Then she makes a tally chart with this data. She checks ✓ the favorite sport of each child and draws a **tally mark** / on the tally chart.

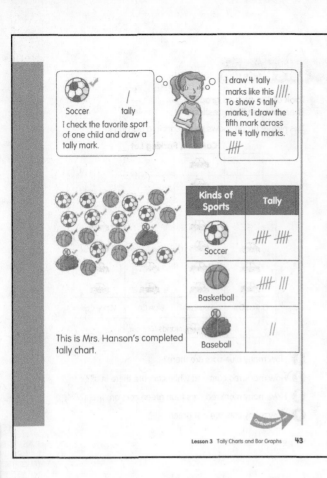

Soccer   tally |

I check the favorite sport of one child and draw a tally mark.

I draw 4 tally marks like this ////. To show 5 tally marks, I draw the fifth mark across the 4 tally marks. ////

Kinds of Sports	Tally
Soccer	//// ////
Basketball	//// ///
Baseball	//

This is Mrs. Hanson's completed tally chart.

Continued on the next page

Lesson 3 Tally Charts and Bar Graphs   **43**

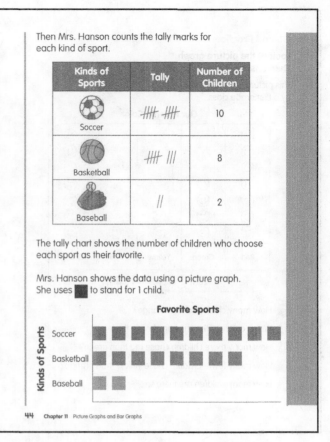

Then Mrs. Hanson counts the tally marks for each kind of sport.

Kinds of Sports	Tally	Number of Children
Soccer	//// ////	10
Basketball	//// ///	8
Baseball	//	2

The tally chart shows the number of children who choose each sport as their favorite.

Mrs. Hanson shows the data using a picture graph. She uses ■ to stand for 1 child.

Favorite Sports

44   **Chapter 11** Picture Graphs and Bar Graphs

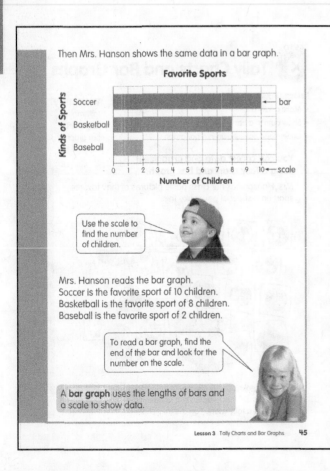

Then Mrs. Hanson shows the same data in a bar graph.

Favorite Sports

Use the scale to find the number of children.

Mrs. Hanson reads the bar graph. Soccer is the favorite sport of 10 children. Basketball is the favorite sport of 8 children. Baseball is the favorite sport of 2 children.

To read a bar graph, find the end of the bar and look for the number on the scale.

A **bar graph** uses the lengths of bars and a scale to show data.

Lesson 3 Tally Charts and Bar Graphs   **45**

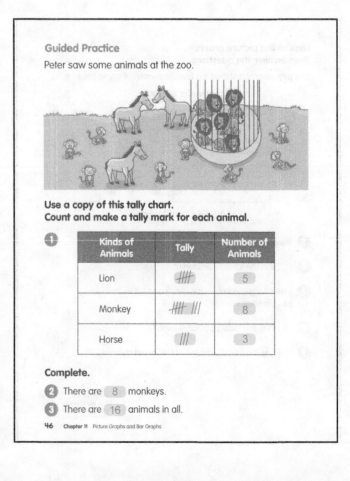

Guided Practice

Peter saw some animals at the zoo.

Use a copy of this tally chart.
Count and make a tally mark for each animal.

❶
Kinds of Animals	Tally	Number of Animals
Lion	////	5
Monkey	//// ///	8
Horse	///	3

Complete.

❷ There are 8 monkeys.

❸ There are 16 animals in all.

46   **Chapter 11** Picture Graphs and Bar Graphs

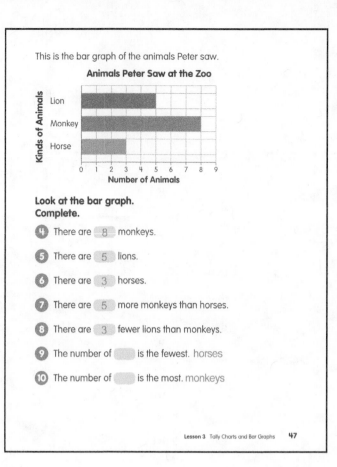

This is the bar graph of the animals Peter saw.

Animals Peter Saw at the Zoo

Look at the bar graph.
Complete.

4 There are 8 monkeys.

5 There are 5 lions.

6 There are 3 horses.

7 There are 5 more monkeys than horses.

8 There are 3 fewer lions than monkeys.

9 The number of ▢ is the fewest. horses

10 The number of ▢ is the most. monkeys

Lesson 3 Tally Charts and Bar Graphs   47

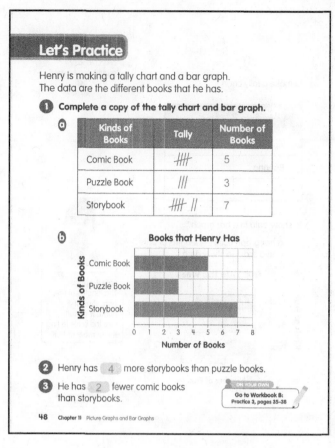

Go to Workbook B:
Practice 3, pages 35–38

Let's Practice

Henry is making a tally chart and a bar graph.
The data are the different books that he has.

1 Complete a copy of the tally chart and bar graph.

a

Kinds of Books	Tally	Number of Books
Comic Book	卌	5
Puzzle Book	|||	3
Storybook	卌 ||	7

b

Books that Henry Has

2 Henry has 4 more storybooks than puzzle books.

3 He has 2 fewer comic books than storybooks.

48   Chapter 11 Picture Graphs and Bar Graphs

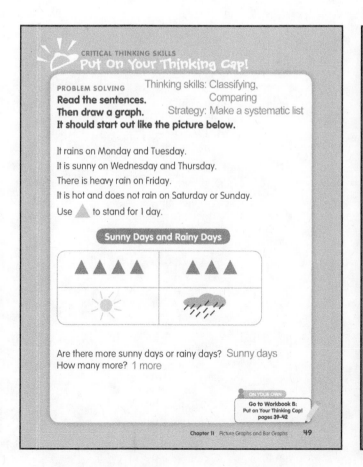

CRITICAL THINKING SKILLS
Put On Your Thinking Cap!

PROBLEM SOLVING
Read the sentences.
Then draw a graph.
It should start out like the picture below.

Thinking skills: Classifying,
Comparing
Strategy: Make a systematic list

It rains on Monday and Tuesday.
It is sunny on Wednesday and Thursday.
There is heavy rain on Friday.
It is hot and does not rain on Saturday or Sunday.
Use ▲ to stand for 1 day.

Sunny Days and Rainy Days

Are there more sunny days or rainy days? Sunny days
How many more? 1 more

Go to Workbook B:
Put on Your Thinking Cap!
pages 39–42

Chapter 11 Picture Graphs and Bar Graphs   49

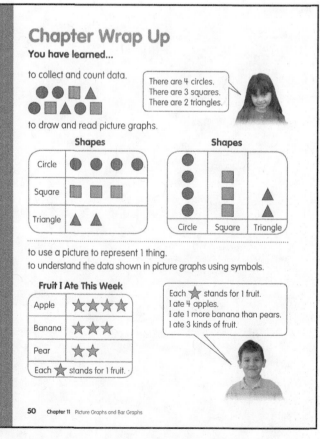

Chapter Wrap Up
You have learned...

to collect and count data.

There are 4 circles.
There are 3 squares.
There are 2 triangles.

to draw and read picture graphs.

Shapes

Circle	● ● ● ●
Square	▪ ▪ ▪
Triangle	▲ ▲

Shapes

Circle	Square	Triangle

to use a picture to represent 1 thing.
to understand the data shown in picture graphs using symbols.

Fruit I Ate This Week

Apple	★ ★ ★ ★
Banana	★ ★ ★
Pear	★ ★
Each ★ stands for 1 fruit.	

Each ★ stands for 1 fruit.
I ate 4 apples.
I ate 1 more banana than pears.
I ate 3 kinds of fruit.

50   Chapter 11 Picture Graphs and Bar Graphs

Student Edition Answers: Chapter 11
Math in Focus Homeschool Answer Key, Grade 1

Chapter 11

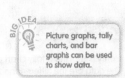

Picture graphs, tally charts, and bar graphs can be used to show data.

to make a tally chart.

Kinds of Fruit	Tally
Apple	////
Banana	///
Pear	//

to show data in a bar graph.

a bar graph uses the lengths of bars and a scale to show data.

Fruit I Ate This Week

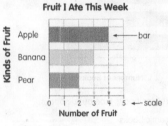

Kinds of Fruit

Apple ← bar

Banana

Pear

0 1 2 3 4 5 ← scale

Number of Fruit

I ate 4 apples. The lengths of the bars show the number of fruit. Use the scale to find the number of fruit.

ON YOUR OWN
Go to Workbook B:
Chapter Review/Test,
pages 43–44

Chapter 11 Picture Graphs and Bar Graphs **51**

CHAPTER
12 Numbers to 40

Lesson 1 Counting to 40
Lesson 2 Place Value
Lesson 3 Comparing, Ordering, and Patterns

BIG IDEA
Count, compare, and order numbers from 1 to 40.

52

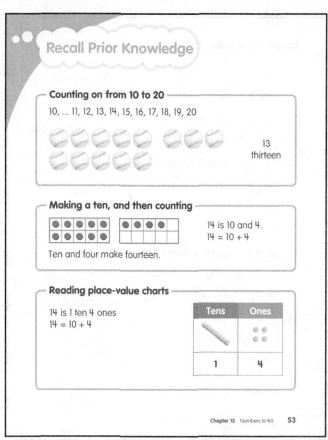

Counting on from 10 to 20

10, ... 11, 12, 13, 14, 15, 16, 17, 18, 19, 20

13
thirteen

Making a ten, and then counting

14 is 10 and 4.
14 = 10 + 4

Ten and four make fourteen.

Reading place-value charts

14 is 1 ten 4 ones
14 = 10 + 4

Tens	Ones
1	4

Chapter 12 Numbers to 40   53

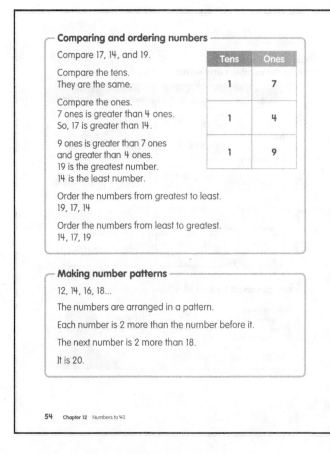

Comparing and ordering numbers

Compare 17, 14, and 19.

Compare the tens.
They are the same.

Compare the ones.
7 ones is greater than 4 ones.
So, 17 is greater than 14.

9 ones is greater than 7 ones
and greater than 4 ones.
19 is the greatest number.
14 is the least number.

Tens	Ones
1	7
1	4
1	9

Order the numbers from greatest to least.
19, 17, 14

Order the numbers from least to greatest.
14, 17, 19

Making number patterns

12, 14, 16, 18...

The numbers are arranged in a pattern.

Each number is 2 more than the number before it.

The next number is 2 more than 18.

It is 20.

54   Chapter 12 Numbers to 40

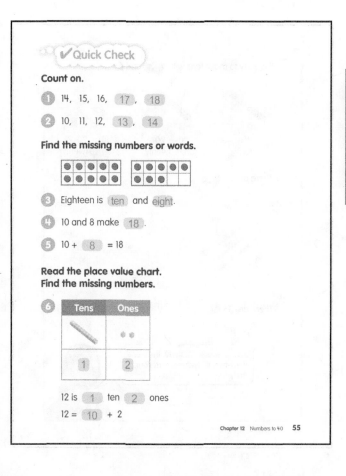

✔ Quick Check

Count on.

1 14, 15, 16, 17, 18

2 10, 11, 12, 13, 14

Find the missing numbers or words.

3 Eighteen is ten and eight.

4 10 and 8 make 18.

5 10 + 8 = 18

Read the place value chart.
Find the missing numbers.

6
Tens	Ones
1	2

12 is 1 ten 2 ones

12 = 10 + 2

Chapter 12 Numbers to 40   55

Compare and order.

16   18   13

7 18 is greater than 16.

8 13 is less than 16.

9 13 is the least number.

10 18 is the greatest number.

11 Order the numbers from greatest to least.

18 , 16 , 13

greatest

Complete the number patterns.

12 11, 13, 15, 17 , 19

13 20, 18, 16 , 14 , 12

Lesson Objectives

- Count on from 21 to 40.
- Read and write 21 to 40 in numbers and words.

Vocabulary	
twenty-one	twenty-two
twenty-three	twenty-four
twenty-five	twenty-six
twenty-seven	twenty-eight
twenty-nine	thirty
forty	

Learn You can count numbers greater than 20 in ones.

Count the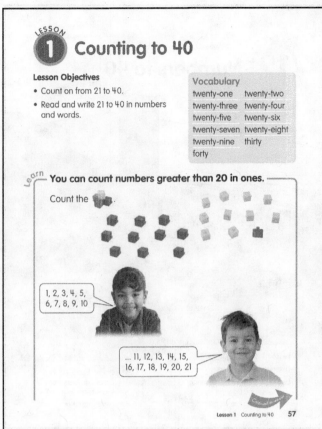

1, 2, 3, 4, 5, 6, 7, 8, 9, 10

... 11, 12, 13, 14, 15, 16, 17, 18, 19, 20, 21

It is easy to make tens with 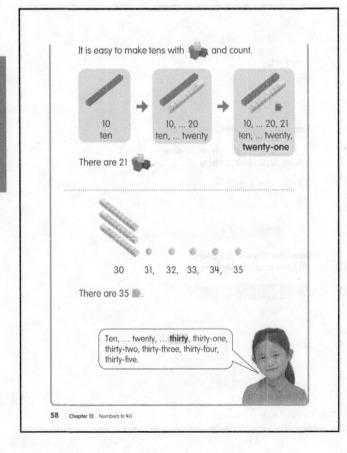 and count.

10 ten	→	10, ... 20 ten, ... twenty	→	10, ... 20, 21 ten, ... twenty, **twenty-one**

There are 21 .

30   31,   32,   33,   34,   35

There are 35 .

Ten, ... twenty, ... **thirty**, thirty-one, thirty-two, thirty-three, thirty-four, thirty-five.

Guided Practice

Count in tens and ones.
Write the numbers and words.

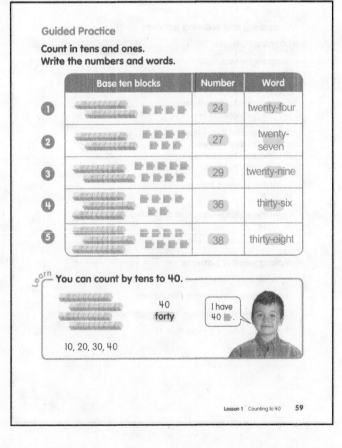

	Base ten blocks	Number	Word
1		24	twenty-four
2		27	twenty-seven
3		29	twenty-nine
4		36	thirty-six
5		38	thirty-eight

Learn You can count by tens to 40.

40 **forty**

I have 40 .

10, 20, 30, 40

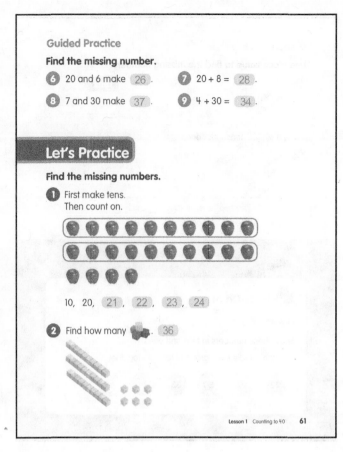

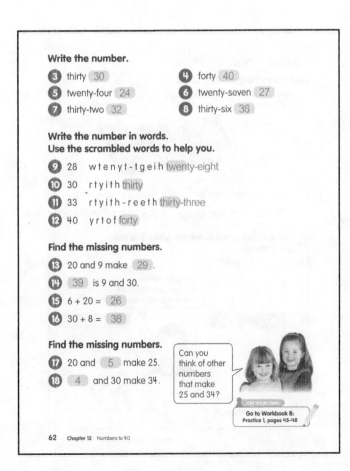

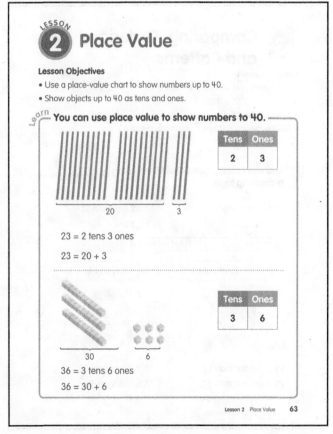

Panel 1 (top-left, page 64)

Guided Practice

Use place value to find the missing numbers.

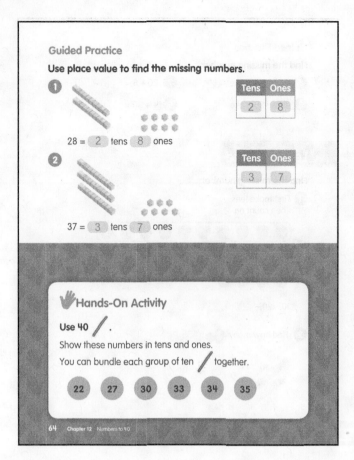

1

Tens	Ones
2	8

28 = 2 tens 8 ones

2

Tens	Ones
3	7

37 = 3 tens 7 ones

✋ **Hands-On Activity**

Use 40 ╱ .

Show these numbers in tens and ones.

You can bundle each group of ten ╱ together.

22 27 30 33 34 35

64 Chapter 12 Numbers to 40

Panel 2 (top-right, page 65)

Let's Practice

Look at each place-value chart.
Find the number it shows.

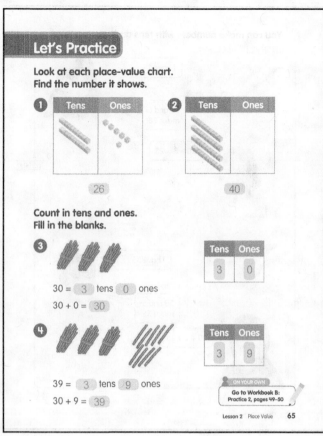

1

Tens	Ones

26

2

Tens	Ones

40

Count in tens and ones.
Fill in the blanks.

3

Tens	Ones
3	0

30 = 3 tens 0 ones
30 + 0 = 30

4

Tens	Ones
3	9

39 = 3 tens 9 ones
30 + 9 = 39

ON YOUR OWN
Go to Workbook B:
Practice 2, pages 49–50

Lesson 2 Place Value 65

Panel 3 (bottom-left, page 66)

Chapter 12

LESSON 3 Comparing, Ordering, and Patterns

Lesson Objectives
- Use a strategy to compare numbers to 40.
- Compare numbers to 40.
- Order numbers to 40.
- Find the missing numbers in a number pattern.

Vocabulary
counting tape

Learn You can count on and count back using a counting tape.

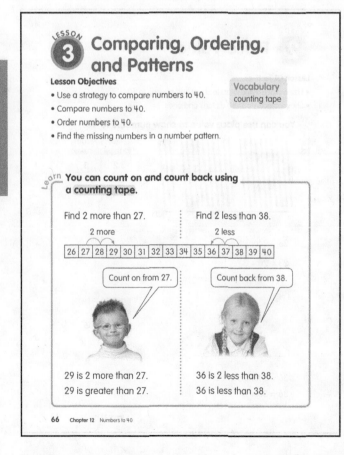

Find 2 more than 27.

2 more

Find 2 less than 38.

2 less

| 26 | 27 | 28 | 29 | 30 | 31 | 32 | 33 | 34 | 35 | 36 | 37 | 38 | 39 | 40 |

Count on from 27.

Count back from 38.

29 is 2 more than 27.
29 is greater than 27.

36 is 2 less than 38.
36 is less than 38.

66 Chapter 12 Numbers to 40

Panel 4 (bottom-right, page 67)

Guided Practice

Find the missing numbers.

This picture shows part of a calendar.

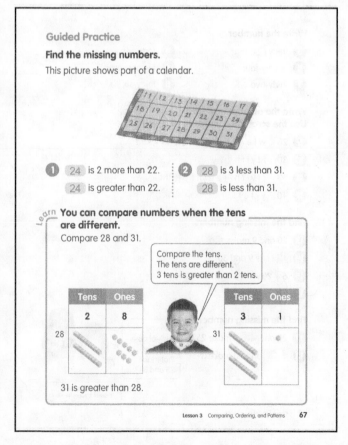

1 24 is 2 more than 22.
24 is greater than 22.

2 28 is 3 less than 31.
28 is less than 31.

Learn You can compare numbers when the tens are different.

Compare 28 and 31.

Compare the tens.
The tens are different.
3 tens is greater than 2 tens.

28

Tens	Ones
2	8

31

Tens	Ones
3	1

31 is greater than 28.

Lesson 3 Comparing, Ordering, and Patterns 67

Student Edition Answers: Chapter 12
Math in Focus Homeschool Answer Key, Grade 1

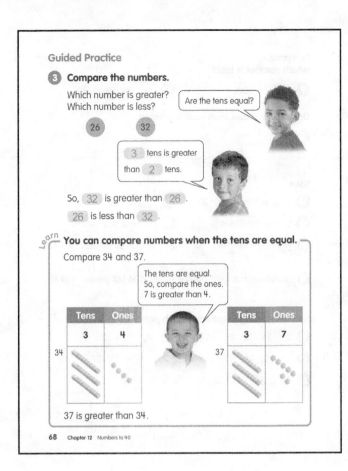

Guided Practice

3 **Compare the numbers.**

Which number is greater?
Which number is less?

26   32

Are the tens equal?

3 tens is greater than 2 tens.

So, 32 is greater than 26.

26 is less than 32.

Learn **You can compare numbers when the tens are equal.**

Compare 34 and 37.

The tens are equal.
So, compare the ones.
7 is greater than 4.

Tens	Ones
3	4

34

Tens	Ones
3	7

37

37 is greater than 34.

68   Chapter 12   Numbers to 40

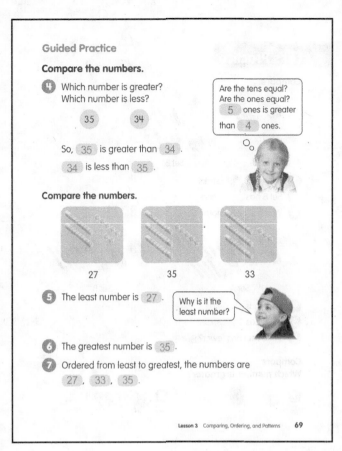

Guided Practice

Compare the numbers.

4 Which number is greater?
Which number is less?

35   34

*Are the tens equal?
Are the ones equal?
5 ones is greater than 4 ones.*

So, 35 is greater than 34.

34 is less than 35.

Compare the numbers.

27   35   33

5 The least number is 27.

Why is it the least number?

6 The greatest number is 35.

7 Ordered from least to greatest, the numbers are
27, 33, 35.

Lesson 3   Comparing, Ordering, and Patterns   69

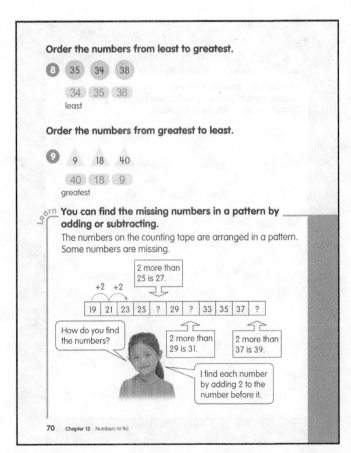

Order the numbers from least to greatest.

8 35   34   38

34   35   38
least

Order the numbers from greatest to least.

9 9   18   40

40   18   9
greatest

Learn **You can find the missing numbers in a pattern by adding or subtracting.**

The numbers on the counting tape are arranged in a pattern.
Some numbers are missing.

2 more than 25 is 27.

+2   +2

| 19 | 21 | 23 | 25 | ? | 29 | ? | 33 | 35 | 37 | ? |

How do you find the numbers?

2 more than 29 is 31.

2 more than 37 is 39.

I find each number by adding 2 to the number before it.

70   Chapter 12   Numbers to 40

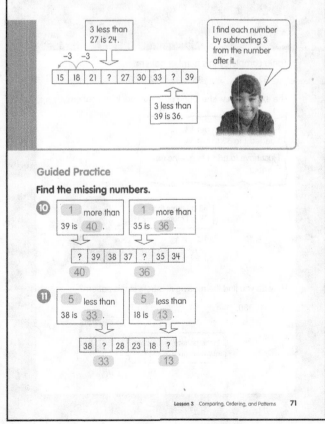

3 less than 27 is 24.

−3   −3

| 15 | 18 | 21 | ? | 27 | 30 | 33 | ? | 39 |

3 less than 39 is 36.

I find each number by subtracting 3 from the number after it.

Guided Practice

Find the missing numbers.

10 1 more than 39 is 40.   1 more than 35 is 36.

| ? | 39 | 38 | 37 | ? | 35 | 34 |

40   36

11 5 less than 38 is 33.   5 less than 18 is 13.

| 38 | ? | 28 | 23 | 18 | ? |

33   13

Lesson 3   Comparing, Ordering, and Patterns   71

Student Edition Answers: Chapter 12
Math in Focus Homeschool Answer Key, Grade 1

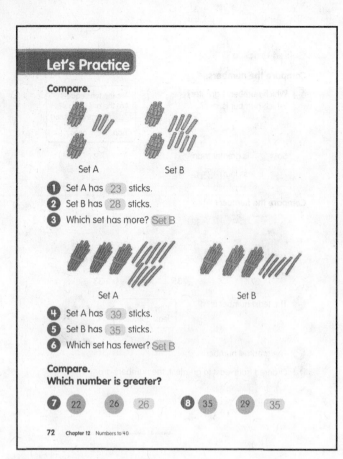

Let's Practice

Compare.

Set A   Set B

1 Set A has `23` sticks.

2 Set B has `28` sticks.

3 Which set has more? `Set B`

Set A   Set B

4 Set A has `39` sticks.

5 Set B has `35` sticks.

6 Which set has fewer? `Set B`

Compare.
Which number is greater?

7 `22`   26   26   **8** 35   29   `35`

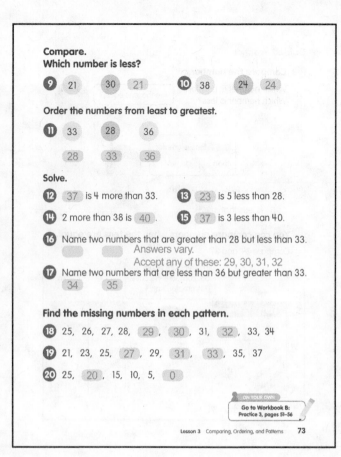

Compare.
Which number is less?

9 `21`   30   21   **10** 38   `24`   24

Order the numbers from least to greatest.

11 33   `28`   36

`28`   `33`   `36`

Solve.

12 `37` is 4 more than 33.   **13** `23` is 5 less than 28.

14 2 more than 38 is `40`.   **15** `37` is 3 less than 40.

16 Name two numbers that are greater than 28 but less than 33.
`  `   `  `   Answers vary.
Accept any of these: 29, 30, 31, 32

17 Name two numbers that are less than 36 but greater than 33.
`34`   `35`

Find the missing numbers in each pattern.

18 25, 26, 27, 28, `29`, `30`, 31, `32`, 33, 34

19 21, 23, 25, `27`, 29, `31`, `33`, 35, 37

20 25, `20`, 15, 10, 5, `0`

> **ON YOUR OWN**
> Go to Workbook B:
> Practice 3, pages 51–56

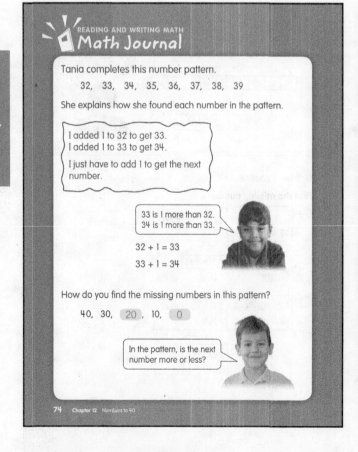

READING AND WRITING MATH
Math Journal

Tania completes this number pattern.

32, 33, 34, 35, 36, 37, 38, 39

She explains how she found each number in the pattern.

> I added 1 to 32 to get 33.
> I added 1 to 33 to get 34.
> I just have to add 1 to get the next number.

> 33 is 1 more than 32.
> 34 is 1 more than 33.

$$32 + 1 = 33$$
$$33 + 1 = 34$$

How do you find the missing numbers in this pattern?

40, 30, `20`, 10, `0`

> In the pattern, is the next number more or less?

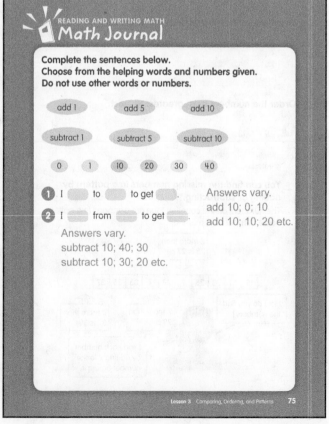

READING AND WRITING MATH
Math Journal

Complete the sentences below.
Choose from the helping words and numbers given.
Do not use other words or numbers.

add 1   add 5   add 10

subtract 1   subtract 5   subtract 10

0   1   10   20   30   40

1 I `  ` to `  ` to get `  `.   Answers vary.
add 10; 0; 10
add 10; 10; 20 etc.

2 I `  ` from `  ` to get `  `.
Answers vary.
subtract 10; 40; 30
subtract 10; 30; 20 etc.

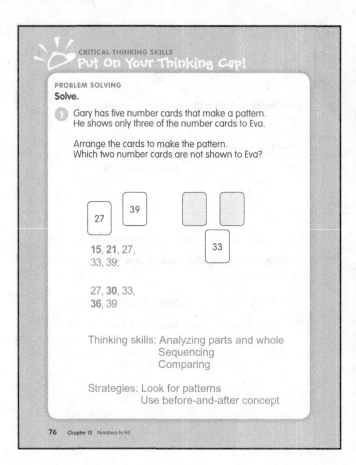

PROBLEM SOLVING
Solve.

1 Gary has five number cards that make a pattern. He shows only three of the number cards to Eva.

Arrange the cards to make the pattern. Which two number cards are not shown to Eva?

27   39   33

15, **21**, 27, 33, 39;

27, **30**, 33, **36**, 39

Thinking skills: Analyzing parts and whole
Sequencing
Comparing

Strategies: Look for patterns
Use before-and-after concept

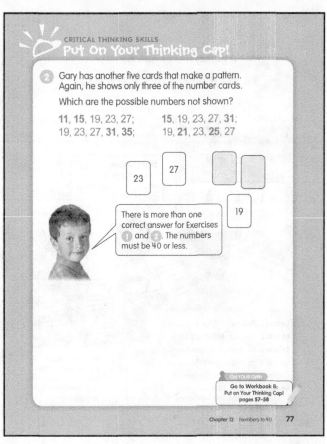

2 Gary has another five cards that make a pattern. Again, he shows only three of the number cards.

Which are the possible numbers not shown?

11, **15**, 19, 23, 27;   **15**, 19, 23, 27, **31**;
19, 23, 27, **31**, **35**;   19, **21**, 23, **25**, 27

23   27   19

There is more than one correct answer for Exercises 1 and 2. The numbers must be 40 or less.

ON YOUR OWN
Go to Workbook B:
Put on Your Thinking Cap!
pages 57–58

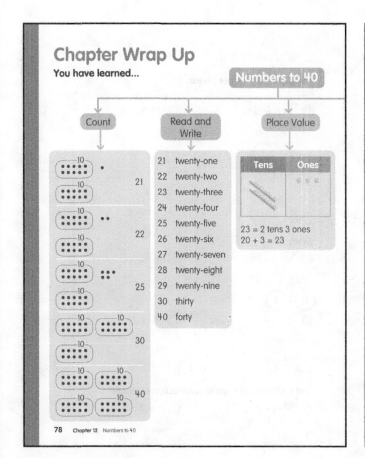

Chapter Wrap Up
You have learned...

Numbers to 40

Count

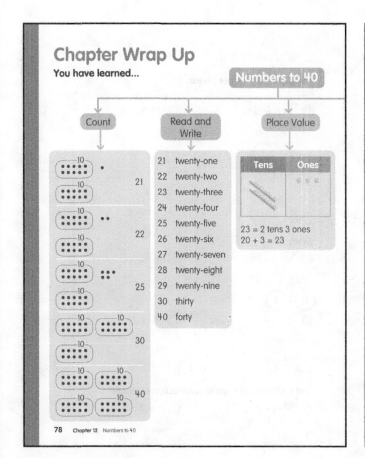

21
22
25
30
40

Read and Write

21	twenty-one
22	twenty-two
23	twenty-three
24	twenty-four
25	twenty-five
26	twenty-six
27	twenty-seven
28	twenty-eight
29	twenty-nine
30	thirty
40	forty

Place Value

Tens	Ones

23 = 2 tens 3 ones
20 + 3 = 23

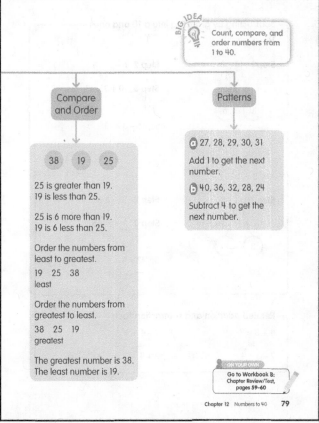

BIG IDEA
Count, compare, and order numbers from 1 to 40.

Compare and Order

38   19   25

25 is greater than 19.
19 is less than 25.

25 is 6 more than 19.
19 is 6 less than 25.

Order the numbers from least to greatest.
19   25   38
least

Order the numbers from greatest to least.
38   25   19
greatest

The greatest number is 38.
The least number is 19.

Patterns

ⓐ 27, 28, 29, 30, 31
Add 1 to get the next number.

ⓑ 40, 36, 32, 28, 24
Subtract 4 to get the next number.

ON YOUR OWN
Go to Workbook B:
Chapter Review/Test,
pages 59–60

Chapter 12

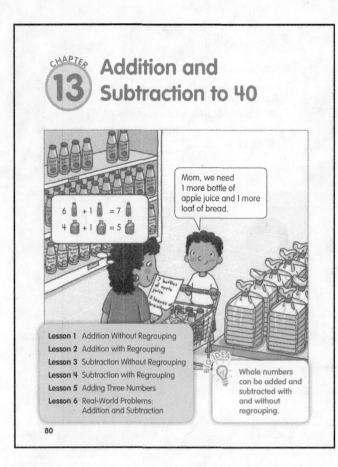

Mom, we need 1 more bottle of apple juice and 1 more loaf of bread.

6 + 1 = 7
4 + 1 = 5

Lesson 1   Addition Without Regrouping
Lesson 2   Addition with Regrouping
Lesson 3   Subtraction Without Regrouping
Lesson 4   Subtraction with Regrouping
Lesson 5   Adding Three Numbers
Lesson 6   Real-World Problems: Addition and Subtraction

BIG IDEA

Whole numbers can be added and subtracted with and without regrouping.

80

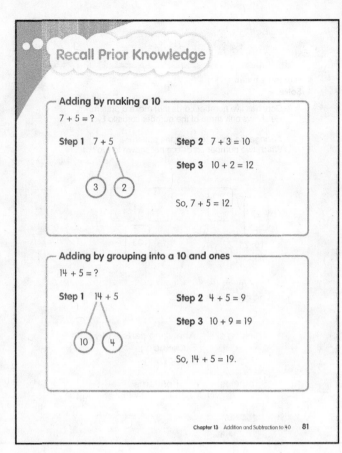

Recall Prior Knowledge

Adding by making a 10

7 + 5 = ?

Step 1   7 + 5
3   2

Step 2   7 + 3 = 10

Step 3   10 + 2 = 12

So, 7 + 5 = 12.

Adding by grouping into a 10 and ones

14 + 5 = ?

Step 1   14 + 5
10   4

Step 2   4 + 5 = 9

Step 3   10 + 9 = 19

So, 14 + 5 = 19.

Chapter 13   Addition and Subtraction to 40   81

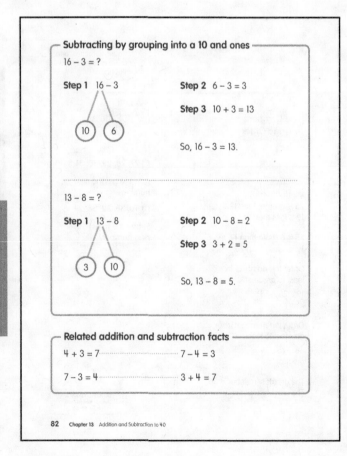

Subtracting by grouping into a 10 and ones

16 − 3 = ?

Step 1   16 − 3
10   6

Step 2   6 − 3 = 3

Step 3   10 + 3 = 13

So, 16 − 3 = 13.

13 − 8 = ?

Step 1   13 − 8
3   10

Step 2   10 − 8 = 2

Step 3   3 + 2 = 5

So, 13 − 8 = 5.

Related addition and subtraction facts

4 + 3 = 7 .... 7 − 4 = 3

7 − 3 = 4 .... 3 + 4 = 7

82   Chapter 13   Addition and Subtraction to 40

Chapter 13

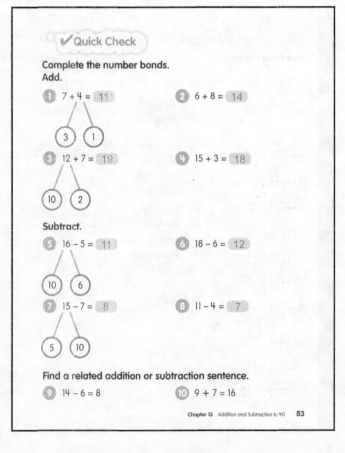

✔ Quick Check

Complete the number bonds.
Add.

1 7 + 4 = 11
   3   1

2 6 + 8 = 14

3 12 + 7 = 19
   10   2

4 15 + 3 = 18

Subtract.

5 16 − 5 = 11
   10   6

6 18 − 6 = 12

7 15 − 7 = 8
   5   10

8 11 − 4 = 7

Find a related addition or subtraction sentence.

9 14 − 6 = 8

10 9 + 7 = 16

Chapter 13   Addition and Subtraction to 40   83

Student Edition Answers: Chapter 13
Math in Focus Homeschool Answer Key, Grade 1

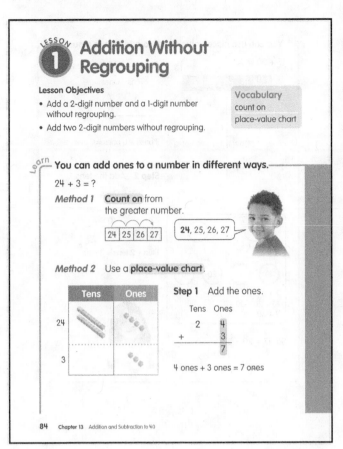

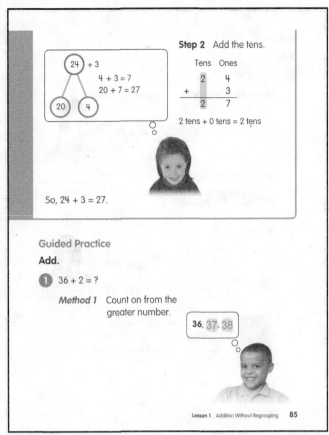

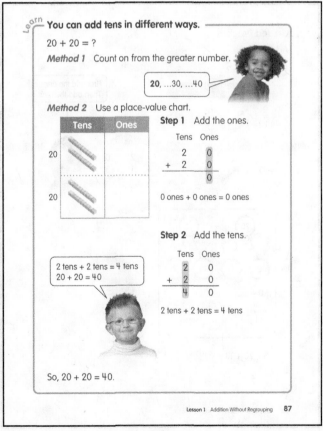

Add.

2 20 + 10 = ?

Method 1 Count on from the greater number.

20, ...30

Method 2 Use a place-value chart.

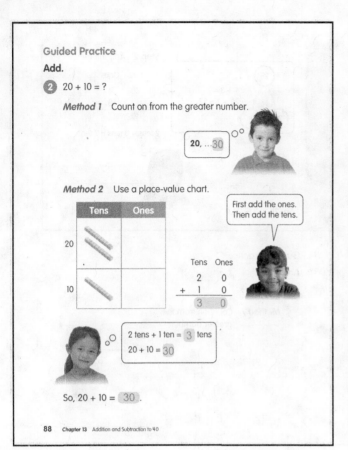

First add the ones.
Then add the tens.

Tens	Ones
20	
10	

```
 Tens  Ones
   2    0
 + 1    0
   3    0
```

2 tens + 1 ten = 3 tens
20 + 10 = 30

So, 20 + 10 = 30 .

---

17 + 20 = ?

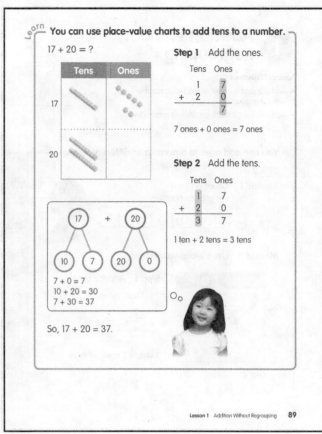

Step 1 Add the ones.

```
 Tens  Ones
   1    7
 + 2    0
        7
```

7 ones + 0 ones = 7 ones

Step 2 Add the tens.

```
 Tens  Ones
   1    7
 + 2    0
   3    7
```

1 ten + 2 tens = 3 tens

17 + 20

10 7   20 0

7 + 0 = 7
10 + 20 = 30
7 + 30 = 37

So, 17 + 20 = 37.

Add.

3 20 + 13 = ?

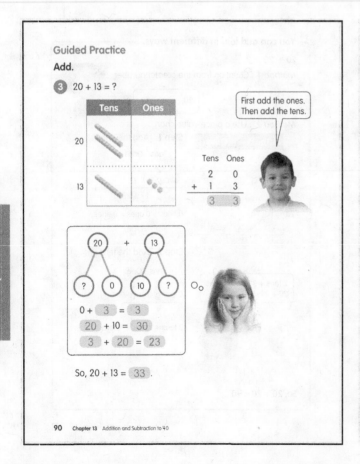

First add the ones.
Then add the tens.

Tens	Ones
20	
13	

```
 Tens  Ones
   2    0
 + 1    3
   3    3
```

20 + 13

? 0   10 ?

0 + 3 = 3
20 + 10 = 30
3 + 20 = 23

So, 20 + 13 = 33 .

---

14 + 25 = ?

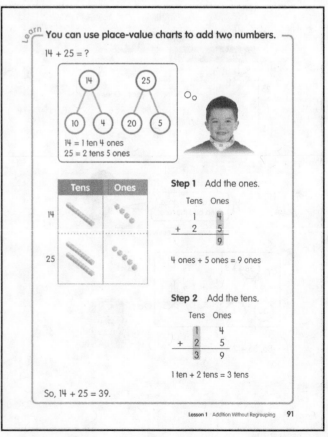

14   25

10 4   20 5

14 = 1 ten 4 ones
25 = 2 tens 5 ones

Tens	Ones
14	
25	

Step 1 Add the ones.

```
 Tens  Ones
   1    4
 + 2    5
        9
```

4 ones + 5 ones = 9 ones

Step 2 Add the tens.

```
 Tens  Ones
   1    4
 + 2    5
   3    9
```

1 ten + 2 tens = 3 tens

So, 14 + 25 = 39.

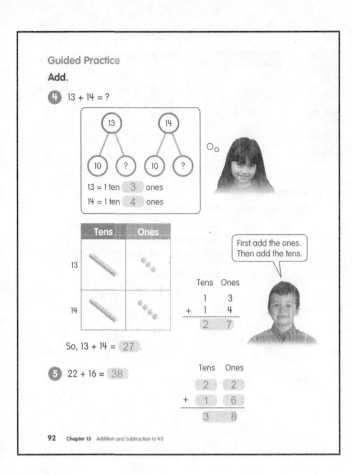

Guided Practice

Add.

④ 13 + 14 = ?

13 = 1 ten [3] ones

14 = 1 ten [4] ones

First add the ones.
Then add the tens.

	Tens	Ones
	1	3
+	1	4
	2	7

So, 13 + 14 = [27].

⑤ 22 + 16 = [38]

	Tens	Ones
	2	2
+	1	6
	3	8

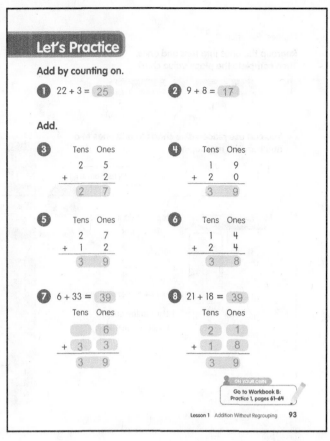

Let's Practice

Add by counting on.

① 22 + 3 = [25]

② 9 + 8 = [17]

Add.

③
	Tens	Ones
	2	5
+		2
	2	7

④
	Tens	Ones
	1	9
+	2	0
	3	9

⑤
	Tens	Ones
	2	7
+	1	2
	3	9

⑥
	Tens	Ones
	1	4
+	2	4
	3	8

⑦ 6 + 33 = [39]

	Tens	Ones
		6
+	3	3
	3	9

⑧ 21 + 18 = [39]

	Tens	Ones
	2	1
+	1	8
	3	9

ON YOUR OWN

Go to Workbook B:
Practice 1, pages 61–64

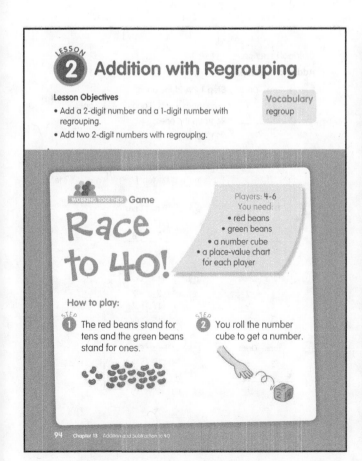

LESSON

2 Addition with Regrouping

Lesson Objectives
- Add a 2-digit number and a 1-digit number with regrouping.
- Add two 2-digit numbers with regrouping.

Vocabulary
regroup

WORKING TOGETHER Game

Race to 40!

Players: 4–6
You need:
- red beans
- green beans
- a number cube
- a place-value chart for each player

How to play:

① The red beans stand for tens and the green beans stand for ones.

② You roll the number cube to get a number.

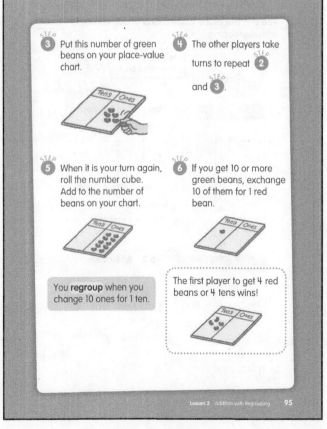

③ Put this number of green beans on your place-value chart.

④ The other players take turns to repeat ② and ③.

⑤ When it is your turn again, roll the number cube. Add to the number of beans on your chart.

⑥ If you get 10 or more green beans, exchange 10 of them for 1 red bean.

You **regroup** when you change 10 ones for 1 ten.

The first player to get 4 red beans or 4 tens wins!

Chapter 13

Guided Practice

Regroup the ones into tens and ones.
Then complete the place-value chart.

1

17 =

Tens	Ones
	17

=

Tens	Ones
1	7

Learn You can use place-value charts to add ones to a number with regrouping.

28 + 6 = ?

28 = 2 tens 8 ones

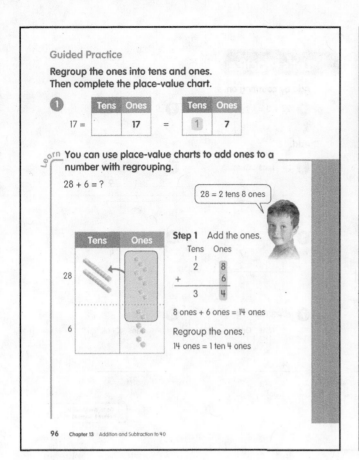

Step 1 Add the ones.

Tens	Ones
2	8
+	6
3	4

8 ones + 6 ones = 14 ones

Regroup the ones.
14 ones = 1 ten 4 ones

Step 2 Add the tens.

Tens	Ones
	8
+	6
3	4

34

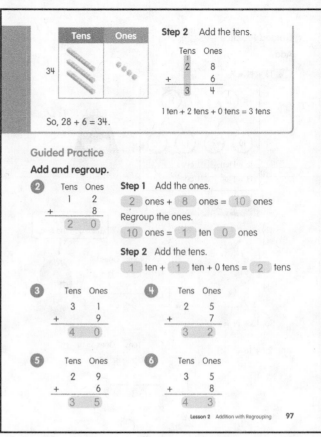

1 ten + 2 tens + 0 tens = 3 tens

So, 28 + 6 = 34.

Guided Practice

Add and regroup.

2

Tens	Ones
1	2
+	8
2	0

Step 1 Add the ones.
2 ones + 8 ones = 10 ones
Regroup the ones.
10 ones = 1 ten 0 ones

Step 2 Add the tens.
1 ten + 1 ten + 0 tens = 2 tens

3

Tens	Ones
3	1
+	9
4	0

4

Tens	Ones
2	5
+	7
3	2

5

Tens	Ones
2	9
+	6
3	5

6

Tens	Ones
3	5
+	8
4	3

Learn You can use place-value charts to add numbers with regrouping.

14 + 18 = ?

14 = 1 ten 4 ones
18 = 1 ten 8 ones

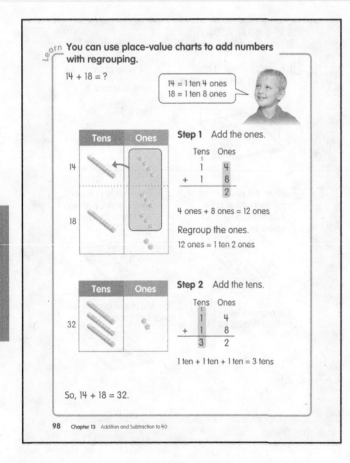

Step 1 Add the ones.

Tens	Ones
1	4
+ 1	8
	2

4 ones + 8 ones = 12 ones

Regroup the ones.
12 ones = 1 ten 2 ones

Step 2 Add the tens.

Tens	Ones
1	4
+ 1	8
3	2

1 ten + 1 ten + 1 ten = 3 tens

So, 14 + 18 = 32.

Guided Practice

Add and regroup.

7

Tens	Ones
1	5
+ 1	6
3	1

Step 1 Add the ones.
5 ones + 6 ones = 11 ones
Regroup the ones.
11 ones = 1 ten 1 one

Step 2 Add the tens.
1 ten + 1 ten + 1 ten = 3 tens

8

Tens	Ones
1	5
+ 1	5
3	0

9

Tens	Ones
1	2
+ 2	8
4	0

10

Tens	Ones
1	2
+ 1	9
3	1

11

Tens	Ones
1	7
+ 1	7
3	4

12

Tens	Ones
2	6
+	8
3	4

13

Tens	Ones
1	9
+	9
2	8

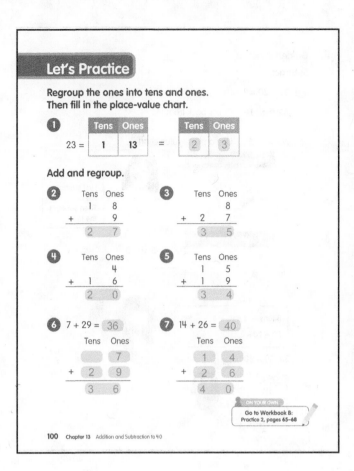

Let's Practice

Regroup the ones into tens and ones.
Then fill in the place-value chart.

1.
Tens	Ones
1	13

23 = | 1 | 13 | =
Tens	Ones
2	3

Add and regroup.

2.
Tens	Ones
1	8
+	9
2	7

3.
Tens	Ones
	8
+ 2	7
3	5

4.
Tens	Ones
	4
+ 1	6
2	0

5.
Tens	Ones
1	5
+ 1	9
3	4

6. 7 + 29 = 36
Tens	Ones
	7
+ 2	9
3	6

7. 14 + 26 = 40
Tens	Ones
1	4
+ 2	6
4	0

ON YOUR OWN
Go to Workbook B:
Practice 2, pages 65–68

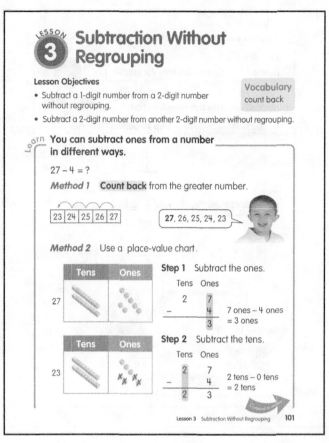

Subtraction Without Regrouping

Lesson Objectives

- Subtract a 1-digit number from a 2-digit number without regrouping.
- Subtract a 2-digit number from another 2-digit number without regrouping.

Vocabulary
count back

Learn You can subtract ones from a number in different ways.

27 – 4 = ?

Method 1 Count back from the greater number.

| 23 | 24 | 25 | 26 | 27 |

27, 26, 25, 24, 23

Method 2 Use a place-value chart.

Step 1 Subtract the ones.

Tens	Ones
2	7
–	4
	3

7 ones – 4 ones = 3 ones

Step 2 Subtract the tens.

Tens	Ones
2	7
–	4
2	3

2 tens – 0 tens = 2 tens

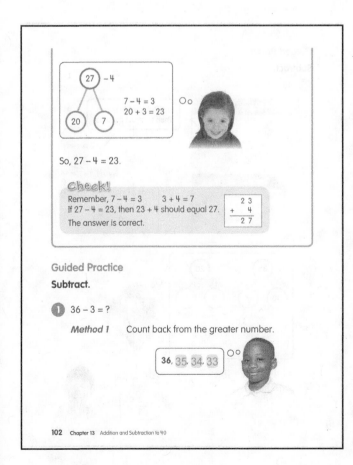

27 – 4

20   7

7 – 4 = 3
20 + 3 = 23

So, 27 – 4 = 23.

Check!

Remember, 7 – 4 = 3   3 + 4 = 7
If 27 – 4 = 23, then 23 + 4 should equal 27.
The answer is correct.

	2	3
+		4
	2	7

Guided Practice

Subtract.

1. 36 – 3 = ?

   Method 1 Count back from the greater number.

   36, 35, 34, 33

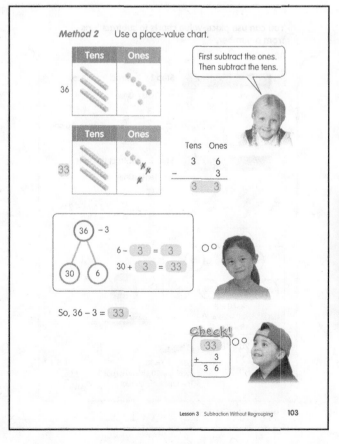

Method 2 Use a place-value chart.

Tens	Ones
36

Tens	Ones
33

First subtract the ones.
Then subtract the tens.

Tens	Ones
3	6
–	3
3	3

36 – 3

30   6

6 – 3 = 3
30 + 3 = 33

So, 36 – 3 = 33.

Check!

	3	3
+		3
	3	6

Chapter 13

You can subtract tens in different ways.

20 − 10 = ?

Method 1   Count back from the greater number.

20, …10

Method 2   Use a place-value chart.

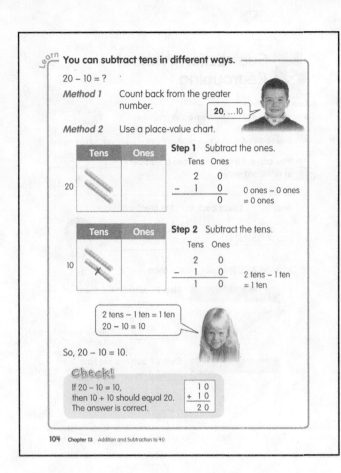

Step 1   Subtract the ones.

```
    Tens  Ones
      2    0
 −    1    0      0 ones − 0 ones
      0           = 0 ones
```

Step 2   Subtract the tens.

```
    Tens  Ones
      2    0
 −    1    0      2 tens − 1 ten
      1    0      = 1 ten
```

2 tens − 1 ten = 1 ten
20 − 10 = 10

So, 20 − 10 = 10.

Check!
If 20 − 10 = 10,
then 10 + 10 should equal 20.
The answer is correct.

```
   1 0
 + 1 0
   2 0
```

Guided Practice

Subtract.

2   30 − 20 = ?

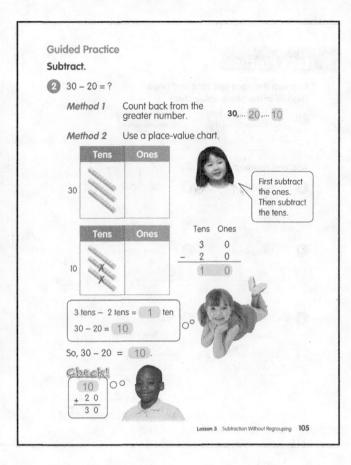

Method 1   Count back from the greater number.

30,… 20,… 10

Method 2   Use a place-value chart.

First subtract the ones. Then subtract the tens.

```
    Tens  Ones
      3    0
 −    2    0
      1    0
```

3 tens − 2 tens = 1 ten
30 − 20 = 10

So, 30 − 20 = 10.

Check!
```
   10
 + 2 0
   3 0
```

You can use place-value charts to subtract tens from a number.

38 − 20 = ?

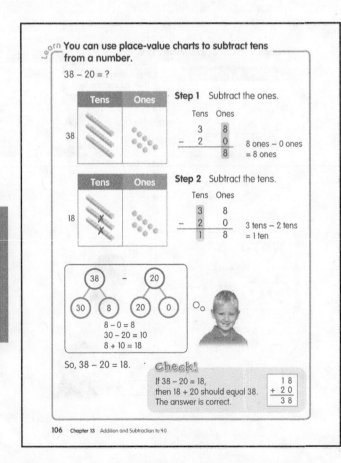

Step 1   Subtract the ones.

```
    Tens  Ones
      3    8
 −    2    0
      8           8 ones − 0 ones
                  = 8 ones
```

Step 2   Subtract the tens.

```
    Tens  Ones
      3    8
 −    2    0
      1    8      3 tens − 2 tens
                  = 1 ten
```

```
     38    −    20
    /  \       /  \
   30   8    20    0
```
8 − 0 = 8
30 − 20 = 10
8 + 10 = 18

So, 38 − 20 = 18.

Check!
If 38 − 20 = 18,
then 18 + 20 should equal 38.
The answer is correct.

```
   1 8
 + 2 0
   3 8
```

Guided Practice

Subtract.

3   35 − 20 = ?

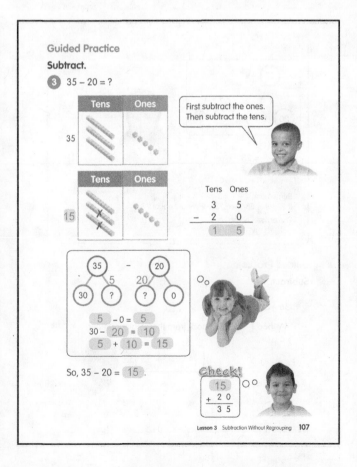

First subtract the ones. Then subtract the tens.

```
    Tens  Ones
      3    5
 −    2    0
      1    5
```

```
     35    −    20
    /  \       /  \
   30   ?    ?     0
```
5 − 0 = 5
30 − 20 = 10
5 + 10 = 15

So, 35 − 20 = 15.

Check!
```
   15
 + 2 0
   3 5
```

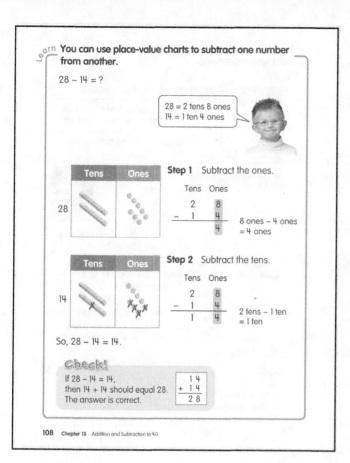

Learn You can use place-value charts to subtract one number from another.

$28 - 14 = ?$

> 28 = 2 tens 8 ones
> 14 = 1 ten 4 ones

Step 1 Subtract the ones.

	Tens	Ones
28		

$$\begin{array}{cc} \text{Tens} & \text{Ones} \\ 2 & 8 \\ - 1 & 4 \\ \hline & 4 \end{array}$$

8 ones – 4 ones = 4 ones

Step 2 Subtract the tens.

	Tens	Ones
14		

$$\begin{array}{cc} \text{Tens} & \text{Ones} \\ 2 & 8 \\ - 1 & 4 \\ \hline 1 & 4 \end{array}$$

2 tens – 1 ten = 1 ten

So, $28 - 14 = 14$.

Check!
If $28 - 14 = 14$,
then $14 + 14$ should equal 28.
The answer is correct.

$$\begin{array}{r} 14 \\ + 14 \\ \hline 28 \end{array}$$

Subtract.

4 $39 - 22 = ?$

> 39 = 3 tens **9** ones
> 22 = **2** tens 2 ones

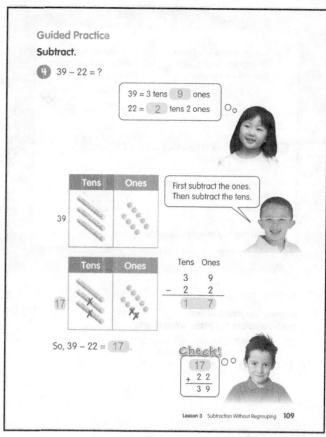

First subtract the ones.
Then subtract the tens.

	Tens	Ones
39		

	Tens	Ones
17		

$$\begin{array}{cc} \text{Tens} & \text{Ones} \\ 3 & 9 \\ - 2 & 2 \\ \hline 1 & 7 \end{array}$$

So, $39 - 22 = 17$.

Check!
$$\begin{array}{r} 17 \\ + 22 \\ \hline 39 \end{array}$$

Let's Practice

Subtract by counting back.

1 $28 - 3 = 25$ **2** $40 - 20 = 20$

Subtract.

3
$$\begin{array}{cc} \text{Tens} & \text{Ones} \\ 2 & 6 \\ - & 5 \\ \hline 2 & 1 \end{array}$$

4
$$\begin{array}{cc} \text{Tens} & \text{Ones} \\ 3 & 6 \\ - 1 & 0 \\ \hline 2 & 6 \end{array}$$

5
$$\begin{array}{cc} \text{Tens} & \text{Ones} \\ 2 & 9 \\ - 1 & 3 \\ \hline 1 & 6 \end{array}$$

6
$$\begin{array}{cc} \text{Tens} & \text{Ones} \\ 3 & 8 \\ - 2 & 5 \\ \hline 1 & 3 \end{array}$$

7 $34 - 3 = 31$

$$\begin{array}{cc} \text{Tens} & \text{Ones} \\ 3 & 4 \\ - & 3 \\ \hline 3 & 1 \end{array}$$

8 $27 - 15 = 12$

$$\begin{array}{cc} \text{Tens} & \text{Ones} \\ 2 & 7 \\ - 1 & 5 \\ \hline 1 & 2 \end{array}$$

ON YOUR OWN
Go to Workbook B:
Practice 3, pages 69–72

LESSON 4 **Subtraction with Regrouping**

Lesson Objectives
- Subtract a 1-digit number from a 2-digit number with regrouping.
- Subtract a 2-digit number from another 2-digit number with regrouping.

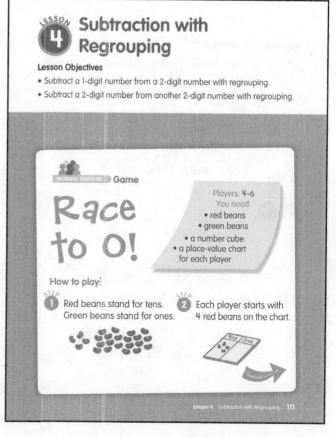

WORKING TOGETHER Game

Race to 0!

Players: 4-6
You need:
- red beans
- green beans
- a number cube
- a place-value chart for each player

How to play:

STEP 1 Red beans stand for tens. Green beans stand for ones.

STEP 2 Each player starts with 4 red beans on the chart.

Chapter 13

95

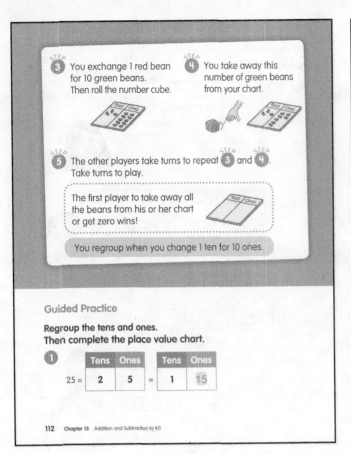

STEP 3 You exchange 1 red bean for 10 green beans. Then roll the number cube.

STEP 4 You take away this number of green beans from your chart.

STEP 5 The other players take turns to repeat **3** and **4**. Take turns to play.

The first player to take away all the beans from his or her chart or get zero wins!

You regroup when you change 1 ten for 10 ones.

Guided Practice

Regroup the tens and ones. Then complete the place value chart.

1

Tens	Ones		Tens	Ones
2	**5**	=	**1**	15

25 =

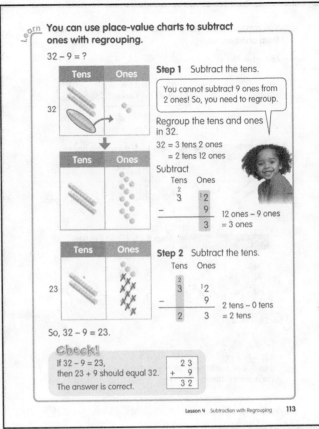

$32 - 9 = ?$

Step 1 Subtract the tens.

You cannot subtract 9 ones from 2 ones! So, you need to regroup.

Regroup the tens and ones in 32.

32 = 3 tens 2 ones
   = 2 tens 12 ones

Subtract

12 ones − 9 ones = 3 ones

Step 2 Subtract the tens.

2 tens − 0 tens = 2 tens

So, $32 - 9 = 23$.

Check!
If $32 - 9 = 23$,
then $23 + 9$ should equal 32.
The answer is correct.

```
  2 3
+   9
-----
  3 2
```

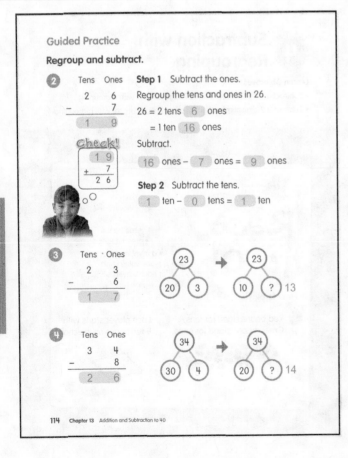

Guided Practice

Regroup and subtract.

2

Tens	Ones
2	6
−	7
1	9

Step 1 Subtract the ones.
Regroup the tens and ones in 26.
26 = 2 tens 6 ones
   = 1 ten 16 ones
Subtract.
16 ones − 7 ones = 9 ones

Check!
```
  1 9
+   7
-----
  2 6
```

Step 2 Subtract the tens.
1 ten − 0 tens = 1 ten

3

Tens	Ones
2	3
−	6
1	7

23 → 20, 3 → 23 → 10, ? = 13

4

Tens	Ones
3	4
−	8
2	6

34 → 30, 4 → 34 → 20, ? = 14

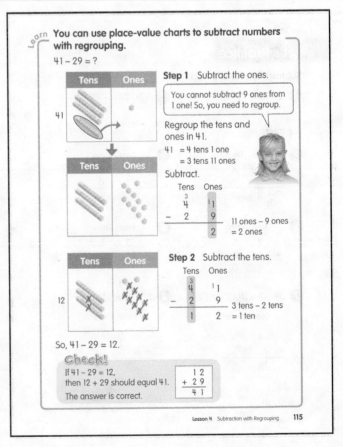

$41 - 29 = ?$

Step 1 Subtract the ones.

You cannot subtract 9 ones from 1 one! So, you need to regroup.

Regroup the tens and ones in 41.

41 = 4 tens 1 one
   = 3 tens 11 ones

Subtract.

11 ones − 9 ones = 2 ones

Step 2 Subtract the tens.

3 tens − 2 tens = 1 ten

So, $41 - 29 = 12$.

Check!
If $41 - 29 = 12$,
then $12 + 29$ should equal 41.
The answer is correct.

```
  1 2
+ 2 9
-----
  4 1
```

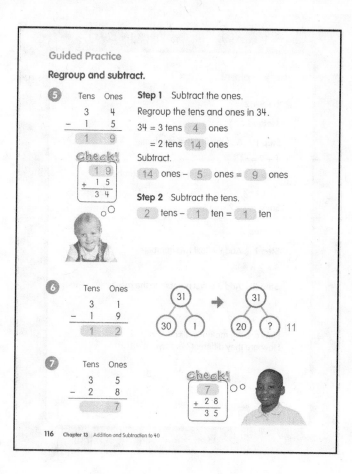

Guided Practice

Regroup and subtract.

5.

Tens	Ones
3	4
− 1	5
1	9

Step 1 Subtract the ones.

Regroup the tens and ones in 34.

34 = 3 tens ⟨4⟩ ones

= 2 tens ⟨14⟩ ones

Subtract.

14 ones − ⟨5⟩ ones = ⟨9⟩ ones

Step 2 Subtract the tens.

⟨2⟩ tens − ⟨1⟩ ten = ⟨1⟩ ten

Check!

1	9
+ 1	5
3	4

6.

Tens	Ones
3	1
− 1	9
1	2

31 → 30 1 → 31 → 20 ? → 11

7.

Tens	Ones
3	5
− 2	8
	7

Check!

7
+ 2 8
3 5

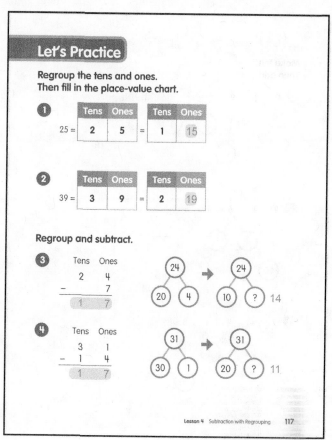

Let's Practice

Regroup the tens and ones.
Then fill in the place-value chart.

1. 25 =

Tens	Ones
2	5

=

Tens	Ones
1	15

2. 39 =

Tens	Ones
3	9

=

Tens	Ones
2	19

Regroup and subtract.

3.

Tens	Ones
2	4
−	7
1	7

24 → 20 4 → 24 → 10 ? → 14

4.

Tens	Ones
3	1
− 1	4
1	7

31 → 30 1 → 31 → 20 ? → 11

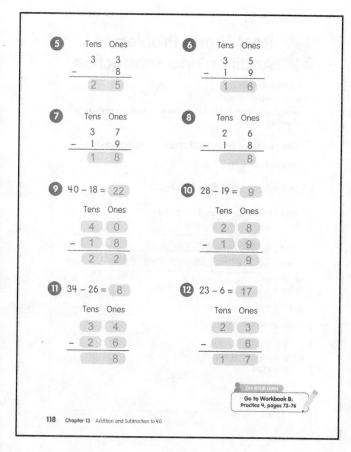

5.

Tens	Ones
3	3
−	8
2	5

6.

Tens	Ones
3	5
− 1	9
1	6

7.

Tens	Ones
3	7
− 1	9
1	8

8.

Tens	Ones
2	6
− 1	8
	8

9. 40 − 18 = ⟨22⟩

Tens	Ones
4	0
− 1	8
2	2

10. 28 − 19 = ⟨9⟩

Tens	Ones
2	8
− 1	9
	9

11. 34 − 26 = ⟨8⟩

Tens	Ones
3	4
− 2	6
	8

12. 23 − 6 = ⟨17⟩

Tens	Ones
2	3
−	6
1	7

ON YOUR OWN

Go to Workbook B:
Practice 4, pages 73–76

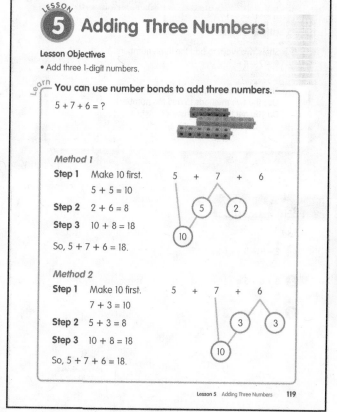

LESSON 5 Adding Three Numbers

Lesson Objectives

• Add three 1-digit numbers.

Learn You can use number bonds to add three numbers.

5 + 7 + 6 = ?

Method 1

Step 1 Make 10 first.

5 + 5 = 10

Step 2 2 + 6 = 8

Step 3 10 + 8 = 18

So, 5 + 7 + 6 = 18.

5 + 7 + 6

(5) (2)

(10)

Method 2

Step 1 Make 10 first.

7 + 3 = 10

Step 2 5 + 3 = 8

Step 3 10 + 8 = 18

So, 5 + 7 + 6 = 18.

5 + 7 + 6

(3) (3)

(10)

Chapter 13

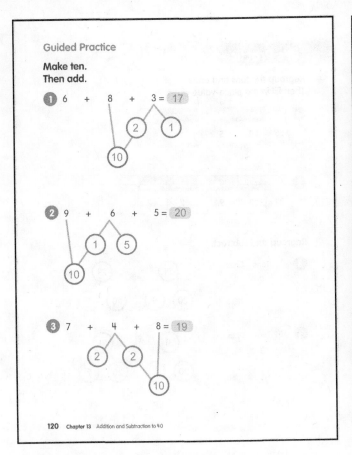

Guided Practice

Make ten.
Then add.

1   6   +   8   +   3 = 17

2   9   +   6   +   5 = 20

3   7   +   4   +   8 = 19

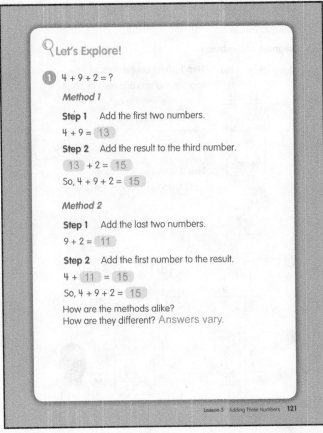

Let's Explore!

1   4 + 9 + 2 = ?

Method 1

Step 1   Add the first two numbers.

4 + 9 = 13

Step 2   Add the result to the third number.

13 + 2 = 15

So, 4 + 9 + 2 = 15

Method 2

Step 1   Add the last two numbers.

9 + 2 = 11

Step 2   Add the first number to the result.

4 + 11 = 15

So, 4 + 9 + 2 = 15

How are the methods alike?
How are they different? Answers vary.

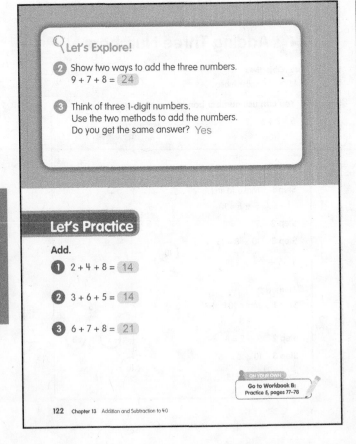

Let's Explore!

2   Show two ways to add the three numbers.
9 + 7 + 8 = 24

3   Think of three 1-digit numbers.
Use the two methods to add the numbers.
Do you get the same answer? Yes

Let's Practice

Add.

1   2 + 4 + 8 = 14

2   3 + 6 + 5 = 14

3   6 + 7 + 8 = 21

ON YOUR OWN
Go to Workbook B:
Practice 5, pages 77–78

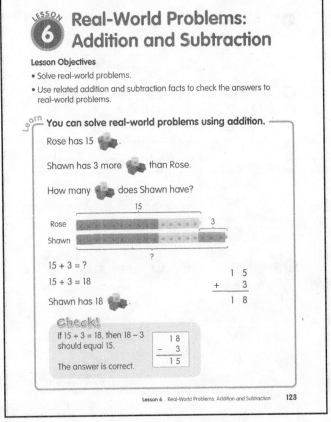

LESSON
6   **Real-World Problems:**
Addition and Subtraction

Lesson Objectives

• Solve real-world problems.
• Use related addition and subtraction facts to check the answers to real-world problems.

Learn   **You can solve real-world problems using addition.**

Rose has 15 .

Shawn has 3 more than Rose.

How many does Shawn have?

15 + 3 = ?

15 + 3 = 18

    1 5
+   3
    1 8

Shawn has 18 .

Check!
If 15 + 3 = 18, then 18 – 3
should equal 15.

    1 8
–   3
    1 5

The answer is correct.

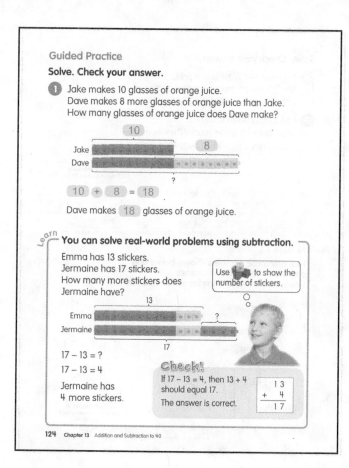

Guided Practice

Solve. Check your answer.

1 Jake makes 10 glasses of orange juice.
Dave makes 8 more glasses of orange juice than Jake.
How many glasses of orange juice does Dave make?

10

Jake
Dave   8
?

10 + 8 = 18

Dave makes 18 glasses of orange juice.

Learn **You can solve real-world problems using subtraction.**

Emma has 13 stickers.
Jermaine has 17 stickers.
How many more stickers does
Jermaine have?

Use ▦ to show the number of stickers.

13

Emma   ?
Jermaine

17

17 − 13 = ?

17 − 13 = 4

Jermaine has
4 more stickers.

Check!
If 17 − 13 = 4, then 13 + 4
should equal 17.
The answer is correct.

$$\begin{array}{r} 1\ 3 \\ +\ \ 4 \\ \hline 1\ 7 \end{array}$$

124   Chapter 13   Addition and Subtraction to 40

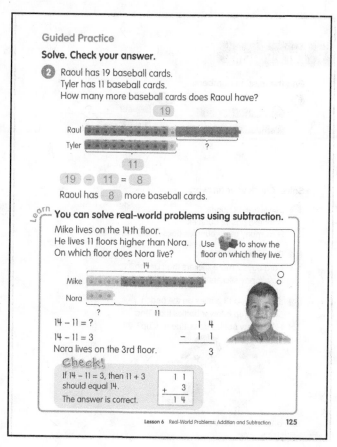

Guided Practice

Solve. Check your answer.

2 Raoul has 19 baseball cards.
Tyler has 11 baseball cards.
How many more baseball cards does Raoul have?

19

Raul
Tyler   ?

11

19 − 11 = 8

Raoul has 8 more baseball cards.

Learn **You can solve real-world problems using subtraction.**

Mike lives on the 14th floor.
He lives 11 floors higher than Nora.
On which floor does Nora live?

Use ▦ to show the floor on which they live.

14

Mike
Nora
?   11

14 − 11 = ?

14 − 11 = 3

Nora lives on the 3rd floor.

$$\begin{array}{r} 1\ 4 \\ -\ 1\ 1 \\ \hline 3 \end{array}$$

Check!
If 14 − 11 = 3, then 11 + 3
should equal 14.
The answer is correct.

$$\begin{array}{r} 1\ 1 \\ +\ \ 3 \\ \hline 1\ 4 \end{array}$$

Lesson 6   Real-World Problems: Addition and Subtraction   125

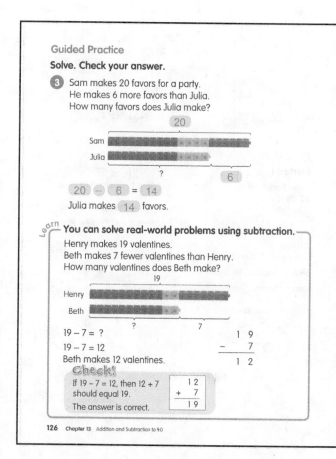

Guided Practice

Solve. Check your answer.

3 Sam makes 20 favors for a party.
He makes 6 more favors than Julia.
How many favors does Julia make?

20

Sam
Julia
?   6

20 − 6 = 14

Julia makes 14 favors.

Learn **You can solve real-world problems using subtraction.**

Henry makes 19 valentines.
Beth makes 7 fewer valentines than Henry.
How many valentines does Beth make?

19

Henry
Beth
?   7

19 − 7 = ?

19 − 7 = 12

Beth makes 12 valentines.

$$\begin{array}{r} 1\ 9 \\ -\ \ 7 \\ \hline 1\ 2 \end{array}$$

Check!
If 19 − 7 = 12, then 12 + 7
should equal 19.
The answer is correct.

$$\begin{array}{r} 1\ 2 \\ +\ \ 7 \\ \hline 1\ 9 \end{array}$$

126   Chapter 13   Addition and Subtraction to 40

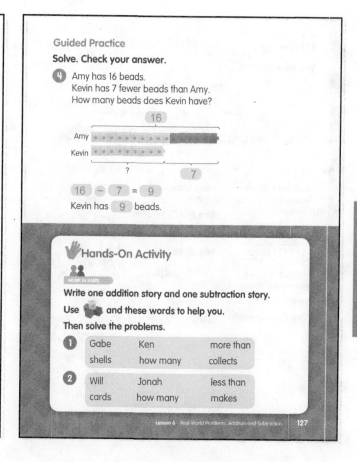

Guided Practice

Solve. Check your answer.

4 Amy has 16 beads.
Kevin has 7 fewer beads than Amy.
How many beads does Kevin have?

16

Amy
Kevin
?   7

16 − 7 = 9

Kevin has 9 beads.

✋ Hands-On Activity

WORK IN PAIRS

Write one addition story and one subtraction story.

Use ▦ and these words to help you.

Then solve the problems.

1
| Gabe | Ken | more than |
| shells | how many | collects |

2
| Will | Jonah | less than |
| cards | how many | makes |

Lesson 6   Real-World Problems: Addition and Subtraction   127

Student Edition Answers: Chapter 13
Math in Focus Homeschool Answer Key, Grade 1

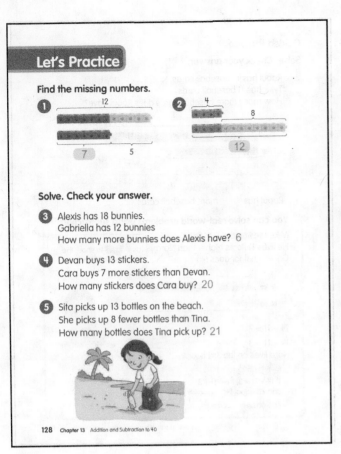

Let's Practice

Find the missing numbers.

1. 12 / 7 / 5

2. 4 / 8 / 12

Solve. Check your answer.

3. Alexis has 18 bunnies.
   Gabriella has 12 bunnies
   How many more bunnies does Alexis have? 6

4. Devan buys 13 stickers.
   Cara buys 7 more stickers than Devan.
   How many stickers does Cara buy? 20

5. Sita picks up 13 bottles on the beach.
   She picks up 8 fewer bottles than Tina.
   How many bottles does Tina pick up? 21

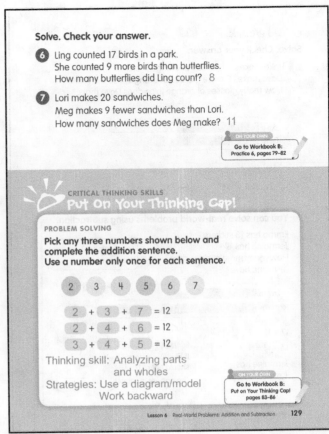

Solve. Check your answer.

6. Ling counted 17 birds in a park.
   She counted 9 more birds than butterflies.
   How many butterflies did Ling count? 8

7. Lori makes 20 sandwiches.
   Meg makes 9 fewer sandwiches than Lori.
   How many sandwiches does Meg make? 11

> ON YOUR OWN
> Go to Workbook B:
> Practice 6, pages 79–82

CRITICAL THINKING SKILLS
Put On Your Thinking Cap!

PROBLEM SOLVING

Pick any three numbers shown below and
complete the addition sentence.
Use a number only once for each sentence.

2　3　4　5　6　7

2 + 3 + 7 = 12
2 + 4 + 6 = 12
3 + 4 + 5 = 12

Thinking skill: Analyzing parts
and wholes
Strategies: Use a diagram/model
Work backward

> ON YOUR OWN
> Go to Workbook B:
> Put on Your Thinking Cap!
> pages 83–86

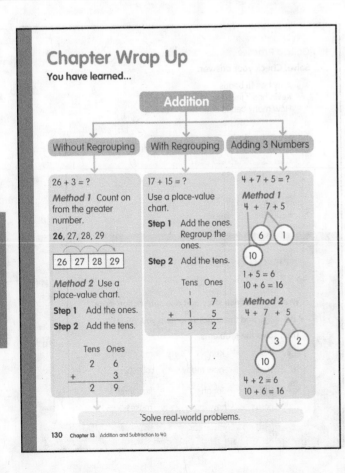

Chapter Wrap Up
You have learned...

Addition

Without Regrouping

26 + 3 = ?

Method 1 Count on from the greater number.

26, 27, 28, 29

| 26 | 27 | 28 | 29 |

Method 2 Use a place-value chart.

Step 1　Add the ones.
Step 2　Add the tens.

Tens　Ones
　2　　6
+　　　3
　2　　9

With Regrouping

17 + 15 = ?

Use a place-value chart.

Step 1　Add the ones. Regroup the ones.

Step 2　Add the tens.

Tens　Ones
　1
　1　　7
+　1　　5
　3　　2

Adding 3 Numbers

4 + 7 + 5 = ?

Method 1
4 + 7 + 5
⟶ 6　1
　10

1 + 5 = 6
10 + 6 = 16

Method 2
4 + 7 + 5
⟶ 3　2
　10

4 + 2 = 6
10 + 6 = 16

`Solve real-world problems.

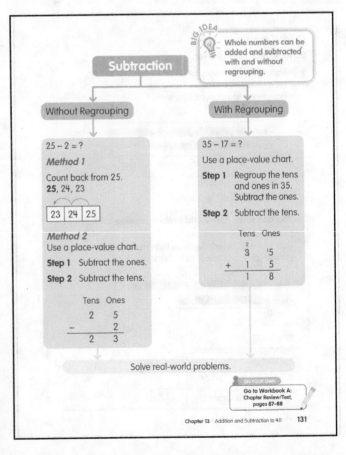

> BIG IDEA
> Whole numbers can be
> added and subtracted
> with and without
> regrouping.

Subtraction

Without Regrouping

25 – 2 = ?

Method 1
Count back from 25.
25, 24, 23

| 23 | 24 | 25 |

Method 2
Use a place-value chart.

Step 1　Subtract the ones.
Step 2　Subtract the tens.

Tens　Ones
　2　　5
–　　　2
　2　　3

With Regrouping

35 – 17 = ?

Use a place-value chart.

Step 1　Regroup the tens and ones in 35. Subtract the ones.

Step 2　Subtract the tens.

Tens　Ones
　2
　3　　15
+　1　　5
　1　　8

Solve real-world problems.

> ON YOUR OWN
> Go to Workbook A:
> Chapter Review/Test,
> pages 87–88

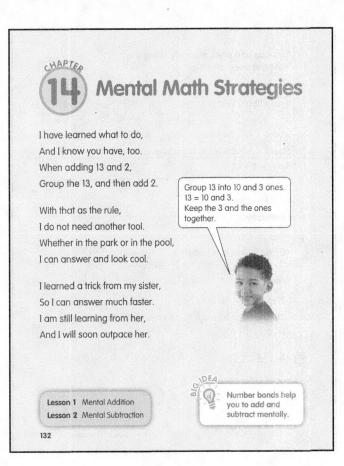

CHAPTER 14 Mental Math Strategies

I have learned what to do,
And I know you have, too.
When adding 13 and 2,
Group the 13, and then add 2.

With that as the rule,
I do not need another tool.
Whether in the park or in the pool,
I can answer and look cool.

I learned a trick from my sister,
So I can answer much faster.
I am still learning from her,
And I will soon outpace her.

Group 13 into 10 and 3 ones.
13 = 10 and 3.
Keep the 3 and the ones together.

Lesson 1 Mental Addition
Lesson 2 Mental Subtraction

132

BIG IDEA Number bonds help you to add and subtract mentally.

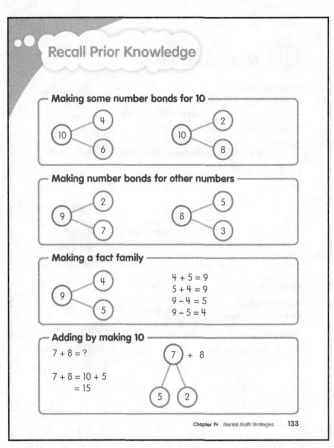

Recall Prior Knowledge

Making some number bonds for 10

10 — 4, 6   10 — 2, 8

Making number bonds for other numbers

9 — 2, 7   8 — 5, 3

Making a fact family

9 — 4, 5

4 + 5 = 9
5 + 4 = 9
9 − 4 = 5
9 − 5 = 4

Adding by making 10

7 + 8 = ?

7 + 8 = 10 + 5
    = 15

7 + 8

5   2

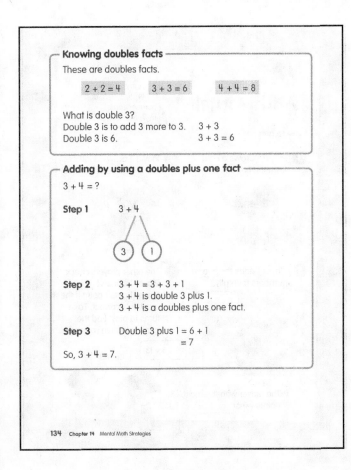

Knowing doubles facts

These are doubles facts.

2 + 2 = 4   3 + 3 = 6   4 + 4 = 8

What is double 3?
Double 3 is to add 3 more to 3.   3 + 3
Double 3 is 6.   3 + 3 = 6

Adding by using a doubles plus one fact

3 + 4 = ?

Step 1   3 + 4

3   1

Step 2   3 + 4 = 3 + 3 + 1
3 + 4 is double 3 plus 1.
3 + 4 is a doubles plus one fact.

Step 3   Double 3 plus 1 = 6 + 1
    = 7

So, 3 + 4 = 7.

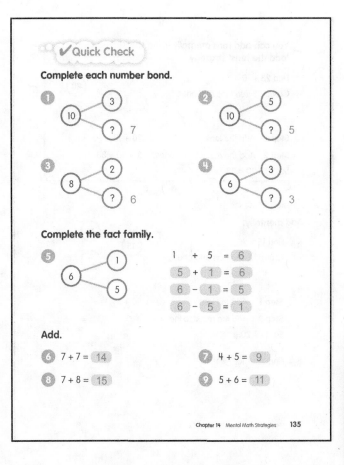

✔ Quick Check

Complete each number bond.

1 10 — 3, ? 7

2 10 — 5, ? 5

3 8 — 2, ? 6

4 6 — 3, ? 3

Complete the fact family.

5 6 — 1, 5

1 + 5 = 6
5 + 1 = 6
6 − 1 = 5
6 − 5 = 1

Add.

6 7 + 7 = 14

7 4 + 5 = 9

8 7 + 8 = 15

9 5 + 6 = 11

Chapter 14

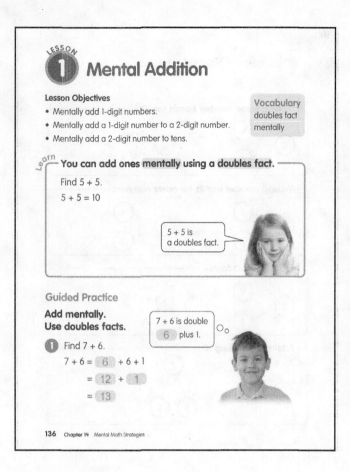

LESSON 1 Mental Addition

Lesson Objectives
- Mentally add 1-digit numbers.
- Mentally add a 1-digit number to a 2-digit number.
- Mentally add a 2-digit number to tens.

Vocabulary
doubles fact
mentally

Learn You can add ones mentally using a doubles fact.

Find 5 + 5.
5 + 5 = 10

5 + 5 is a doubles fact.

Guided Practice

Add mentally.
Use doubles facts.

7 + 6 is double 6 plus 1.

1 Find 7 + 6.

$7 + 6 = 6 + 6 + 1$

$= 12 + 1$

$= 13$

136 Chapter 14 Mental Math Strategies

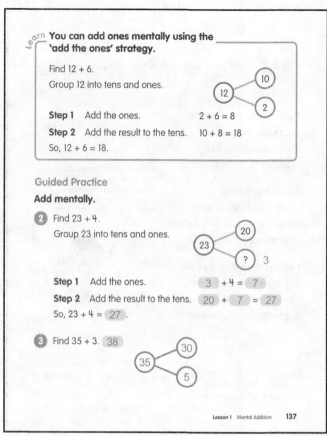

Learn You can add ones mentally using the 'add the ones' strategy.

Find 12 + 6.
Group 12 into tens and ones.

12 → 10, 2

Step 1 Add the ones. 2 + 6 = 8

Step 2 Add the result to the tens. 10 + 8 = 18

So, 12 + 6 = 18.

Guided Practice

Add mentally.

2 Find 23 + 4.
Group 23 into tens and ones.

23 → 20, ? 3

Step 1 Add the ones. 3 + 4 = 7

Step 2 Add the result to the tens. 20 + 7 = 27

So, 23 + 4 = 27.

3 Find 35 + 3. 38

35 → 30, 5

Lesson 1 Mental Addition 137

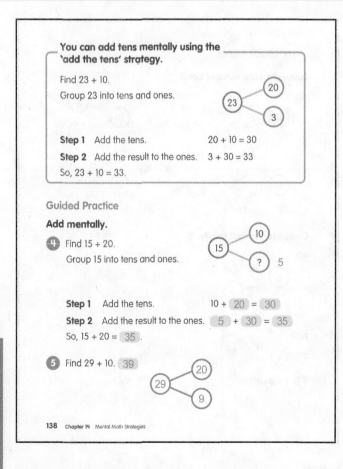

You can add tens mentally using the 'add the tens' strategy.

Find 23 + 10.
Group 23 into tens and ones.

23 → 20, 3

Step 1 Add the tens. 20 + 10 = 30

Step 2 Add the result to the ones. 3 + 30 = 33

So, 23 + 10 = 33.

Guided Practice

Add mentally.

4 Find 15 + 20.
Group 15 into tens and ones.

15 → 10, ? 5

Step 1 Add the tens. 10 + 20 = 30

Step 2 Add the result to the ones. 5 + 30 = 35

So, 15 + 20 = 35.

5 Find 29 + 10. 39

29 → 20, 9

138 Chapter 14 Mental Math Strategies

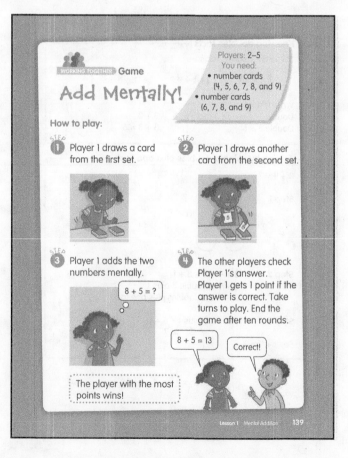

WORKING TOGETHER Game

Add Mentally!

Players: 2–5
You need:
- number cards (4, 5, 6, 7, 8, and 9)
- number cards (6, 7, 8, and 9)

How to play:

STEP 1 Player 1 draws a card from the first set.

STEP 2 Player 1 draws another card from the second set.

STEP 3 Player 1 adds the two numbers mentally.

8 + 5 = ?

STEP 4 The other players check Player 1's answer. Player 1 gets 1 point if the answer is correct. Take turns to play. End the game after ten rounds.

8 + 5 = 13   Correct!

The player with the most points wins!

Lesson 1 Mental Addition 139

Chapter 14

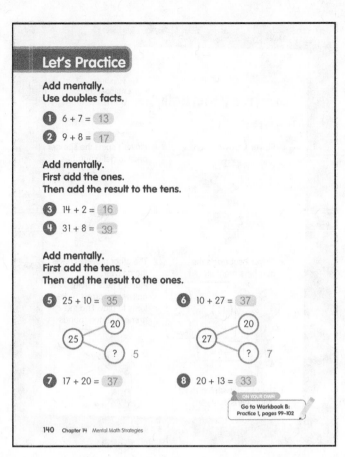

Let's Practice

Add mentally.
Use doubles facts.

1. 6 + 7 = 13

2. 9 + 8 = 17

Add mentally.
First add the ones.
Then add the result to the tens.

3. 14 + 2 = 16

4. 31 + 8 = 39

Add mentally.
First add the tens.
Then add the result to the ones.

5. 25 + 10 = 35

6. 10 + 27 = 37

7. 17 + 20 = 37

8. 20 + 13 = 33

ON YOUR OWN
Go to Workbook B:
Practice 1, pages 99–102

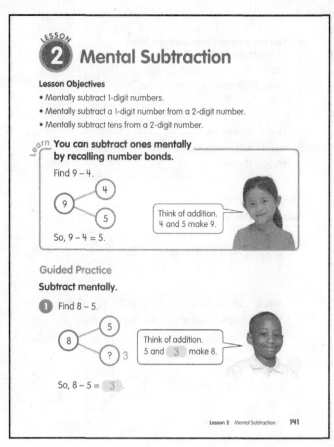

2 Mental Subtraction

Lesson Objectives
• Mentally subtract 1-digit numbers.
• Mentally subtract a 1-digit number from a 2-digit number.
• Mentally subtract tens from a 2-digit number.

Learn You can subtract ones mentally by recalling number bonds.

Find 9 – 4.

Think of addition. 4 and 5 make 9.

So, 9 – 4 = 5.

Guided Practice

Subtract mentally.

1. Find 8 – 5.

Think of addition. 5 and 3 make 8.

So, 8 – 5 = 3.

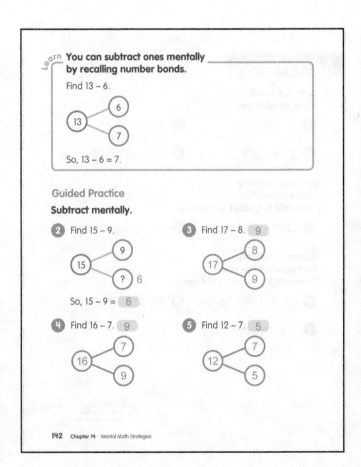

Learn You can subtract ones mentally by recalling number bonds.

Find 13 – 6.

So, 13 – 6 = 7.

Guided Practice

Subtract mentally.

2. Find 15 – 9.

So, 15 – 9 = 6.

3. Find 17 – 8. 9

4. Find 16 – 7. 9

5. Find 12 – 7. 5

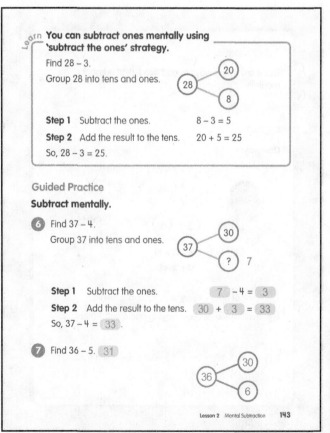

Learn You can subtract ones mentally using 'subtract the ones' strategy.

Find 28 – 3.
Group 28 into tens and ones.

Step 1 Subtract the ones. 8 – 3 = 5
Step 2 Add the result to the tens. 20 + 5 = 25
So, 28 – 3 = 25.

Guided Practice

Subtract mentally.

6. Find 37 – 4.
Group 37 into tens and ones.

Step 1 Subtract the ones. 7 – 4 = 3
Step 2 Add the result to the tens. 30 + 3 = 33
So, 37 – 4 = 33.

7. Find 36 – 5. 31

Chapter 14

Student Edition Answers: Chapter 14
Math in Focus Homeschool Answer Key, Grade 1

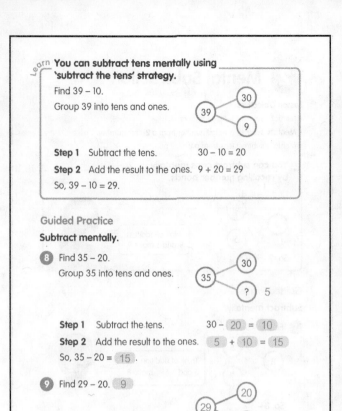

Learn You can subtract tens mentally using 'subtract the tens' strategy.

Find 39 − 10.

Group 39 into tens and ones.

39 → 30, 9

Step 1 Subtract the tens.   30 − 10 = 20

Step 2 Add the result to the ones.   9 + 20 = 29

So, 39 − 10 = 29.

Guided Practice

Subtract mentally.

8 Find 35 − 20.

Group 35 into tens and ones.

35 → 30, ? 5

Step 1 Subtract the tens.   30 − 20 = 10

Step 2 Add the result to the ones.   5 + 10 = 15

So, 35 − 20 = 15.

9 Find 29 − 20.   9

29 → 20, 9

144   Chapter 14   Mental Math Strategies

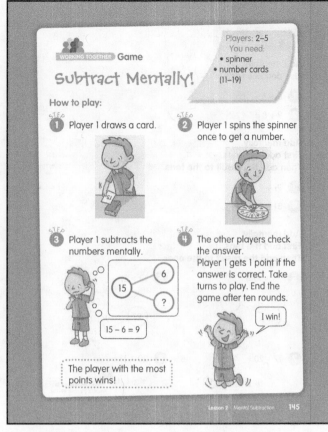

WORKING TOGETHER Game

Players: 2–5
You need:
• spinner
• number cards (11–19)

Subtract Mentally!

How to play:

STEP 1 Player 1 draws a card.

STEP 2 Player 1 spins the spinner once to get a number.

STEP 3 Player 1 subtracts the numbers mentally.

15 → 6, ?

15 − 6 = 9

STEP 4 The other players check the answer.
Player 1 gets 1 point if the answer is correct. Take turns to play. End the game after ten rounds.

I win!

The player with the most points wins!

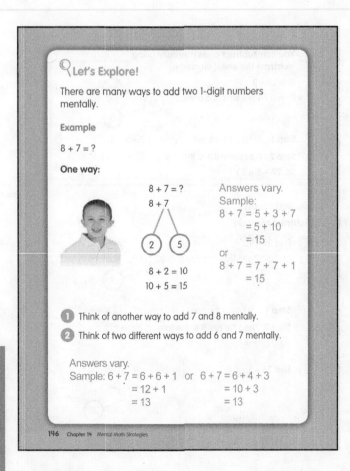

Let's Explore!

There are many ways to add two 1-digit numbers mentally.

Example

8 + 7 = ?

One way:

8 + 7 = ?

8 + 7

2 5

8 + 2 = 10

10 + 5 = 15

Answers vary.
Sample:
8 + 7 = 5 + 3 + 7
       = 5 + 10
       = 15
or
8 + 7 = 7 + 7 + 1
       = 15

1 Think of another way to add 7 and 8 mentally.

2 Think of two different ways to add 6 and 7 mentally.

Answers vary.
Sample: 6 + 7 = 6 + 6 + 1   or   6 + 7 = 6 + 4 + 3
              = 12 + 1   = 10 + 3
              = 13   = 13

146   Chapter 14   Mental Math Strategies

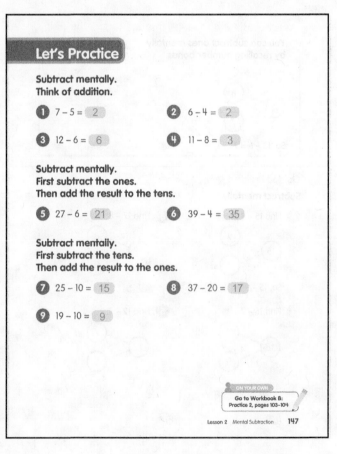

Let's Practice

Subtract mentally.
Think of addition.

1 7 − 5 = 2

2 6 − 4 = 2

3 12 − 6 = 6

4 11 − 8 = 3

Subtract mentally.
First subtract the ones.
Then add the result to the tens.

5 27 − 6 = 21

6 39 − 4 = 35

Subtract mentally.
First subtract the tens.
Then add the result to the ones.

7 25 − 10 = 15

8 37 − 20 = 17

9 19 − 10 = 9

ON YOUR OWN
Go to Workbook B:
Practice 2, pages 103–104

Lesson 2   Mental Subtraction   147

Chapter 14

Student Edition Answers: Chapter 14
Math in Focus Homeschool Answer Key, Grade 1

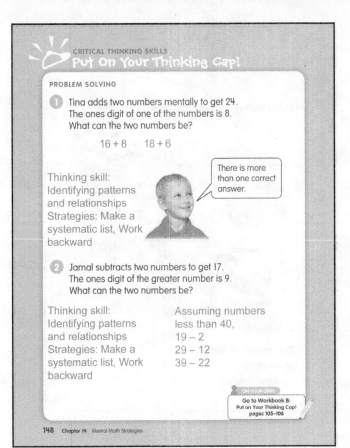

Put On Your Thinking Cap!

PROBLEM SOLVING

1. Tina adds two numbers mentally to get 24.
The ones digit of one of the numbers is 8.
What can the two numbers be?

$$16 + 8 \qquad 18 + 6$$

Thinking skill:
Identifying patterns
and relationships
Strategies: Make a
systematic list, Work
backward

There is more than one correct answer.

2. Jamal subtracts two numbers to get 17.
The ones digit of the greater number is 9.
What can the two numbers be?

Thinking skill:
Identifying patterns
and relationships
Strategies: Make a
systematic list, Work
backward

Assuming numbers
less than 40,
$19 - 2$
$29 - 12$
$39 - 22$

ON YOUR OWN
Go to Workbook B:
Put on Your Thinking Cap!
pages 105–106

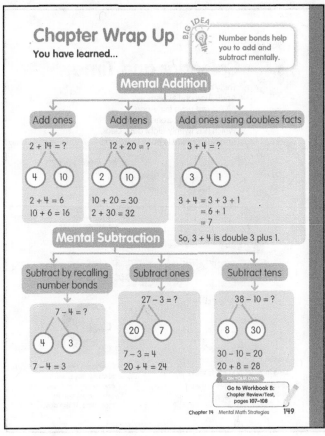

Chapter Wrap Up
You have learned...

BIG IDEA Number bonds help you to add and subtract mentally.

Mental Addition

Add ones

$2 + 14 = ?$

(4) (10)

$2 + 4 = 6$
$10 + 6 = 16$

Add tens

$12 + 20 = ?$

(2) (10)

$10 + 20 = 30$
$2 + 30 = 32$

Add ones using doubles facts

$3 + 4 = ?$

(3) (1)

$3 + 4 = 3 + 3 + 1$
$= 6 + 1$
$= 7$

So, $3 + 4$ is double 3 plus 1.

Mental Subtraction

Subtract by recalling number bonds

$7 - 4 = ?$

(4) (3)

$7 - 4 = 3$

Subtract ones

$27 - 3 = ?$

(20) (7)

$7 - 3 = 4$
$20 + 4 = 24$

Subtract tens

$38 - 10 = ?$

(8) (30)

$30 - 10 = 20$
$20 + 8 = 28$

ON YOUR OWN
Go to Workbook B:
Chapter Review/Test,
pages 107–108

105

CHAPTER 15 Calendar and Time

Thirty days have September,
April, June and November.
All the rest have thirty-one,
Except February alone,
Which has twenty-eight days clear,
And twenty-nine in each leap year.

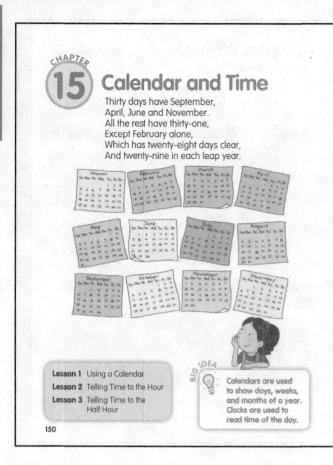

Lesson 1 Using a Calendar
Lesson 2 Telling Time to the Hour
Lesson 3 Telling Time to the Half Hour

150

BIG IDEA
Calendars are used to show days, weeks, and months of a year. Clocks are used to read time of the day.

Using ordinal numbers and position

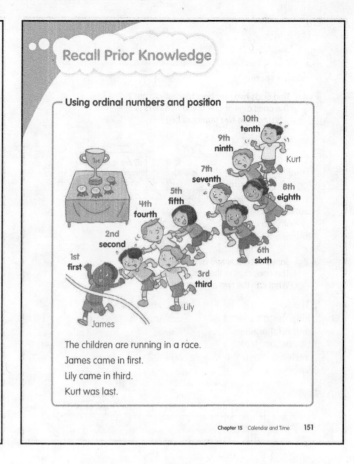

The children are running in a race.
James came in first.
Lily came in third.
Kurt was last.

Chapter 15 Calendar and Time   151

✔ Quick Check

The children are running in a race.

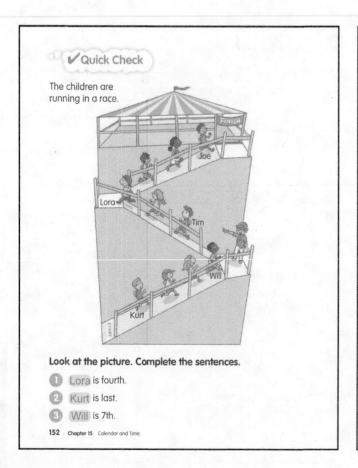

Look at the picture. Complete the sentences.

1. **Lora** is fourth.
2. **Kurt** is last.
3. **Will** is 7th.

152   Chapter 15   Calendar and Time

LESSON 1 Using a Calendar

Lesson Objectives
- Read a calendar.
- Know the days of the week and months of the year.
- Write the date.
- Know the seasons of the year.

Vocabulary
calendar days
weeks   months
year   date
warmer   colder
seasons

Learn You can read a calendar.

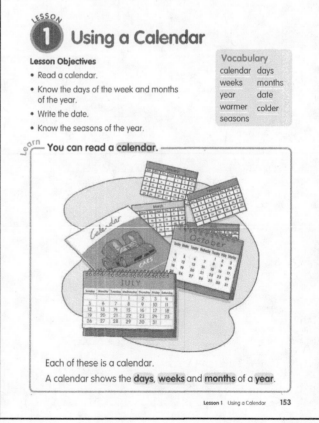

Each of these is a calendar.
A calendar shows the **days**, **weeks** and **months** of a **year**.

Lesson 1 Using a Calendar   153

Student Edition Answers: Chapter 15
Math in Focus Homeschool Answer Key, Grade 1

You can know the days of the week.

There are 7 days in one week.
The first day of the week is Sunday.
The last day of the week is Saturday.

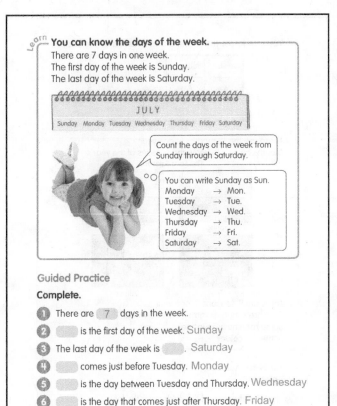

JULY

Sunday Monday Tuesday Wednesday Thursday Friday Saturday

Count the days of the week from Sunday through Saturday.

You can write Sunday as Sun.
Monday → Mon.
Tuesday → Tue.
Wednesday → Wed.
Thursday → Thu.
Friday → Fri.
Saturday → Sat.

Guided Practice

Complete.

1. There are (7) days in the week.

2. ▢ is the first day of the week. Sunday

3. The last day of the week is ▢. Saturday

4. ▢ comes just before Tuesday. Monday

5. ▢ is the day between Tuesday and Thursday. Wednesday

6. ▢ is the day that comes just after Thursday. Friday

154 **Chapter 15** Calendar and Time

Hands-On Activity

WORK IN PAIRS

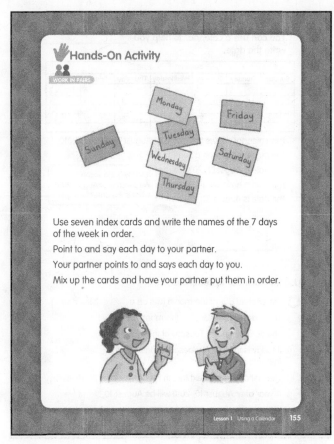

Use seven index cards and write the names of the 7 days of the week in order.

Point to and say each day to your partner.

Your partner points to and says each day to you.

Mix up the cards and have your partner put them in order.

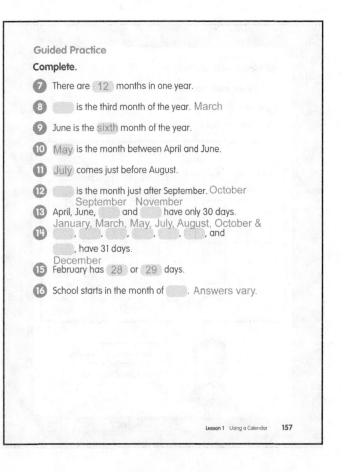

Lesson 1 Using a Calendar 155

You can know the months of the year.

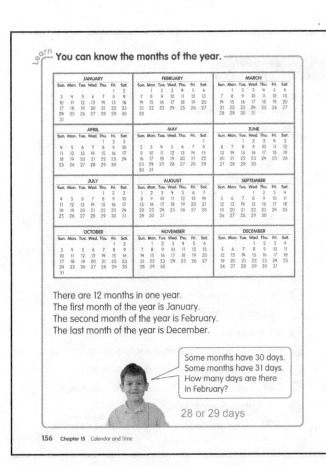

There are 12 months in one year.
The first month of the year is January.
The second month of the year is February.
The last month of the year is December.

Some months have 30 days.
Some months have 31 days.
How many days are there in February?

28 or 29 days

156 **Chapter 15** Calendar and Time

Guided Practice

Complete.

7. There are (12) months in one year.

8. ▢ is the third month of the year. March

9. June is the sixth month of the year.

10. May is the month between April and June.

11. July comes just before August.

12. ▢ is the month just after September. October
September November

13. April, June, ▢ and ▢ have only 30 days.
January, March, May, July, August, October &

14. ▢, ▢, ▢, ▢, ▢, ▢, and
▢, have 31 days.
December

15. February has (28) or (29) days.

16. School starts in the month of ▢. Answers vary.

Lesson 1 Using a Calendar 157

Learn You can use a calendar to help you write the date.

August 2010						
Sunday	**Monday**	**Tuesday**	**Wednesday**	**Thursday**	**Friday**	**Saturday**
1	2	3	4	5	6	7
8	9	10	11	12	13	14
15	16	17	18	19	20	21
22	23	24	25	26	27	28
29	30	31				

This calendar shows the month of August in the year 2010.

The month begins on a Sunday.

The date is August 1, 2010.

The month ends on a Tuesday.

The date is August 31, 2010.

If today is the second Wednesday of August 2010, what is the date?

August 11, 2010

Guided Practice

Use the calendar to complete.

17 The second day of the month falls on a ▢. Monday

18 There are ▢4 Fridays in this month of August.

19 The date of the first Tuesday of the month is ▢ August 3, 2010

20 If today is the last Wednesday of the month, the date is ▢. August 25, 2010

21 The first day of the next month falls on a ▢. Wednesday

22 A year after August 10, 2010 will be August 10, 2011.

Learn You can know the months and seasons of the year.

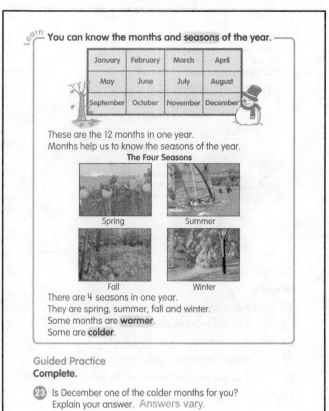

January	February	March	April
May	June	July	August
September	October	November	December

These are the 12 months in one year.

Months help us to know the seasons of the year.

The Four Seasons

Spring   Summer

Fall   Winter

There are 4 seasons in one year.

They are spring, summer, fall and winter.

Some months are **warmer**.

Some are **colder**.

Guided Practice

Complete.

23 Is December one of the colder months for you? Explain your answer. Answers vary.

✋**Hands-On Activity**

Make your own calendar.

Show special days.

Birthdays, holidays and school days, are some special days.

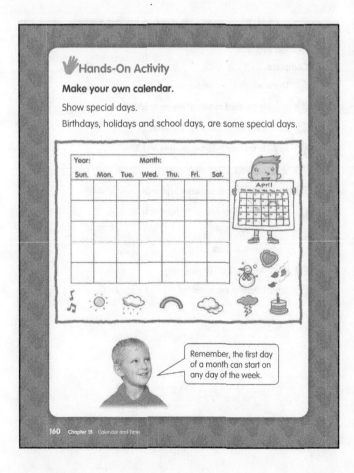

Remember, the first day of a month can start on any day of the week.

Let's Practice

Fill in the blanks.

Use the calendar to help you.

2010

1 The fourth month of the year is April.

2 The date one week after May 8, 2010 is May 15, 2010

3 The season for the month of January is ▢. winter

4 The date for the second Tuesday of March is ▢ March 9, 2010

5 Independence Day, the Fourth of July, falls on a ▢. Sunday

6 ▢ is the date two weeks before August 26, 2010. August 12, 2010

7 Summer vacation starts in the month of ▢. Answers vary.

8 ▢ is the only month with 28 days. February

ON YOUR OWN
Go to Workbook B: Practice 1, page 109–112

Student Edition Answers: Chapter 15
Math in Focus Homeschool Answer Key, Grade 1

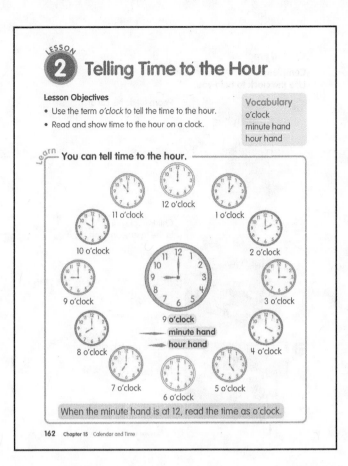

2 Telling Time to the Hour

Lesson Objectives
- Use the term *o'clock* to tell the time to the hour.
- Read and show time to the hour on a clock.

Vocabulary
o'clock
minute hand
hour hand

Learn You can tell time to the hour.

12 o'clock
11 o'clock
1 o'clock
10 o'clock
2 o'clock
9 o'clock
3 o'clock
8 o'clock
4 o'clock
7 o'clock
5 o'clock
6 o'clock

9 o'clock
minute hand
hour hand

When the minute hand is at 12, read the time as o'clock.

Guided Practice

Answer the question.

It is now 12 o'clock.

No, it is 5 o'clock.

Lance

Sherry

1 Who is correct? _____. Sherry

Tell the time.
Complete.

2 11 o'clock

3 2 o'clock

4 10 o'clock

5 3 o'clock

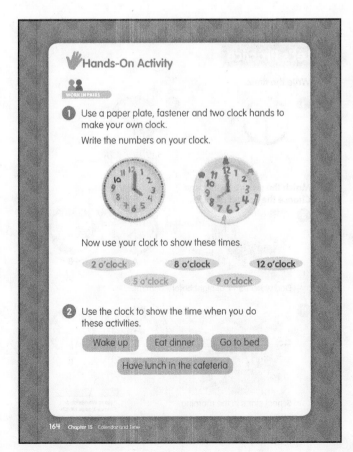

Hands-On Activity

WORK IN PAIRS

1 Use a paper plate, fastener and two clock hands to make your own clock.

Write the numbers on your clock.

Now use your clock to show these times.

2 o'clock   8 o'clock   12 o'clock
5 o'clock   9 o'clock

2 Use the clock to show the time when you do these activities.

Wake up   Eat dinner   Go to bed

Have lunch in the cafeteria

Let's Practice

Write the time.

1 2 o'clock

2 7 o'clock

Match the picture to the time.
Choose the correct clock.

3

Math class starts in the morning.

4

Lunch time is at 12 o'clock.

ON YOUR OWN
Go to Workbook B:
Practice 2, page 113–118

LESSON 3 — Telling Time to the Half Hour

Lesson Objectives
- Read time to the half hour.
- Use the term 'half past'.
- Relate time to daily activities.

Vocabulary
half past
half hour

Learn You can tell time to the **half hour.**

Leo wakes up at 7 o'clock in the morning.

Leo eats breakfast at **half past** 7.

When the minute hand is at 6, it is half past the hour.

The hour hand has moved too!

166   Chapter 15   Calendar and Time

Guided Practice

Complete.
Use the clock to help you.

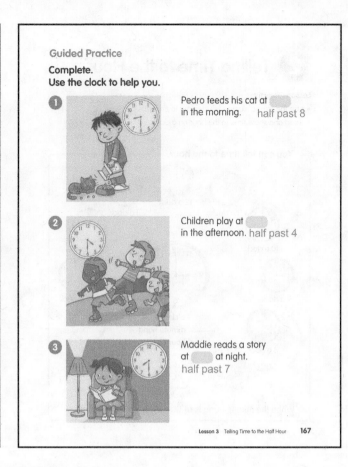

1. Pedro feeds his cat at ____ in the morning.   half past 8

2. Children play at ____ in the afternoon.   half past 4

3. Maddie reads a story at ____ at night.   half past 7

Lesson 3   Telling Time to the Half Hour   167

Complete.
Use the clock to help you.

4. Pa Lion and Baby Lion go to the carnival at ____.   half past 2

5. At ____, Pa Lion plays a game.   3 o'clock

6. Pa Lion wins the game and gets a toy chick at ____.   half past 3

7. At ____, Pa Lion and Baby Lion take a ride on the Ferris wheel.   half past 4

168   Chapter 15   Calendar and Time

Let's Practice

Write the time.

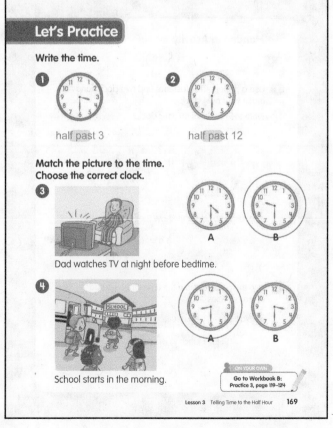

1. half past 3

2. half past 12

Match the picture to the time.
Choose the correct clock.

3.

A   B

Dad watches TV at night before bedtime.

4.

A   B

School starts in the morning.

ON YOUR OWN
Go to Workbook B:
Practice 3, page 119–124

Lesson 3   Telling Time to the Half Hour   169

Student Edition Answers: Chapter 15
Math in Focus Homeschool Answer Key, Grade 1

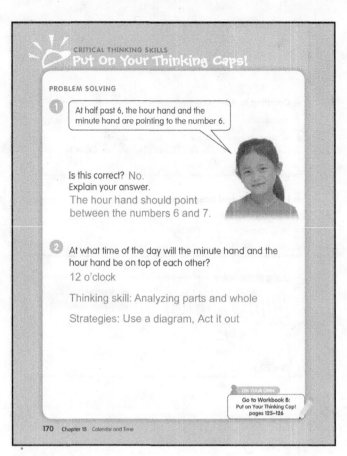

CRITICAL THINKING SKILLS
Put On Your Thinking Caps!

PROBLEM SOLVING

1 At half past 6, the hour hand and the minute hand are pointing to the number 6.

Is this correct? No.
Explain your answer.
The hour hand should point between the numbers 6 and 7.

2 At what time of the day will the minute hand and the hour hand be on top of each other?
12 o'clock

Thinking skill: Analyzing parts and whole

Strategies: Use a diagram, Act it out

ON YOUR OWN
Go to Workbook B:
Put on Your Thinking Cap!
pages 125–126

Chapter Wrap Up
You have learned...

BIG IDEA
Calendars are used to show days, weeks, and months of a year. Clocks are used to read time of the day.

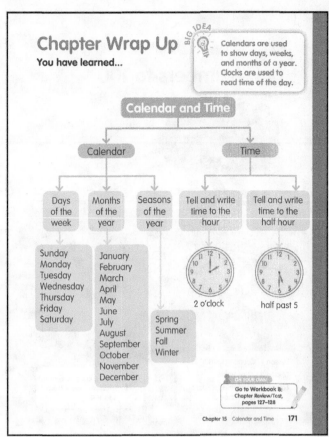

ON YOUR OWN
Go to Workbook B:
Chapter Review/Test,
pages 127–128

111

CHAPTER 16 Numbers to 100

Lesson 1 Counting to 100
Lesson 2 Place Value
Lesson 3 Comparing, Ordering, and Patterns

BIG IDEA
Count, compare, and order numbers from 1 to 100.

172

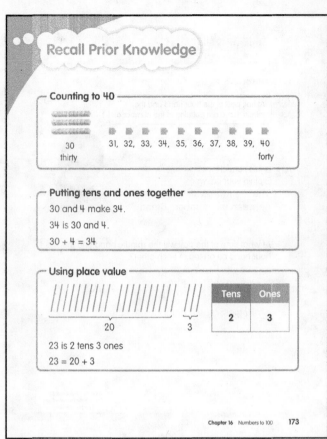

Recall Prior Knowledge

Counting to 40

30
thirty

31, 32, 33, 34, 35, 36, 37, 38, 39, 40
forty

Putting tens and ones together

30 and 4 make 34.
34 is 30 and 4.
30 + 4 = 34

Using place value

20   3

Tens	Ones
2	3

23 is 2 tens 3 ones
23 = 20 + 3

Comparing and ordering numbers

Compare 36, 39, and 40.

Compare the tens.
4 tens is greater than 3 tens.
40 is the greatest number.

In 36 and 39, the tens are the same.
So, compare the ones.

6 ones is less than 9 ones.
So, 36 is less than 39.
36 is the least number.

Tens	Ones
3	6
3	9
4	0

Order the numbers from greatest to least.
40, 39, 36

Making number patterns

24, 27, 30, 33, 36, 39
The numbers are arranged in a pattern.
Each number is 3 more than the number before it.

✔ Quick Check

Count on.

1 27, 28, 29, 30 , 31 , 32

2 35, 36, 37, 38 , 39 , 40

Find the missing numbers.

3 20 and 8 make 28 .

4 35 is 30 and 5.

5 30 + 7 = 37

6 26 = 2 tens 6 ones

7 2 tens 9 ones = 29

Compare and order.

28   32   19

8 The least number is 19 .

9 The greatest number is 32 .

10 Order the numbers from least to greatest.
19 , 28 , 32
least

Complete the number pattern.

11 31, 33, 35, 37 , 39 , 41

12 30, 27, 24, 21 , 18 , 15 , 12

Student Edition Answers: Chapter 16
Math in Focus Homeschool Answer Key, Grade 1

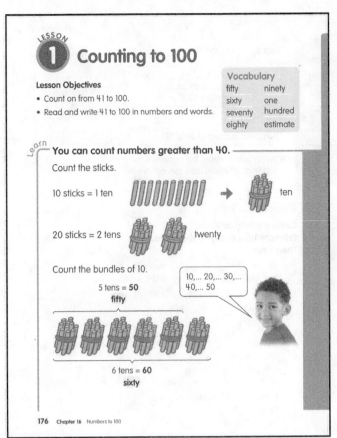

LESSON 1 Counting to 100

Lesson Objectives
• Count on from 41 to 100.
• Read and write 41 to 100 in numbers and words.

Vocabulary

fifty	ninety
sixty	one
seventy	hundred
eighty	estimate

Learn You can count numbers greater than 40.

Count the sticks.

10 sticks = 1 ten → ten

20 sticks = 2 tens → twenty

Count the bundles of 10.

5 tens = **50**
fifty

10,... 20,... 30,...
40,... 50

6 tens = **60**
sixty

176 Chapter 16 Numbers to 100

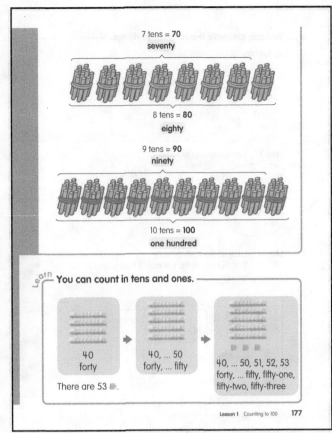

7 tens = **70**
seventy

8 tens = **80**
eighty

9 tens = **90**
ninety

10 tens = **100**
one hundred

Learn You can count in tens and ones.

40
forty

40, ... 50
forty, ... fifty

40, ... 50, 51, 52, 53
forty, ... fifty, fifty-one,
fifty-two, fifty-three

There are 53.

Lesson 1 Counting to 100 177

Guided Practice

Count in tens and ones.
Then find the missing numbers.

1

10, ... 20, ... 30, ... 40, ... 50 , ... 60 , ... 70 .

71, 72 , 73 , 74 , 75

There are 75 .

Ten, ... twenty, ...
thirty, ... forty, ...
seventy-one, ...

Learn You can count in tens.

10, 20, 30, 40, 50,
60, 70, 80, 90, 100!
10 tens = 100!

178 Chapter 16 Numbers to 100

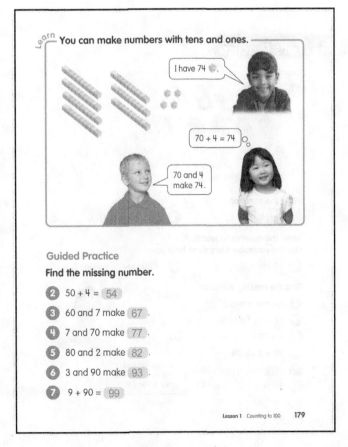

Learn You can make numbers with tens and ones.

I have 74.

70 + 4 = 74

70 and 4
make 74.

Guided Practice

Find the missing number.

2 50 + 4 = 54

3 60 and 7 make 67 .

4 7 and 70 make 77 .

5 80 and 2 make 82 .

6 3 and 90 make 93 .

7 9 + 90 = 99

Lesson 1 Counting to 100 179

Student Edition Answers: Chapter 16
Math in Focus Homeschool Answer Key, Grade 1

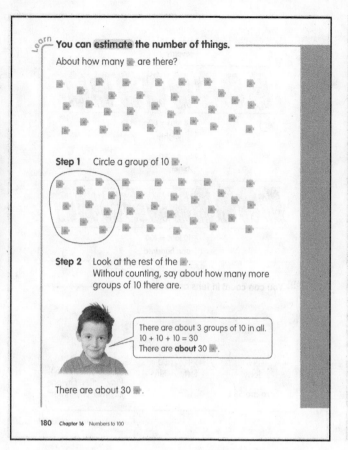

Learn You can **estimate** the number of things.

About how many 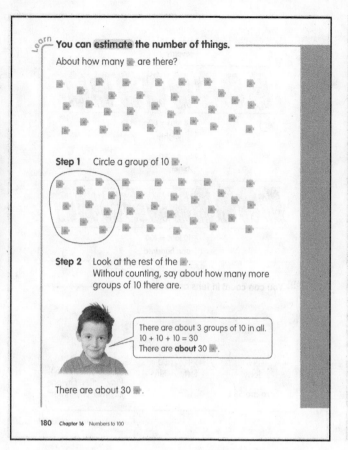 are there?

Step 1 Circle a group of 10 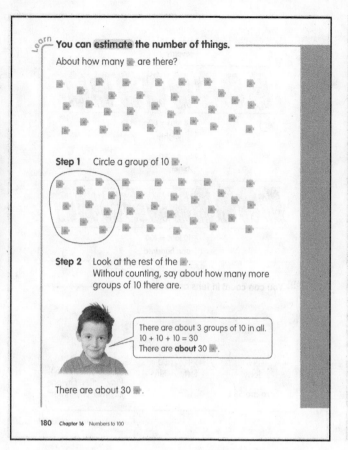.

Step 2 Look at the rest of the 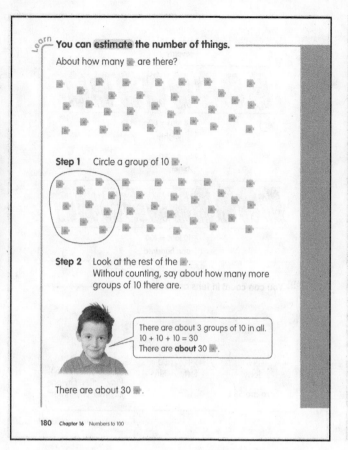.
Without counting, say about how many more groups of 10 there are.

There are about 3 groups of 10 in all.
10 + 10 + 10 = 30
There are **about** 30 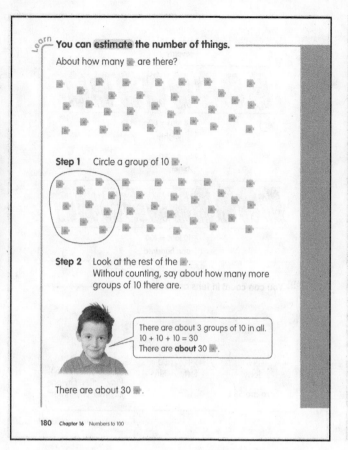.

There are about 30 .

180 Chapter 16 Numbers to 100

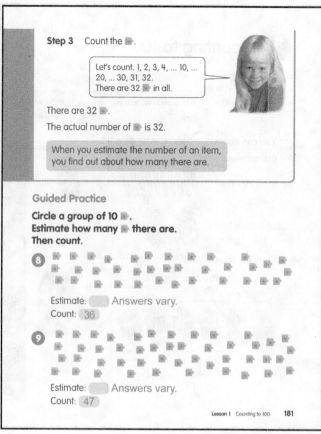

Step 3 Count the .

Let's count. 1, 2, 3, 4, ... 10, ... 20, ... 30, 31, 32.
There are 32 in all.

There are 32 .

The actual number of is 32.

When you estimate the number of an item, you find out about how many there are.

Guided Practice

Circle a group of 10 .
Estimate how many there are.
Then count.

8

Estimate: ___ Answers vary.
Count: 36

9

Estimate: ___ Answers vary.
Count: 47

Lesson 1 Counting to 100 181

Let's Practice

Count.

1

10, ... 20, ... 30, ... 40, ... 50, ... 60, ... 70 , ... 80 ,
... 90 , 91, 92 , 93 , 94 , 95
There are 95 sticks.

Write the number.

2 forty-eight 48   **3** one hundred 100

Write the number in words.
Use the scrambled words to help you.

4 50 yfitf fifty   **5** 91 ntieny-noe ninety one

Find the missing numbers.

6 80 and 5 make 85 .

7 57 is 7 and 50.

8 9 + 70 = 97

9 90 + 8 = 98

10 80 and 9 make 89.

11 40 and 7 make 47.

Can you think of other numbers that make 89 and 47?

182 Chapter 16 Numbers to 100

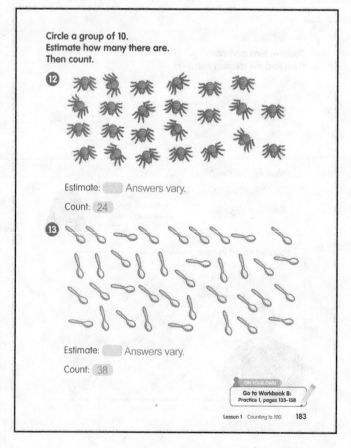

Circle a group of 10.
Estimate how many there are.
Then count.

12

Estimate: ___ Answers vary.

Count: 24

13

Estimate: ___ Answers vary.

Count: 38

ON YOUR OWN
Go to Workbook B:
Practice 1, pages 135–138

Lesson 1 Counting to 100 183

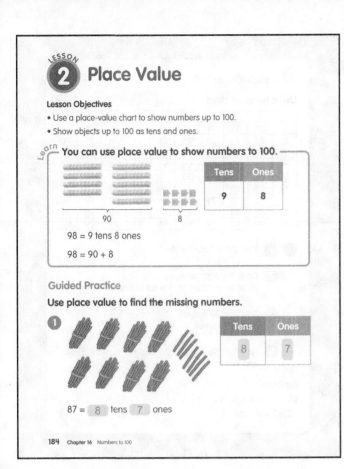

LESSON 2 Place Value

Lesson Objectives
• Use a place-value chart to show numbers up to 100.
• Show objects up to 100 as tens and ones.

Learn You can use place value to show numbers to 100.

Tens	Ones
9	8

90   8

98 = 9 tens 8 ones

98 = 90 + 8

Guided Practice

Use place value to find the missing numbers.

1

Tens	Ones
8	7

87 = **8** tens **7** ones

184   Chapter 16   Numbers to 100

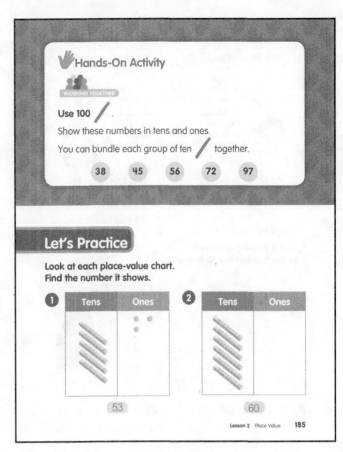

✋ Hands-On Activity

WORKING TOGETHER

Use 100 /.

Show these numbers in tens and ones.
You can bundle each group of ten / together.

38   45   56   72   97

Let's Practice

Look at each place-value chart.
Find the number it shows.

1

Tens	Ones

53

2

Tens	Ones

60

Lesson 2   Place Value   185

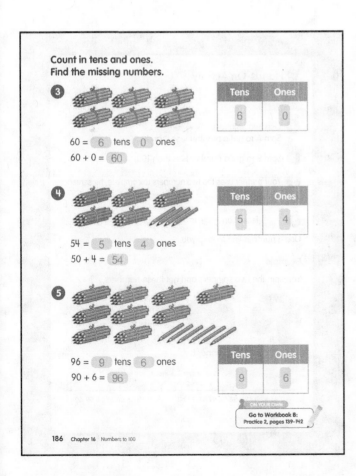

Count in tens and ones.
Find the missing numbers.

3

Tens	Ones
6	0

60 = **6** tens **0** ones

60 + 0 = **60**

4

Tens	Ones
5	4

54 = **5** tens **4** ones

50 + 4 = **54**

5

Tens	Ones
9	6

96 = **9** tens **6** ones

90 + 6 = **96**

ON YOUR OWN
Go to Workbook B:
Practice 2, pages 139–142

186   Chapter 16   Numbers to 100

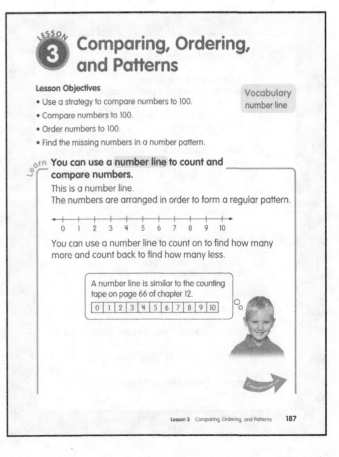

LESSON 3 Comparing, Ordering, and Patterns

Lesson Objectives
• Use a strategy to compare numbers to 100.
• Compare numbers to 100.
• Order numbers to 100.
• Find the missing numbers in a number pattern.

Vocabulary
number line

Learn You can use a number line to count and compare numbers.

This is a number line.
The numbers are arranged in order to form a regular pattern.

0 1 2 3 4 5 6 7 8 9 10

You can use a number line to count on to find how many more and count back to find how many less.

A number line is similar to the counting tape on page 66 of chapter 12.

0 1 2 3 4 5 6 7 8 9 10

Lesson 3   Comparing, Ordering, and Patterns   187

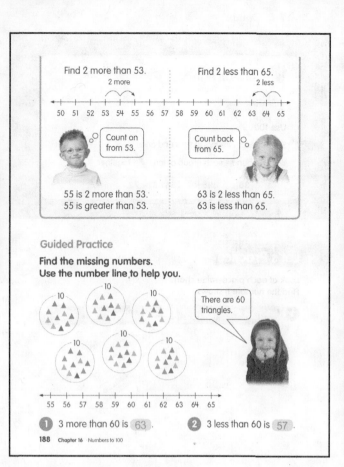

Guided Practice

Find the missing numbers.
Use the number line to help you.

There are 60 triangles.

1. 3 more than 60 is 63.
2. 3 less than 60 is 57.

188   Chapter 16   Numbers to 100

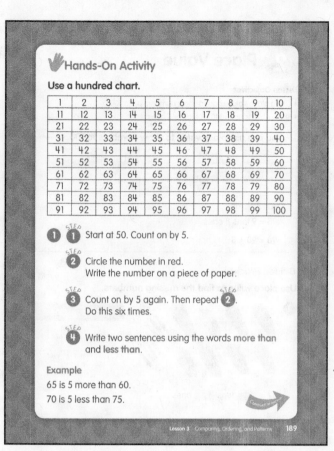

Hands-On Activity

Use a hundred chart.

1	2	3	4	5	6	7	8	9	10
11	12	13	14	15	16	17	18	19	20
21	22	23	24	25	26	27	28	29	30
31	32	33	34	35	36	37	38	39	40
41	42	43	44	45	46	47	48	49	50
51	52	53	54	55	56	57	58	59	60
61	62	63	64	65	66	67	68	69	70
71	72	73	74	75	76	77	78	79	80
81	82	83	84	85	86	87	88	89	90
91	92	93	94	95	96	97	98	99	100

1. **STEP 1** Start at 50. Count on by 5.

   STEP 2 Circle the number in red.
   Write the number on a piece of paper.

   STEP 3 Count on by 5 again. Then repeat 2.
   Do this six times.

   STEP 4 Write two sentences using the words more than and less than.

Example
65 is 5 more than 60.
70 is 5 less than 75.

Lesson 3   Comparing, Ordering, and Patterns   189

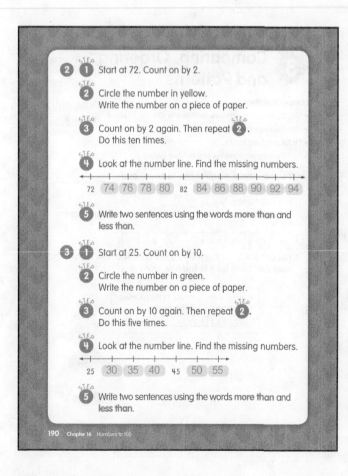

2. **STEP 1** Start at 72. Count on by 2.

   STEP 2 Circle the number in yellow.
   Write the number on a piece of paper.

   STEP 3 Count on by 2 again. Then repeat 2.
   Do this ten times.

   STEP 4 Look at the number line. Find the missing numbers.

   72 74 76 78 80 82 84 86 88 90 92 94

   STEP 5 Write two sentences using the words more than and less than.

3. **STEP 1** Start at 25. Count on by 10.

   STEP 2 Circle the number in green.
   Write the number on a piece of paper.

   STEP 3 Count on by 10 again. Then repeat 2.
   Do this five times.

   STEP 4 Look at the number line. Find the missing numbers.

   25 30 35 40 45 50 55

   STEP 5 Write two sentences using the words more than and less than.

190   Chapter 16   Numbers to 100

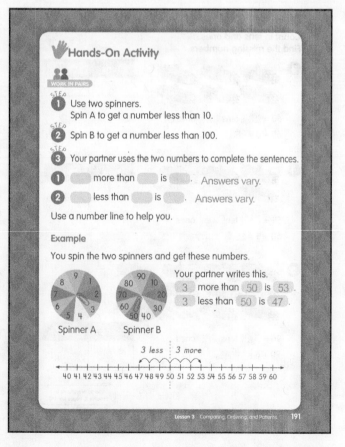

Hands-On Activity

WORK IN PAIRS

1. Use two spinners.
   Spin A to get a number less than 10.

2. Spin B to get a number less than 100.

3. Your partner uses the two numbers to complete the sentences.

1. [ ] more than [ ] is [ ]. Answers vary.

2. [ ] less than [ ] is [ ]. Answers vary.

Use a number line to help you.

Example

You spin the two spinners and get these numbers.

Spinner A   Spinner B

Your partner writes this.
3 more than 50 is 53.
3 less than 50 is 47.

Lesson 3   Comparing, Ordering, and Patterns   191

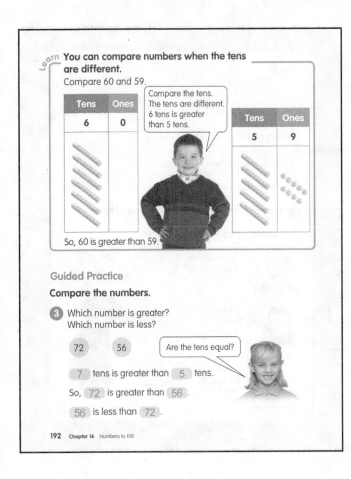

You can compare numbers when the tens are different.

Compare 60 and 59.

Tens	Ones
6	0

Compare the tens. The tens are different. 6 tens is greater than 5 tens.

Tens	Ones
5	9

So, 60 is greater than 59.

Guided Practice

Compare the numbers.

3. Which number is greater? Which number is less?

   72   56

   Are the tens equal?

   7 tens is greater than 5 tens.
   So, 72 is greater than 56.
   56 is less than 72.

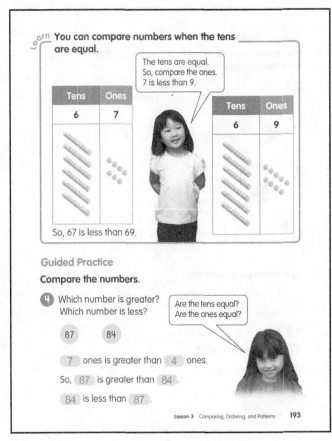

You can compare numbers when the tens are equal.

Tens	Ones
6	7

The tens are equal. So, compare the ones. 7 is less than 9.

Tens	Ones
6	9

So, 67 is less than 69.

Guided Practice

Compare the numbers.

4. Which number is greater? Which number is less?

   87   84

   Are the tens equal? Are the ones equal?

   7 ones is greater than 4 ones.
   So, 87 is greater than 84.
   84 is less than 87.

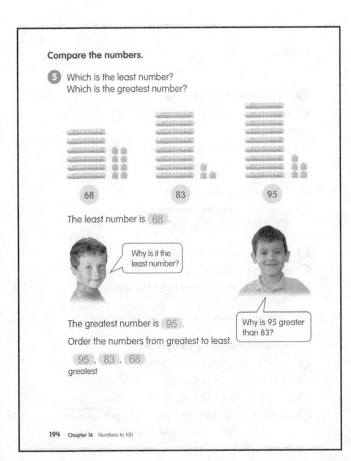

Compare the numbers.

5. Which is the least number? Which is the greatest number?

   68   83   95

   The least number is 68.

   Why is it the least number?

   The greatest number is 95.
   Order the numbers from greatest to least.

   Why is 95 greater than 83?

   95, 83, 68
   greatest

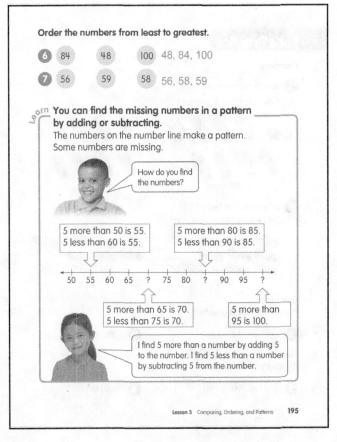

Order the numbers from least to greatest.

6. 84   48   100   48, 84, 100

7. 56   59   58   56, 58, 59

You can find the missing numbers in a pattern by adding or subtracting.

The numbers on the number line make a pattern. Some numbers are missing.

How do you find the numbers?

5 more than 50 is 55.
5 less than 60 is 55.

5 more than 80 is 85.
5 less than 90 is 85.

50 55 60 65 ? 75 80 ? 90 95 ?

5 more than 65 is 70.
5 less than 75 is 70.

5 more than 95 is 100.

I find 5 more than a number by adding 5 to the number. I find 5 less than a number by subtracting 5 from the number.

Guided Practice

The numbers on the number line make a pattern.
Find the missing numbers.

8

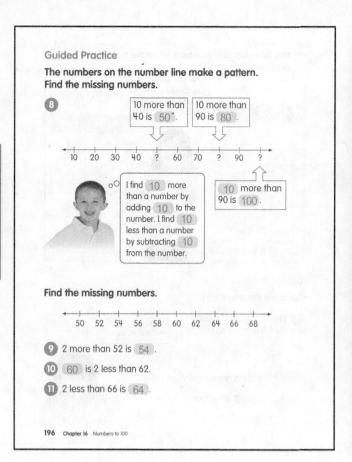

| 10 more than 40 is 50. | 10 more than 90 is 80. |

10 20 30 40 ? 60 70 ? 90 ?

I find 10 more than a number by adding 10 to the number. I find 10 less than a number by subtracting 10 from the number.

10 more than 90 is 100.

Find the missing numbers.

50 52 54 56 58 60 62 64 66 68

9 2 more than 52 is 54.

10 60 is 2 less than 62.

11 2 less than 66 is 64.

What's My Number?

How to play:

STEP 1 Think of a number between 50 and 100.

STEP 2 Players take turns asking you questions to find the number.

STEP 3 You can answer only **Yes** or **No** to the questions.

STEP 4 See who gets the right number first!

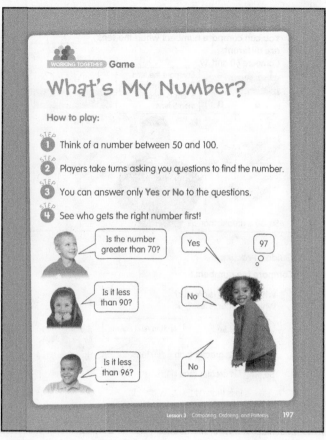

Is the number greater than 70? Yes 97

Is it less than 90? No

Is it less than 96? No

Let's Practice

Compare.

1 Which set has more? A
Which number is greater? 86

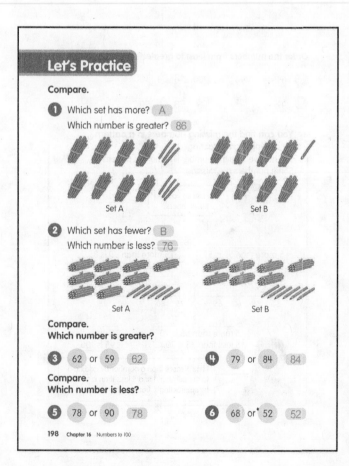

Set A   Set B

2 Which set has fewer? B
Which number is less? 76

Set A   Set B

Compare.
Which number is greater?

3 62 or 59 62   **4** 79 or 84 84

Compare.
Which number is less?

5 78 or 90 78   **6** 68 or 52 52

Compare.

71 78 85

7 Which number is the least? 71

8 Which number is the greatest? 85

Complete.

82 53 95 60 79

9 Which number is the greatest? 95

10 Which number is the least? 53

11 Order the numbers from least to greatest.
53, 60, 79, 82, 95
least

12 What is 5 more than 95? 100

13 What is 5 less than 95? 90

14 Name two numbers greater than 53 but less than 79.
___ ___ Answers vary.
Accept any two numbers from 54 to 78

15 Name two numbers less than 82 but greater than 79.
80 81

Find the missing numbers in each pattern.

16 56, 57, 58, 59, 60, 61, 62, 63, 64, 65

17 81, 83, 85, 87, 89, 91, 93

18 100, 99, 98, 97, 96, 95

19 95, 85, 75, 65, 55, 45, 35

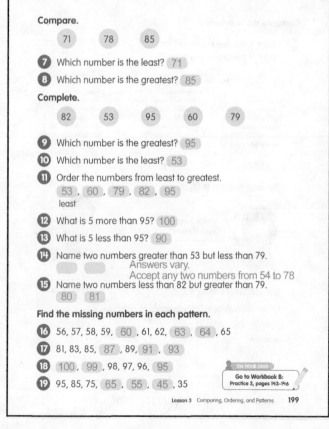

ON YOUR OWN
Go to Workbook B:
Practice 3, pages 143–146

118

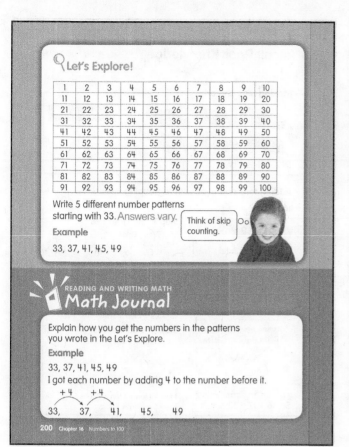

Let's Explore!

1	2	3	4	5	6	7	8	9	10
11	12	13	14	15	16	17	18	19	20
21	22	23	24	25	26	27	28	29	30
31	32	33	34	35	36	37	38	39	40
41	42	43	44	45	46	47	48	49	50
51	52	53	54	55	56	57	58	59	60
61	62	63	64	65	66	67	68	69	70
71	72	73	74	75	76	77	78	79	80
81	82	83	84	85	86	87	88	89	90
91	92	93	94	95	96	97	98	99	100

Write 5 different number patterns
starting with 33. Answers vary.

> Think of skip counting.

Example

33, 37, 41, 45, 49

Math Journal
READING AND WRITING MATH

Explain how you get the numbers in the patterns
you wrote in the Let's Explore.

Example

33, 37, 41, 45, 49

I got each number by adding 4 to the number before it.

$$\overset{+4}{33,} \quad \overset{+4}{37,} \quad 41, \quad 45, \quad 49$$

CRITICAL THINKING SKILLS
Put On Your Thinking Cap!

PROBLEM SOLVING

Put each number card into the number machine to
make a pattern of 5 numbers.

For each card, the rule for the pattern is shown.

Example

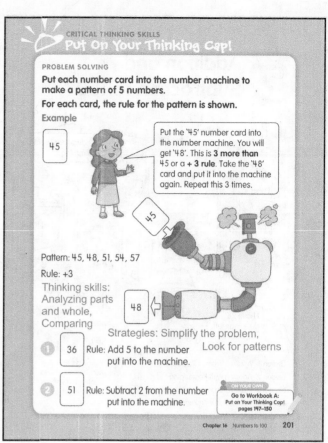

| 45 |

> Put the '45' number card into
> the number machine. You will
> get '48'. This is **3 more than**
> 45 or a **+ 3 rule**. Take the '48'
> card and put it into the machine
> again. Repeat this 3 times.

Pattern: 45, 48, 51, 54, 57

Rule: +3

Thinking skills:
Analyzing parts
and whole,
Comparing

| 48 |

Strategies: Simplify the problem,
Look for patterns

1) | 36 | Rule: Add 5 to the number
put into the machine.

2) | 51 | Rule: Subtract 2 from the number
put into the machine.

> ON YOUR OWN
> Go to Workbook A:
> Put on Your Thinking Cap!
> pages 147–150

Chapter Wrap Up
You have learned...

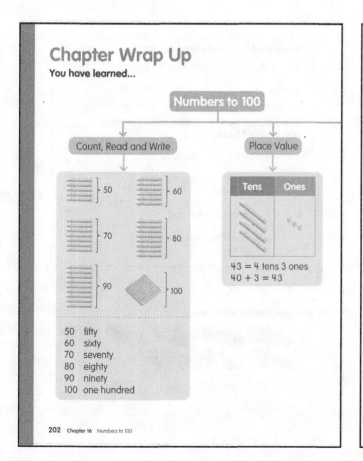

Numbers to 100

Count, Read and Write

{ 50   { 60
{ 70   { 80
{ 90   { 100

50	fifty
60	sixty
70	seventy
80	eighty
90	ninety
100	one hundred

Place Value

Tens	Ones

43 = 4 tens 3 ones
40 + 3 = 43

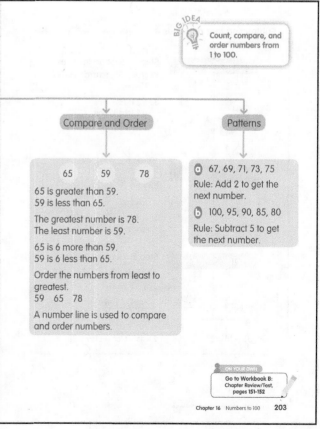

> BIG IDEA
> Count, compare, and
> order numbers from
> 1 to 100.

Compare and Order

| 65 | 59 | 78 |

65 is greater than 59.
59 is less than 65.

The greatest number is 78.
The least number is 59.

65 is 6 more than 59.
59 is 6 less than 65.

Order the numbers from least to
greatest.
59 65 78

A number line is used to compare
and order numbers.

Patterns

(a) 67, 69, 71, 73, 75

Rule: Add 2 to get the
next number.

(b) 100, 95, 90, 85, 80

Rule: Subtract 5 to get
the next number.

> ON YOUR OWN
> Go to Workbook B:
> Chapter Review/Test,
> pages 151–152

119

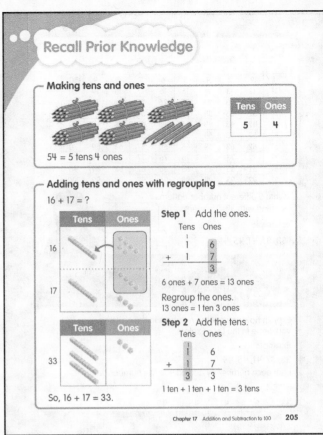

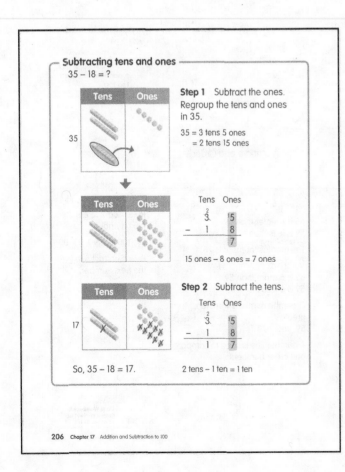

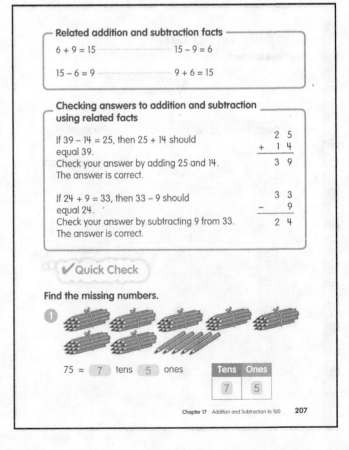

120

Find the missing numbers.

2 17 − 8 = 9

3 11 + 5 = 16

Show how to check that the answers are correct.

4
```
  2 4        3 2
+   8      −   8
  3 2        2 4
```

5
```
  3 2        1 9
− 1 3      + 1 3
  1 9        3 2
```

Add. Show how to check your answer.

6 23 + 6 = 29

7 19 + 8 = 27

8 14 + 15 = 29

9 23 + 17 = 40

Subtract. Show how to check your answer.

10 37 − 5 = 32

11 30 − 8 = 22

12 25 − 14 = 11

13 32 − 16 = 16

---

1 Addition Without Regrouping

Lesson Objectives
- Add a 2-digit number and a 1-digit number without regrouping.
- Add two 2-digit numbers without regrouping.

Learn **You can add ones to a number in different ways.**

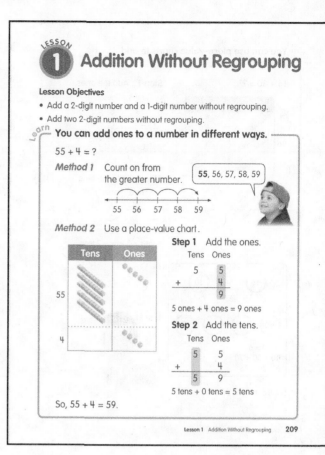

55 + 4 = ?

Method 1   Count on from the greater number.

55, 56, 57, 58, 59

55   56   57   58   59

Method 2   Use a place-value chart.

Tens	Ones

55

4

Step 1   Add the ones.
```
Tens  Ones
  5      5
+        4
         9
```
5 ones + 4 ones = 9 ones

Step 2   Add the tens.
```
Tens  Ones
  5      5
+        4
  5      9
```
5 tens + 0 tens = 5 tens

So, 55 + 4 = 59.

Chapter 17

Guided Practice

Complete.

1 82 + 7 = ?

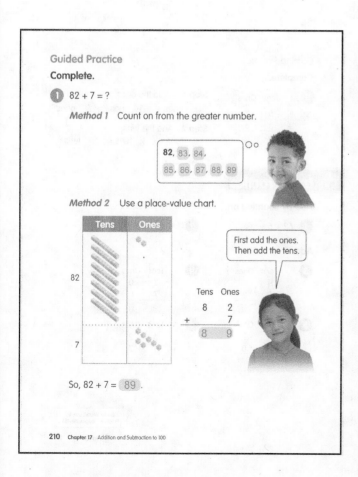

Method 1   Count on from the greater number.

82, 83, 84, 85, 86, 87, 88, 89

Method 2   Use a place-value chart.

Tens	Ones

82

7

First add the ones.
Then add the tens.

```
Tens  Ones
  8      2
+        7
  8      9
```

So, 82 + 7 = 89.

Learn **You can use place-value charts to add tens.**

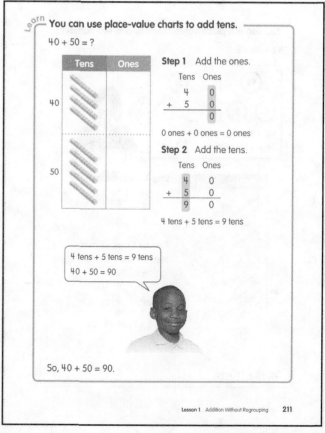

40 + 50 = ?

Tens	Ones

40

50

Step 1   Add the ones.
```
Tens  Ones
  4      0
+ 5      0
         0
```
0 ones + 0 ones = 0 ones

Step 2   Add the tens.
```
Tens  Ones
  4      0
+ 5      0
  9      0
```
4 tens + 5 tens = 9 tens

4 tens + 5 tens = 9 tens
40 + 50 = 90

So, 40 + 50 = 90.

121

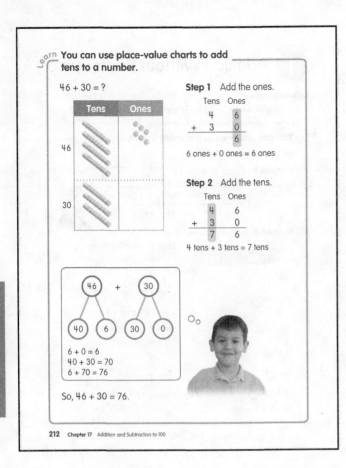

Learn You can use place-value charts to add tens to a number.

$46 + 30 = ?$

Tens	Ones
46	
30	

Step 1 Add the ones.

	Tens	Ones
	4	6
+	3	0
		6

6 ones + 0 ones = 6 ones

Step 2 Add the tens.

	Tens	Ones
	4	6
+	3	0
	7	6

4 tens + 3 tens = 7 tens

```
    46    +    30
   /  \       /  \
  40   6     30   0

  6 + 0 = 6
  40 + 30 = 70
  6 + 70 = 76
```

So, $46 + 30 = 76$.

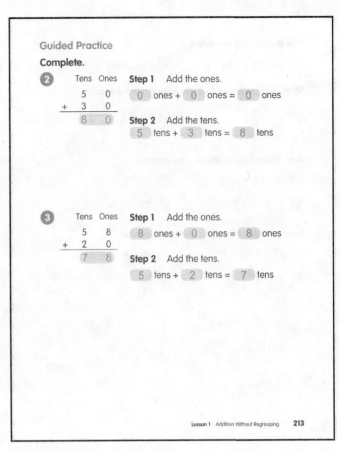

Guided Practice

Complete.

2

	Tens	Ones
	5	0
+	3	0
	8	0

Step 1 Add the ones.
(0) ones + (0) ones = (0) ones

Step 2 Add the tens.
(5) tens + (3) tens = (8) tens

3

	Tens	Ones
	5	8
+	2	0
	7	8

Step 1 Add the ones.
(8) ones + (0) ones = (8) ones

Step 2 Add the tens.
(5) tens + (2) tens = (7) tens

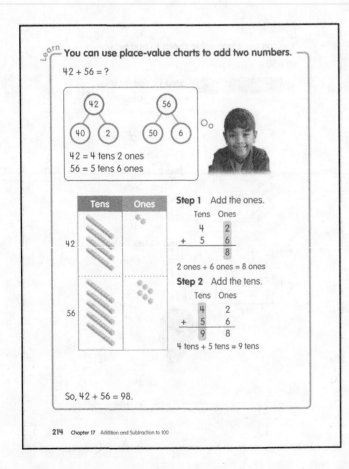

Learn You can use place-value charts to add two numbers.

$42 + 56 = ?$

```
    42          56
   /  \        /  \
  40   2      50   6

  42 = 4 tens 2 ones
  56 = 5 tens 6 ones
```

Tens	Ones
42	
56	

Step 1 Add the ones.

	Tens	Ones
	4	2
+	5	6
		8

2 ones + 6 ones = 8 ones

Step 2 Add the tens.

	Tens	Ones
	4	2
+	5	6
	9	8

4 tens + 5 tens = 9 tens

So, $42 + 56 = 98$.

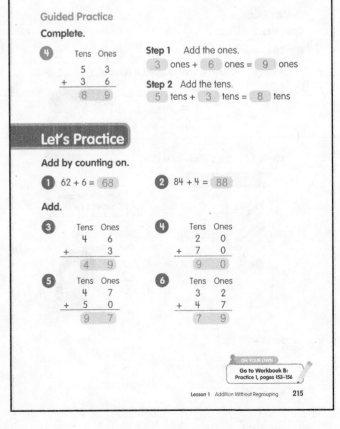

Guided Practice

Complete.

4

	Tens	Ones
	5	3
+	3	6
	8	9

Step 1 Add the ones.
(3) ones + (6) ones = (9) ones

Step 2 Add the tens.
(5) tens + (3) tens = (8) tens

Let's Practice

Add by counting on.

1 $62 + 6 = $ (68)   **2** $84 + 4 = $ (88)

Add.

3

	Tens	Ones
	4	6
+		3
	4	9

4

	Tens	Ones
	2	0
+	7	0
	9	0

5

	Tens	Ones
	4	7
+	5	0
	9	7

6

	Tens	Ones
	3	2
+	4	7
	7	9

ON YOUR OWN
Go to Workbook B:
Practice 1, pages 153–156

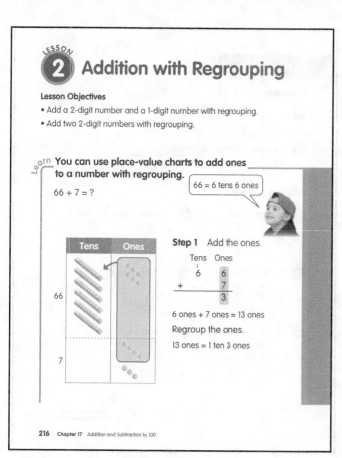

LESSON 2 Addition with Regrouping

Lesson Objectives
- Add a 2-digit number and a 1-digit number with regrouping.
- Add two 2-digit numbers with regrouping.

Learn You can use place-value charts to add ones to a number with regrouping.

$66 + 7 = ?$

> $66 = 6$ tens 6 ones

Tens	Ones

66

7

Step 1 Add the ones.

```
   Tens Ones
     6    6
 +        7
          3
```

6 ones + 7 ones = 13 ones
Regroup the ones.
13 ones = 1 ten 3 ones

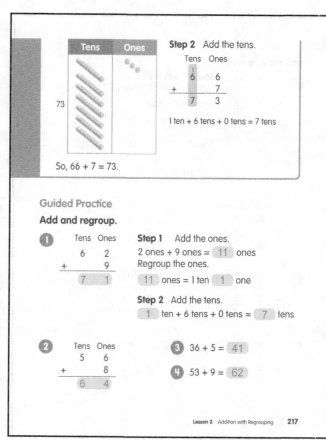

Tens	Ones

73

Step 2 Add the tens.

```
   Tens Ones
     6    6
 +        7
     7    3
```

1 ten + 6 tens + 0 tens = 7 tens

So, $66 + 7 = 73$.

Guided Practice

Add and regroup.

1
```
   Tens Ones
     6    2
 +        9
     7    1
```

Step 1 Add the ones.
2 ones + 9 ones = 11 ones
Regroup the ones.
11 ones = 1 ten 1 one

Step 2 Add the tens.
1 ten + 6 tens + 0 tens = 7 tens

2
```
   Tens Ones
     5    6
 +        8
     6    4
```

3 $36 + 5 = 41$

4 $53 + 9 = 62$

216 Chapter 17 Addition and Subtraction to 100

Lesson 2 Addition with Regrouping 217

Chapter 17

✋ Hands-On Activity

WORKING TOGETHER

Use a spinner.

spinner

STEP 1 Spin to get a number.

6!

STEP 2 Add this number to 52 and solve.

$52 + \_\_\_ = \_\_\_$
Answers vary.

$52 + 6 = ?$

STEP 3 Spin to get another number.
Add this number to 64 and solve.

$64 + \_\_\_ = \_\_\_$
Answers vary.

STEP 4 Have someone in your group check your work.
Take turns to spin numbers and solve.

218 Chapter 17 Addition and Subtraction to 100

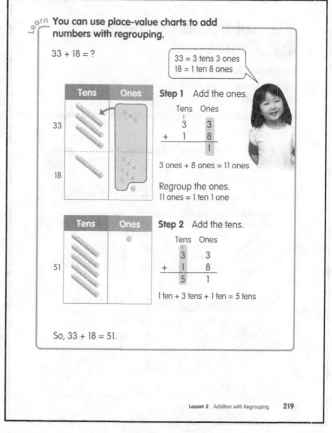

Learn You can use place-value charts to add numbers with regrouping.

$33 + 18 = ?$

> $33 = 3$ tens 3 ones
> $18 = 1$ ten 8 ones

Tens	Ones

33

18

Step 1 Add the ones.

```
   Tens Ones
     3    3
 +   1    8
          1
```

3 ones + 8 ones = 11 ones
Regroup the ones.
11 ones = 1 ten 1 one

Tens	Ones

51

Step 2 Add the tens.

```
   Tens Ones
     3    3
 +   1    8
     5    1
```

1 ten + 3 tens + 1 ten = 5 tens

So, $33 + 18 = 51$.

Lesson 2 Addition with Regrouping 219

Student Edition Answers: Chapter 17
Math in Focus Homeschool Answer Key, Grade 1

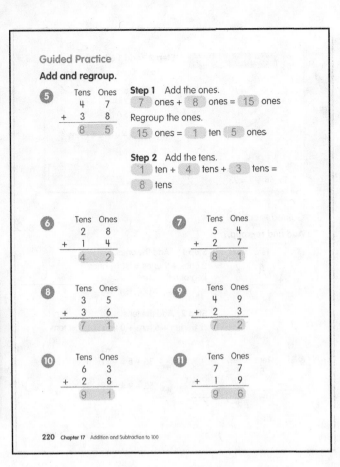

Guided Practice

Add and regroup.

5

Tens	Ones
4	7
+ 3	8
8	5

Step 1 Add the ones.
7 ones + 8 ones = 15 ones
Regroup the ones.
15 ones = 1 ten 5 ones

Step 2 Add the tens.
1 ten + 4 tens + 3 tens = 8 tens

6

Tens	Ones
2	8
+ 1	4
4	2

7

Tens	Ones
5	4
+ 2	7
8	1

8

Tens	Ones
3	5
+ 3	6
7	1

9

Tens	Ones
4	9
+ 2	3
7	2

10

Tens	Ones
6	3
+ 2	8
9	1

11

Tens	Ones
7	7
+ 1	9
9	6

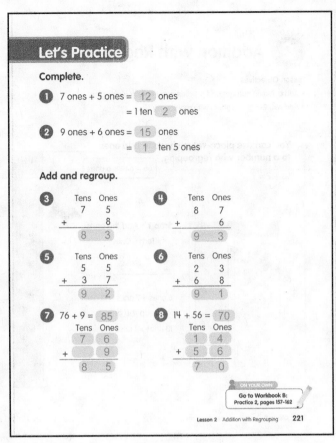

Let's Practice

Complete.

1 7 ones + 5 ones = 12 ones
= 1 ten 2 ones

2 9 ones + 6 ones = 15 ones
= 1 ten 5 ones

Add and regroup.

3

Tens	Ones
7	5
+	8
8	3

4

Tens	Ones
8	7
+	6
9	3

5

Tens	Ones
5	5
+ 3	7
9	2

6

Tens	Ones
2	3
+ 6	8
9	1

7 76 + 9 = 85

Tens	Ones
7	6
+	9
8	5

8 14 + 56 = 70

Tens	Ones
1	4
+ 5	6
7	0

ON YOUR OWN
Go to Workbook B:
Practice 2, pages 157–162

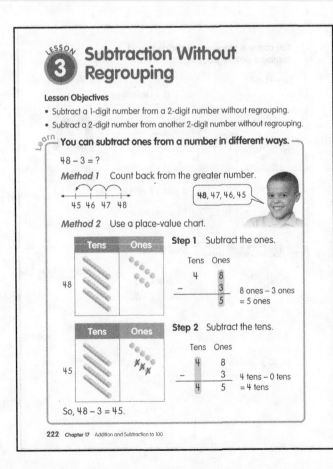

LESSON
3

Subtraction Without Regrouping

Lesson Objectives
- Subtract a 1-digit number from a 2-digit number without regrouping.
- Subtract a 2-digit number from another 2-digit number without regrouping.

Learn **You can subtract ones from a number in different ways.**

48 − 3 = ?

Method 1 Count back from the greater number.

45 46 47 48

48, 47, 46, 45

Method 2 Use a place-value chart.

Tens	Ones

48

Step 1 Subtract the ones.

Tens	Ones
4	8
−	3
	5

8 ones − 3 ones = 5 ones

45

Step 2 Subtract the tens.

Tens	Ones
4	8
−	3
4	5

4 tens − 0 tens = 4 tens

So, 48 − 3 = 45.

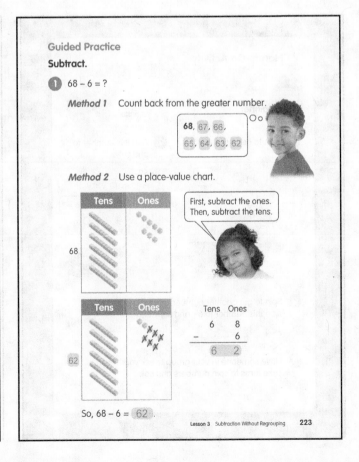

Guided Practice

Subtract.

1 68 − 6 = ?

Method 1 Count back from the greater number.

68, 67, 66,
65, 64, 63, 62

Method 2 Use a place-value chart.

Tens	Ones

68

First, subtract the ones.
Then, subtract the tens.

Tens	Ones

62

Tens	Ones
6	8
−	6
6	2

So, 68 − 6 = 62.

Chapter 17

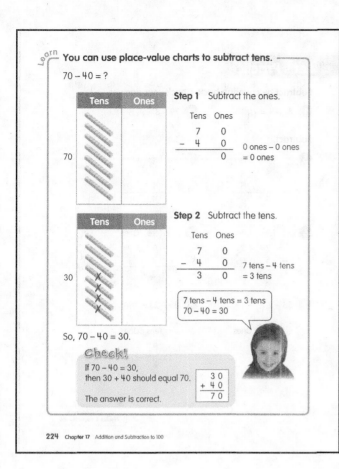

Learn **You can use place-value charts to subtract tens.**

$70 - 40 = ?$

Step 1 Subtract the ones.

```
   Tens  Ones
    7     0
 -  4     0      0 ones – 0 ones
 ─────────      = 0 ones
          0
```

Step 2 Subtract the tens.

```
   Tens  Ones
    7     0
 -  4     0      7 tens – 4 tens
 ─────────      = 3 tens
    3     0
```

7 tens – 4 tens = 3 tens
70 – 40 = 30

So, $70 - 40 = 30$.

Check!
If 70 – 40 = 30,
then 30 + 40 should equal 70.

```
   3 0
 + 4 0
 ─────
   7 0
```

The answer is correct.

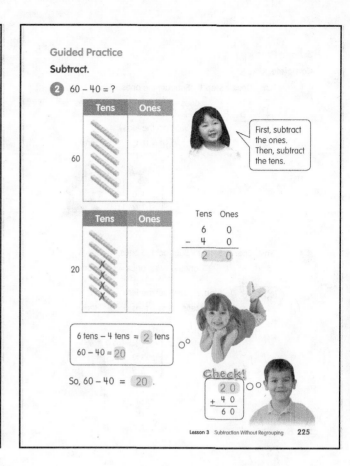

Guided Practice

Subtract.

2 $60 - 40 = ?$

```
   Tens  Ones
    6     0
 -  4     0
 ─────────
    2     0
```

First, subtract
the ones.
Then, subtract
the tens.

6 tens – 4 tens = [2] tens
60 – 40 = [20]

So, $60 - 40 = $ [20].

Check!
```
   2 0
 + 4 0
 ─────
   6 0
```

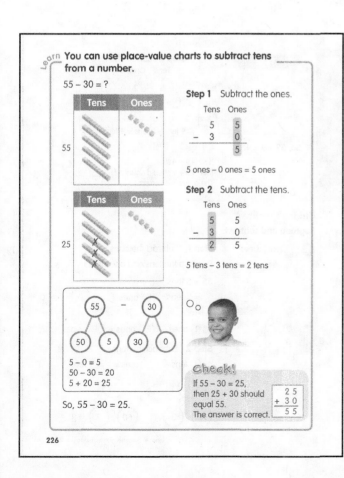

Learn **You can use place-value charts to subtract tens from a number.**

$55 - 30 = ?$

Step 1 Subtract the ones.

```
   Tens  Ones
    5     5
 -  3     0
 ─────────
          5
```

5 ones – 0 ones = 5 ones

Step 2 Subtract the tens.

```
   Tens  Ones
    5     5
 -  3     0
 ─────────
    2     5
```

5 tens – 3 tens = 2 tens

```
    55  –  30
   /  \    /  \
  50   5  30   0
```

5 – 0 = 5
50 – 30 = 20
5 + 20 = 25

So, $55 - 30 = 25$.

Check!
If 55 – 30 = 25,
then 25 + 30 should
equal 55.
The answer is correct.

```
   2 5
 + 3 0
 ─────
   5 5
```

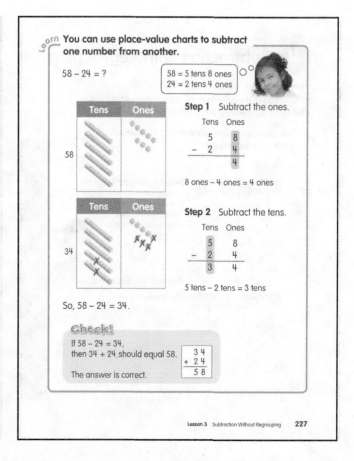

Learn **You can use place-value charts to subtract one number from another.**

$58 - 24 = ?$

58 = 5 tens 8 ones
24 = 2 tens 4 ones

Step 1 Subtract the ones.

```
   Tens  Ones
    5     8
 -  2     4
 ─────────
          4
```

8 ones – 4 ones = 4 ones

Step 2 Subtract the tens.

```
   Tens  Ones
    5     8
 -  2     4
 ─────────
    3     4
```

5 tens – 2 tens = 3 tens

So, $58 - 24 = 34$.

Check!
If 58 – 24 = 34,
then 34 + 24 should equal 58.
The answer is correct.

```
   3 4
 + 2 4
 ─────
   5 8
```

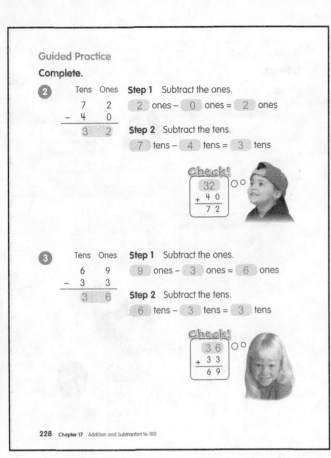

Guided Practice

Complete.

2

Tens	Ones
7	2
− 4	0
3	2

Step 1 Subtract the ones.
2 ones − 0 ones = 2 ones

Step 2 Subtract the tens.
7 tens − 4 tens = 3 tens

Check!
| 32 |
| + 4 0 |
| 7 2 |

3

Tens	Ones
6	9
− 3	3
3	6

Step 1 Subtract the ones.
9 ones − 3 ones = 6 ones

Step 2 Subtract the tens.
6 tens − 3 tens = 3 tens

Check!
| 3 6 |
| + 3 3 |
| 6 9 |

228 Chapter 17 Addition and Subtraction to 100

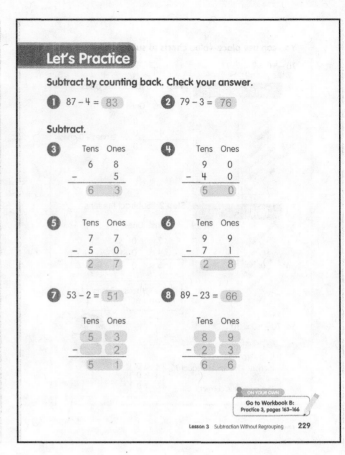

Let's Practice

Subtract by counting back. Check your answer.

1 87 − 4 = 83   **2** 79 − 3 = 76

Subtract.

3
Tens	Ones
6	8
−	5
6	3

4
Tens	Ones
9	0
− 4	0
5	0

5
Tens	Ones
7	7
− 5	0
2	7

6
Tens	Ones
9	9
− 7	1
2	8

7 53 − 2 = 51   **8** 89 − 23 = 66

Tens	Ones
5	3
−	2
5	1

Tens	Ones
8	9
− 2	3
6	6

ON YOUR OWN
Go to Workbook B:
Practice 3, pages 163–166

Lesson 3 Subtraction Without Regrouping 229

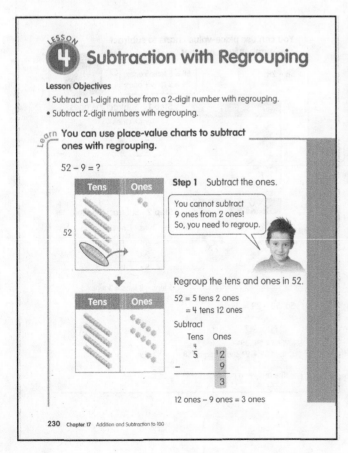

LESSON 4 Subtraction with Regrouping

Lesson Objectives
- Subtract a 1-digit number from a 2-digit number with regrouping.
- Subtract 2-digit numbers with regrouping.

Learn You can use place-value charts to subtract ones with regrouping.

52 − 9 = ?

Tens	Ones

52

Step 1 Subtract the ones.

You cannot subtract 9 ones from 2 ones! So, you need to regroup.

Tens	Ones

Regroup the tens and ones in 52.

52 = 5 tens 2 ones
= 4 tens 12 ones

Subtract

Tens	Ones
4 5	1 2
−	9
	3

12 ones − 9 ones = 3 ones

230 Chapter 17 Addition and Subtraction to 100

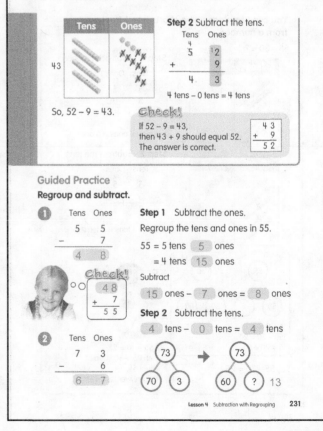

Tens	Ones

43

Step 2 Subtract the tens.

Tens	Ones
4 5	1 2
+	9
4	3

4 tens − 0 tens = 4 tens

So, 52 − 9 = 43.

Check!
If 52 − 9 = 43,
then 43 + 9 should equal 52.
The answer is correct.
| 4 3 |
| + 9 |
| 5 2 |

Guided Practice

Regroup and subtract.

1
Tens	Ones
5	5
−	7
4	8

Step 1 Subtract the ones.

Regroup the tens and ones in 55.

55 = 5 tens 5 ones
= 4 tens 15 ones

Subtract

15 ones − 7 ones = 8 ones

Step 2 Subtract the tens.

4 tens − 0 tens = 4 tens

Check!
| 4 8 |
| + 7 |
| 5 5 |

2
Tens	Ones
7	3
−	6
6	7

73 → 70 3

73 → 60 ? 13

Lesson 4 Subtraction with Regrouping 231

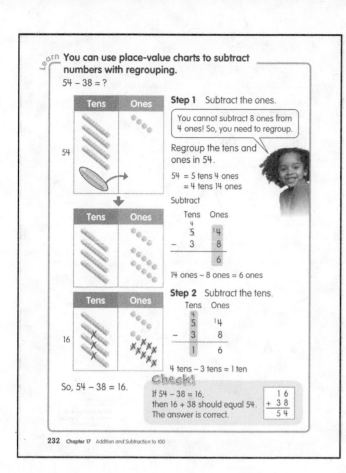

Learn You can use place-value charts to subtract numbers with regrouping.

54 − 38 = ?

Step 1 Subtract the ones.

You cannot subtract 8 ones from 4 ones! So, you need to regroup.

Regroup the tens and ones in 54.

54 = 5 tens 4 ones
= 4 tens 14 ones

Subtract

```
    Tens   Ones
      4
      5     ¹4
  −   3      8
  ─────────────
             6
```

14 ones − 8 ones = 6 ones

Step 2 Subtract the tens.

```
    Tens   Ones
      4
      5     ¹4
  −   3      8
  ─────────────
      1      6
```

4 tens − 3 tens = 1 ten

So, 54 − 38 = 16.

Check!
If 54 − 38 = 16,
then 16 + 38 should equal 54.
The answer is correct.

```
    1 6
  + 3 8
  ─────
    5 4
```

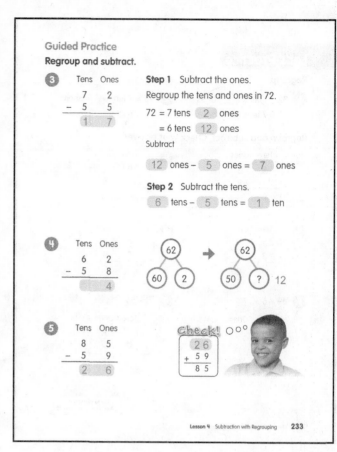

Guided Practice

Regroup and subtract.

3.
```
   Tens   Ones
     7      2
  −  5      5
  ──────────────
     1      7
```

Step 1 Subtract the ones.
Regroup the tens and ones in 72.

72 = 7 tens 2 ones
   = 6 tens 12 ones

Subtract

12 ones − 5 ones = 7 ones

Step 2 Subtract the tens.

6 tens − 5 tens = 1 ten

4.
```
   Tens   Ones
     6      2
  −  5      8
  ──────────────
            4
```

62 → 62
60 2   50 ? 12

5.
```
   Tens   Ones
     8      5
  −  5      9
  ──────────────
     2      6
```

Check!
```
    2 6
  + 5 9
  ─────
    8 5
```

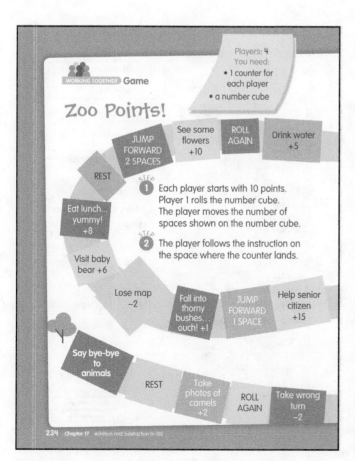

Zoo Points!

Players: 4
You need:
• 1 counter for each player
• a number cube

WORKING TOGETHER **Game**

JUMP FORWARD 2 SPACES
See some flowers +10
ROLL AGAIN
Drink water +5
REST
Eat lunch... yummy! +8
Visit baby bear +6
Lose map −2
Fall into thorny bushes... ouch! +1
JUMP FORWARD 1 SPACE
Help senior citizen +15
Say bye-bye to animals
REST
Take photos of camels +2
ROLL AGAIN
Take wrong turn −2

STEP 1 Each player starts with 10 points. Player 1 rolls the number cube. The player moves the number of spaces shown on the number cube.

STEP 2 The player follows the instruction on the space where the counter lands.

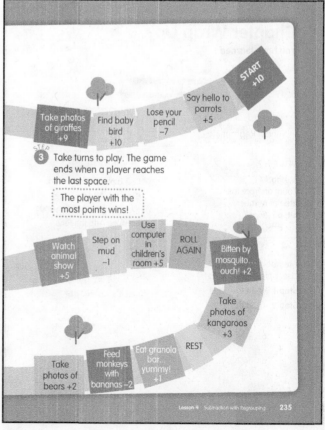

START +10
Say hello to parrots +5
Lose your pencil −7
Find baby bird +10
Take photos of giraffes +9
Watch animal show +5
Step on mud −1
Use computer in children's room +5
ROLL AGAIN
Bitten by mosquito... ouch! +2
Take photos of kangaroos +3
REST
Eat granola bar, yummy! +1
Feed monkeys with bananas −2
Take photos of bears +2

STEP 3 Take turns to play. The game ends when a player reaches the last space.

The player with the most points wins!

127

Student Edition Answers: Chapter 17
Math in Focus Homeschool Answer Key, Grade 1

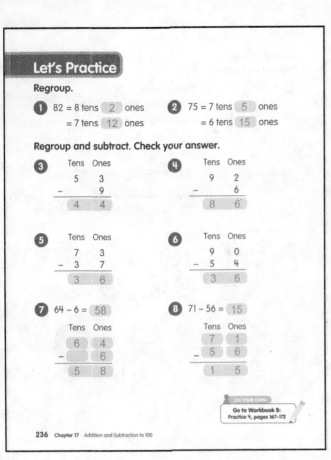

Let's Practice

Regroup.

1. 82 = 8 tens [2] ones
   = 7 tens [12] ones

2. 75 = 7 tens [5] ones
   = 6 tens [15] ones

Regroup and subtract. Check your answer.

3.
Tens	Ones
5	3
−	9
[4]	[4]

4.
Tens	Ones
9	2
−	6
[8]	[6]

5.
Tens	Ones
7	3
− 3	7
[3]	[6]

6.
Tens	Ones
9	0
− 5	4
[3]	[6]

7. 64 − 6 = [58]
Tens	Ones
[6]	[4]
−	[6]
[5]	[8]

8. 71 − 56 = [15]
Tens	Ones
[7]	[1]
− [5]	[6]
[1]	[5]

ON YOUR OWN
Go to Workbook B:
Practice 4, pages 167–172

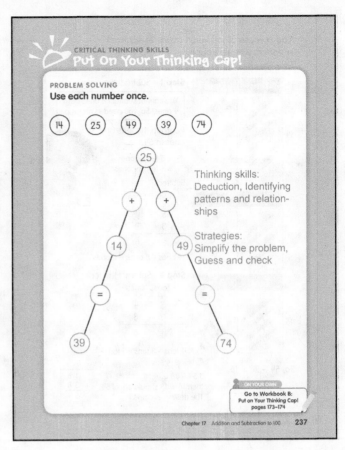

CRITICAL THINKING SKILLS
Put On Your Thinking Cap!

PROBLEM SOLVING
Use each number once.

(14) (25) (49) (39) (74)

(25)

(+)   (+)

(14)   (49)

(=)   (=)

(39)   (74)

Thinking skills:
Deduction, Identifying
patterns and relation-
ships

Strategies:
Simplify the problem,
Guess and check

ON YOUR OWN
Go to Workbook B:
Put on Your Thinking Cap!
pages 173–174

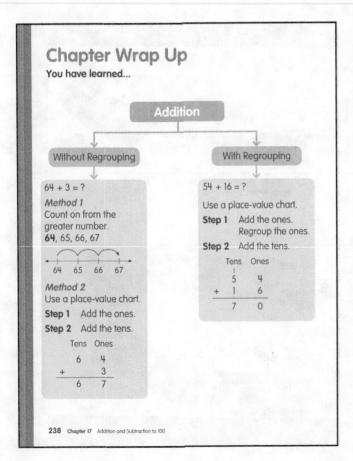

Chapter Wrap Up

You have learned...

Addition

Without Regrouping

64 + 3 = ?

Method 1
Count on from the
greater number.
64, 65, 66, 67

64 65 66 67

Method 2
Use a place-value chart.
Step 1   Add the ones.
Step 2   Add the tens.

Tens	Ones
6	4
+	3
6	7

With Regrouping

54 + 16 = ?

Use a place-value chart.
Step 1   Add the ones.
          Regroup the ones.
Step 2   Add the tens.

Tens	Ones
5	4
+ 1	6
7	0

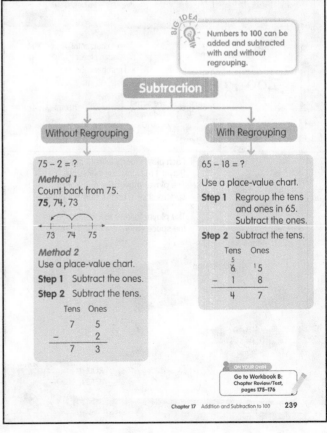

BIG IDEA
Numbers to 100 can be
added and subtracted
with and without
regrouping.

Subtraction

Without Regrouping

75 − 2 = ?

Method 1
Count back from 75.
75, 74, 73

73 74 75

Method 2
Use a place-value chart.
Step 1   Subtract the ones.
Step 2   Subtract the tens.

Tens	Ones
7	5
−	2
7	3

With Regrouping

65 − 18 = ?

Use a place-value chart.
Step 1   Regroup the tens
          and ones in 65.
          Subtract the ones.
Step 2   Subtract the tens.

Tens	Ones
6	5
− 1	8
4	7

ON YOUR OWN
Go to Workbook B:
Chapter Review/Test,
pages 175–176

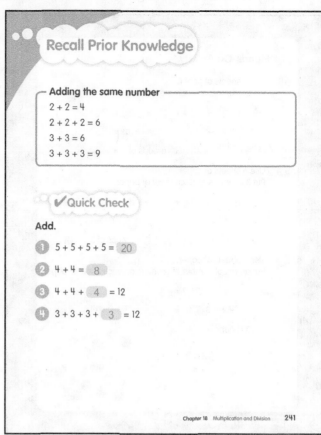

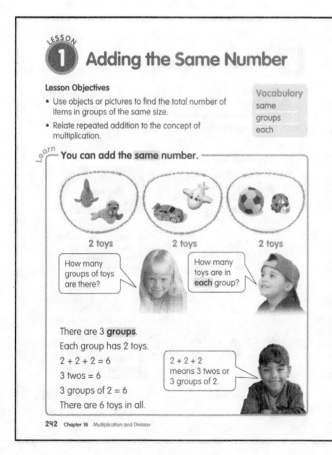

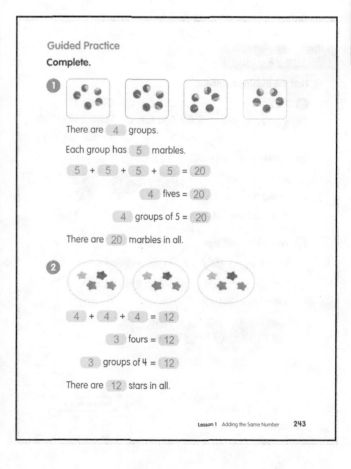

129

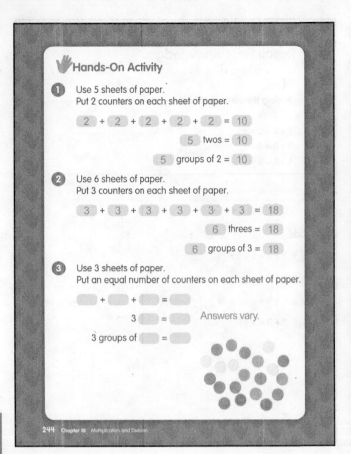

Hands-On Activity

1 Use 5 sheets of paper.
Put 2 counters on each sheet of paper.

2 + 2 + 2 + 2 + 2 = 10

5 twos = 10

5 groups of 2 = 10

2 Use 6 sheets of paper.
Put 3 counters on each sheet of paper.

3 + 3 + 3 + 3 + 3 + 3 = 18

6 threes = 18

6 groups of 3 = 18

3 Use 3 sheets of paper.
Put an equal number of counters on each sheet of paper.

⬜ + ⬜ + ⬜ = ⬜

3 ⬜ = ⬜   Answers vary.

3 groups of ⬜ = ⬜

244 Chapter 18 Multiplication and Division

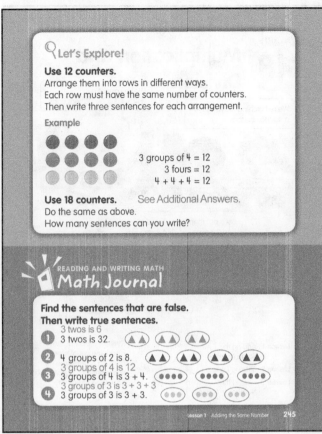

Let's Explore!

Use 12 counters.
Arrange them into rows in different ways.
Each row must have the same number of counters.
Then write three sentences for each arrangement.

Example

3 groups of 4 = 12
3 fours = 12
4 + 4 + 4 = 12

Use 18 counters.   See Additional Answers.
Do the same as above.
How many sentences can you write?

READING AND WRITING MATH
Math Journal

Find the sentences that are false.
Then write true sentences.

1 3 twos is 6
3 twos is 32. ▲▲ ▲▲ ▲▲

2 4 groups of 2 is 8. ◀▶ ◀▶ ◀▶ ◀▶
3 groups of 4 is 12

3 3 groups of 4 is 3 + 4. ●●●● ●●●● ●●●●
3 groups of 3 is 3 + 3 + 3

4 3 groups of 3 is 3 + 3. ●●● ●●● ●●●

Lesson 1 Adding the Same Number 245

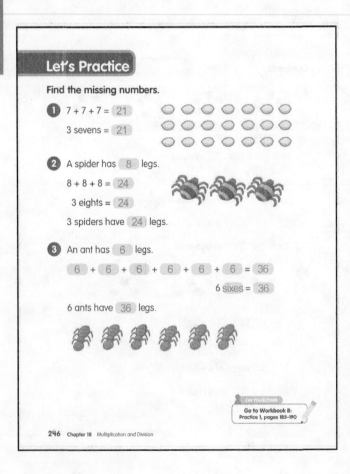

Let's Practice

Find the missing numbers.

1 7 + 7 + 7 = 21

3 sevens = 21

2 A spider has 8 legs.

8 + 8 + 8 = 24

3 eights = 24

3 spiders have 24 legs.

3 An ant has 6 legs.

6 + 6 + 6 + 6 + 6 + 6 = 36

6 sixes = 36

6 ants have 36 legs.

ON YOUR OWN
Go to Workbook B:
Practice 1, pages 185–190

246 Chapter 18 Multiplication and Division

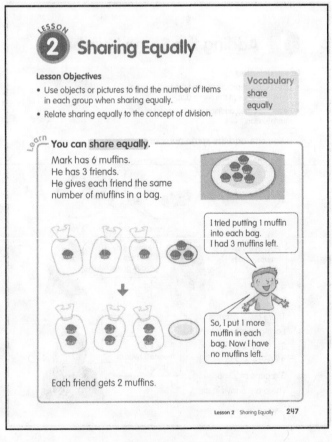

LESSON
2 Sharing Equally

Lesson Objectives
- Use objects or pictures to find the number of items in each group when sharing equally.
- Relate sharing equally to the concept of division.

Vocabulary
share
equally

You can share equally.

Mark has 6 muffins.
He has 3 friends.
He gives each friend the same number of muffins in a bag.

I tried putting 1 muffin into each bag. I had 3 muffins left.

So, I put 1 more muffin in each bag. Now I have no muffins left.

Each friend gets 2 muffins.

Lesson 2 Sharing Equally 247

Chapter 18

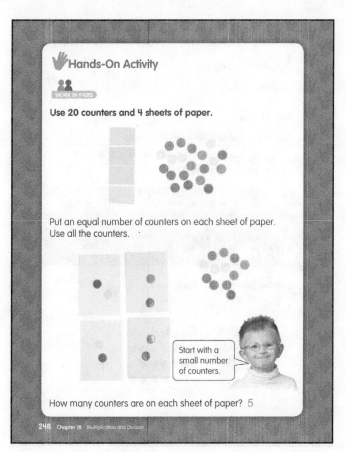

Hands-On Activity

WORK IN PAIRS

Use 20 counters and 4 sheets of paper.

Put an equal number of counters on each sheet of paper.
Use all the counters.

Start with a small number of counters.

How many counters are on each sheet of paper? 5

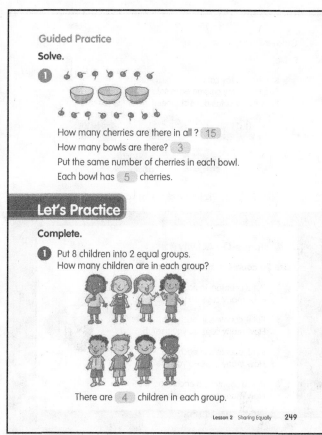

Solve.

1.

How many cherries are there in all ? 15
How many bowls are there? 3
Put the same number of cherries in each bowl.
Each bowl has 5 cherries.

Let's Practice

Complete.

1. Put 8 children into 2 equal groups.
How many children are in each group?

There are 4 children in each group.

2. There are 12 beads of different colors in a box.
Put the beads into 4 equal groups.
How many beads are in each group?

There are 3 beads in each group.

3. Mr. Armstrong has 18 crayons.
He gives the crayons equally to 6 children.
How many crayons does each child get?

Each child gets 3 crayons.

4. Mrs. Curley bakes 20 muffins.
She packs them into 5 boxes equally.
How many muffins are in each box?

There are 4 muffins in each box.

ON YOUR OWN
Go to Workbook B:
Practice 2, pages 191–198

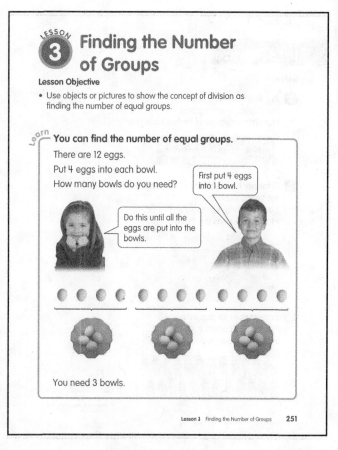

LESSON 3 Finding the Number of Groups

Lesson Objective

• Use objects or pictures to show the concept of division as finding the number of equal groups.

You can find the number of equal groups.

There are 12 eggs.
Put 4 eggs into each bowl.
How many bowls do you need?

First put 4 eggs into 1 bowl.

Do this until all the eggs are put into the bowls.

You need 3 bowls.

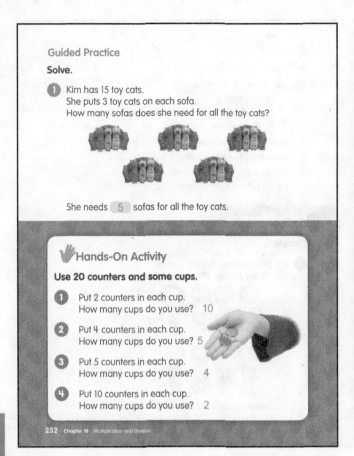

Guided Practice

Solve.

1. Kim has 15 toy cats.
   She puts 3 toy cats on each sofa.
   How many sofas does she need for all the toy cats?

   She needs 5 sofas for all the toy cats.

✋ **Hands-On Activity**

Use 20 counters and some cups.

1. Put 2 counters in each cup.
   How many cups do you use? 10

2. Put 4 counters in each cup.
   How many cups do you use? 5

3. Put 5 counters in each cup.
   How many cups do you use? 4

4. Put 10 counters in each cup.
   How many cups do you use? 2

252 Chapter 18 Multiplication and Division

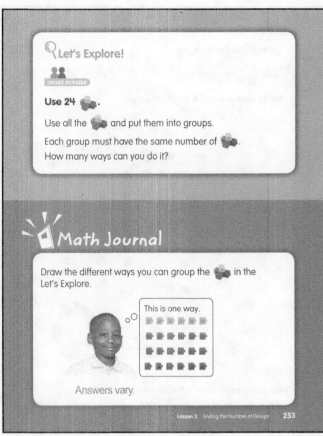

🔍 **Let's Explore!**

👥 WORK IN PAIRS

Use 24 🧊.

Use all the 🧊 and put them into groups.

Each group must have the same number of 🧊.
How many ways can you do it?

📱 **Math Journal**

Draw the different ways you can group the 🧊 in the Let's Explore.

This is one way.

Answers vary.

Lesson 3 Finding the Number of Groups 253

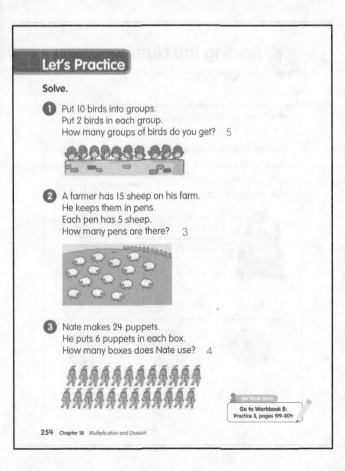

Let's Practice

Solve.

1. Put 10 birds into groups.
   Put 2 birds in each group.
   How many groups of birds do you get? 5

2. A farmer has 15 sheep on his farm.
   He keeps them in pens.
   Each pen has 5 sheep.
   How many pens are there? 3

3. Nate makes 24 puppets.
   He puts 6 puppets in each box.
   How many boxes does Nate use? 4

ON YOUR OWN
Go to Workbook B:
Practice 3, pages 199–204

254 Chapter 18 Multiplication and Division

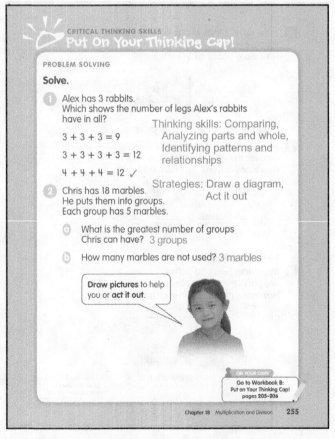

🎓 CRITICAL THINKING SKILLS
Put On Your Thinking Cap!

PROBLEM SOLVING

Solve.

1. Alex has 3 rabbits.
   Which shows the number of legs Alex's rabbits have in all?

   $3 + 3 + 3 = 9$

   $3 + 3 + 3 + 3 = 12$

   $4 + 4 + 4 = 12$ ✓

   Thinking skills: Comparing, Analyzing parts and whole, Identifying patterns and relationships

   Strategies: Draw a diagram, Act it out

2. Chris has 18 marbles.
   He puts them into groups.
   Each group has 5 marbles.

   a. What is the greatest number of groups Chris can have? 3 groups

   b. How many marbles are not used? 3 marbles

   Draw pictures to help you or **act it out.**

ON YOUR OWN
Go to Workbook B:
Put on Your Thinking Cap!
pages 205–206

Chapter 18 Multiplication and Division 255

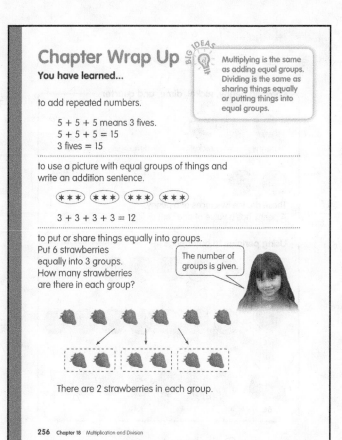

Chapter Wrap Up

You have learned...

BIG IDEAS — Multiplying is the same as adding equal groups. Dividing is the same as sharing things equally or putting things into equal groups.

to add repeated numbers.

5 + 5 + 5 means 3 fives.
5 + 5 + 5 = 15
3 fives = 15

to use a picture with equal groups of things and write an addition sentence.

3 + 3 + 3 + 3 = 12

to put or share things equally into groups.
Put 6 strawberries equally into 3 groups. How many strawberries are there in each group?

The number of groups is given.

There are 2 strawberries in each group.

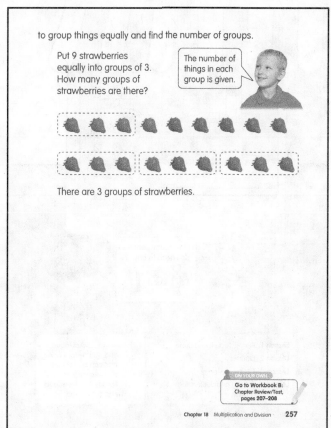

to group things equally and find the number of groups.

Put 9 strawberries equally into groups of 3. How many groups of strawberries are there?

The number of things in each group is given.

There are 3 groups of strawberries.

ON YOUR OWN
Go to Workbook B: Chapter Review/Test, pages 207–208

Chapter 18

Lesson 1 Penny, Nickel, and Dime
Lesson 2 Quarter
Lesson 3 Counting Money
Lesson 4 Adding and Subtracting Money

Penny, nickel, dime, and quarter are coins that can be counted and exchanged. Money can be added and subtracted.

258

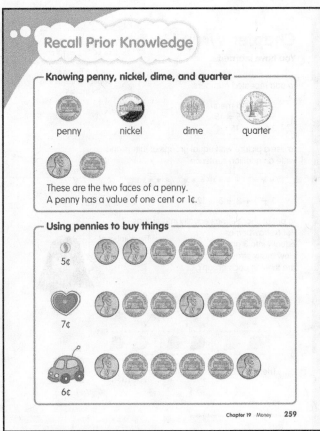

Knowing penny, nickel, dime, and quarter

penny   nickel   dime   quarter

These are the two faces of a penny.
A penny has a value of one cent or 1¢.

Using pennies to buy things

5¢

7¢

6¢

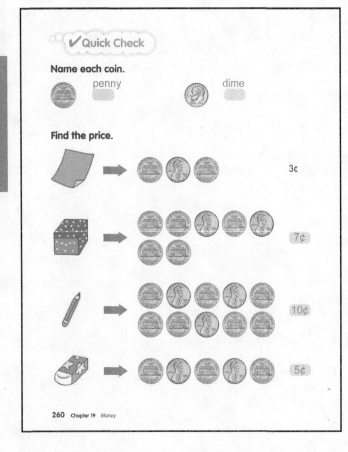

✔ Quick Check

Name each coin.

penny   dime

Find the price.

3¢

7¢

10¢

5¢

260 Chapter 19 Money

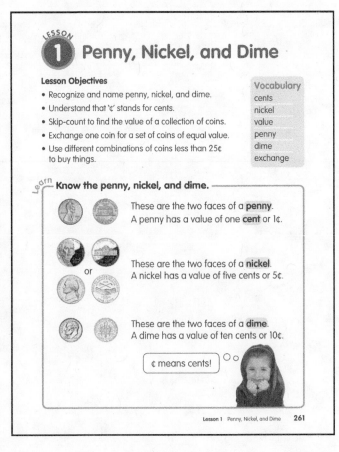

LESSON
1 Penny, Nickel, and Dime

Lesson Objectives

• Recognize and name penny, nickel, and dime.
• Understand that '¢' stands for cents.
• Skip-count to find the value of a collection of coins.
• Exchange one coin for a set of coins of equal value.
• Use different combinations of coins less than 25¢ to buy things.

Vocabulary
cents
nickel
value
penny
dime
exchange

Know the penny, nickel, and dime.

These are the two faces of a penny.
A penny has a value of one cent or 1¢.

or

These are the two faces of a nickel.
A nickel has a value of five cents or 5¢.

These are the two faces of a dime.
A dime has a value of ten cents or 10¢.

¢ means cents!

Lesson 1 Penny, Nickel, and Dime 261

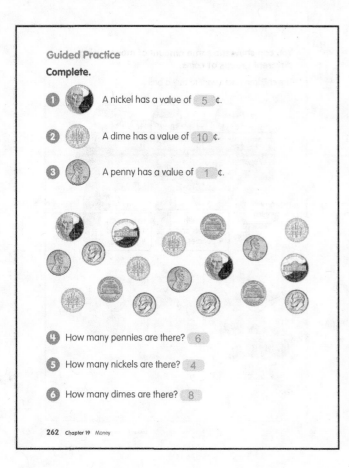

Guided Practice

Complete.

1. A nickel has a value of 5 ¢.

2. A dime has a value of 10 ¢.

3. A penny has a value of 1 ¢.

4. How many pennies are there? 6

5. How many nickels are there? 4

6. How many dimes are there? 8

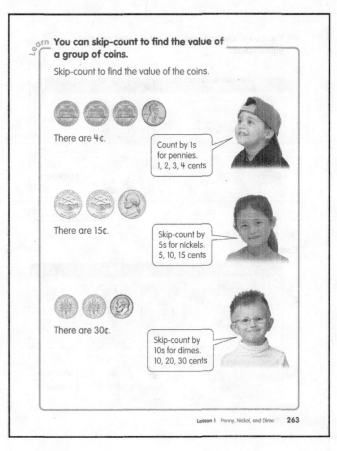

You can skip-count to find the value of a group of coins.

Skip-count to find the value of the coins.

There are 4¢.

> Count by 1s for pennies.
> 1, 2, 3, 4 cents

There are 15¢.

> Skip-count by 5s for nickels.
> 5, 10, 15 cents

There are 30¢.

> Skip-count by 10s for dimes.
> 10, 20, 30 cents

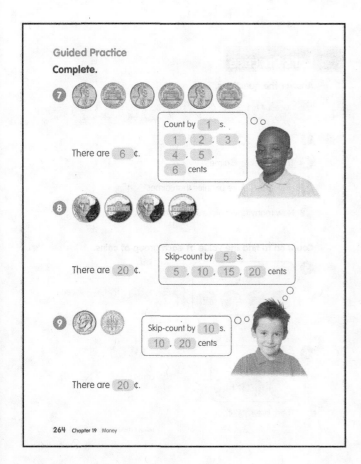

Guided Practice

Complete.

7. There are 6 ¢.

> Count by 1 s.
> 1 , 2 , 3 ,
> 4 , 5 ,
> 6 cents

8. There are 20 ¢.

> Skip-count by 5 s.
> 5 , 10 , 15 , 20 cents

9. Skip-count by 10 s.
> 10 , 20 cents

There are 20 ¢.

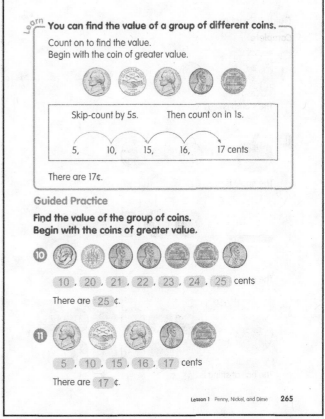

You can find the value of a group of different coins.

Count on to find the value.
Begin with the coin of greater value.

> Skip-count by 5s.   Then count on in 1s.
> 5,   10,   15,   16,   17 cents

There are 17¢.

Guided Practice

Find the value of the group of coins.
Begin with the coins of greater value.

10. 10 , 20 , 21 , 22 , 23 , 24 , 25 cents

There are 25 ¢.

11. 5 , 10 , 15 , 16 , 17 cents

There are 17 ¢.

Chapter 19

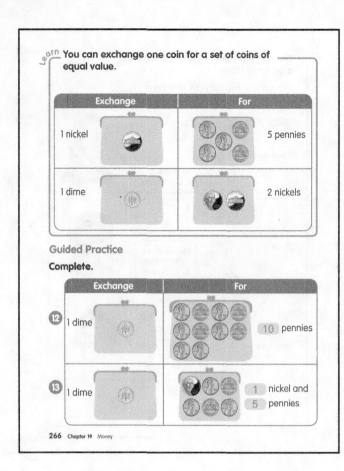

Learn You can exchange one coin for a set of coins of equal value.

Exchange		For	
1 nickel			5 pennies
1 dime			2 nickels

Guided Practice

Complete.

Exchange		For	
⑫ 1 dime			**10** pennies
⑬ 1 dime			**1** nickel and **5** pennies

Learn You can show the same amount of money using different groups of coins.

The children each want to buy a ball.

I'll pay with 14 pennies.

I'll pay with 2 nickels and 4 pennies.

I'll pay with 1 dime and 4 pennies.

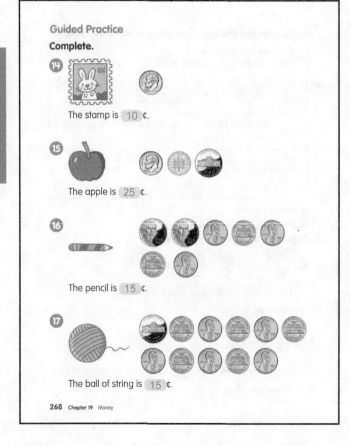

Guided Practice

Complete.

⑭ The stamp is **10** ¢.

⑮ The apple is **25** ¢.

⑯ The pencil is **15** ¢.

⑰ The ball of string is **15** ¢.

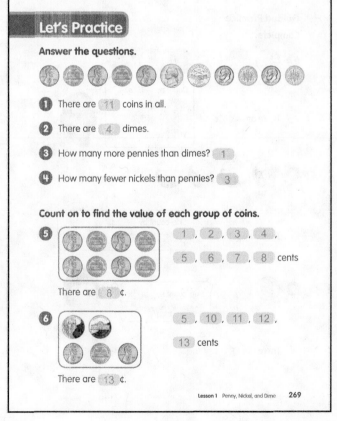

Let's Practice

Answer the questions.

❶ There are **11** coins in all.

❷ There are **4** dimes.

❸ How many more pennies than dimes? **1**

❹ How many fewer nickels than pennies? **3**

Count on to find the value of each group of coins.

❺ **1**, **2**, **3**, **4**, **5**, **6**, **7**, **8** cents

There are **8** ¢.

❻ **5**, **10**, **11**, **12**, **13** cents

There are **13** ¢.

Student Edition Answers: Chapter 19
Math in Focus Homeschool Answer Key, Grade 1

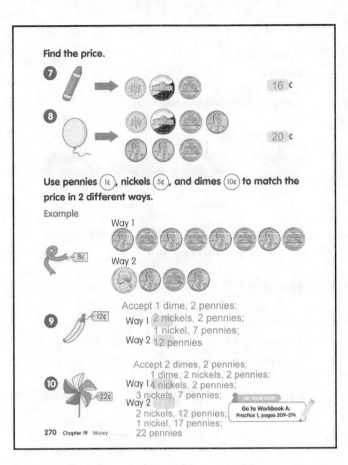

Find the price.

7 16 ¢

8 20 ¢

Use pennies (1¢)**, nickels** (5¢)**, and dimes** (10¢) **to match the price in 2 different ways.**

Example

Way 1

Way 2

8¢

9 12¢

Way 1 | Accept 1 dime, 2 pennies; 2 nickels, 2 pennies; 1 nickel, 7 pennies;
Way 2 | 12 pennies

10 22¢

Way 1 | Accept 2 dimes, 2 pennies; 1 dime, 2 nickels, 2 pennies; 4 nickels, 2 pennies; 3 nickels, 7 pennies;
Way 2 | 2 nickels, 12 pennies; 1 nickel, 17 pennies; 22 pennies

Go to Workbook A: Practice 1, pages 209–214

270 Chapter 19 Money

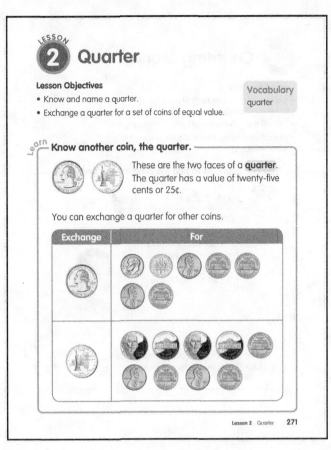

2 Quarter

Lesson Objectives
- Know and name a quarter.
- Exchange a quarter for a set of coins of equal value.

Vocabulary
quarter

Know another coin, the quarter.

These are the two faces of a **quarter**. The quarter has a value of twenty-five cents or 25¢.

You can exchange a quarter for other coins.

Exchange	For

Lesson 2 Quarter **271**

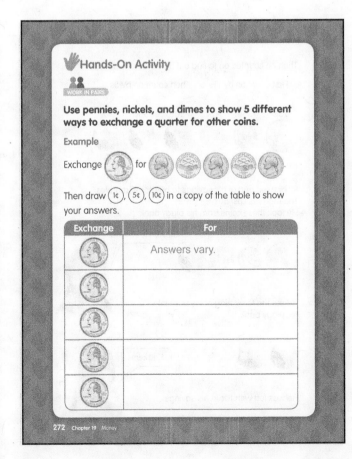

✋ **Hands-On Activity**

👥👥 WORK IN PAIRS

Use pennies, nickels, and dimes to show 5 different ways to exchange a quarter for other coins.

Example

Exchange ___ for ___

Then draw (1¢), (5¢), (10¢) in a copy of the table to show your answers.

Exchange	For
	Answers vary.

272 Chapter 19 Money

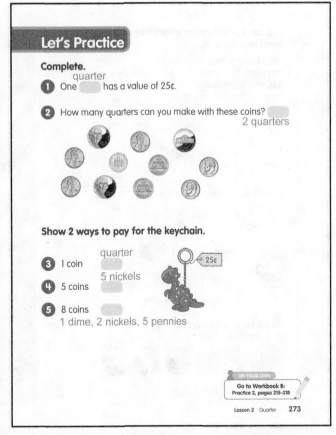

Let's Practice

Complete.

1 One [quarter] has a value of 25¢.

2 How many quarters can you make with these coins? [2 quarters]

Show 2 ways to pay for the keychain.

25¢

3 1 coin [quarter]

4 5 coins [5 nickels]

5 8 coins [1 dime, 2 nickels, 5 pennies]

Go to Workbook B: Practice 2, pages 215–218

Lesson 2 Quarter **273**

Chapter 19

LESSON 3 Counting Money

Lesson Objectives

- Count money in cents up to $1 using the 'count on' strategy.
- Choose the correct value of coins when buying items.
- Use different combinations of coins to show the same value.

Learn **You can count on to find the amount of money.**

75¢

Count on from the coins of the greatest value.
25, 50, 60, 70, 75 cents

Count on in 25s for quarters, 10s for dimes, 5s for nickels and 1s for pennies.

274 Chapter 19 Money

Guided Practice

Complete.

Matt buys some things.
Count on to find the price of each keychain.

airplane keychain   car keychain   helicopter keychain   truck keychain

1 He pays ⬤⬤⬤⬤ for the airplane keychain.
The airplane keychain costs **66** ¢.

2 He pays ⬤⬤⬤⬤ for the car keychain.
The car keychain costs **45** ¢.

3 He pays ⬤⬤⬤ for the helicopter keychain.
The helicopter keychain costs **60** ¢.

4 He pays ⬤⬤⬤⬤⬤ for the truck keychain.
The truck keychain costs **52** ¢.

Lesson 3 Counting Money 275

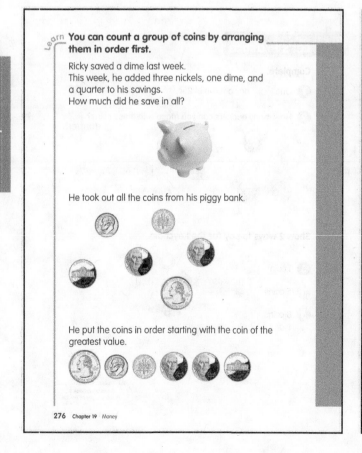

Learn **You can count a group of coins by arranging them in order first.**

Ricky saved a dime last week.
This week, he added three nickels, one dime, and a quarter to his savings.
How much did he save in all?

He took out all the coins from his piggy bank.

He put the coins in order starting with the coin of the greatest value.

276 Chapter 19 Money

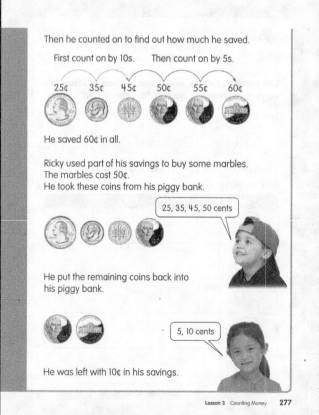

Then he counted on to find out how much he saved.

First count on by 10s.   Then count on by 5s.

25¢   35¢   45¢   50¢   55¢   60¢

He saved 60¢ in all.

Ricky used part of his savings to buy some marbles.
The marbles cost 50¢.
He took these coins from his piggy bank.

25, 35, 45, 50 cents

He put the remaining coins back into his piggy bank.

5, 10 cents

He was left with 10¢ in his savings.

Lesson 3 Counting Money 277

Chapter 19

Student Edition Answers: Chapter 19
Math in Focus Homeschool Answer Key, Grade 1

Guided Practice

Look at the coins.
Fill in the blanks.

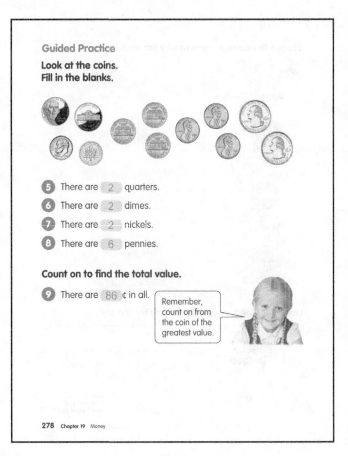

5 There are `2` quarters.

6 There are `2` dimes.

7 There are `2` nickels.

8 There are `6` pennies.

Count on to find the total value.

9 There are `86` ¢ in all.

Remember, count on from the coin of the greatest value.

Guided Practice

Complete.

10 Tell which of these coins make 62¢. Answers vary.

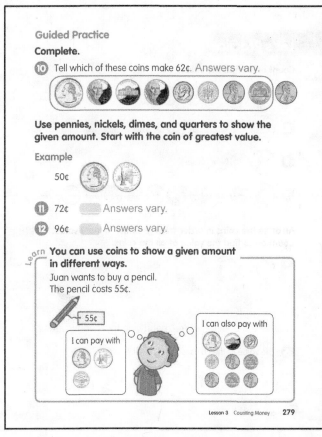

Use pennies, nickels, dimes, and quarters to show the given amount. Start with the coin of greatest value.

Example

50¢

11 72¢   Answers vary.

12 96¢   Answers vary.

You can use coins to show a given amount in different ways.

Juan wants to buy a pencil.
The pencil costs 55¢.

55¢

I can pay with

I can also pay with

Guided Practice

Use coins to show 2 ways of paying for each thing.

Example

Way 1

85¢

Way 2

15   95¢

Answers vary.
Way 1
Way 2

16   86¢

Answers vary.
Way 1
Way 2

17   45¢

Answers vary.
Way 1
Way 2

18   75¢

Answers vary.
Way 1
Way 2

19   99¢

Answers vary.
Way 1
Way 2

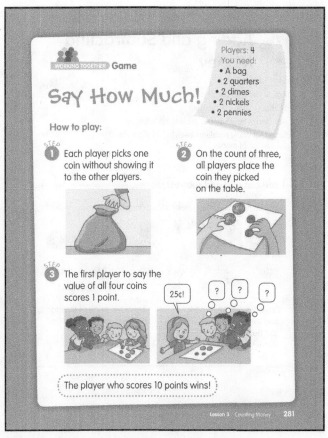

WORKING TOGETHER Game

Say How Much!

Players: 4
You need:
- A bag
- 2 quarters
- 2 dimes
- 2 nickels
- 2 pennies

How to play:

STEP 1 Each player picks one coin without showing it to the other players.

STEP 2 On the count of three, all players place the coin they picked on the table.

STEP 3 The first player to say the value of all four coins scores 1 point.

25¢!   ?   ?   ?

The player who scores 10 points wins!

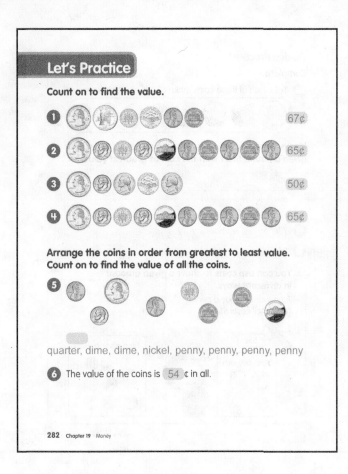

Let's Practice

Count on to find the value.

1. 67¢

2. 65¢

3. 50¢

4. 65¢

Arrange the coins in order from greatest to least value.
Count on to find the value of all the coins.

5.

quarter, dime, dime, nickel, penny, penny, penny, penny

6. The value of the coins is 54 ¢ in all.

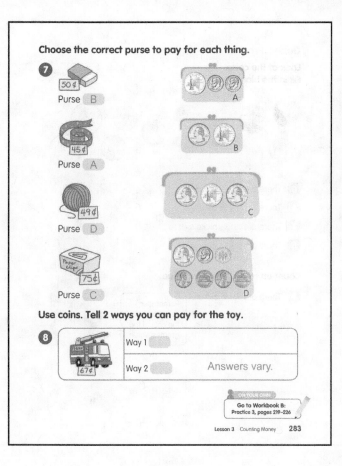

Choose the correct purse to pay for each thing.

7.
Purse B 50¢
Purse A 45¢
Purse D 49¢
Purse C 75¢ Paper clips

A
B
C
D

Use coins. Tell 2 ways you can pay for the toy.

8.
67¢
Way 1
Way 2   Answers vary.

ON YOUR OWN
Go to Workbook B:
Practice 3, pages 219–226

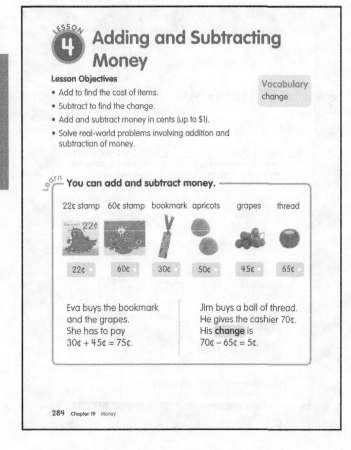

LESSON 4 Adding and Subtracting Money

Lesson Objectives
- Add to find the cost of items.
- Subtract to find the change.
- Add and subtract money in cents (up to $1).
- Solve real-world problems involving addition and subtraction of money.

Vocabulary
change

Learn You can add and subtract money.

22¢ stamp 60¢ stamp bookmark apricots grapes thread

22¢   60¢   30¢   50¢   45¢   65¢

Eva buys the bookmark
and the grapes.
She has to pay
30¢ + 45¢ = 75¢.

Jim buys a ball of thread.
He gives the cashier 70¢.
His **change** is
70¢ − 65¢ = 5¢.

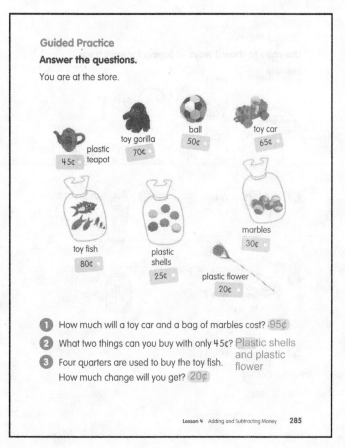

Guided Practice
Answer the questions.
You are at the store.

plastic teapot 45¢
toy gorilla 70¢
ball 50¢
toy car 65¢
toy fish 80¢
plastic shells 25¢
plastic flower 20¢
marbles 30¢

1. How much will a toy car and a bag of marbles cost? 95¢

2. What two things can you buy with only 45¢? Plastic shells and plastic flower

3. Four quarters are used to buy the toy fish.
How much change will you get? 20¢

140

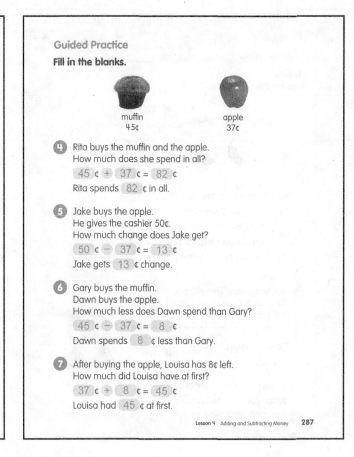

Learn — You can solve real-world money problems.

Stickers

car 15¢   ship 20¢

bus 25¢   bicycle 5¢

airplane 35¢

Mike buys the car, ship, and bicycle stickers.

15¢ + 20¢ + 5¢ = 40¢

He spends 40¢ in all.

Lily buys the car sticker.
She gives the cashier a quarter.

25¢ − 15¢ = 10¢

She gets 10¢ as change.

Salmah has 17¢.
She wants to buy the airplane sticker.

35¢ − 17¢ = 18¢

She needs 18¢ more.

Peter buys the bus sticker.
He has a nickel left.

25¢ + 5¢ = 30¢

He had 30¢ at first.

286   Chapter 19   Money

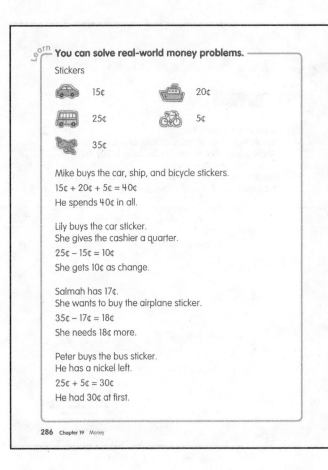

Guided Practice

Fill in the blanks.

muffin 45¢   apple 37¢

4   Rita buys the muffin and the apple.
How much does she spend in all?
45 ¢ + 37 ¢ = 82 ¢
Rita spends 82 ¢ in all.

5   Jake buys the apple.
He gives the cashier 50¢.
How much change does Jake get?
50 ¢ − 37 ¢ = 13 ¢
Jake gets 13 ¢ change.

6   Gary buys the muffin.
Dawn buys the apple.
How much less does Dawn spend than Gary?
45 ¢ − 37 ¢ = 8 ¢
Dawn spends 8 ¢ less than Gary.

7   After buying the apple, Louisa has 8¢ left.
How much did Louisa have at first?
37 ¢ + 8 ¢ = 45 ¢
Louisa had 45 ¢ at first.

Lesson 4   Adding and Subtracting Money   287

Let's Explore!

These are some things on sale.

bread 60¢   toy clock 65¢   pencil case 90¢   nuts 80¢

marbles 35¢   animal crackers 83¢   paper clips 20¢   ball 75¢

1   Paula wants to buy something to eat.
She has 80¢.
What can she buy?   bread or nuts

2   Dwayne has 95¢.
After buying something to eat, he has 15¢ left.
What is the food that he buys? nuts

3   Juanita has 4 quarters.
List any two things she can buy.
Then show how much she spends.
bread and paper clips 80¢; bread and marbles 95¢;
toy clock and paper clips 85¢; toy clock and marbles
100¢; paper clips and marbles 55¢; ball and paper
clips 95¢; nuts and paper clips 100¢

288   Chapter 19   Money

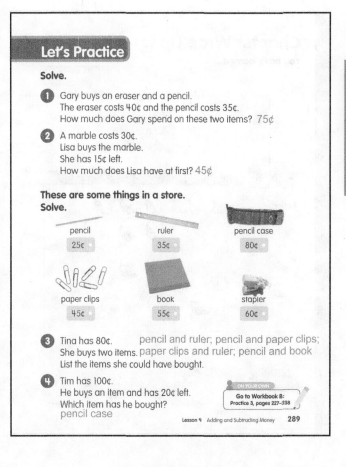

Let's Practice

Solve.

1   Gary buys an eraser and a pencil.
The eraser costs 40¢ and the pencil costs 35¢.
How much does Gary spend on these two items? 75¢

2   A marble costs 30¢.
Lisa buys the marble.
She has 15¢ left.
How much does Lisa have at first? 45¢

These are some things in a store.
Solve.

pencil 25¢   ruler 35¢   pencil case 80¢

paper clips 45¢   book 55¢   stapler 60¢

3   Tina has 80¢.   pencil and ruler; pencil and paper clips;
She buys two items. paper clips and ruler; pencil and book
List the items she could have bought.

4   Tim has 100¢.
He buys an item and has 20¢ left.
Which item has he bought?
pencil case

ON YOUR OWN

Go to Workbook B:
Practice 3, pages 227–238

Lesson 4   Adding and Subtracting Money   289

Chapter 19

PROBLEM SOLVING
Answer the questions.

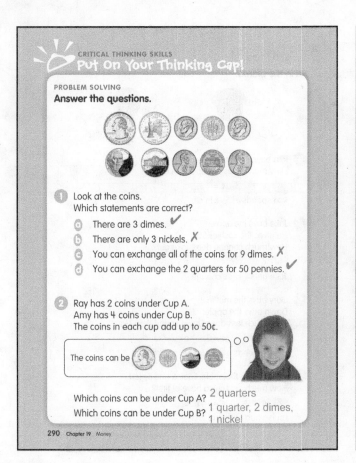

1. Look at the coins.
   Which statements are correct?
   a. There are 3 dimes. ✔
   b. There are only 3 nickels. ✗
   c. You can exchange all of the coins for 9 dimes. ✗
   d. You can exchange the 2 quarters for 50 pennies. ✔

2. Ray has 2 coins under Cup A.
   Amy has 4 coins under Cup B.
   The coins in each cup add up to 50¢.

   The coins can be [coins]

   Which coins can be under Cup A? 2 quarters
   Which coins can be under Cup B? 1 quarter, 2 dimes, 1 nickel

3. 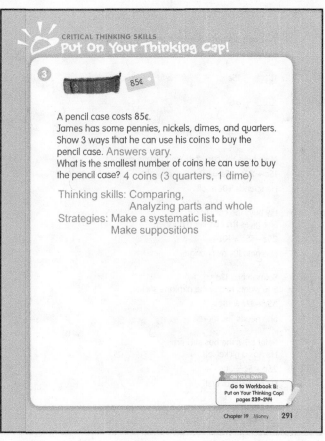 85¢

A pencil case costs 85¢.
James has some pennies, nickels, dimes, and quarters.
Show 3 ways that he can use his coins to buy the
pencil case. Answers vary.
What is the smallest number of coins he can use to buy
the pencil case? 4 coins (3 quarters, 1 dime)

Thinking skills: Comparing,
                 Analyzing parts and whole
Strategies: Make a systematic list,
            Make suppositions

ON YOUR OWN
Go to Workbook B:
Put on Your Thinking Cap!
pages 239–244

Chapter Wrap Up

You have learned...

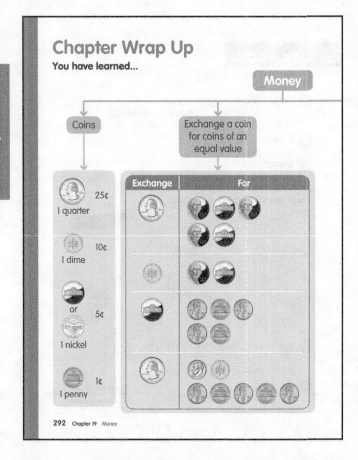

Money

Coins

Exchange a coin
for coins of an
equal value

Exchange	For
1 quarter	[coins]
1 dime	25¢
1 nickel or	10¢
1 penny	5¢
	1¢

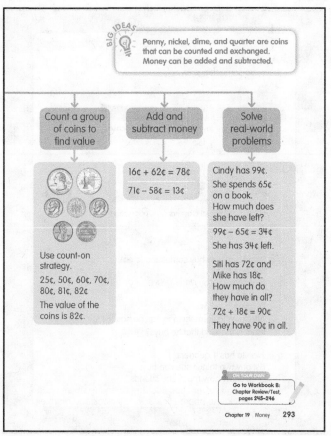

BIG IDEAS
Penny, nickel, dime, and quarter are coins
that can be counted and exchanged.
Money can be added and subtracted.

Count a group
of coins to
find value

Add and
subtract money

Solve
real-world
problems

Use count-on
strategy.
25¢, 50¢, 60¢, 70¢,
80¢, 81¢, 82¢
The value of the
coins is 82¢.

16¢ + 62¢ = 78¢
71¢ − 58¢ = 13¢

Cindy has 99¢.
She spends 65¢
on a book.
How much does
she have left?
99¢ − 65¢ = 34¢
She has 34¢ left.

Siti has 72¢ and
Mike has 18¢.
How much do
they have in all?
72¢ + 18¢ = 90¢
They have 90¢ in all.

ON YOUR OWN
Go to Workbook B:
Chapter Review/Test,
pages 245–246

Chapter 19

Math in Focus
Workbook Answers
Grade 1

Name: _____ Date: _____

1 Numbers to 10

Practice 1 Counting to 10

Count.
Write the numbers.

Example

_2_

1. _3_

2. _7_

3. _10_

Count.
Write the numbers.

4.

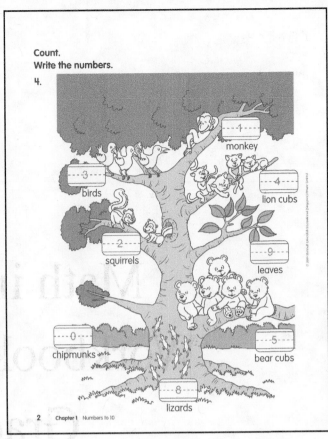

_1_ monkey

_3_ birds

_4_ lion cubs

_2_ squirrels

_9_ leaves

_0_ chipmunks

_5_ bear cubs

_8_ lizards

Name: _____ Date: _____

Draw.

5. A cow has 2 horns.

6. A chair has 4 legs.

7. An ant has 6 legs.

8. Each ladybug has 10 spots.

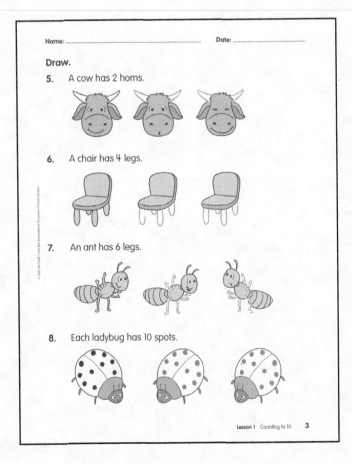

How many insects are there?
Match.

9.

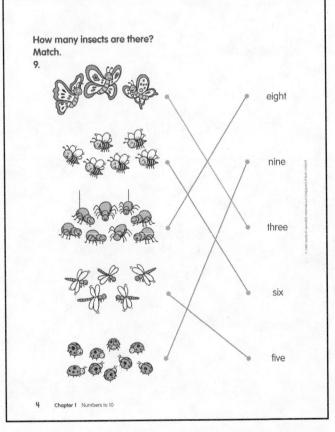

eight

nine

three

six

five

144

Name: _____ Date: _____

Count the things on the snowman.
Circle the correct words.

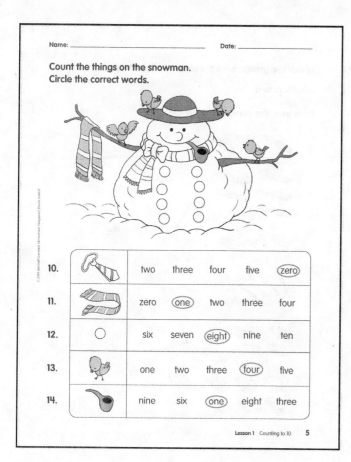

10.	tie image	two	three	four	five	(zero)
11.	scarf image	zero	(one)	two	three	four
12.	button image	six	seven	(eight)	nine	ten
13.	bird image	one	two	three	(four)	five
14.	pipe image	nine	six	(one)	eight	three

Lesson 1 Counting to 10   5

Match the numbers to the words.
15.

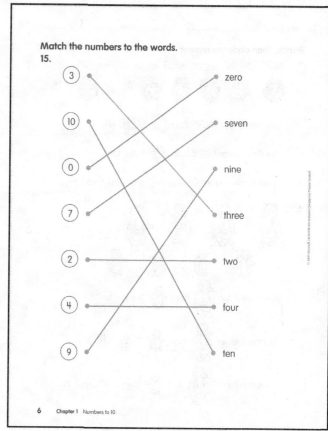

3 — seven
10 — nine
0 — three
7 — zero
2 — two
4 — ten
9 — four

6   Chapter 1   Numbers to 10

Practice 2   Comparing Numbers

Count.
Circle the groups that have the same number.

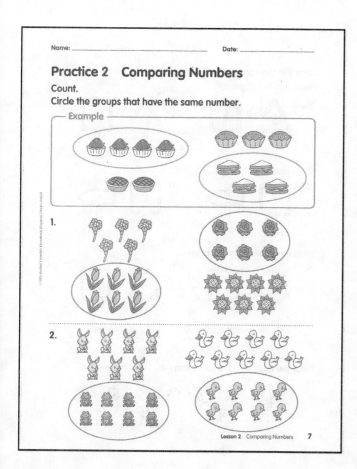

Example

1.

2.

Lesson 2 Comparing Numbers   7

Match. Then circle the answer to each question.

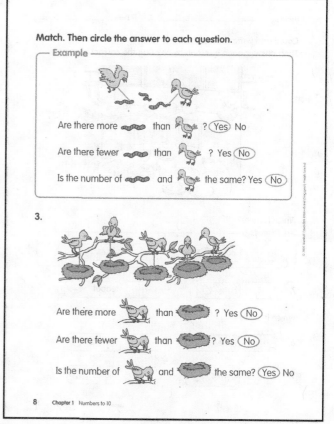

Example

Are there more 🐛 than 🐦? (Yes) No

Are there fewer 🐛 than 🐦? Yes (No)

Is the number of 🐛 and 🐦 the same? Yes (No)

3.

Are there more 🐦 than 🪹? Yes (No)

Are there fewer 🐦 than 🪹? Yes (No)

Is the number of 🐦 and 🪹 the same? (Yes) No

8   Chapter 1   Numbers to 10

Workbook Answers: Chapter 1
Math in Focus Homeschool Answer Key, Grade 1

Page 9

Name: _____ **Date:** _____

Match. Then circle the answer.

4.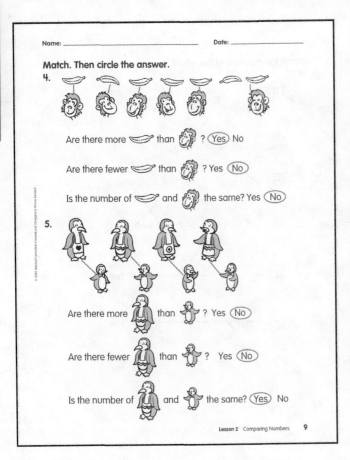

Are there more 🍌 than 🐵 ? (Yes) No

Are there fewer 🍌 than 🐵 ? Yes (No)

Is the number of 🍌 and 🐵 the same? Yes (No)

5.

Are there more 🐧 than 🐧 ? Yes (No)

Are there fewer 🐧 than 🐧 ? Yes (No)

Is the number of 🐧 and 🐧 the same? (Yes) No

Lesson 2 Comparing Numbers **9**

Page 10

Which two groups have the same number of things?

Join them to a -------.

Then write the number in each -------.

6.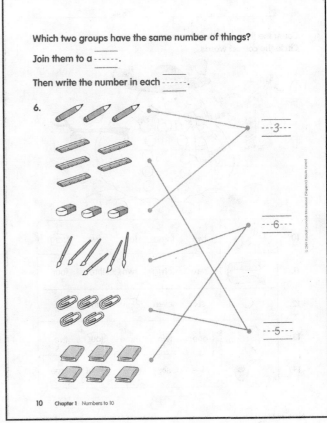

------3------

------6------

------5------

10 Chapter 1 Numbers to 10

Page 11

Name: _____ **Date:** _____

Count and write the number.
Then answer each question by coloring the correct box.

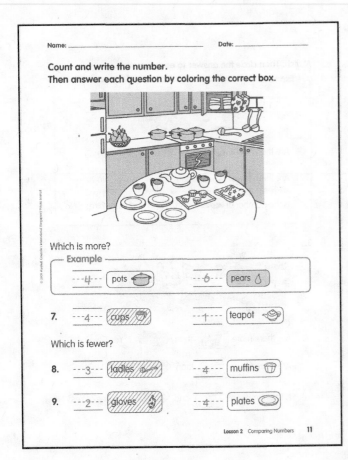

Which is more?

Example

---4--- pots 🍲   ---6--- pears 🍐

7. ---4--- cups 🍵   ---1--- teapot 🫖

Which is fewer?

8. ---3--- ladles 🥄   ---4--- muffins 🧁

9. ---2--- gloves 🧤   ---4--- plates 🍽

Lesson 2 Comparing Numbers **11**

Page 12

Color the correct signs.
Which number is greater?

10. 5 |8| 11. |10| 9

Which number is less?

12. 7 |3| 13. |1| 6

Write the numbers in the blanks.

14. 2 0   15. 9 3

---2--- is greater than ---0---   ---3--- is less than ---9---.

Color the flags with the same number.

16.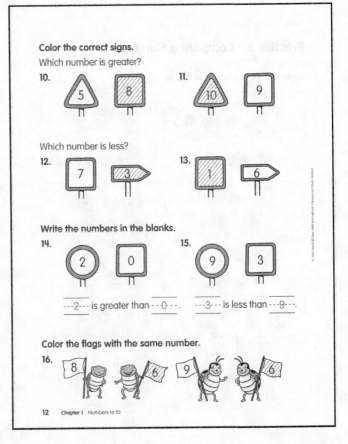

|8| 🐛 🐛 6   9 🐛 🐛 |6|

12 Chapter 1 Numbers to 10

Workbook Answers: Chapter 1
Math in Focus Homeschool Answer Key, Grade 1

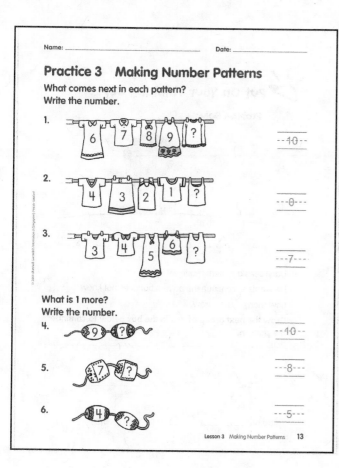

Practice 3   Making Number Patterns

What comes next in each pattern?
Write the number.

1. 6 7 8 9 ? ----10----

2. 4 3 2 1 ? ----0----

3. 3 4 5 6 ? ----7----

What is 1 more?
Write the number.

4. 9 ? ----10----

5. 7 ? ----8----

6. 4 ? ----5----

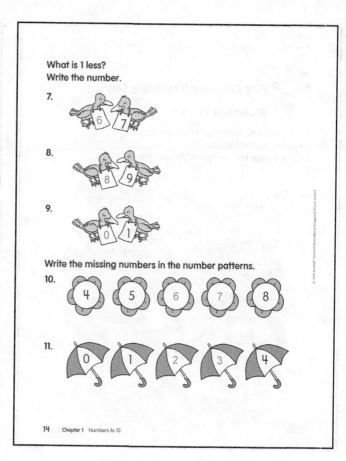

What is 1 less?
Write the number.

7. 6 7

8. 8 9

9. 0 1

Write the missing numbers in the number patterns.

10. 4 5 6 7 8

11. 0 1 2 3 4

Write the missing numbers in the number patterns.

12. 6 7 8 9 10

13. 6 5 4 3 2

14. 3 2 1 0

15. 9 8 7 6 5

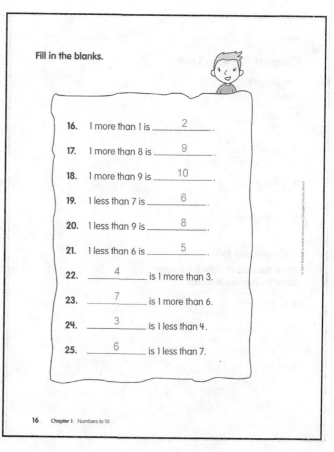

Fill in the blanks.

16. 1 more than 1 is ____2____.

17. 1 more than 8 is ____9____.

18. 1 more than 9 is ____10____.

19. 1 less than 7 is ____6____.

20. 1 less than 9 is ____8____.

21. 1 less than 6 is ____5____.

22. ____4____ is 1 more than 3.

23. ____7____ is 1 more than 6.

24. ____3____ is 1 less than 4.

25. ____6____ is 1 less than 7.

147

Workbook Answers: Chapter 1
Math in Focus Homeschool Answer Key, Grade 1

Name: _____ Date: _____

Put On Your Thinking Cap!

Challenging Practice

Mother Hen's eggs have numbers that are
greater than 2 and less than 8.
Color the eggs that belong to Mother Hen.

Chapter 1 Numbers to 10   17

Name: _____ Date: _____

Put On Your Thinking Cap!

Problem Solving

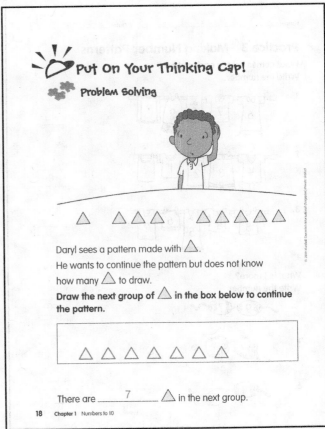

Daryl sees a pattern made with △.

He wants to continue the pattern but does not know

how many △ to draw.

**Draw the next group of △ in the box below to continue
the pattern.**

△ △ △ △ △ △ △

There are _____7_____ △ in the next group.

18   Chapter 1 Numbers to 10

Chapter Review/Test

Vocabulary

Match.

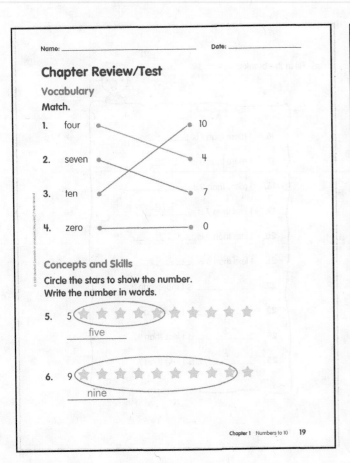

1. four — 10
2. seven — 4
3. ten — 7
4. zero — 0

(matches: four → 4, seven → 7, ten → 10, zero → 0)

Concepts and Skills

Circle the stars to show the number.
Write the number in words.

5. 5   ★★★★★ ★ ★ ★ ★ ★
   five

6. 9   ★★★★★★★★★ ★
   nine

Chapter 1 Numbers to 10   19

Fill in the blanks with *greater than, less than or the same as.*

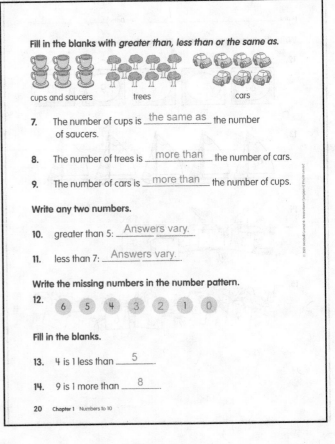

cups and saucers   trees   cars

7. The number of cups is ___the same as___ the number
   of saucers.

8. The number of trees is ___more than___ the number of cars.

9. The number of cars is ___more than___ the number of cups.

Write any two numbers.

10. greater than 5: _Answers vary._

11. less than 7: _Answers vary._

Write the missing numbers in the number pattern.

12. 6 5 4 3 2 1 0

Fill in the blanks.

13. 4 is 1 less than ___5___

14. 9 is 1 more than ___8___

20   Chapter 1 Numbers to 10

Workbook Answers: Chapter 1
Math in Focus Homeschool Answer Key, Grade 1

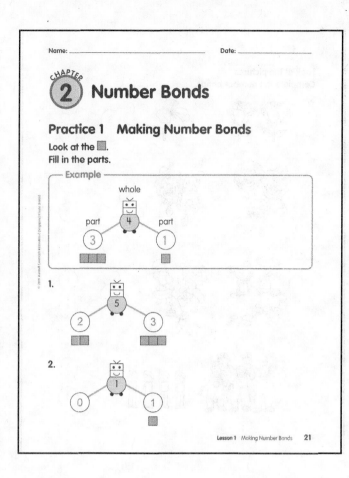

CHAPTER 2 Number Bonds

Practice 1 Making Number Bonds

Look at the ☐.
Fill in the parts.

Example

whole
part 4 part
3 · · 1

1. 5 / 2 · · 3
2. 1 / 0 · · 1

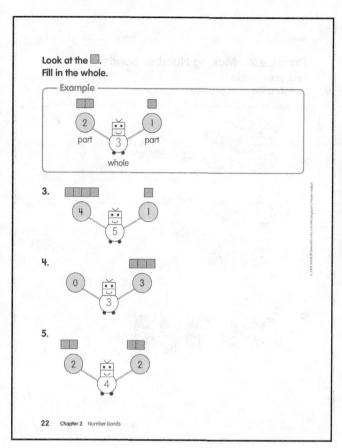

Look at the ☐.
Fill in the whole.

Example
2 part · 3 · 1 part
whole

3. 4 · 5 · 1
4. 0 · 3 · 3
5. 2 · 4 · 2

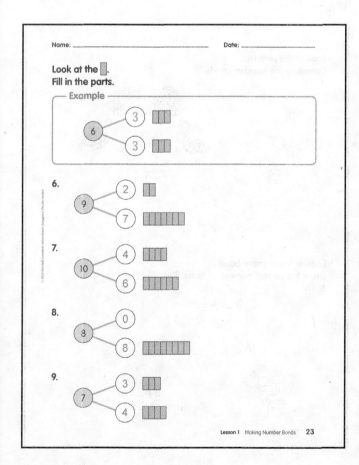

Look at the ☐.
Fill in the parts.

Example
6 — 3
— 3

6. 9 — 2
— 7
7. 10 — 4
— 6
8. 8 — 0
— 8
9. 7 — 3
— 4

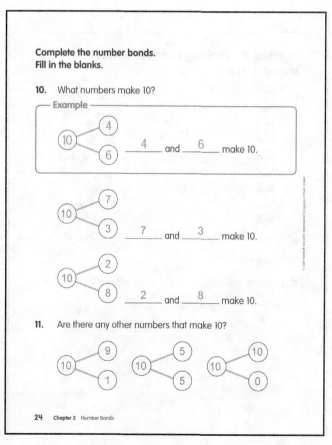

Complete the number bonds.
Fill in the blanks.

10. What numbers make 10?

Example
10 — 4
— 6
___4___ and ___6___ make 10.

10 — 7
— 3
___7___ and ___3___ make 10.

10 — 2
— 8
___2___ and ___8___ make 10.

11. Are there any other numbers that make 10?

10 — 9
— 1
10 — 5
— 5
10 — 10
— 0

Practice 2   Making Number Bonds

Look at the pictures.
Complete the number bonds.

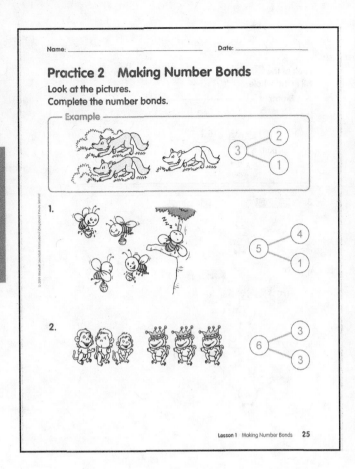

Name: _____   Date: _____

Example

1.

2.

Look at the pictures.
Complete the number bonds.

3.

4.

5.

6.

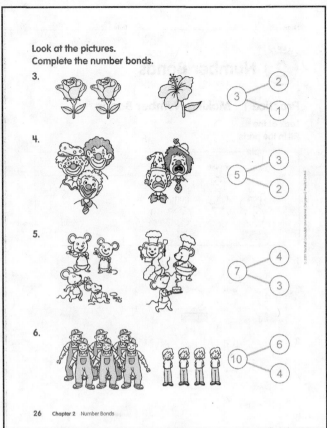

Practice 3   Making Number Bonds

Match to make 8.

Name: _____   Date: _____

1.

Match the numbers.

2. Match to make 6.   3. Match to make 9.

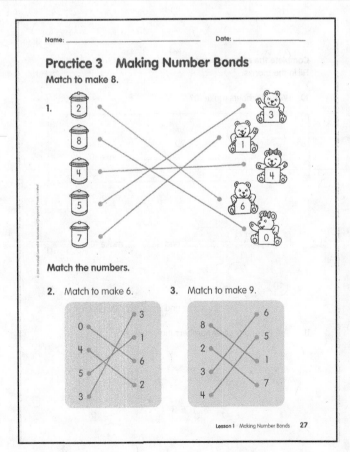

Look at the picture.
Complete the number bonds.
4.

Look at the number bond.
Draw the correct number of butterflies.
5.

Two butterflies   Two butterflies

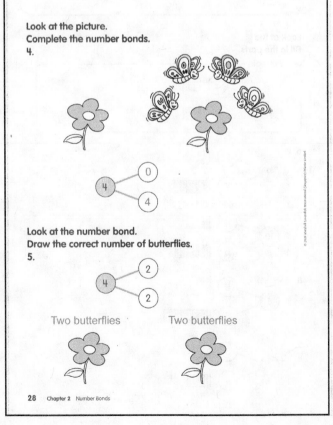

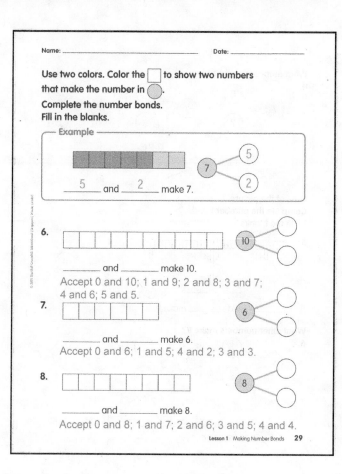

Name: _____ Date: _____

Use two colors. Color the ☐ to show two numbers
that make the number in ◯.
Complete the number bonds.
Fill in the blanks.

Example

__5__ and __2__ make 7.

7 → 5, 2

6.

_____ and _____ make 10.
Accept 0 and 10; 1 and 9; 2 and 8; 3 and 7;
4 and 6; 5 and 5.

10

7.

_____ and _____ make 6.
Accept 0 and 6; 1 and 5; 4 and 2; 3 and 3.

6

8.

_____ and _____ make 8.
Accept 0 and 8; 1 and 7; 2 and 6; 3 and 5; 4 and 4.

8

Lesson 1 Making Number Bonds **29**

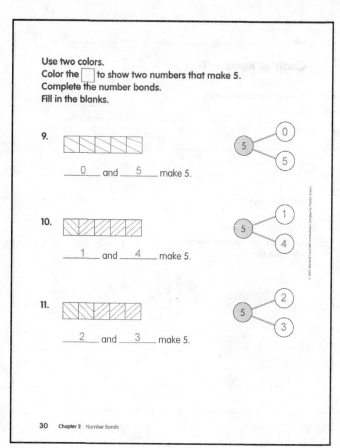

Use two colors.
Color the ☐ to show two numbers that make 5.
Complete the number bonds.
Fill in the blanks.

9.

__0__ and __5__ make 5.

5 → 0, 5

10.

__1__ and __4__ make 5.

5 → 1, 4

11.

__2__ and __3__ make 5.

5 → 2, 3

30 Chapter 2 Number Bonds

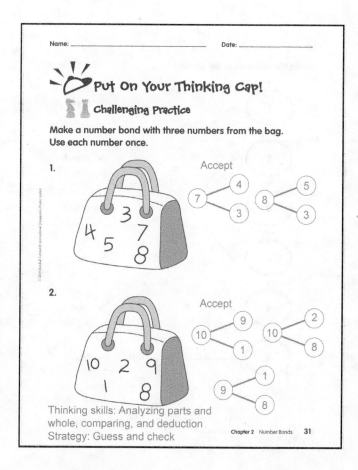

Name: _____ Date: _____

Put On Your Thinking Cap!

Challenging Practice

Make a number bond with three numbers from the bag.
Use each number once.

1.

3 4 5 7 8

Accept

7 → 4, 3   8 → 5, 3

2.

10 2 9 1 8

Accept

10 → 9, 1   10 → 2, 8

9 → 1, 8

Thinking skills: Analyzing parts and
whole, comparing, and deduction
Strategy: Guess and check

Chapter 2 Number Bonds **31**

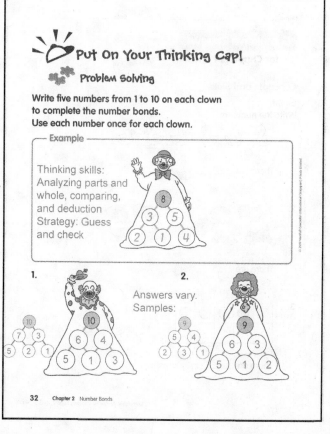

Put On Your Thinking Cap!

Problem Solving

Write five numbers from 1 to 10 on each clown
to complete the number bonds.
Use each number once for each clown.

Example

Thinking skills:
Analyzing parts and
whole, comparing,
and deduction
Strategy: Guess
and check

8
3 5
2 1 4

1.

10
6 4
5 1 3

10
7 3
5 2 1

2.

Answers vary.
Samples:

9
6 3
5 1 2

9
5 4
2 3 1

32 Chapter 2 Number Bonds

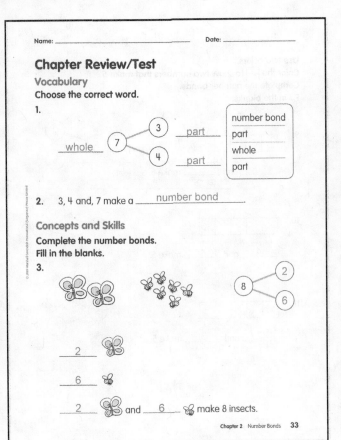

Chapter Review/Test

Vocabulary
Choose the correct word.

1.

whole 7 — 3 part
        — 4 part

number bond
part
whole
part

2. 3, 4 and, 7 make a ___number bond___

Concepts and Skills
Complete the number bonds.
Fill in the blanks.

3.

8 — 2
    6

__2__ 🦋
__6__ 🐝
__2__ 🦋 and __6__ 🐝 make 8 insects.

Chapter 2   Number Bonds   33

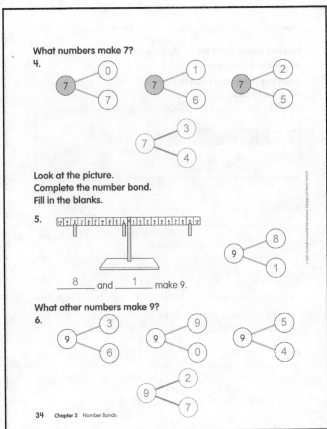

What numbers make 7?

4.

7 — 0 / 7   7 — 1 / 6   7 — 2 / 5

7 — 3 / 4

Look at the picture.
Complete the number bond.
Fill in the blanks.

5.

__8__ and __1__ make 9.

9 — 8 / 1

What other numbers make 9?

6.

9 — 3 / 6   9 — 9 / 0   9 — 5 / 4

9 — 2 / 7

34   Chapter 2   Number Bonds

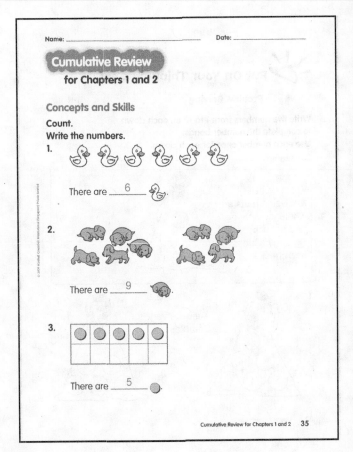

Cumulative Review
for Chapters 1 and 2

Concepts and Skills
Count.
Write the numbers.

1.

There are __6__ 🦆.

2.

There are __9__ 🐕.

3.

There are __5__ ⬤.

Cumulative Review for Chapters 1 and 2   35

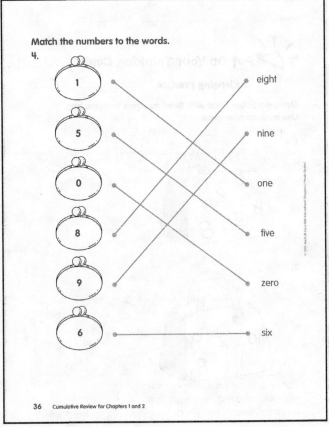

Match the numbers to the words.

4.

1 — one
5 — zero
0 — eight
8 — nine
9 — five
6 — six

36   Cumulative Review for Chapters 1 and 2

Workbook Answers: Chapters 1-2 Review
Math in Focus Homeschool Answer Key, Grade 1

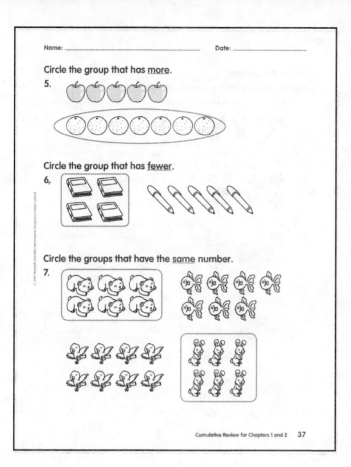

Name: _____ Date: _____

Circle the group that has **more**.

5.

Circle the group that has **fewer**.

6.

Circle the groups that have the **same** number.

7.

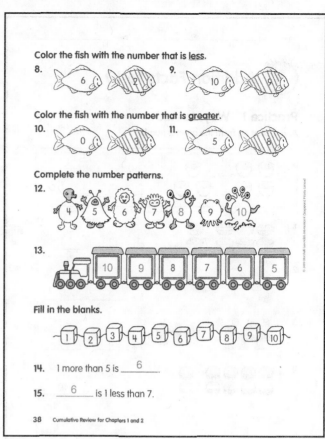

Color the fish with the number that is **less**.

8.   6   2   9.   10   9

Color the fish with the number that is **greater**.

10.   0   3   11.   5   8

Complete the number patterns.

12.   4   5   6   7   8   9   10

13.   10   9   8   7   6   5

Fill in the blanks.

1   2   3   4   5   6   7   8   9   10

14.   1 more than 5 is _____6_____.

15.   ____6____ is 1 less than 7.

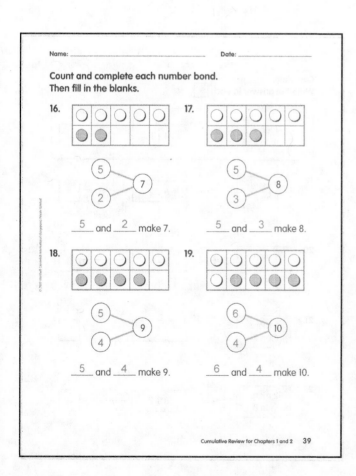

Name: _____ Date: _____

Count and complete each number bond.
Then fill in the blanks.

16.

5
2   7

__5__ and __2__ make 7.

17.

5
3   8

__5__ and __3__ make 8.

18.

5
4   9

__5__ and __4__ make 9.

19.

6
4   10

__6__ and __4__ make 10.

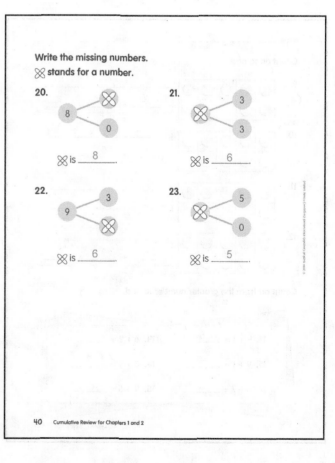

Write the missing numbers.
�֎ stands for a number.

20.

8   �֎
0

✖ is ____8____.

21.

✖   3
3

✖ is ____6____.

22.

9   3
✖

✖ is ____6____.

23.

✖   5
0

✖ is ____5____.

153

Workbook Answers: Chapters 1-2 Review
Math in Focus Homeschool Answer Key, Grade 1

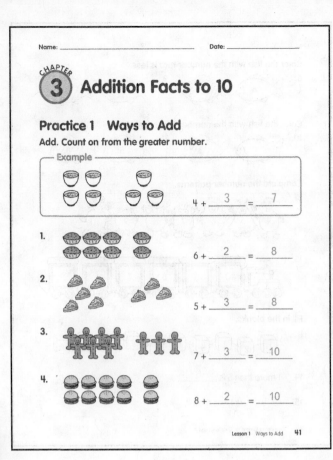

Name: _____ Date: _____

3 Addition Facts to 10

Practice 1 Ways to Add

Add. Count on from the greater number.

Example

$4 + \underline{3} = \underline{7}$

1. $6 + \underline{2} = \underline{8}$

2. $5 + \underline{3} = \underline{8}$

3. $7 + \underline{3} = \underline{10}$

4. $8 + \underline{2} = \underline{10}$

Lesson 1 Ways to Add 41

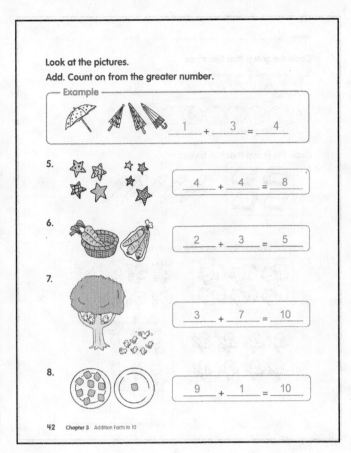

Look at the pictures.
Add. Count on from the greater number.

Example

$\underline{1} + \underline{3} = \underline{4}$

5. $\underline{4} + \underline{4} = \underline{8}$

6. $\underline{2} + \underline{3} = \underline{5}$

7. $\underline{3} + \underline{7} = \underline{10}$

8. $\underline{9} + \underline{1} = \underline{10}$

42 Chapter 3 Addition Facts to 10

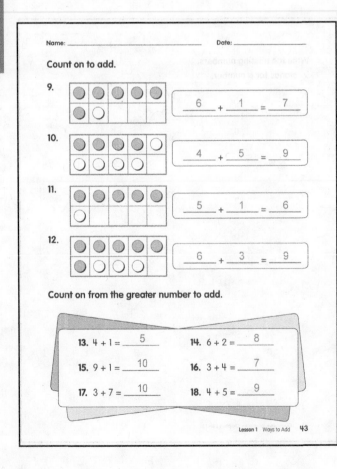

Name: _____ Date: _____

Count on to add.

9. $\underline{6} + \underline{1} = \underline{7}$

10. $\underline{4} + \underline{5} = \underline{9}$

11. $\underline{5} + \underline{1} = \underline{6}$

12. $\underline{6} + \underline{3} = \underline{9}$

Count on from the greater number to add.

13. $4 + 1 = \underline{5}$ 14. $6 + 2 = \underline{8}$

15. $9 + 1 = \underline{10}$ 16. $3 + 4 = \underline{7}$

17. $3 + 7 = \underline{10}$ 18. $4 + 5 = \underline{9}$

Lesson 1 Ways to Add 43

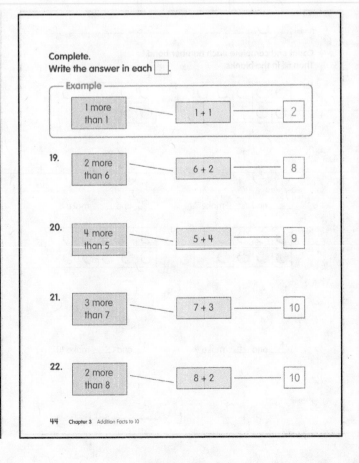

Complete.
Write the answer in each ☐.

Example

| 1 more than 1 | 1 + 1 | 2 |

19. | 2 more than 6 | 6 + 2 | 8 |

20. | 4 more than 5 | 5 + 4 | 9 |

21. | 3 more than 7 | 7 + 3 | 10 |

22. | 2 more than 8 | 8 + 2 | 10 |

44 Chapter 3 Addition Facts to 10

Practice 2   Ways to Add
Complete the number bonds.
Then fill in the blanks.

Example

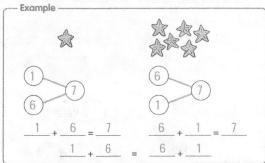

Number bond: 1, 6 → 7

$$\underline{1} + \underline{6} = \underline{7}$$
$$\underline{1} + \underline{6} = $$

Number bond: 6, 1 → 7

$$\underline{6} + \underline{1} = \underline{7}$$
$$\underline{6} + \underline{1}$$

1.

Number bond: 8, 2 → 10

$$\underline{8} + \underline{2} = \underline{10}$$
$$\underline{8} + \underline{2} = $$

Number bond: 2, 8 → 10

$$\underline{2} + \underline{8} = \underline{10}$$
$$\underline{2} + \underline{8}$$

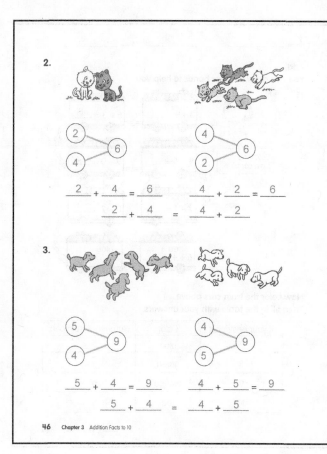

2.

Number bond: 2, 4 → 6

$$\underline{2} + \underline{4} = \underline{6}$$
$$\underline{2} + \underline{4} = $$

Number bond: 4, 2 → 6

$$\underline{4} + \underline{2} = \underline{}$$
$$\underline{4} + \underline{2}$$

3.

Number bond: 5, 4 → 9

$$\underline{5} + \underline{4} = \underline{9}$$
$$\underline{5} + \underline{4} = $$

Number bond: 4, 5 → 9

$$\underline{4} + \underline{5} = \underline{9}$$
$$\underline{4} + \underline{5}$$

Complete the number bonds.
Then fill in the blanks.

4. $1 + \underline{4} = 5$ Number bond: 1, 4 → 5

5. $4 + \underline{1} = 5$ Number bond: 4, 1 → 5

6. $\underline{3} + 5 = 8$ Number bond: 3, 5 → 8

7. $\underline{5} + 3 = 8$ Number bond: 5, 3 → 8

8. $10 + \underline{0} = 10$ Number bond: 10, 0 → 10

9. $\underline{0} + 10 = 10$ Number bond: 0, 10 → 10

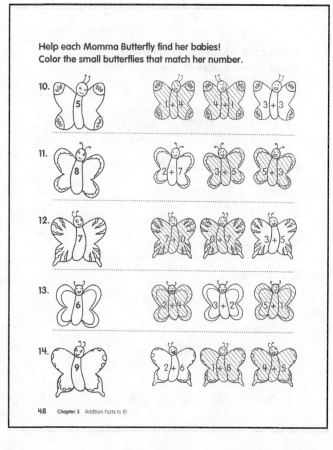

Help each Momma Butterfly find her babies!
Color the small butterflies that match her number.

10. 5 — $1+4$, $4+1$, $3+3$

11. 8 — $2+7$, $3+5$, $5+3$

12. 7 — $7+0$, $0+7$, $3+5$

13. 6 — $2+4$, $3+2$, $5+1$

14. 9 — $2+6$, $1+8$, $4+5$

Name: _____ Date: _____

Add.
You can draw number bonds to help you.
15.

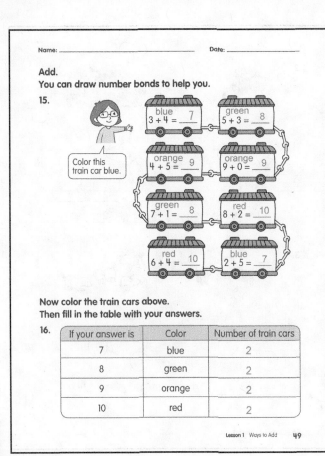

Color this train car blue.

blue
3 + 4 = 7

green
5 + 3 = 8

orange
4 + 5 = 9

orange
9 + 0 = 9

green
7 + 1 = 8

red
8 + 2 = 10

red
6 + 4 = 10

blue
2 + 5 = 7

Now color the train cars above.
Then fill in the table with your answers.

16.

If your answer is	Color	Number of train cars
7	blue	2
8	green	2
9	orange	2
10	red	2

Solve.
17. A ball falls into the number machine.
Which ball is it?
Write the correct number on the ball below.

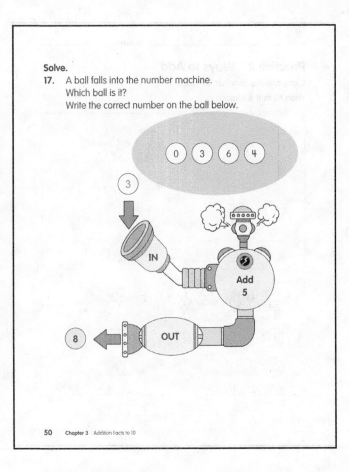

0 3 6 4

3

IN

Add 5

OUT

8

Name: _____ Date: _____

Practice 3   Making Addition Stories
Use the pictures to make addition stories.
Use number bonds to help you.

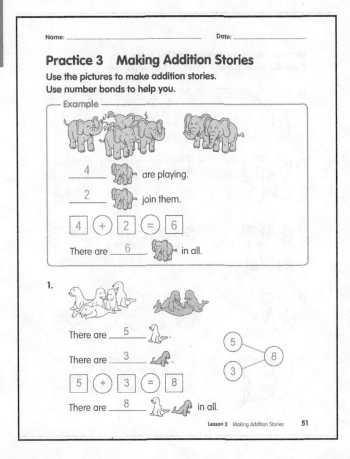

Example

_____4_____ are playing.

_____2_____ join them.

4 + 2 = 6

There are _____6_____ in all.

1.

There are _____5_____ .

There are _____3_____ .

5 + 3 = 8

There are _____8_____ in all.

5
3
8

2.

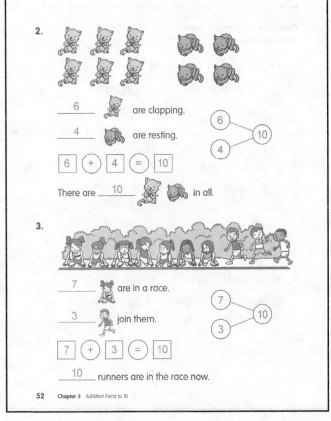

_____6_____ are clapping.

_____4_____ are resting.

6 + 4 = 10

There are _____10_____ in all.

6
4
10

3.

_____7_____ are in a race.

_____3_____ join them.

7 + 3 = 10

_____10_____ runners are in the race now.

7
3
10

156

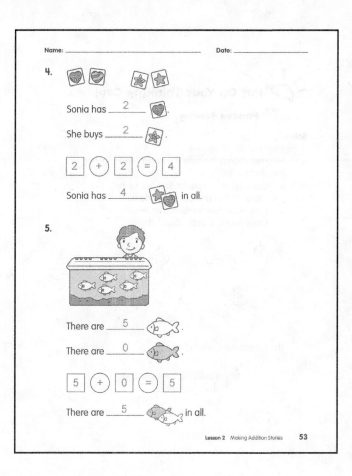

Name: _____ Date: _____

4.

Sonia has ___2___ .

She buys ___2___ .

| 2 | + | 2 | = | 4 |

Sonia has ___4___ in all.

5.

There are ___5___ .

There are ___0___ .

| 5 | + | 0 | = | 5 |

There are ___5___ in all.

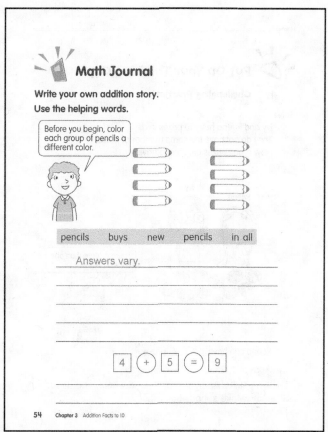

Math Journal

Write your own addition story.
Use the helping words.

Before you begin, color each group of pencils a different color.

| pencils | buys | new | pencils | in all |

Answers vary.

_____

_____

_____

| 4 | + | 5 | = | 9 |

_____

Chapter 3

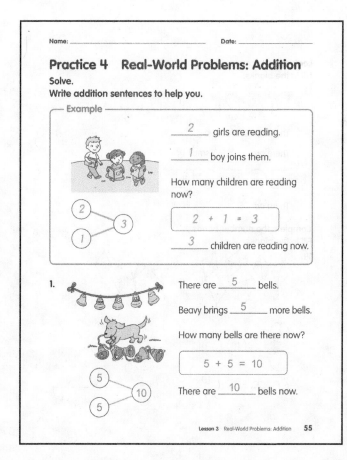

Name: _____ Date: _____

Practice 4   Real-World Problems: Addition
Solve.
Write addition sentences to help you.

Example

___2___ girls are reading.

___1___ boy joins them.

How many children are reading now?

| 2 | + | 1 | = | 3 |

___3___ children are reading now.

1.

There are ___5___ bells.

Beavy brings ___5___ more bells.

How many bells are there now?

| 5 | + | 5 | = | 10 |

There are ___10___ bells now.

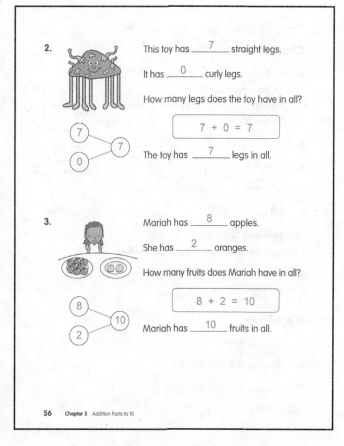

2.

This toy has ___7___ straight legs.

It has ___0___ curly legs.

How many legs does the toy have in all?

| 7 + 0 = 7 |

The toy has ___7___ legs in all.

3.

Mariah has ___8___ apples.

She has ___2___ oranges.

How many fruits does Mariah have in all?

| 8 + 2 = 10 |

Mariah has ___10___ fruits in all.

Name: _____ Date: _____

Put On Your Thinking Cap!
Challenging Practice

Solve.

Ivy and Reena have 10 prizes in all.
They do not have the same number of prizes.
How many prizes can Reena have?

Reena   Ivy

There is more than one
correct answer!

Reena can have _____ prizes.

Accept 1; 2; 3; 4; 6; 7; 8; 9.

Thinking skills: Analyzing parts and whole, and deduction
Strategy: Make suppositions

Chapter 3   Addition Facts to 10   **57**

Name: _____ Date: _____

Put On Your Thinking Cap!
Problem Solving

Solve.

Lilian has these candles.
Help her choose the correct number candle for her
friend's birthday.

- Cross out two numbers that add up to 5.
- Cross out two numbers that add up to 10.
- Look at the two numbers that are left.
  Cross out the number that is the less.

2   4   6

3   5   7

The correct number candle is _____7_____.

Thinking skill: Analizing parts and whole,
                 and deduction
Strategy: Act it out

58   Chapter 3   Addition Facts to 10

Name: _____ Date: _____

Chapter Review/Test

Vocabulary

Choose the correct word.

1. You can ____add____ by counting on from
   the greater number.

2. 2 + 3 = 5 is an ___addition sentence___

3. 3 plus 4 is ___equal to___ 7.

4. "+" is read as ___plus___

5. 6 is 2 ___more than___ 4.

plus
add
equal to
more than
addition sentence

Concepts and Skills

Add by counting on from the greater number.

6. 3 + 6 = ___9___   7. 7 + 1 = ___8___

8. 2 + 8 = ___10___   9. 1 + 9 = ___10___

Fill in the blanks.

10. ___9___ is 3 more than 6.

11. ___7___ is 2 more than 5.

12. ___8___ is 4 more than 4.

Chapter 3   Addition Facts to 10   **59**

Look at the pictures.
Fill in the blanks.

13.

There are ___2___ big .

There are ___6___ small .

2	+	6	=	8

There are ___8___ in all.

Complete the number bonds.
Fill in the blanks.

14.

6 + ___4___ = ___10___   4 + ___6___ = ___10___

6 + 4 = 4 + ___6___

60   Chapter 3   Addition Facts to 10

Workbook Answers: Chapter 3
Math in Focus Homeschool Answer Key, Grade 1

Problem Solving

Solve.

15. Carlos has 3 brown belts.
    He has 2 black belts.
    How many belts does he have in all?

◐	○	○	●	●

    3 + 2 = _____5_____

    Carlos has _____5_____ belts in all.

16. Jane has 4 bows.
    She gets 3 more bows.
    How many bows does she have now?

◐	○	○	○	●
●	●			

    4 + 3 = _____7_____

    Jane has _____7_____ bows now.

Draw ◐.
Then solve.

17. How many toys are there in all?

○	○	○	○	○
○	○	○		

    3 + _____5_____ = _____8_____

    There are _____8_____ toys in all.

Look at the ▭▭▭▭▭ in question 17 to answer the questions.

Circle the correct answer.

18. a. Are there more 🦆 or more 🧸?
    There are more (🦆 🧸).

    b. How many more?

    5 is [3] (2) more than 3.

Chapter 3

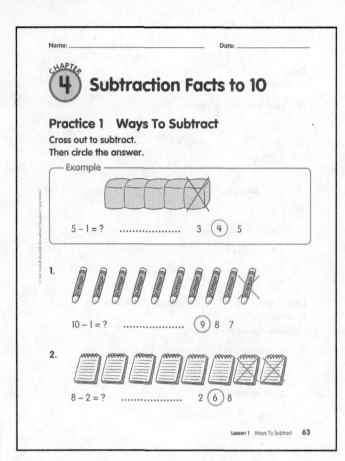

Name: _____ Date: _____

CHAPTER 4 Subtraction Facts to 10

Practice 1 Ways To Subtract

Cross out to subtract.
Then circle the answer.

┌─ Example ──────────────────────────────┐
│   │
│   5 – 1 = ? .... 3 ④ 5   │
└──┘

1.

10 – 1 = ? .... ⑨ 8 7

2.

8 – 2 = ? .... 2 ⑥ 8

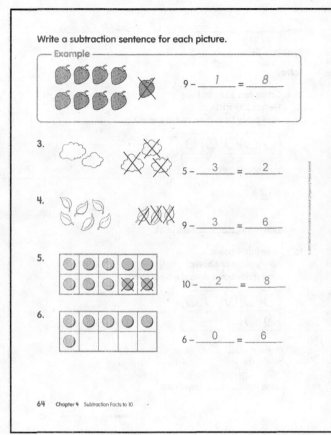

Write a subtraction sentence for each picture.

┌─ Example ──────────────────────────────┐
│   │
│   9 – __1__ = __8__   │
└──┘

3.

5 – __3__ = __2__

4.

9 – __3__ = __6__

5.

10 – __2__ = __8__

6.

6 – __0__ = __6__

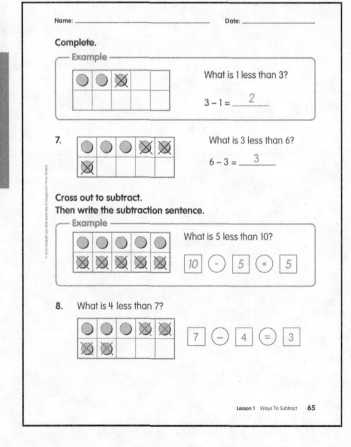

Name: _____ Date: _____

Complete.

┌─ Example ──────────────────────────────┐
│   What is 1 less than 3? │
│   3 – 1 = __2__   │
└──┘

7.   What is 3 less than 6?
                      6 – 3 = __3__

Cross out to subtract.
Then write the subtraction sentence.

┌─ Example ──────────────────────────────┐
│   What is 5 less than 10? │
│   10 – 5 = 5   │
└──┘

8. What is 4 less than 7?

    7 – 4 = 3

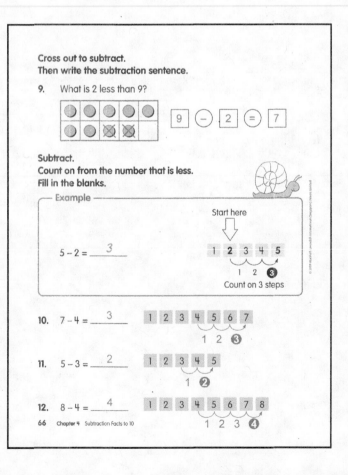

Cross out to subtract.
Then write the subtraction sentence.

9. What is 2 less than 9?

    9 – 2 = 7

Subtract.
Count on from the number that is less.
Fill in the blanks.

┌─ Example ──────────────────────────────┐
│   Start here   │
│   │
│   5 – 2 = __3__   1 2 3 4 5   │
│   1 2 ③   │
│   Count on 3 steps   │
└──┘

10. 7 – 4 = __3__   1 2 3 4 5 6 7
                        1 2 ③

11. 5 – 3 = __2__   1 2 3 4 5
                        1 ②

12. 8 – 4 = __4__   1 2 3 4 5 6 7 8
                        1 2 3 ④

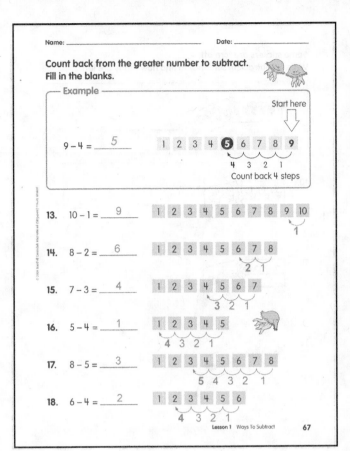

Name: _____ **Date:** _____

Count back from the greater number to subtract.
Fill in the blanks.

Example

9 − 4 = __5__   1 2 3 4 **5** 6 7 8 **9**
                     4 3 2 1
                Count back 4 steps

13. 10 − 1 = __9__   1 2 3 4 5 6 7 8 9 10
                                          1

14. 8 − 2 = __6__   1 2 3 4 5 6 7 8
                                 2 1

15. 7 − 3 = __4__   1 2 3 4 5 6 7
                            3 2 1

16. 5 − 4 = __1__   1 2 3 4 5
                    4 3 2 1

17. 8 − 5 = __3__   1 2 3 4 5 6 7 8
                        5 4 3 2 1

18. 6 − 4 = __2__   1 2 3 4 5 6
                    4 3 2 1

Lesson 1 Ways To Subtract   67

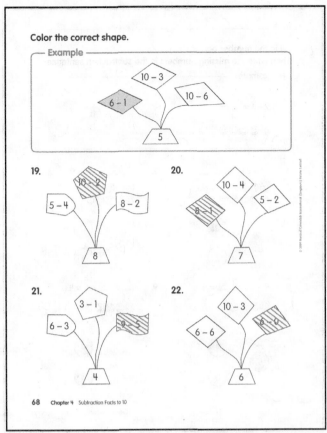

Color the correct shape.

Example

10 − 3   **6 − 1**   10 − 6

5

19.   10 − 2
       5 − 4   8 − 2
       8

20.   10 − 4
       8 − 1   5 − 2
       7

21.   3 − 1
       6 − 3   9 − 5
       4

22.   10 − 3
       6 − 6   6 − 0
       6

68   Chapter 4   Subtraction Facts to 10

Name: _____ **Date:** _____

Practice 2   Ways To Subtract

Fill in each number bond.
Then complete the subtraction sentence.

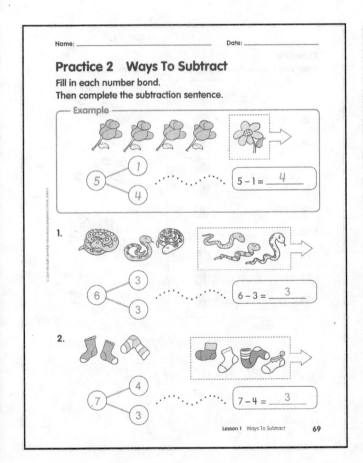

Example

5 — 1 / 4   5 − 1 = __4__

1. 6 — 3 / 3   6 − 3 = __3__

2. 7 — 4 / 3   7 − 4 = __3__

Lesson 1 Ways To Subtract   69

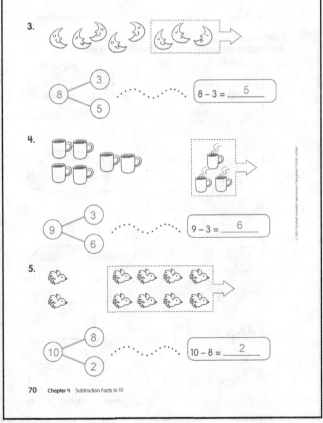

3. 8 — 3 / 5   8 − 3 = __5__

4. 9 — 3 / 6   9 − 3 = __6__

5. 10 — 8 / 2   10 − 8 = __2__

70   Chapter 4   Subtraction Facts to 10

Name: _____ Date: _____

Fill in the number bonds.
Then write the missing numbers in the subtraction sentences.

Example

$7 - 1 =$ _6_

⊘😊😊😊😊😊😊

(7) — (1)
(6)

6. $10 - 3 =$ _7_

⊘⊘⊘😊😊
😊😊😊😊😊

(10) — (3)
(7)

7. _10_ $- 1 = 9$

⊘😊😊😊😊
😊😊😊😊😊

(10) — (9)
(1)

8. $4 -$ _0_ $= 4$

😊😊😊😊

(4) — (4)
(0)

9. _9_ $- 5 = 4$

⊘⊘⊘⊘⊘
😊😊😊😊

(9) — (4)
(5)

Some stickers are torn off.
Write a subtraction sentence to find how many are left.

Example

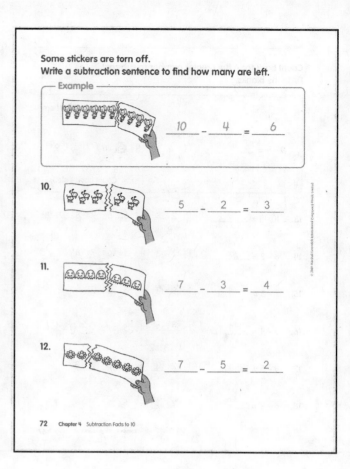

_10_ $-$ _4_ $=$ _6_

10.

_5_ $-$ _2_ $=$ _3_

11.

_7_ $-$ _3_ $=$ _4_

12.

_7_ $-$ _5_ $=$ _2_

Name: _____ Date: _____

Subtract.
Then match the answers to show where each animal lives.

13. **Example**

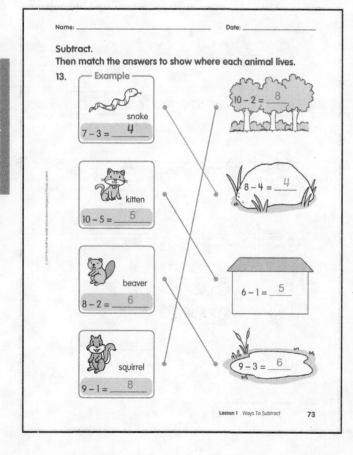

snake
$7 - 3 =$ _4_

$10 - 2 =$ _8_

kitten
$10 - 5 =$ _5_

$8 - 4 =$ _4_

beaver
$8 - 2 =$ _6_

$6 - 1 =$ _5_

squirrel
$9 - 1 =$ _8_

$9 - 3 =$ _6_

Complete.
Then write the letters in the correct ☐ to solve the riddle.

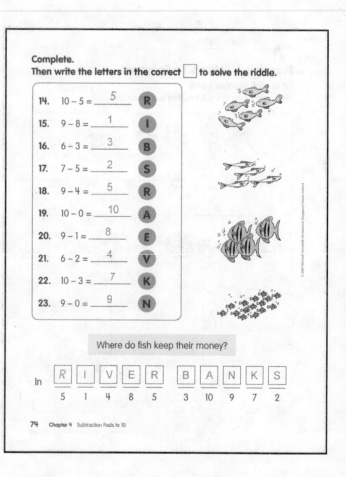

14. $10 - 5 =$ _5_ (R)
15. $9 - 8 =$ _1_ (I)
16. $6 - 3 =$ _3_ (B)
17. $7 - 5 =$ _2_ (S)
18. $9 - 4 =$ _5_ (R)
19. $10 - 0 =$ _10_ (A)
20. $9 - 1 =$ _8_ (E)
21. $6 - 2 =$ _4_ (V)
22. $10 - 3 =$ _7_ (K)
23. $9 - 0 =$ _9_ (N)

Where do fish keep their money?

In | R | I | V | E | R | | B | A | N | K | S |
   | 5 | 1 | 4 | 8 | 5 | | 3 | 10 | 9 | 7 | 2 |

162

Practice 3   Making Subtraction Stories

Look at the pictures.
Make subtraction stories.
Write subtraction sentences for each story.

Example

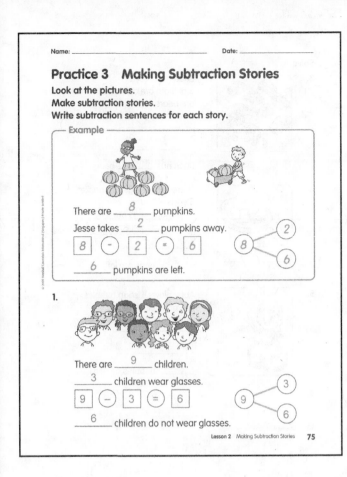

There are ___8___ pumpkins.
Jesse takes ___2___ pumpkins away.

$8 - 2 = 6$

8 — 2
        6

___6___ pumpkins are left.

1.

There are ___9___ children.
___3___ children wear glasses.

$9 - 3 = 6$

9 — 3
        6

___6___ children do not wear glasses.

Lesson 2   Making Subtraction Stories   **75**

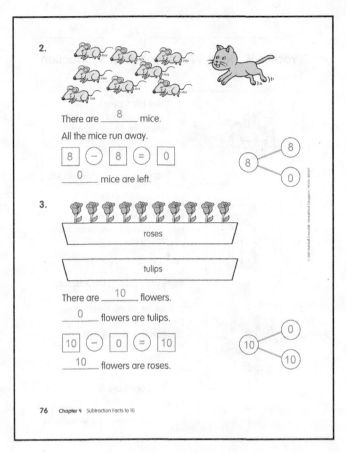

2.

There are ___8___ mice.
All the mice run away.

$8 - 8 = 0$

8 — 8
        0

___0___ mice are left.

3.

roses

tulips

There are ___10___ flowers.
___0___ flowers are tulips.

$10 - 0 = 10$

10 — 0
        10

___10___ flowers are roses.

76   Chapter 4   Subtraction Facts to 10

4.

Lola has ___9___ crayons.

She gives ___7___ crayons to Pete.

$9 - 7 = 2$

Lola has ___2___ crayons left.

Lesson 2   Making Subtraction Stories   **77**

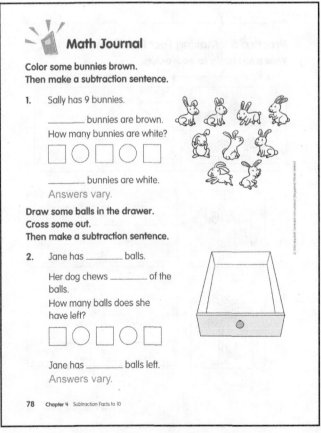

Math Journal

Color some bunnies brown.
Then make a subtraction sentence.

1.   Sally has 9 bunnies.

_____ bunnies are brown.
How many bunnies are white?

☐ ◯ ☐ ◯ ☐

_____ bunnies are white.
Answers vary.

Draw some balls in the drawer.
Cross some out.
Then make a subtraction sentence.

2.   Jane has _____ balls.

Her dog chews _____ of the balls.

How many balls does she have left?

☐ ◯ ☐ ◯ ☐

Jane has _____ balls left.
Answers vary.

78   Chapter 4   Subtraction Facts to 10

Chapter 4

Workbook Answers: Chapter 4
Math in Focus Homeschool Answer Key, Grade 1

Practice 4   Real-World Problems: Subtraction
Solve.

— Example —

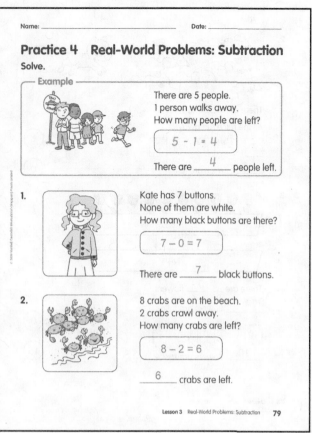

There are 5 people.
1 person walks away.
How many people are left?

$5 - 1 = 4$

There are ____4____ people left.

1.

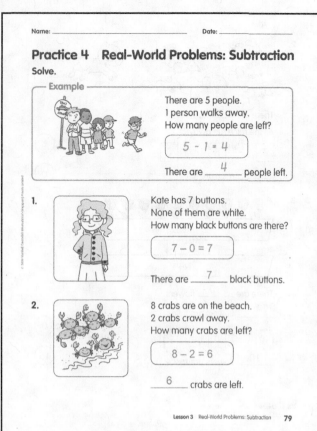

Kate has 7 buttons.
None of them are white.
How many black buttons are there?

$7 - 0 = 7$

There are ____7____ black buttons.

2.

8 crabs are on the beach.
2 crabs crawl away.
How many crabs are left?

$8 - 2 = 6$

____6____ crabs are left.

Solve.

3.

Brian has 9 toys.
6 of them are cars and the rest
are bears.
How many bears does Brian have?

$9 - 6 = 3$

Brian has ____3____ bears.

4.

There are 10 eggs in a basket.
3 eggs roll out.
How many eggs are left?

$10 - 3 = 7$

____7____ eggs are left.

5.

Abby blows 4 soap bubbles.
She pops all of them.
How many bubbles are left?

$4 - 4 = 0$

____0____ bubbles are left.

Practice 5   Making Fact Families
Write a fact family for each picture.

— Example —

big dolphin

small dolphins

1	+	2	= 3
2	+	1	= 3
3	−	1	= 2
3	−	2	= 1

1.

4	+	3	= 7
3	+	4	= 7
7	−	3	= 4
7	−	4	= 3

2.

6	+	3	= 9
3	+	6	= 9
9	−	3	= 6
9	−	6	= 3

Solve.
Use related facts to help you.

3. Simone has some tomatoes.
She throws away 5 rotten tomatoes.
She has 4 tomatoes left.
How many tomatoes did she have at first?

$\boxed{9} - 5 = 4$

$5 + 4 = \boxed{9}$ is the related addition fact.

She had ____9____ tomatoes at first.

4. Marcus has 6 magnets.
Susan gives him some magnets.
Marcus now has 9 magnets.
How many magnets did Susan give Marcus?

$6 + \boxed{3} = 9$

$9 - 6 = \boxed{3}$ is the related subtraction fact.

Susan gave Marcus ____3____ magnets.

Find the missing number.
Use related facts to help you.

5. $\boxed{5} + 5 = 10$ **6.** $2 + \boxed{5} = 7$

7. $\boxed{10} - 8 = 2$ **8.** $9 - \boxed{6} = 3$

Panel 1 (top left)

Name: _____ Date: _____

 **Put On Your Thinking Cap!**
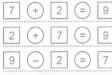 **Challenging Practice**

Pick three numbers to make a fact family.
Then write each fact family.

1.

```
5 + 2 = 7
2 + 5 = 7
7 - 5 = 2
7 - 2 = 5
```

2.
```
7 + 2 = 9
2 + 7 = 9
9 - 2 = 7
9 - 7 = 2
```

Thinking skill: Analyzing parts and whole,
Strategies: Solving part of the problem, and
guess and check

Chapter 4 Subtraction Facts to 10   **83**

Panel 2 (top right)

 Put On Your Thinking Cap!
 Problem Solving

Read this riddle.   Thinking skills: Analyzing parts and
whole, and deduction
Strategy: Solving part of the problem

Example

I think of two numbers.
When I add the numbers, the answer is 5.

0 + 5 = 5
1 + 4 = 5
2 + 3 = 5

When I subtract the numbers, the answer is 1.

5 – 0 = 5   ✗
4 – 1 = 3   ✗
3 – 2 = 1   ✓

What are the two numbers?
The two numbers are 2 and 3.

 What numbers make 5?

Now you try.

I think of two numbers.
When I add the numbers, the answer is 8.
When I subtract the numbers, the answer is less than 6.
What can the two numbers be?
The two numbers can be _____ and _____.

Accept 2 and 6; 3 and 5; 4 and 4.

 There is more than one correct answer.

84   Chapter 4   Subtraction Facts to 10

Panel 3 (bottom left)

Name: _____ Date: _____

Chapter Review/Test
Vocabulary
Choose the correct word.

1. + is plus, – is ___minus___.

2. 3 is ___less than___ 7.

3. 8 – 2 means to ___take away___ 2 from 8.

4. 4 – 3 = 1 is a ___subtraction sentence___

| subtraction sentence |
| take away |
| minus |
| less than |

Concepts and Skills
Complete each subtraction sentence.

5.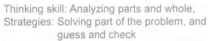

8 – ___3___ = ___5___

6. What is 4 less than 6?

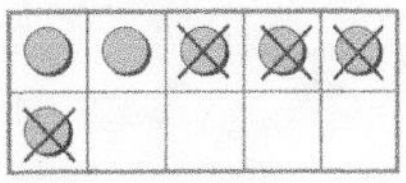

6 – ___4___ = ___2___

Chapter 4 Subtraction Facts to 10   **85**

Panel 4 (bottom right)

7. What is 3 less than 9?
9 – ___3___ = ___6___

Count on from the number which is less.

8. 6 – 3 = ___3___

9. 9 – 7 = ___2___

Count back from the greater number.

10. 10 – 5 = ___5___

11. 7 – 6 = ___1___

Complete the number bond.
Then complete the subtraction sentence.

12. 7 – 2 = ?

7 – 2 = ___5___

13. ? – 2 = 8

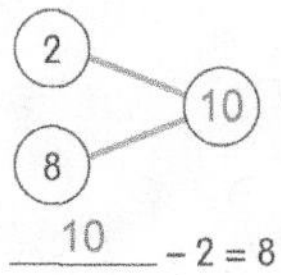

___10___ – 2 = 8

Subtract.
Use related facts.

14. 8 – 4 = ___4___   15. 7 – 3 = ___4___

16. 10 – ___3___ = 7   17. 5 – ___0___ = 5

86   Chapter 4   Subtraction Facts to 10

Chapter 4

Name: _____   Date: _____

Write a subtraction story.   Answers vary.

18.

There are 9 children.
_____

5 children are jumping.
_____

_____

_____9_____ − _____5_____ = _____4_____

4 children are not jumping.
_____

Write a fact family.

19.

_____6_____ + _____4_____ = _____10_____
_____4_____ + _____6_____ = _____10_____
_____10_____ − _____4_____ = _____6_____
_____10_____ − _____6_____ = _____4_____

Problem Solving

Draw ⬤.
Cross them out to solve.
Then write a number sentence.

20. James has 9 fish in his fish tank.
He gives his friend 4 fish.
How many fish does he have left?

_____9_____ − _____4_____ = _____5_____

James has _____5_____ fish left.

Solve.
Use related facts to help you.

21. Mr. Peterson bakes 10 pies.
He eats some of them.
He now has 8 pies.
How many pies did he eat?

10 − _____2_____ = 8

Mr. Peterson ate _____2_____ pies.

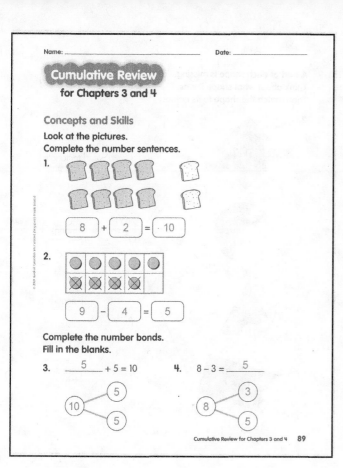

Name: _____   Date: _____

Cumulative Review
for Chapters 3 and 4

Concepts and Skills
Look at the pictures.
Complete the number sentences.

1.

$8 + 2 = 10$

2.

$9 - 4 = 5$

Complete the number bonds.
Fill in the blanks.

3. $\underline{\quad 5 \quad} + 5 = 10$

4. $8 - 3 = \underline{\quad 5 \quad}$

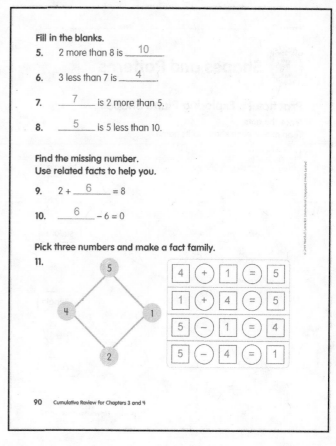

Fill in the blanks.

5. 2 more than 8 is $\underline{\quad 10 \quad}$

6. 3 less than 7 is $\underline{\quad 4 \quad}$

7. $\underline{\quad 7 \quad}$ is 2 more than 5.

8. $\underline{\quad 5 \quad}$ is 5 less than 10.

Find the missing number.
Use related facts to help you.

9. $2 + \underline{\quad 6 \quad} = 8$

10. $\underline{\quad 6 \quad} - 6 = 0$

Pick three numbers and make a fact family.
11.

$4 + 1 = 5$

$1 + 4 = 5$

$5 - 1 = 4$

$5 - 4 = 1$

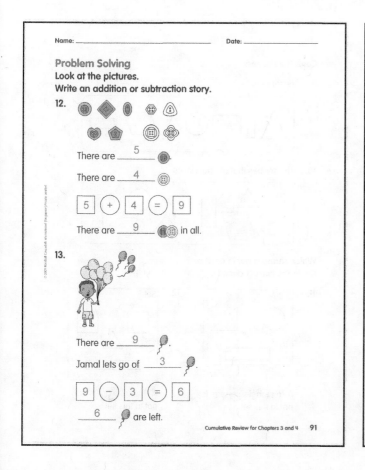

Name: _____   Date: _____

Problem Solving
Look at the pictures.
Write an addition or subtraction story.

12.

There are $\underline{\quad 5 \quad}$.

There are $\underline{\quad 4 \quad}$.

$5 + 4 = 9$

There are $\underline{\quad 9 \quad}$ in all.

13.

There are $\underline{\quad 9 \quad}$.

Jamal lets go of $\underline{\quad 3 \quad}$.

$9 - 3 = 6$

$\underline{\quad 6 \quad}$ are left.

Solve.
Write addition or subtraction sentences.

14. Ellen has 3 spoons.
Her sister gives her 5 spoons.
How many spoons does Ellen have now?

$3 + 5 = 8$

Ellen has $\underline{\quad 8 \quad}$ spoons now.

15. There are 8 fish in a fish tank.
6 are angelfish and the rest are goldfish.
How many goldfish are there?

$8 - 6 = 2$

There are $\underline{\quad 2 \quad}$ goldfish.

Workbook Answers: Chapters 3-4 Review
Math in Focus Homeschool Answer Key, Grade 1

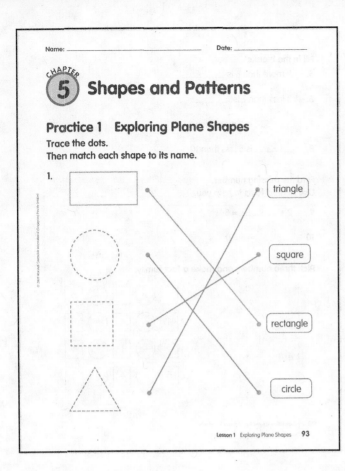

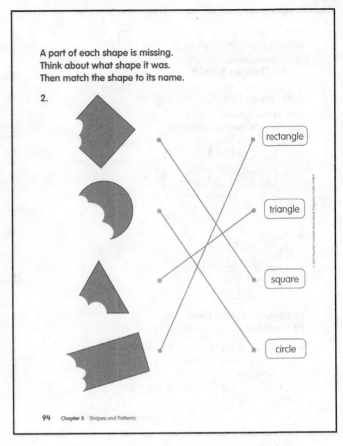

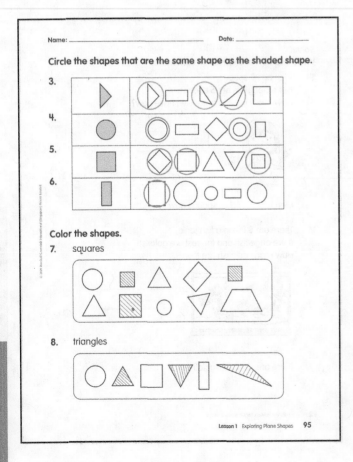

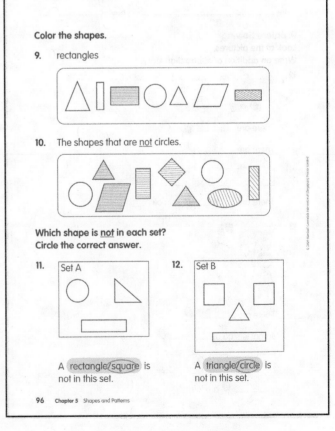

Chapter 5 Shapes and Patterns

Practice 1 Exploring Plane Shapes
Trace the dots.
Then match each shape to its name.

1.
triangle
square
rectangle
circle

A part of each shape is missing.
Think about what shape it was.
Then match the shape to its name.

2.
rectangle
triangle
square
circle

Circle the shapes that are the same shape as the shaded shape.

3.
4.
5.
6.

Color the shapes.

7. squares

8. triangles

Color the shapes.

9. rectangles

10. The shapes that are not circles.

Which shape is not in each set?
Circle the correct answer.

11. Set A

A rectangle/square is
not in this set.

12. Set B

A triangle/circle is
not in this set.

Lesson 1 Exploring Plane Shapes 93

94 Chapter 5 Shapes and Patterns

Lesson 1 Exploring Plane Shapes 95

96 Chapter 5 Shapes and Patterns

www.harcourtschoolsupply.com

168

Workbook Answers: Chapter 5
Math in Focus Homeschool Answer Key, Grade 1

Chapter 5

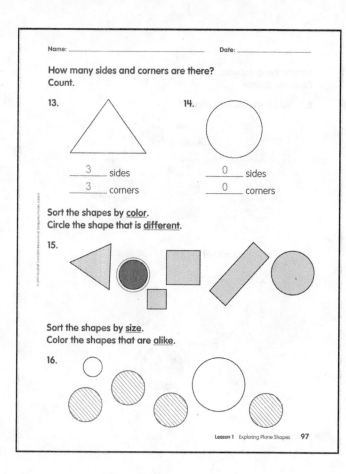

How many sides and corners are there?
Count.

13.

_3_ sides
_3_ corners

14.

_0_ sides
_0_ corners

Sort the shapes by color.
Circle the shape that is different.

15.

Sort the shapes by size.
Color the shapes that are alike.

16.

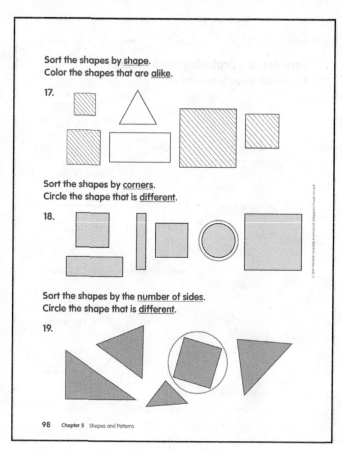

Sort the shapes by shape.
Color the shapes that are alike.

17.

Sort the shapes by corners.
Circle the shape that is different.

18.

Sort the shapes by the number of sides.
Circle the shape that is different.

19.

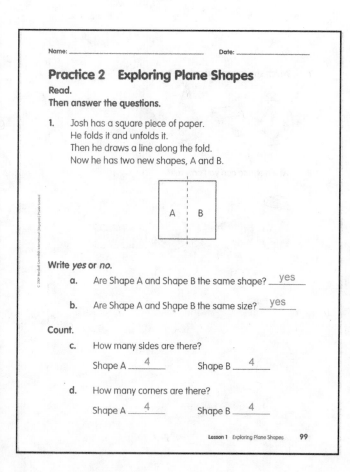

Name: _____   Date: _____

Practice 2   Exploring Plane Shapes
Read.
Then answer the questions.

1. Josh has a square piece of paper.
    He folds it and unfolds it.
    Then he draws a line along the fold.
    Now he has two new shapes, A and B.

Write yes or no.

a. Are Shape A and Shape B the same shape? ___yes___

b. Are Shape A and Shape B the same size? ___yes___

Count.

c. How many sides are there?

    Shape A ___4___   Shape B ___4___

d. How many corners are there?

    Shape A ___4___   Shape B ___4___

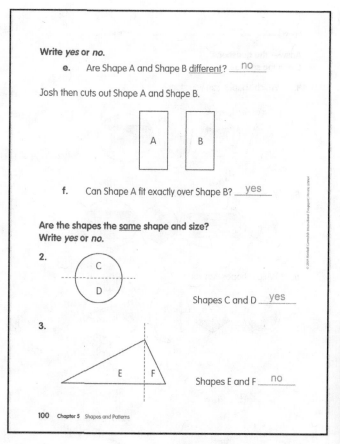

Write yes or no.

e. Are Shape A and Shape B different? ___no___

Josh then cuts out Shape A and Shape B.

f. Can Shape A fit exactly over Shape B? ___yes___

Are the shapes the same shape and size?
Write yes or no.

2.

Shapes C and D ___yes___

3.

Shapes E and F ___no___

Name: _____ Date: _____

Practice 3 Exploring Solid Shapes
Match each shape to its name.

1.

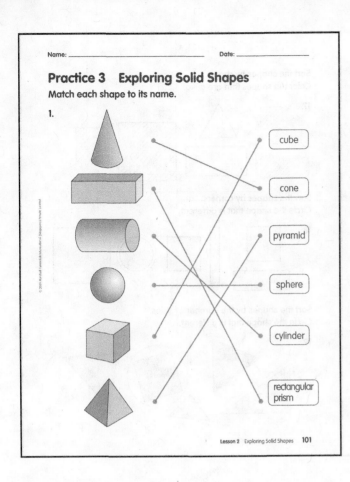

cube

cone

pyramid

sphere

cylinder

rectangular prism

Answer the questions.
Circle the shapes.

2. Which shapes are <u>not</u> cylinders?

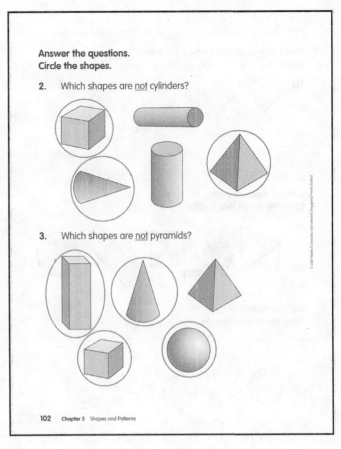

3. Which shapes are <u>not</u> pyramids?

Name: _____ Date: _____

Answer the questions.
Circle the shapes.

4. Which shapes can you stack?

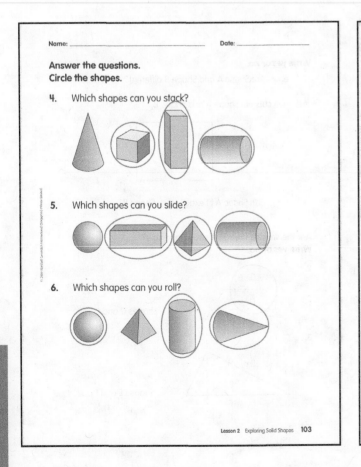

5. Which shapes can you slide?

6. Which shapes can you roll?

---

7. Which shape can you <u>only</u> slide?

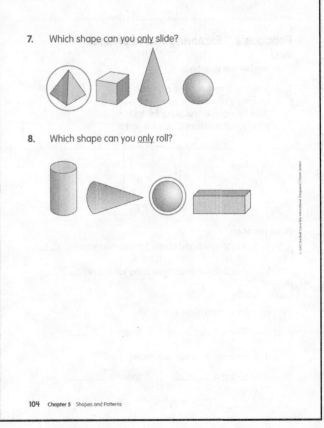

8. Which shape can you <u>only</u> roll?

170

Chapter 5

Practice 4 Making Pictures and Models with Shapes

Find the shapes in the pictures.
Count how many of each shape there are.
Write the number.

1.

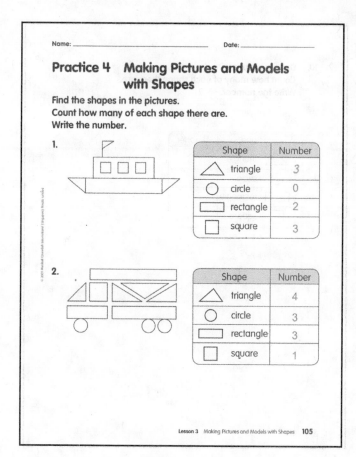

Shape		Number
△	triangle	3
○	circle	0
▭	rectangle	2
☐	square	3

2.

Shape		Number
△	triangle	4
○	circle	3
▭	rectangle	3
☐	square	1

Match the pieces to make a shape.
Name the shapes.
Use the words in the box.

circle
square
triangle
rectangle

3.

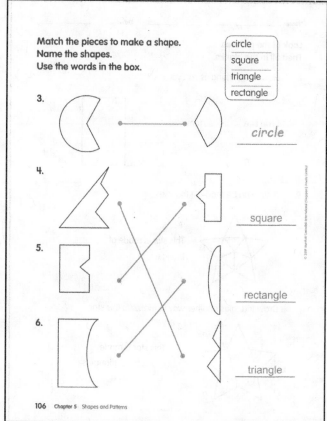

circle

4.

square

5.

rectangle

6.

triangle

Cut out the shapes below and make a picture.
Paste the picture here or use your own paper.
You do not need to use all the shapes.

7.

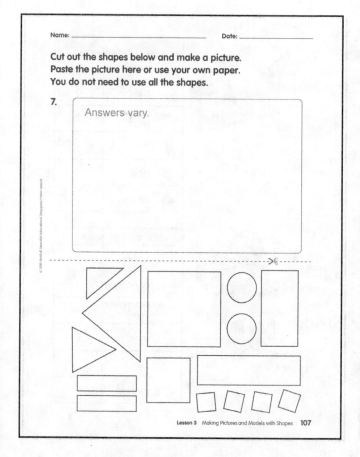

Answers vary.

BLANK

Chapter 5

Name: _____ Date: _____

Look at the pictures.
Then fill in the blanks.

8. How many triangles can you see?

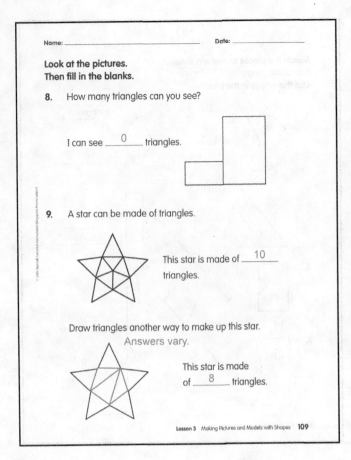

I can see ___0___ triangles.

9. A star can be made of triangles.

This star is made of ___10___ triangles.

Draw triangles another way to make up this star.

Answers vary.

This star is made of ___8___ triangles.

10. Draw a picture with shapes.
Count how many of each shape there are.
Write the number.

Answers vary.

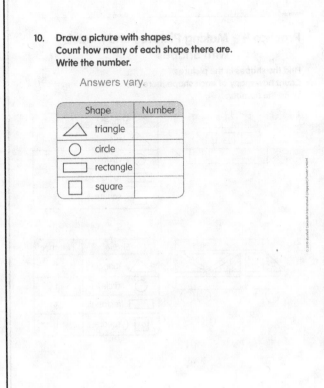

Shape	Number
triangle	
circle	
rectangle	
square	

Name: _____ Date: _____

Practice 5 Making Pictures and Models with Shapes

Look at the pictures.
Count how many of each solid shape there are.
Write the number.

1.

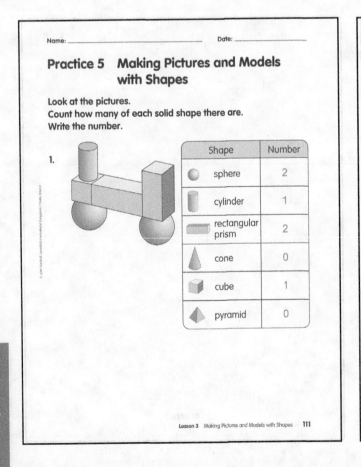

Shape	Number
sphere	2
cylinder	1
rectangular prism	2
cone	0
cube	1
pyramid	0

2.

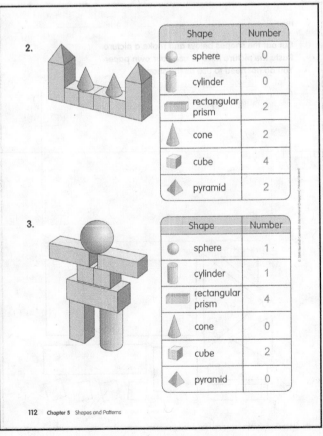

Shape	Number
sphere	0
cylinder	0
rectangular prism	2
cone	2
cube	4
pyramid	2

3.

Shape	Number
sphere	1
cylinder	1
rectangular prism	4
cone	0
cube	2
pyramid	0

Name: _____ Date: _____

Practice 6 Seeing Shapes Around Us

Trace the shape of each thing.
Then color.

1.

● Circles - red	■ Squares - yellow
▲ Triangles - blue	▬ Rectangles - green

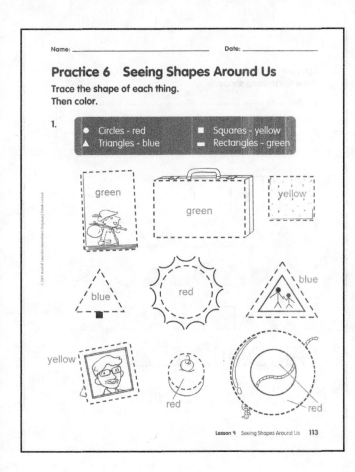

Look at the pictures.
Circle the correct things.

2. the thing that has the shape of a square

3. the thing that does <u>not</u> have the shape of a circle

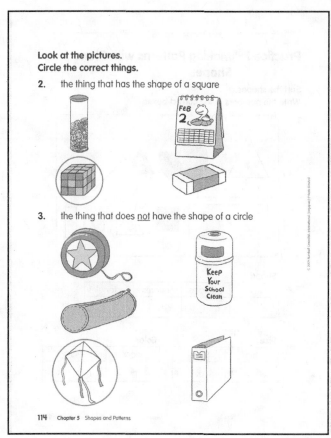

Name: _____ Date: _____

Match.

4.

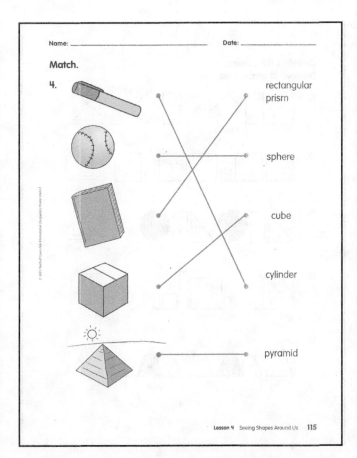

rectangular prism

sphere

cube

cylinder

pyramid

Look at the picture.
Color the shapes in the picture.

5.

Shape	Color
cube	blue
sphere	red
cone	yellow

Shape	Color
pyramid	purple
rectangular prism	green
cylinder	orange

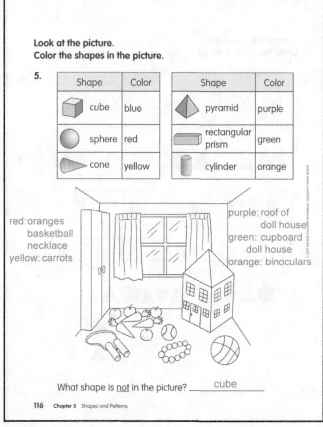

red: oranges
basketball
necklace
yellow: carrots

purple: roof of doll house
green: cupboard doll house
orange: binoculars

What shape is <u>not</u> in the picture? ____cube____

Chapter 5

Practice 7 Making Patterns with Plane Shapes

Sort the shapes.
Write the numbers in the correct boxes.

1.

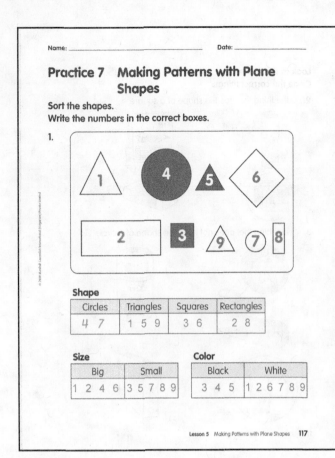

Shape

Circles	Triangles	Squares	Rectangles
4 7	1 5 9	3 6	2 8

Size

Big	Small
1 2 4 6	3 5 7 8 9

Color

Black	White
3 4 5	1 2 6 7 8 9

Lesson 5 Making Patterns with Plane Shapes   117

Complete the patterns.
Draw the missing shape.

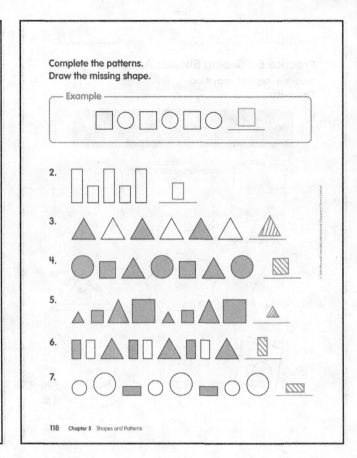

118   Chapter 5   Shapes and Patterns

Complete the patterns.
Circle the missing shape.

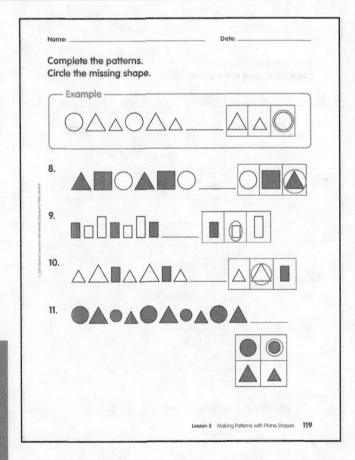

Lesson 5 Making Patterns with Plane Shapes   119

Complete the patterns.
Draw what comes next.

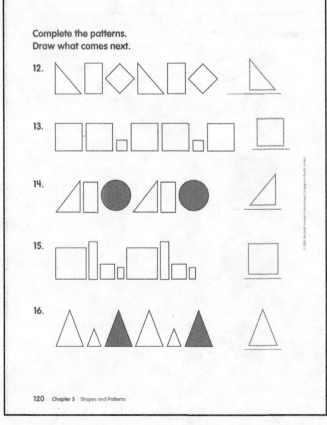

120   Chapter 5   Shapes and Patterns

Name: _____   Date: _____

Cut out the shapes below.
Make two patterns.
You do not need to use all the shapes.

17.   Paste your first pattern here.

Answers vary.

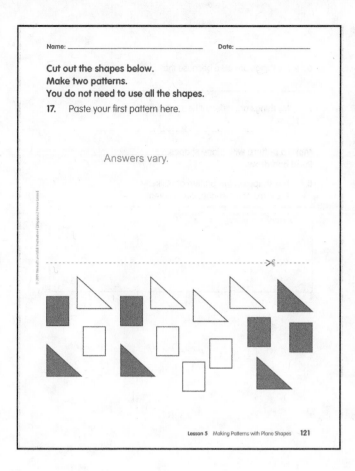

18.   Paste your second pattern here.

Answers vary.

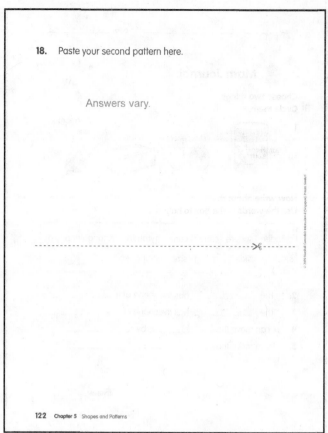

Name: _____   Date: _____

Practice 8   Making Patterns with Solid Shapes

Complete the patterns.
Circle the shape that comes next.

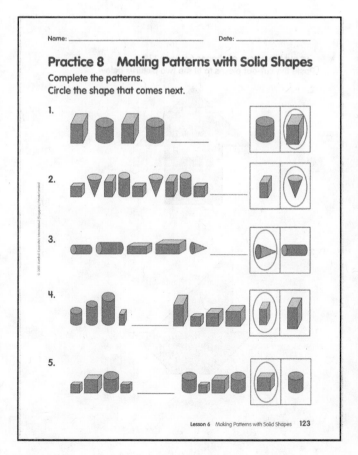

1.

2.

3.

4.

5.

Circle the mistake in the pattern.
Then make a ✔ for the correct shape.

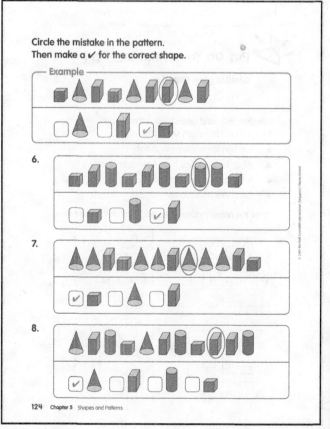

— Example —

6.

7.

8.

175

Workbook Answers: Chapter 5
Math in Focus Homeschool Answer Key, Grade 1

Chapter 5

Name: _____ Date: _____

Math Journal

Choose two things.
Circle them.

1.

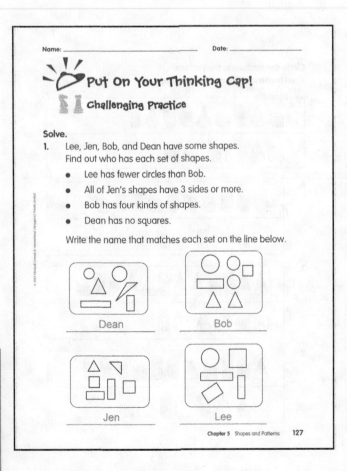

jar Peanut Butter   sharpener   brick   ice-cream cone

Answers vary.

Now write about them.
Use the words in the box to help you.

cylinder	sphere	cube	cone	pyramid	rectangular prism
stacking	sliding	rolling	size	shape	

2. The _____ has the shape of a _____
3. The _____ has the shape of a _____
4. I can move the _____ by _____.
5. I can move the _____ by _____.

Continued on next page

---

6. My things are alike because they _____
_____

7. My things are different because they _____
_____

Make a pattern with plane shapes.
Read and draw.

8. The shapes in this pattern are alike.
The sizes of the shapes are different.

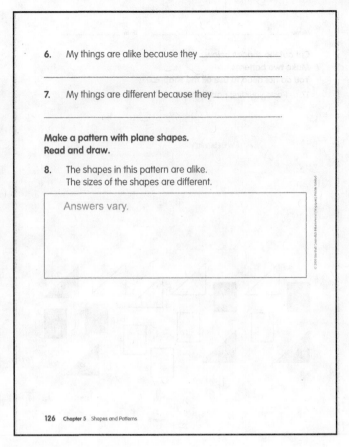

Answers vary.

Name: _____ Date: _____

Put On Your Thinking Cap!

Challenging Practice

Solve.

1. Lee, Jen, Bob, and Dean have some shapes.
Find out who has each set of shapes.

- Lee has fewer circles than Bob.
- All of Jen's shapes have 3 sides or more.
- Bob has four kinds of shapes.
- Dean has no squares.

Write the name that matches each set on the line below.

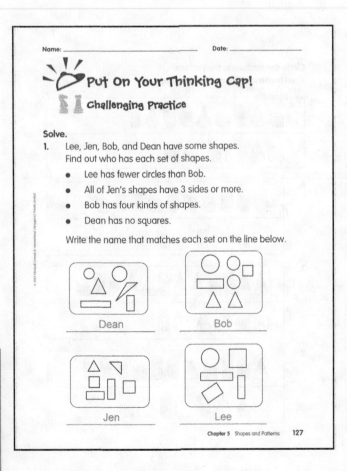

Dean   Bob

Jen   Lee

Cut out the pieces of shapes on page 129.
Paste the cut-out pieces to fit the two pictures below.

2.

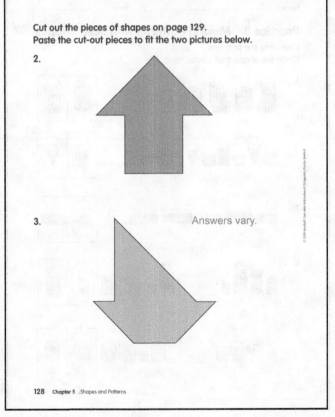

3. Answers vary.

Name: _____ Date: _____

2.

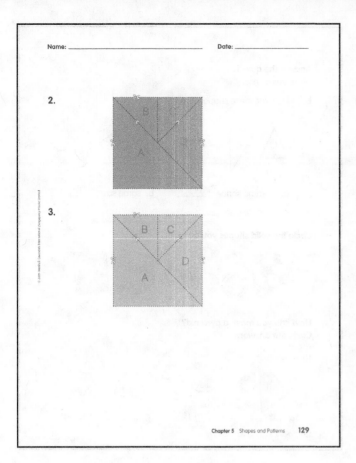

3.

BLANK

Name: _____ Date: _____

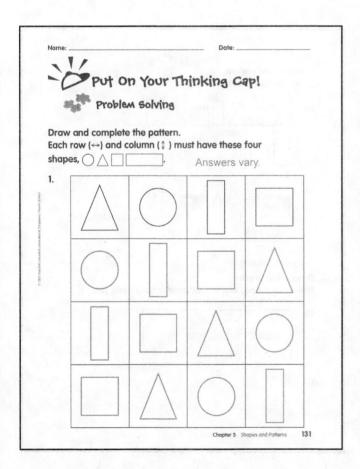

☀ Put On Your Thinking Cap!

🧩 Problem Solving

Draw and complete the pattern.
Each row (↔) and column (↕) must have these four
shapes, ○ △ □ ▭.

Answers vary.

1.

Draw and complete the pattern.
Each row (↔) and column must have these four shapes,
○ □ □ △.

2.

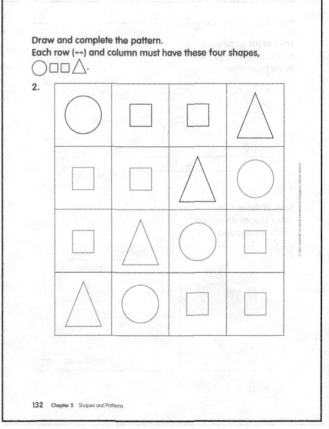

177

Chapter 5

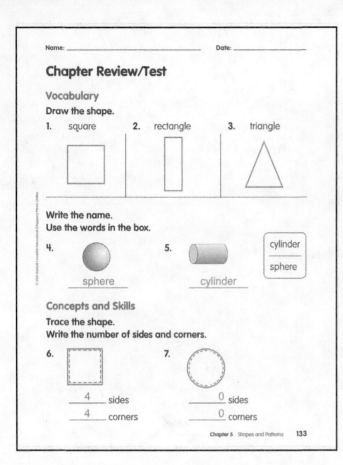

Chapter Review/Test

Vocabulary
Draw the shape.

1. square   2. rectangle   3. triangle

Write the name.
Use the words in the box.

4. sphere   5. cylinder

cylinder
sphere

Concepts and Skills
Trace the shape.
Write the number of sides and corners.

6. __4__ sides   __4__ corners

7. __0__ sides   __0__ corners

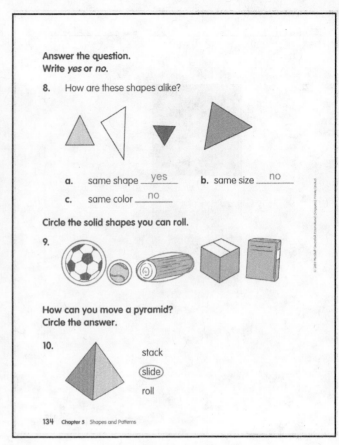

Answer the question.
Write *yes* or *no*.

8. How are these shapes alike?

a. same shape __yes__   b. same size __no__
c. same color __no__

Circle the solid shapes you can roll.

9.

How can you move a pyramid?
Circle the answer.

10. stack
(slide)
roll

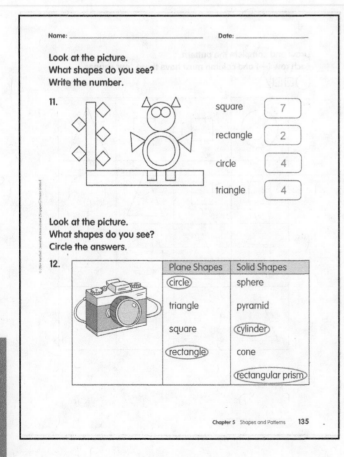

Look at the picture.
What shapes do you see?
Write the number.

11.

square — 7
rectangle — 2
circle — 4
triangle — 4

Look at the picture.
What shapes do you see?
Circle the answers.

12.

Plane Shapes	Solid Shapes
(circle)	sphere
triangle	pyramid
square	(cylinder)
(rectangle)	cone
	(rectangular prism)

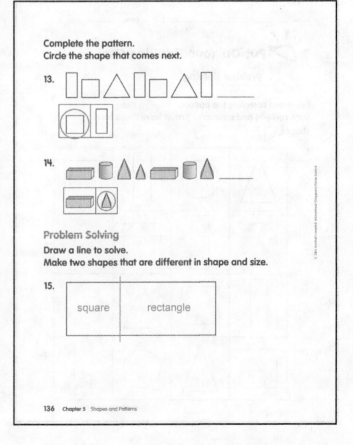

Complete the pattern.
Circle the shape that comes next.

13.

14.

Problem Solving
Draw a line to solve.
Make two shapes that are different in shape and size.

15.

square   rectangle

178

Chapter 5

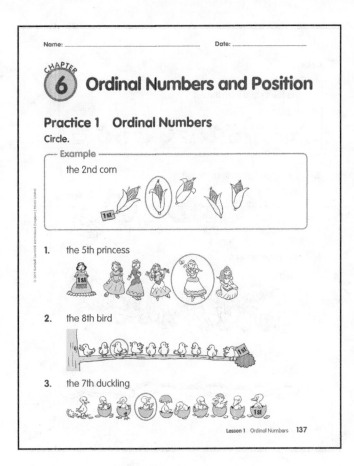

Name: _____ Date: _____

CHAPTER 6 Ordinal Numbers and Position

Practice 1 Ordinal Numbers
Circle.

┌─ Example ─────────────────────────┐
│ the 2nd corn   │
│   │
└───────────────────────────────────┘

1. the 5th princess

2. the 8th bird

3. the 7th duckling

Lesson 1 Ordinal Numbers 137

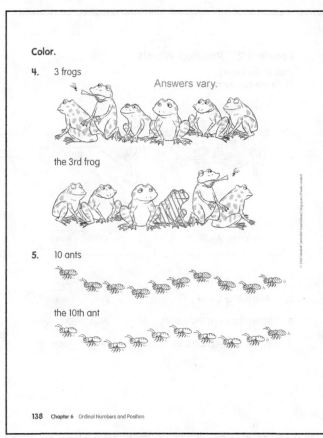

Color.

4. 3 frogs   Answers vary.

the 3rd frog

5. 10 ants

the 10th ant

138 Chapter 6 Ordinal Numbers and Position

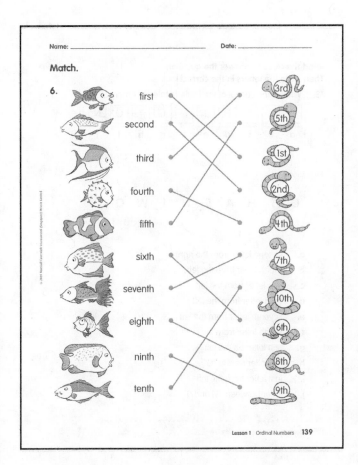

Name: _____ Date: _____

Match.

6.

first — (3rd)
second — (5th)
third — (1st)
fourth — (2nd)
fifth — (4th)
sixth — (7th)
seventh — (10th)
eighth — (6th)
ninth — (8th)
tenth — (9th)

Lesson 1 Ordinal Numbers 139

Look at the picture.
Answer the questions.

7. Who is first in the race? _____Dora_____

8. Who is fourth in the race? _____Wanda_____

9. In which position is Tandi? _____6th/sixth_____

10. In which position is Jenn? _____5th/fifth_____

11. Who is last? _____Meg_____

140 Chapter 6 Ordinal Numbers and Position

Workbook Answers: Chapter 6
Math in Focus Homeschool Answer Key, Grade 1

Practice 2   Position Words

Look at the picture.
Circle the correct name.

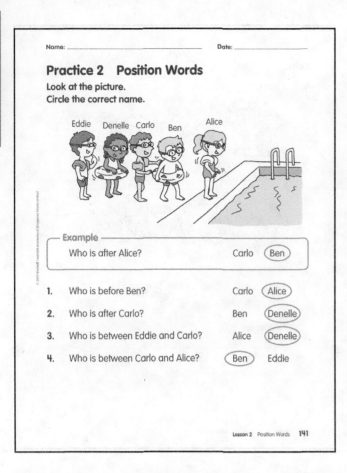

Eddie   Denelle   Carlo   Ben   Alice

Example

| Who is after Alice? | Carlo | (Ben) |

1. Who is before Ben?   Carlo   (Alice)

2. Who is after Carlo?   Ben   (Denelle)

3. Who is between Eddie and Carlo?   Alice   (Denelle)

4. Who is between Carlo and Alice?   (Ben)   Eddie

Color.

Example

the fourth bird from the left

Left   Right

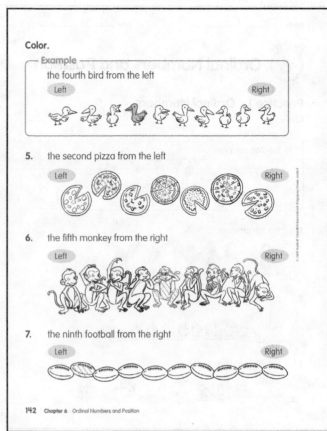

5. the second pizza from the left

Left   Right

6. the fifth monkey from the right

Left   Right

7. the ninth football from the right

Left   Right

Look at the picture.
Fill in the blanks with the words in the box.

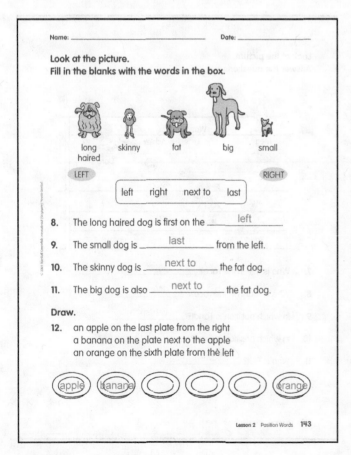

long haired   skinny   fat   big   small

LEFT   RIGHT

| left | right | next to | last |

8. The long haired dog is first on the __left__

9. The small dog is __last__ from the left.

10. The skinny dog is __next to__ the fat dog.

11. The big dog is also __next to__ the fat dog.

Draw.

12. an apple on the last plate from the right
    a banana on the plate next to the apple
    an orange on the sixth plate from the left

(apple) (banana) ( ) ( ) ( ) (orange)

Read the clues to answer the question.
Then write the letters in the correct ☐.

13. What is the capital of the United States of America?

| W | A | S | H | I | N | G | T | O | N | D.C. |
| a | b | c | d | e | f | g | h | i | j |

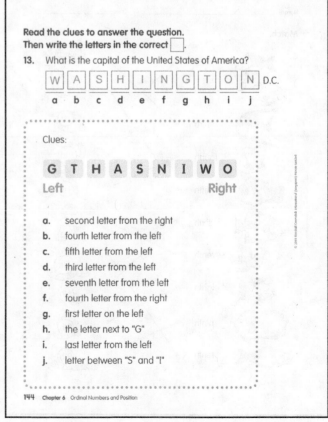

Clues:

G T H A S N I W O

Left   Right

a. second letter from the right

b. fourth letter from the left

c. fifth letter from the left

d. third letter from the left

e. seventh letter from the left

f. fourth letter from the right

g. first letter on the left

h. the letter next to "G"

i. last letter from the left

j. letter between "S" and "I"

180

Name: _____ Date: _____

Practice 3   Position Words

Color.

1. the rabbit below the black rabbit pink
    the rabbit above the black rabbit gray
    the rabbit under the paper brown
    the hair of the boy behind the shelf yellow
    the hair of the boy in front of the shelf red

yellow

gray

red

pink   brown

Lesson 2   Position Words   **145**

Look at the picture.
Fill in the blanks with the words in the box.

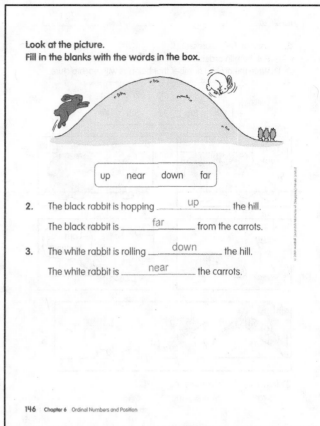

up	near	down	far

2. The black rabbit is hopping _____ up _____ the hill.

    The black rabbit is _____ far _____ from the carrots.

3. The white rabbit is rolling _____ down _____ the hill.

    The white rabbit is _____ near _____ the carrots.

146   Chapter 6   Ordinal Numbers and Position

Name: _____ Date: _____

Put On Your Thinking Cap!

Challenging Practice

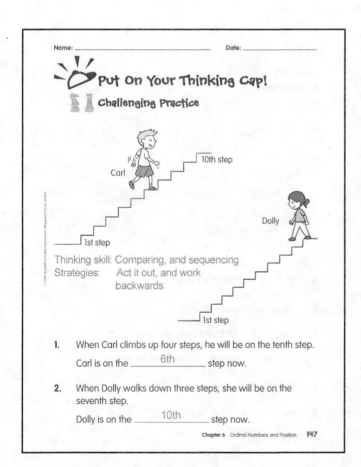

Carl

10th step

1st step

Dolly

1st step

Thinking skill: Comparing, and sequencing
Strategies: Act it out, and work
                 backwards

1. When Carl climbs up four steps, he will be on the tenth step.

    Carl is on the _____ 6th _____ step now.

2. When Dolly walks down three steps, she will be on the
    seventh step.

    Dolly is on the _____ 10th _____ step now.

Chapter 6   Ordinal Numbers and Position   **147**

Put On Your Thinking Cap!

Problem Solving

1. There are four rabbits, A, B, C, and D.
    Read the clues.
    Fill in the circles with the correct letters.

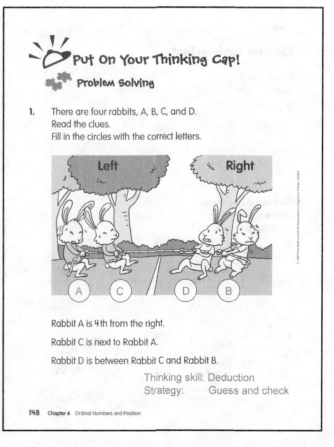

Left   Right

A   C   D   B

Rabbit A is 4th from the right.

Rabbit C is next to Rabbit A.

Rabbit D is between Rabbit C and Rabbit B.

Thinking skill: Deduction
Strategy: Guess and check

148   Chapter 6   Ordinal Numbers and Position

---

2. Look at the pictures.
Put them in order.
Write the ordinal number that belongs with each picture.

| 7th | 4th | 6th | 2nd | 1st |
| 8th | 3rd | 9th | 5th | 10th |

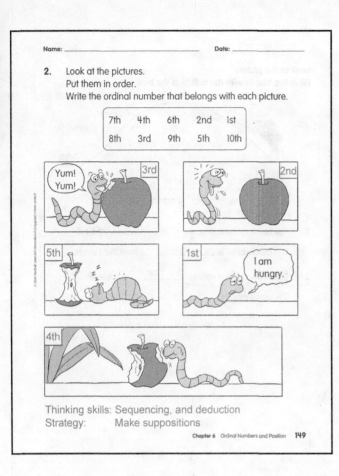

Thinking skills: Sequencing, and deduction
Strategy: Make suppositions

Chapter 6 Ordinal Numbers and Position   **149**

---

3. Michael has some cards in these shapes.

He makes this pattern:

Continue the pattern.
What is the shape of the tenth card from the left?

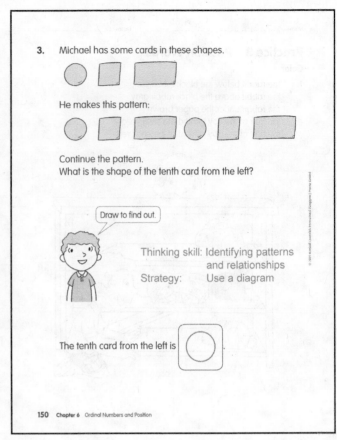

The tenth card from the left is

150 Chapter 6 Ordinal Numbers and Position

Name: _____   Date: _____

Chapter Review/Test

Vocabulary
Match.

1. 7th ——————— ninth
    3rd ——————— fifth
    5th ——————— seventh
    10th ——————— third
    9th ——————— tenth

Look at the chipmunks.
Where is the acorn?
Circle the correct word.

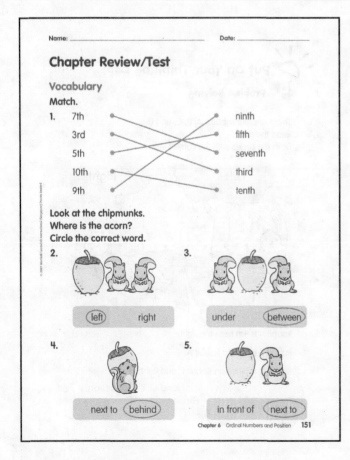

Chapter 6 Ordinal Numbers and Position   **151**

Concepts and Skills
Read and draw.

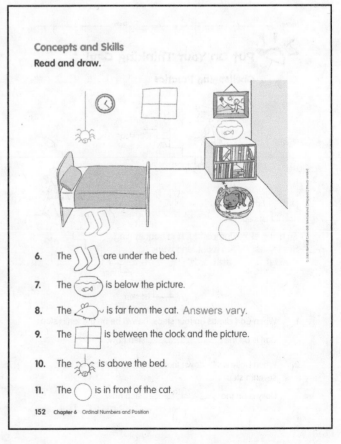

6.   The 🧦 are under the bed.

7.   The 🐟 is below the picture.

8.   The 🐭 is far from the cat. Answers vary.

9.   The ▦ is between the clock and the picture.

10. The 🕷 is above the bed.

11. The ◯ is in front of the cat.

152 Chapter 6 Ordinal Numbers and Position

182

Name: _____ Date: _____

Look at the picture.
Fill in the blanks.

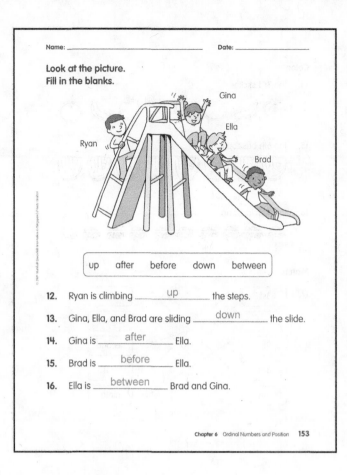

Gina
Ella
Ryan
Brad

| up | after | before | down | between |

12. Ryan is climbing ____up____ the steps.

13. Gina, Ella, and Brad are sliding ____down____ the slide.

14. Gina is ____after____ Ella.

15. Brad is ____before____ Ella.

16. Ella is ____between____ Brad and Gina.

Chapter 6 Ordinal Numbers and Position **153**

Problem Solving
Color.
17.

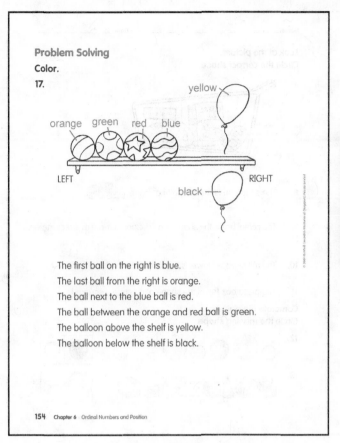

orange green red blue
yellow
LEFT
black
RIGHT

The first ball on the right is blue.
The last ball from the right is orange.
The ball next to the blue ball is red.
The ball between the orange and red ball is green.
The balloon above the shelf is yellow.
The balloon below the shelf is black.

154 Chapter 6 Ordinal Numbers and Position

Name: _____ Date: _____

Cumulative Review
for Chapters 5 and 6

Concepts and Skills

Look at the picture.
Count and write the number of shapes you see.

1.

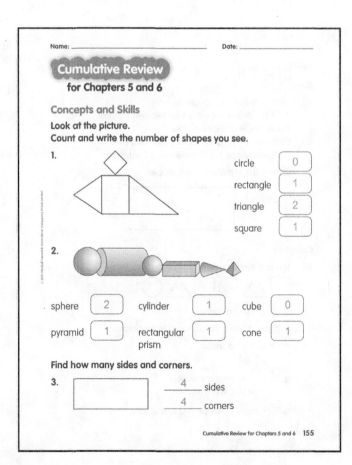

circle **0**
rectangle **1**
triangle **2**
square **1**

2.

sphere **2** cylinder **1** cube **0**

pyramid **1** rectangular prism **1** cone **1**

Find how many sides and corners.

3.

____4____ sides
____4____ corners

Cumulative Review for Chapters 5 and 6 **155**

Sort the shapes by size.
Color the shapes that are different.
4.

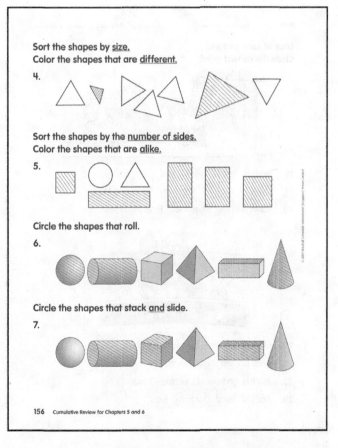

Sort the shapes by the number of sides.
Color the shapes that are alike.
5.

Circle the shapes that roll.
6.

Circle the shapes that stack and slide.
7.

156 Cumulative Review for Chapters 5 and 6

183

Workbook Answers: Chapters 5-6 Review
Math in Focus Homeschool Answer Key, Grade 1

Name: _____ Date: _____

Look at the picture.
Circle the correct shape.

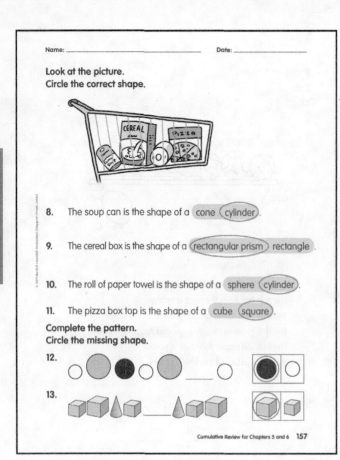

8. The soup can is the shape of a (cone (cylinder)).

9. The cereal box is the shape of a ((rectangular prism) rectangle).

10. The roll of paper towel is the shape of a (sphere (cylinder)).

11. The pizza box top is the shape of a (cube (square)).

Complete the pattern.
Circle the missing shape.

12.

13.

Cumulative Review for Chapters 5 and 6   157

Color.

14. the 3rd sticker

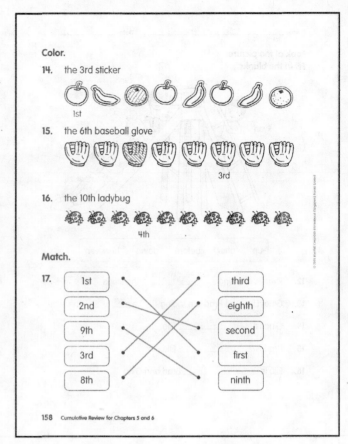

1st

15. the 6th baseball glove

3rd

16. the 10th ladybug

4th

Match.

17.

1st		third
2nd		eighth
9th		second
3rd		first
8th		ninth

158   Cumulative Review for Chapters 5 and 6

Name: _____ Date: _____

Look at each picture.
Circle the correct word.

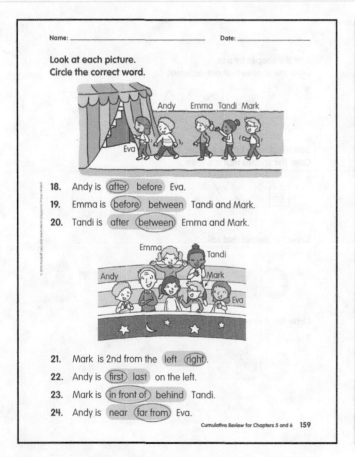

18. Andy is ((after) before) Eva.

19. Emma is ((before) between) Tandi and Mark.

20. Tandi is (after (between)) Emma and Mark.

21. Mark is 2nd from the (left (right)).

22. Andy is ((first) last) on the left.

23. Mark is ((in front of) behind) Tandi.

24. Andy is (near (far from)) Eva.

Cumulative Review for Chapters 5 and 6   159

Problem Solving

Solve.

25. Shantel draws a rectangle.
Then she draws a line to make two new shapes.
The two new shapes are alike.
Each new shape is the same shape and size.
Each new shape has 3 corners and 3 sides.

Draw a line to make the two shapes.

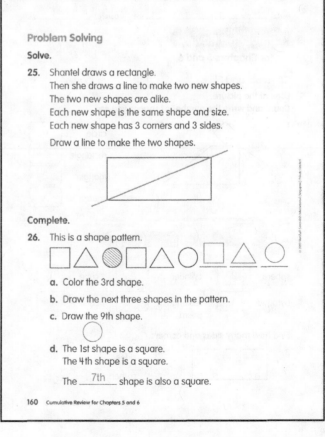

Complete.

26. This is a shape pattern.

a. Color the 3rd shape.

b. Draw the next three shapes in the pattern.

c. Draw the 9th shape.

d. The 1st shape is a square.
The 4th shape is a square.

The ___7th___ shape is also a square.

160   Cumulative Review for Chapters 5 and 6

184

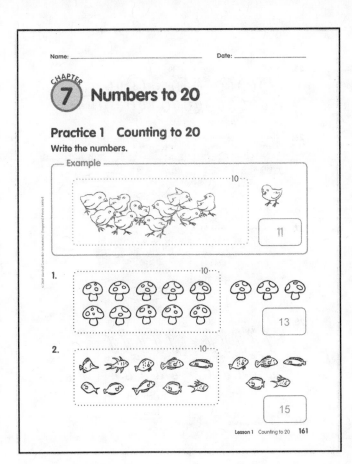

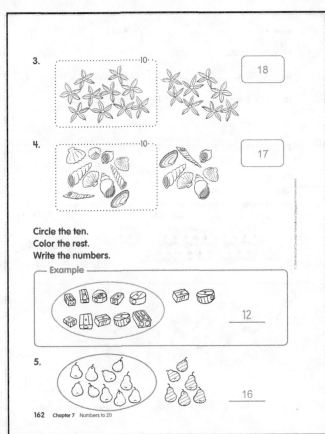

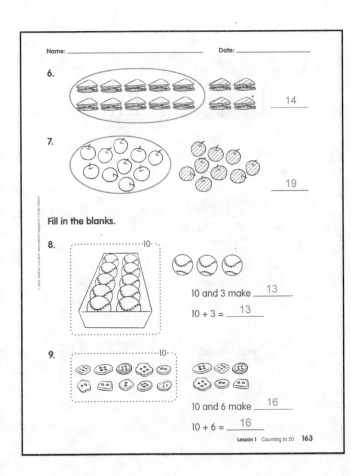

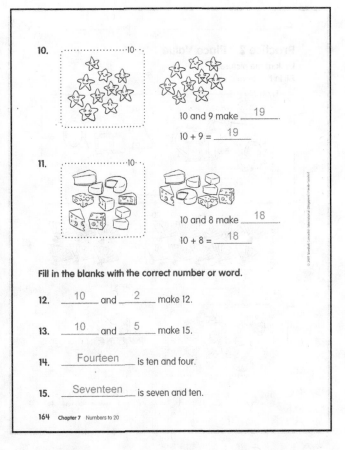

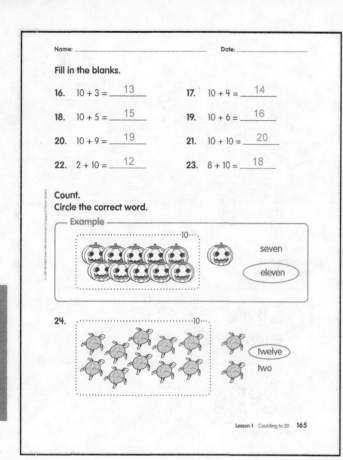

Name: _____ Date: _____

Fill in the blanks.

16. 10 + 3 = __13__   17. 10 + 4 = __14__

18. 10 + 5 = __15__   19. 10 + 6 = __16__

20. 10 + 9 = __19__   21. 10 + 10 = __20__

22. 2 + 10 = __12__   23. 8 + 10 = __18__

Count.
Circle the correct word.

Example

seven
(eleven)

24.

twelve
two

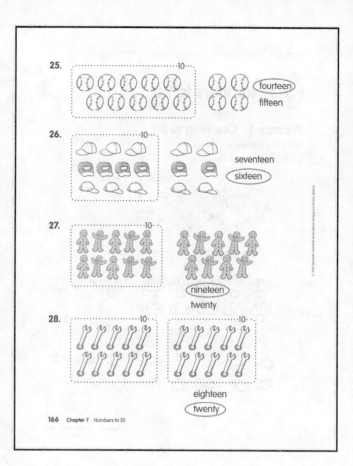

25.

fourteen
fifteen

26.

seventeen
(sixteen)

27.

(nineteen)
twenty

28.

eighteen
(twenty)

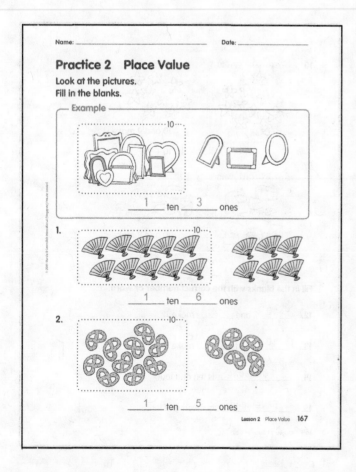

Name: _____ Date: _____

Practice 2 Place Value

Look at the pictures.
Fill in the blanks.

Example

__1__ ten __3__ ones

1.

__1__ ten __6__ ones

2.

__1__ ten __5__ ones

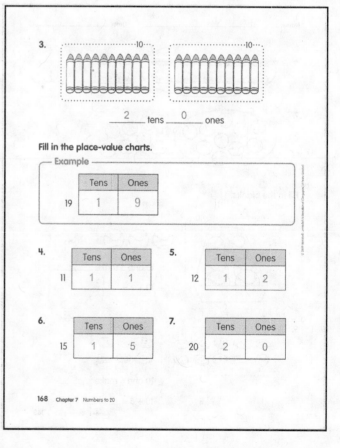

3.

__2__ tens __0__ ones

Fill in the place-value charts.

Example

	Tens	Ones
19	1	9

4.		Tens	Ones
	11	1	1

5.		Tens	Ones
	12	1	2

6.		Tens	Ones
	15	1	5

7.		Tens	Ones
	20	2	0

186

Name: _____   Date: _____

Show the number.
Draw ▯ for tens and □ for ones.

┌─ Example ──────────────────────────┐
│   │
│ | Tens | Ones   │
│ | ▯ | □ □ □   │
│   13   │
│   │
└────────────────────────────────────┘

8. | Tens | Ones | **9.** | Tens | Ones |
        | ▯ | □ □ | | ▯ | □ □ □ |
   12   16 | □ □ □ |

10. | Tens | Ones | **11.** | Tens | Ones |
        | ▯ | □ □ □ | | ▯ | □ □ □ |
        | | □ □ □ | | □ □ □ |
   18 | □ □ | 19 | □ □ □ |

Look at the place-value charts.
Write the numbers.

12. | Tens | Ones | **13.** | Tens | Ones |
        | ▮ | ● ● ● | | | ● ● ● |
                                       | | ● ● ● |
                              _13_ | ● | _17_

14. | Tens | Ones | **15.** | Tens | Ones |
        | ▮ | ● ● | | ▮ | ● |
        | | ● ● |
                  _14_   _11_

Fill in the blanks.

16. 13 = 1 ten ____3____ ones

17. 17 = ____1____ ten 7 ones

18. 15 = 1 ten ____5____ ones

19. 12 = ____1____ ten 2 ones

20. 19 = 1 ten ____9____ ones

Name: _____   Date: _____

Practice 3   Comparing Numbers

Write the number in each set.
Then fill in the blanks.

┌─ Example ──────────────────────────────────┐
│   │
│ 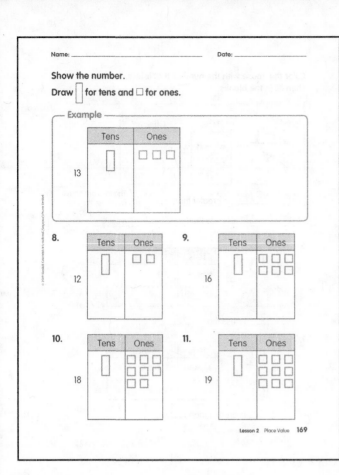   │
│   │
│   Set A: __15__   Set B: __12__   │
│   │
│ Set __A__ has __3__ more kangaroos than   │
│ Set __B__ .   │
└──┘

1.

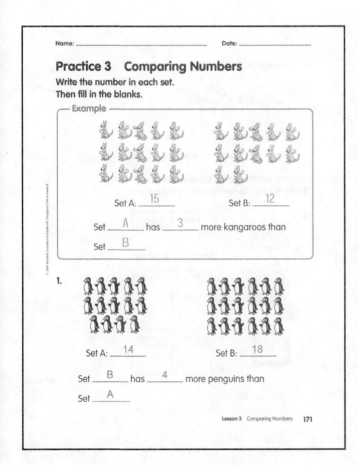

   Set A: __14__   Set B: __18__

Set __B__ has __4__ more penguins than
Set __A__ .

Write the number in each set.
Then fill in the blanks.

2.

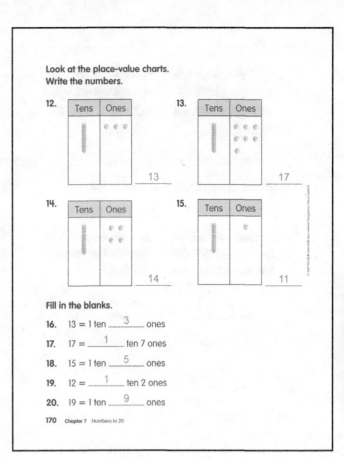

   Set A: __19__   Set B: __11__

Set __A__ has __8__ more crocodiles than
Set __B__ .

3.

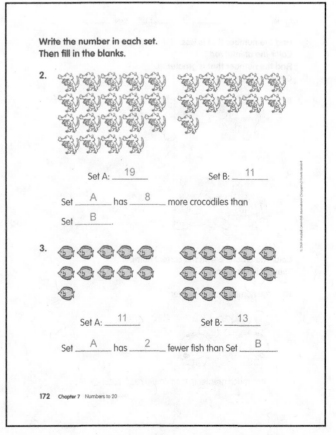

   Set A: __11__   Set B: __13__

Set __A__ has __2__ fewer fish than Set __B__ .

187

Name: _____ Date: _____

4.

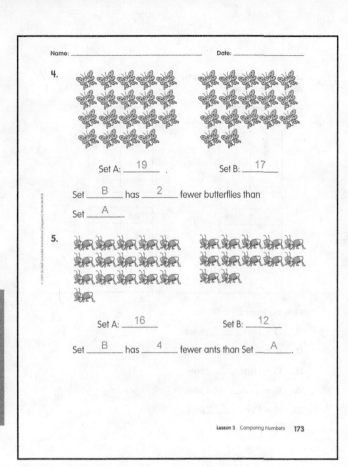

Set A: ___19___ . Set B: ___17___

Set ___B___ has ___2___ fewer butterflies than

Set ___A___

5.

Set A: ___16___ Set B: ___12___

Set ___B___ has ___4___ fewer ants than Set ___A___ .

Color the house with the number that is less.
Then fill in the blanks.

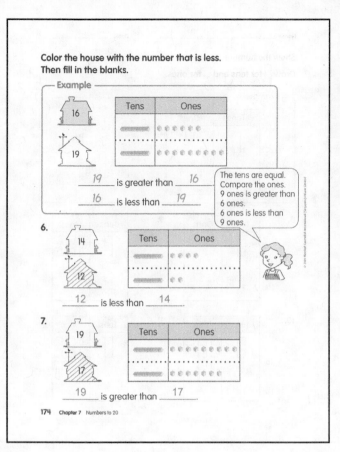

Example

	Tens	Ones
16		
19		

___19___ is greater than ___16___

___16___ is less than ___19___

The tens are equal.
Compare the ones.
9 ones is greater than
6 ones.
6 ones is less than
9 ones.

6.

	Tens	Ones
14		
12		

___12___ is less than ___14___

7.

	Tens	Ones
19		
17		

___19___ is greater than ___17___

Name: _____ Date: _____

Find the number that is less.
Color the animal red.
Find the number that is greater.
Color the animal blue.

8.

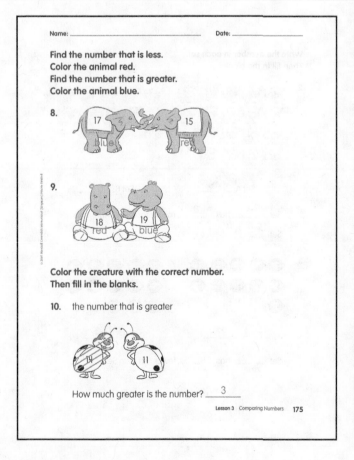

17 blue 15 red

9.

18 red 19 blue

Color the creature with the correct number.
Then fill in the blanks.

10. the number that is greater

14 11

How much greater is the number? ___3___

11. the number that is less

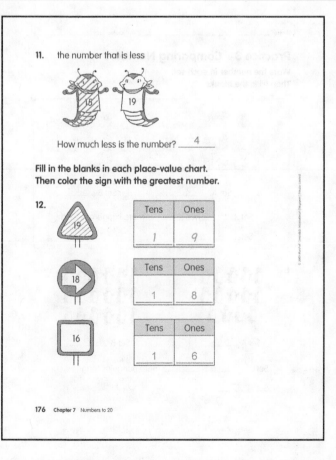

15 19

How much less is the number? ___4___

Fill in the blanks in each place-value chart.
Then color the sign with the greatest number.

12.

19

Tens	Ones
1	9

18

Tens	Ones
1	8

16

Tens	Ones
1	6

Name: _____ Date: _____

Fill in the blanks in each place-value chart.
Then color the sign with the least number.

13.

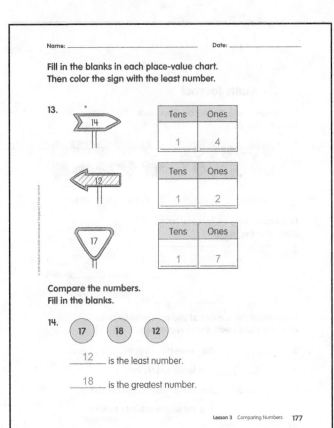

Tens	Ones
1	4

Tens	Ones
1	2

Tens	Ones
1	7

Compare the numbers.
Fill in the blanks.

14.

17 18 12

___12___ is the least number.

___18___ is the greatest number.

Compare the numbers.
Fill in the blanks.

15.

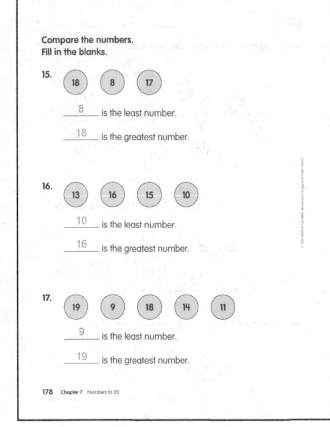

18 8 17

___8___ is the least number.

___18___ is the greatest number.

16.

13 16 15 10

___10___ is the least number.

___16___ is the greatest number.

17.

19 9 18 14 11

___9___ is the least number.

___19___ is the greatest number.

Name: _____ Date: _____

Practice 4   Making Patterns and Ordering Numbers

Solve.

1. Alex uses circles to make a pattern.
   How many circles come next in the pattern?
   Draw the circles in the empty box.
   Write the number of circles below this box.

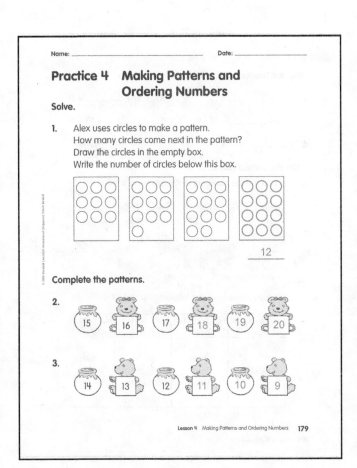

___12___

Complete the patterns.

2.

15 16 17 18 19 20

3.

14 13 12 11 10 9

Look at the numbers.
Fill in the blanks.

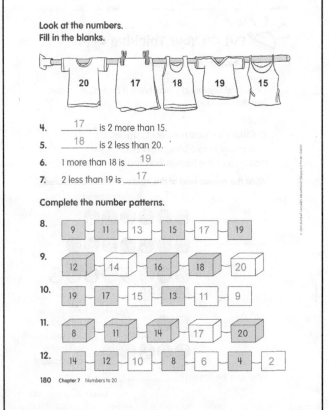

20 17 18 19 15

4. ___17___ is 2 more than 15.
5. ___18___ is 2 less than 20.
6. 1 more than 18 is ___19___
7. 2 less than 19 is ___17___

Complete the number patterns.

8. 9 11 13 15 17 19

9. 12 14 16 18 20

10. 19 17 15 13 11 9

11. 8 11 14 17 20

12. 14 12 10 8 6 4 2

Workbook Answers: Chapter 7
Math in Focus Homeschool Answer Key, Grade 1

Name: _____ Date: _____

Help Rosa order the bowling pins and balls.

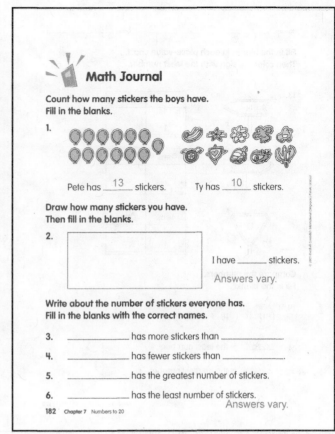

13. Write the numbers on the ⚲ in order from least to greatest.

| 12 | 13 | 15 | 18 | 20 |

least

14. Write the numbers on the ◯ in order from greatest to least.

| 17 | 16 | 14 | 11 | 8 |

greatest

Lesson 4 Making Patterns and Ordering Numbers **181**

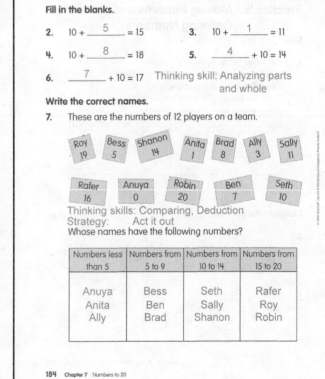

Math Journal

Count how many stickers the boys have.
Fill in the blanks.

1.

Pete has __13__ stickers.   Ty has __10__ stickers.

Draw how many stickers you have.
Then fill in the blanks.

2.

I have _____ stickers.

Answers vary.

Write about the number of stickers everyone has.
Fill in the blanks with the correct names.

3. _____ has more stickers than _____.

4. _____ has fewer stickers than _____.

5. _____ has the greatest number of stickers.

6. _____ has the least number of stickers.

Answers vary.

182 Chapter 7 Numbers to 20

Name: _____ Date: _____

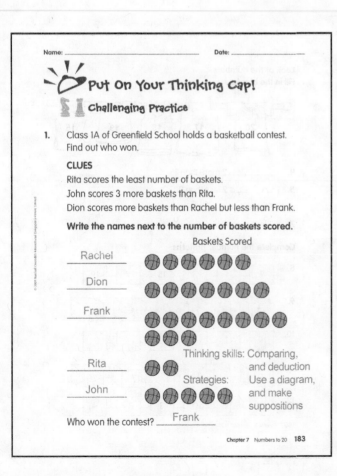

🎓 **Put On Your Thinking Cap!**

♟ **Challenging Practice**

1. Class 1A of Greenfield School holds a basketball contest.
   Find out who won.

   CLUES
   Rita scores the least number of baskets.
   John scores 3 more baskets than Rita.
   Dion scores more baskets than Rachel but less than Frank.

   Write the names next to the number of baskets scored.

   Baskets Scored

   Rachel

   Dion

   Frank

   Rita Thinking skills: Comparing, and deduction

   John Strategies: Use a diagram, and make suppositions

   Who won the contest? __Frank__

   Chapter 7 Numbers to 20 **183**

Fill in the blanks.

2. $10 + \underline{5} = 15$ 3. $10 + \underline{1} = 11$

4. $10 + \underline{8} = 18$ 5. $\underline{4} + 10 = 14$

6. $\underline{7} + 10 = 17$ Thinking skill: Analyzing parts and whole

Write the correct names.

7. These are the numbers of 12 players on a team.

| Roy 19 | Bess 5 | Shanon 14 | Anita 1 | Brad 8 | Ally 3 | Sally 11 |

| Rafer 16 | Anuya 0 | Robin 20 | Ben 7 | Seth 10 |

Thinking skills: Comparing, Deduction
Strategy: Act it out
Whose names have the following numbers?

Numbers less than 5	Numbers from 5 to 9	Numbers from 10 to 14	Numbers from 15 to 20
Anuya Anita Ally	Bess Ben Brad	Seth Sally Shanon	Rafer Roy Robin

184 Chapter 7 Numbers to 20

Use the clues on the next page.
Help Tony find which numbers his counters covered.
Thinking skills: Deduction, and comparing
Strategy: Guess and check

Continued on next page

Chapter 7 Numbers to 20 **185**

Read what Tony's friends said.
Circle the numbers that were covered on Tony's card.

First, cover the greatest number.

Next, cover the number that is 2 less than the greatest number.

Then, cover the number that is the least.

There are two more numbers. I remember that one of these numbers is 3 less than the other.

Tony's card.

①	9	13	⑱
5	3	7	17
⑯	11	⑮	⑫

Accept 9 and 12

186 Chapter 7 Numbers to 20

Chapter 7

Name: _____ Date: _____

Chapter Review/Test

Vocabulary

Unscramble the letters to spell each number.

1. 15 f i e e t f n
   fifteen

2. 11 e v l e e n
   eleven

3. 18 e g e e t h n i
   eighteen

4. 20 t w y n e t
   twenty

Fill in the blank with the correct word.

place-value chart	compare

5. You can show numbers as tens and ones in
   a ___place-value chart___

6. When you ___compare___ 12 and 15, 12 is the number that is less.

Concepts and Skills

Count. Write the number.

7.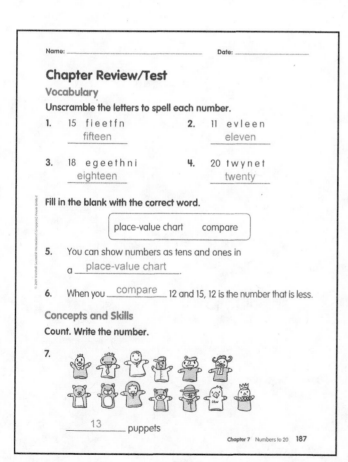

___13___ puppets

Chapter 7 Numbers to 20 **187**

8.

___17___ faces.

Fill in the blanks.

9.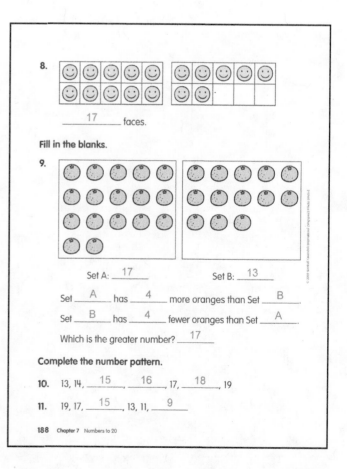

Set A: ___17___   Set B: ___13___

Set ___A___ has ___4___ more oranges than Set ___B___.

Set ___B___ has ___4___ fewer oranges than Set ___A___.

Which is the greater number? ___17___

Complete the number pattern.

10. 13, 14, ___15___, ___16___, 17, ___18___, 19

11. 19, 17, ___15___, 13, 11, ___9___

188 Chapter 7 Numbers to 20

Workbook Answers: Chapter 7
Math in Focus Homeschool Answer Key, Grade 1

Name: _____ Date: _____

Write the numbers in order from least to greatest.

12.

| 17 | 3 | 0 | 10 | 15 |

_0_ , _3_ , _10_ , _15_ , _17_

Write the numbers in order from greatest to least.

13.

| 11 | 19 | 8 | 9 | 14 |

_19_ , _14_ , _11_ , _9_ , _8_

Problem Solving

Read the clues.

Then cross out the numbers to solve.

┌─ Example ──────────────────────────────┐
│   │
│ | 10̸ | 11̸ | 12̸ | 13̸ | 14̸ | 15 | 16̸ | 17̸ | 18̸ | 19̸ | 20 | │
│   │
│ I am greater than 13.   │
│ I am less than 17.   │
│ Of the numbers that are left: │
│   I am not the least.   │
│   I am not the greatest.   │
│ What number am I? ___15___   │
└──┘

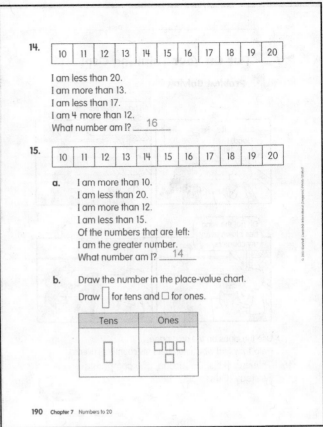

14.

| 10 | 11 | 12 | 13 | 14 | 15 | 16 | 17 | 18 | 19 | 20 |

I am less than 20.
I am more than 13.
I am less than 17.
I am 4 more than 12.
What number am I? ___16___

15.

| 10 | 11 | 12 | 13 | 14 | 15 | 16 | 17 | 18 | 19 | 20 |

a. I am more than 10.
    I am less than 20.
    I am more than 12.
    I am less than 15.
    Of the numbers that are left:
    I am the greater number.
    What number am I? ___14___

b. Draw the number in the place-value chart.
    Draw | for tens and □ for ones.

Tens	Ones
▯	□ □ □ □

CHAPTER 8 — Addition and Subtraction Facts to 20

Practice 1 Ways to Add

Make a 10.
Then add.

Example

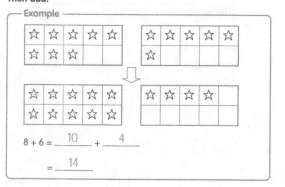

$8 + 6 = \underline{\quad 10 \quad} + \underline{\quad 4 \quad}$

$ = \underline{\quad 14 \quad}$

1.

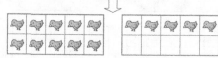

$7 + 5 = \underline{\quad 10 \quad} + \underline{\quad 2 \quad}$

$ = \underline{\quad 12 \quad}$

2.

$9 + 6 = \underline{\quad 10 \quad} + \underline{\quad 5 \quad}$

$ = \underline{\quad 15 \quad}$

Draw ◯ in the ⬚⬚⬚⬚⬚ to make a 10.
Then add.

Example

$6 + 5 = \underline{\quad 10 \quad} + \underline{\quad 1 \quad}$

$ = \underline{\quad 11 \quad}$

3.

$8 + 8 = \underline{\quad 10 \quad} + \underline{\quad 6 \quad}$

$ = \underline{\quad 16 \quad}$

4.

$9 + 5 = \underline{\quad 10 \quad} + \underline{\quad 4 \quad}$

$ = \underline{\quad 14 \quad}$

5.

$8 + 7 = \underline{\quad 10 \quad} + \underline{\quad 5 \quad}$

$ = \underline{\quad 15 \quad}$

Chapter 8

Name: _____ Date: _____

Draw ● in the ⬜ to show the numbers.

Then draw ● in the ⬜ and add.

┌─ Example ─────────────────────────────┐

$9 + 6 =$ ___10___ $+$ ___5___

$=$ ___15___

└───────────────────────────────────────┘

6.

$7 + 6 =$ ___10___ $+$ ___3___

$=$ ___13___

Make a 10.
Then add.

┌─ Example ─────────────────────────────┐

$3 + 8 =$ ___11___

(1) (2)   ___8___ $+$ ___2___ $=$ ___10___

___10___ $+$ ___1___ $=$ ___11___

└───────────────────────────────────────┘

7. $5 + 9 =$ ___14___

(4) (1)

___1___ $+$ ___9___ $=$ ___10___

___10___ $+$ ___4___ $=$ ___14___

8. $6 + 6 =$ ___12___

(2) (4)

___4___ $+$ ___6___ $=$ ___10___

___10___ $+$ ___2___ $=$ ___12___

9. $7 + 8 =$ ___15___

(5) (2)

___2___ $+$ ___8___ $=$ ___10___

___10___ $+$ ___5___ $=$ ___15___

10. $9 + 9 =$ ___18___

(8) (1)

___1___ $+$ ___9___ $=$ ___10___

___10___ $+$ ___8___ $=$ ___18___

Name: _____ Date: _____

Practice 2 Ways to Add

Group the numbers into a 10 and ones.
Then add.

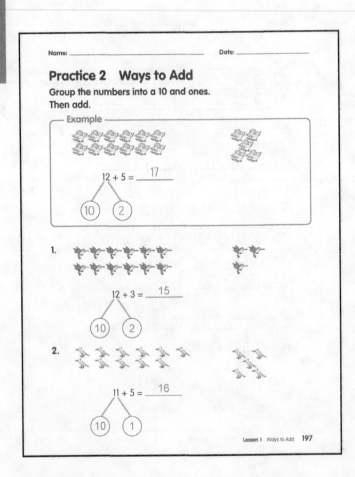

┌─ Example ─────────────────────────────┐

$12 + 5 =$ ___17___

(10) (2)

└───────────────────────────────────────┘

1.

$12 + 3 =$ ___15___

(10) (2)

2.

$11 + 5 =$ ___16___

(10) (1)

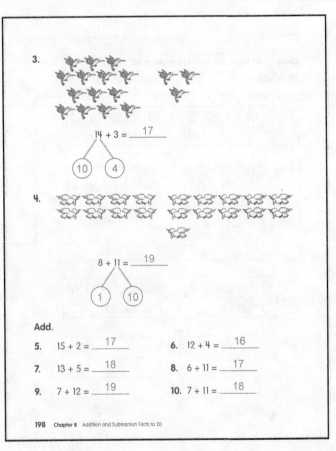

3.

$14 + 3 =$ ___17___

(10) (4)

4.

$8 + 11 =$ ___19___

(1) (10)

Add.

5. $15 + 2 =$ ___17___   6. $12 + 4 =$ ___16___

7. $13 + 5 =$ ___18___   8. $6 + 11 =$ ___17___

9. $7 + 12 =$ ___19___   10. $7 + 11 =$ ___18___

Practice 3 Ways to Add
Complete each addition sentence.

— Example —

What is double 1?

Double 1 means to add __1__ more to 1.

1 + __1__ = __2__

1. What is double 2?

Double 2 means to add __2__ more to 2.

__2__ + __2__ = __4__

2. What is double 3?

Double 3 means to add __3__ more to 3.

__3__ + __3__ = __6__

3. 4 + 4 = __8__

4. 5 + 5 = __10__

Complete each addition sentence.

5. a. 3 + 3 = __6__
   3 + 4 = __7__

   b. 3 + 3 is double __3__.
   3 + 4 is double __3__ plus __1__.

Complete the number bonds.
Then fill in the blanks.

— Example —

6 + 7 = ?

6 + 7 is double 6 plus __1__.

6 + 6 + __1__

= 12 + __1__

= 13

6. 7 + 8 = ?

7 + 8 is double __7__ plus 1.

7 + __7__ + 1

= __14__ + 1

= 15

7. 5 + 4 = ?

5 + 4 is double __4__ plus 1.

__4__ + __4__ + __1__

= __9__

Use doubles facts to complete the addition sentences.

— Example —

[2] + [2] = 4

8. [0] + [0] = 0

9. [6] + [6] = 12

10. [5] + [5] = 10

11. [8] + [8] = 16

12. [9] + [9] = 18

13. [10] + [10] = 20

Add the doubles-plus one numbers.
Use doubles facts to help you.
Then write the doubles fact you used.

— Example —

5 + 6 = __11__

Doubles fact: __5__ + __5__ = __10__

14. 7 + 6 = __13__

Doubles fact: __6__ + __6__ = __12__

15. 7 + 8 = __15__

Doubles fact: __7__ + __7__ = __14__

16. 9 + 10 = __19__

Doubles fact: __9__ + __9__ = __18__

17. 8 + 9 = __17__

Doubles fact: __8__ + __8__ = __16__

Practice 4 Ways to Subtract

Group the numbers into a 10 and ones.
Then subtract.

Example

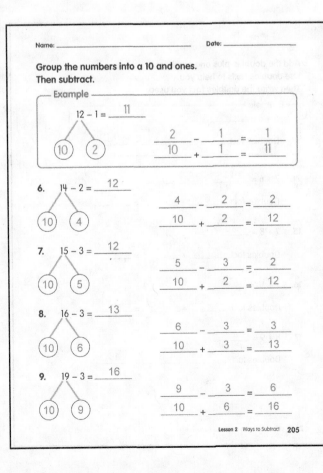

$13 - 2 = $ _11_

(10) (3)

1.

$17 - 3 = $ _14_

(10) (7)

2.

$18 - 0 = $ _18_

(10) (8)

3.

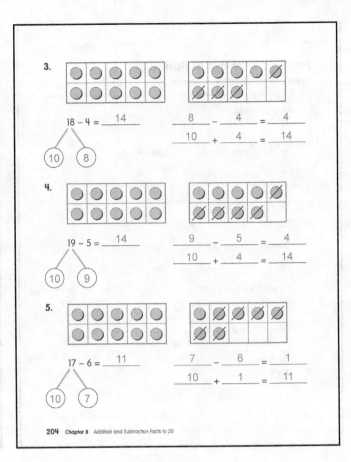

$18 - 4 = $ _14_

(10) (8)

$8 - 4 = 4$

$10 + 4 = 14$

4.

$19 - 5 = $ _14_

(10) (9)

$9 - 5 = 4$

$10 + 4 = 14$

5.

$17 - 6 = $ _11_

(10) (7)

$7 - 6 = 1$

$10 + 1 = 11$

Group the numbers into a 10 and ones.
Then subtract.

Example

$12 - 1 = $ _11_

(10) (2)

$2 - 1 = 1$

$10 + 1 = 11$

6. $14 - 2 = $ _12_

(10) (4)

$4 - 2 = 2$

$10 + 2 = 12$

7. $15 - 3 = $ _12_

(10) (5)

$5 - 3 = 2$

$10 + 2 = 12$

8. $16 - 3 = $ _13_

(10) (6)

$6 - 3 = 3$

$10 + 3 = 13$

9. $19 - 3 = $ _16_

(10) (9)

$9 - 3 = 6$

$10 + 6 = 16$

Group the numbers into a 10 and ones.
Then subtract.

Example

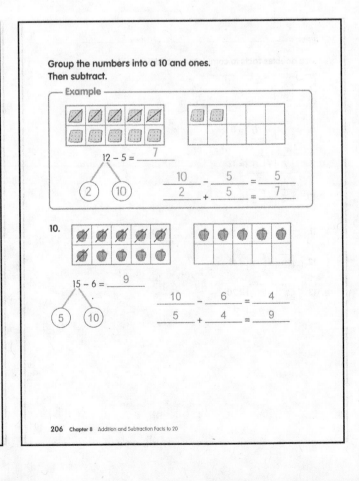

$12 - 5 = $ _7_

(2) (10)

$10 - 5 = 5$

$2 + 5 = 7$

10.

$15 - 6 = $ _9_

(5) (10)

$10 - 6 = 4$

$5 + 4 = 9$

196

Workbook Answers: Chapter 8
Math in Focus Homeschool Answer Key, Grade 1

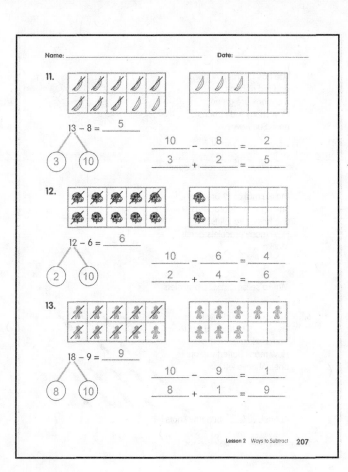

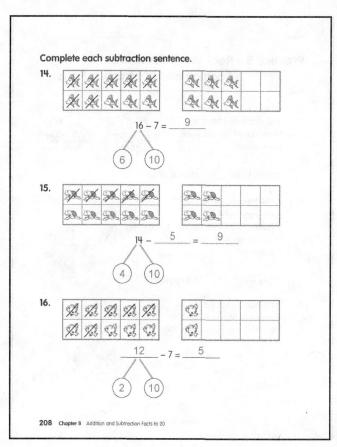

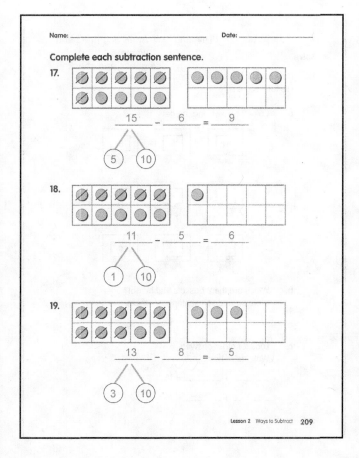

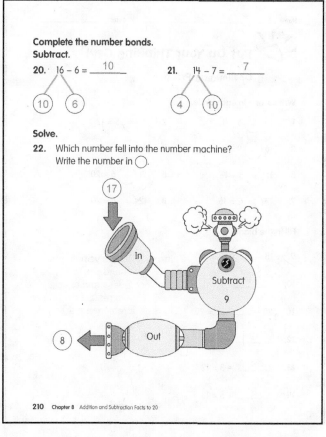

Name: _____ Date: _____

Practice 5 Real-World Problems: Addition and Subtraction Facts

Solve.

1. Mandy has 5 toy bears.
    She also has 5 toy dogs.
    How many toys does she
    have in all?

    $5 + 5 = 10$

    Mandy has ___10___ toys in all.

2. 6 children are on the
    merry-go-round.
    6 more children join them.
    How many children are
    there now?

    $6 + 6 = 12$

    There are ___12___ children now.

3. Sam has 8 marbles.
    Lamont gives him 9 marbles.
    How many marbles does Sam
    have now?

    $8 + 9 = 17$

    Sam has ___17___ marbles now.

4. Sue has 13 green ribbons
    and red ribbons.
    5 ribbons are green.
    How many red ribbons
    does Sue have?

    $13 - 5 = 8$

    Sue has ___8___ red ribbons.

5. Malika makes 12 bracelets.
    She sells some bracelets.
    She has 4 bracelets left.
    How many bracelets does
    Malika sell?

    $12 - 4 = 8$

    Malika sells ___8___ bracelets.

6. Al makes 16 butterfly knots.
    He gives 9 butterfly knots to
    his friends.
    How many butterfly knots
    does Al have left?

    $16 - 9 = 7$

    Al has ___7___ butterfly knots left.

Name: _____ Date: _____

Put On Your Thinking Cap!
Challenging Practice

Write + or − in each circle.

1. $10 \bigcirc 6 = 4$ → $10 \ominus 6 = 4$

2. $7 \oplus 5 = 12$

3. $16 \ominus 9 = 7$

4. $9 \oplus 7 = 16$

5. $11 \oplus 3 = 14$

6. $14 \oplus 6 = 20$

7. $17 \ominus 2 = 15$

8. $12 \oplus 8 = 20$

Fill in the blanks.

9. $18 - \underline{8} = 10$

10. $\underline{20} - 9 = 11$

11. $20 - \underline{0} = 20$

12. $\underline{12} - 6 = 6$

13. $\underline{9} + 3 = 12$

14. $\underline{8} + 5 = 13$

Thinking skill: Analyzing parts
and whole
Strategies: Guess and check,
and restate the
problem another way

Thinking skill: Analyzing parts and
whole
Strategy: Use guess and check

Solve.

15. Dane gets 2 baskets in a computer game.
    His total score is 16.

    a. Color 2 baskets that he gets.

    | 11 | 5 | 3 |
    | 4 | 8 | 6 |
    | 7 | 12 | 9 |

    Accept
    11, 5;
    7, 9;
    4, 12.

    b. Which are the 2 baskets that he got?
        Write an addition sentence for them.

        _____ + _____ = 16

        Accept
        $11 + 5 = 16$
        $7 + 9 = 16$
        $4 + 12 = 16$

    c. Look for other answers.
        Write them here.

        _____ + _____ = 16

        _____ + _____ = 16

Name: _____ Date: _____

 **Put On Your Thinking Cap!**

Problem Solving

Solve.

Ed did 6 more cartwheels than Lila.
How many cartwheels did
Ed and Lila each do?

Write four possible pairs of numbers.
The total number of cartwheels cannot be more than 20.

1. If Lila did _____ cartwheels, then Ed did _____ cartwheels.

2. If Lila did _____ cartwheels, then Ed did _____ cartwheels.

3. If Ed did _____ cartwheels, then Lila did _____ cartwheels.

4. If Ed did _____ cartwheels, then Lila did _____ cartwheels.

Answers vary.

Thinking skills: Identifying patterns
and relationships,
and comparing
Strategy: Guess and check

Chapter 8 Addition and Subtraction Facts to 20 **215**

Fill the ◯ with any of these numbers.
Use each number once.

5.

2 3 5 6

The numbers in each
line must add up to 12.
For example,
$1 + 4 + 7 = 12$

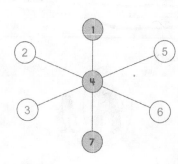

216 Chapter 8 Addition and Subtraction Facts to 20

Name: _____ Date: _____

Chapter Review/Test
Vocabulary
Circle the correct answers.

1. Which numbers are the <u>same</u>?
   ④ 9 6 0 ④

2. Which fact is a doubles fact?
   $9 + 1 = 10$ $4 + 8 = 12$ $（9 + 9 = 18）$

3. Which fact is a doubles plus one fact?
   $（1 + 2 = 3）$ $3 + 3 = 6$ $9 + 2 = 11$

Concepts and Skills
Fill in the blanks.

4. $6 + 5 =$ __11__   5. $9 + 6 =$ __15__

Complete the number bonds.
Then fill in the blanks.

6. $15 + 4 =$ __19__
   ⑩ ⑤

7. $6 + 14 =$ __20__
   ④ ⑩

8. $16 - 4 =$ __12__
   ⑩ ⑥

9. $14 - 8 =$ __6__
   ④ ⑩

Chapter 8 Addition and Subtraction Facts to 20 **217**

Fill in the blanks.

10. $11 + 9 =$ __20__   11. $12 - 5 =$ __7__

Problem Solving
Solve.

12. Andy has 9 stickers.
    His sister gives him 5 more.
    How many stickers does
    Andy have in all?

    $9 + 5 = 14$

    Andy has __14__ stickers in all.

13. Tia has 14 hair clips.
    She gives 7 hair clips to her sister.
    How many hair clips does Tia
    have left?

    $14 - 7 = 7$

    Tia has __7__ hair clips left.

14. I am double 6 plus 1 more.
    What number am I?

    $6 + 6 + 1 = 13$

    I am the number __13__

218 Chapter 8 Addition and Subtraction Facts to 20

199

Name: _____ Date: _____

CHAPTER 9 Length

Practice 1   Comparing Two Things
Circle the correct answer.

┌─ Example ─────────────────────────────┐
│ Which is longer?   │
│ 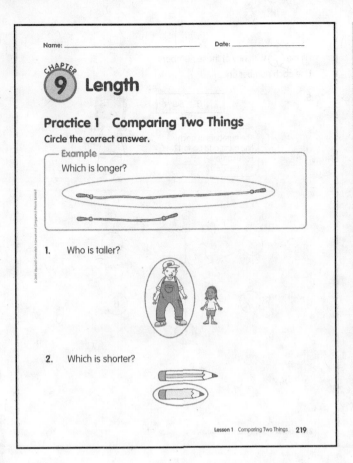   │
└───────────────────────────────────────┘

1.   Who is taller?

2.   Which is shorter?

Fill in the blanks.

┌─ Example ─────────────────────────────┐
│ Which is longer?   │
│ Which is shorter?   │
│ 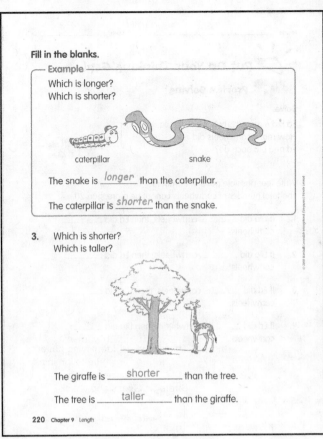   │
│ caterpillar   snake   │
│   │
│ The snake is _longer_ than the caterpillar. │
│ The caterpillar is _shorter_ than the snake. │
└───────────────────────────────────────┘

3.   Which is shorter?
     Which is taller?

The giraffe is ___shorter___ than the tree.

The tree is ___taller___ than the giraffe.

Name: _____ Date: _____

4.   Which is longer?
     Which is shorter

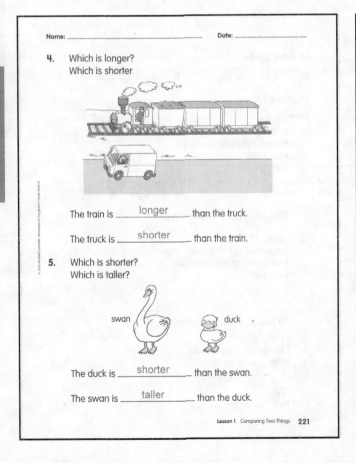

The train is ___longer___ than the truck.

The truck is ___shorter___ than the train.

5.   Which is shorter?
     Which is taller?

swan   duck

The duck is ___shorter___ than the swan.

The swan is ___taller___ than the duck.

Draw.

┌─ Example ─────────────────────────────┐
│ a longer arrow   │
│ ──────────────▶   │
│ ──────────────────▶   │
└───────────────────────────────────────┘

6.   a shorter tree

Accept all drawings of
trees that are shorter.

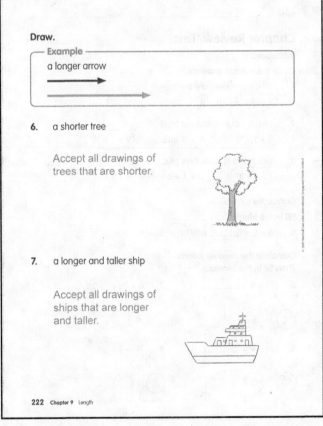

7.   a longer and taller ship

Accept all drawings of
ships that are longer
and taller.

Name: _____ Date: _____

Practice 2   Comparing More Than Two Things
Look at the picture.
Fill in the blanks with the correct names.

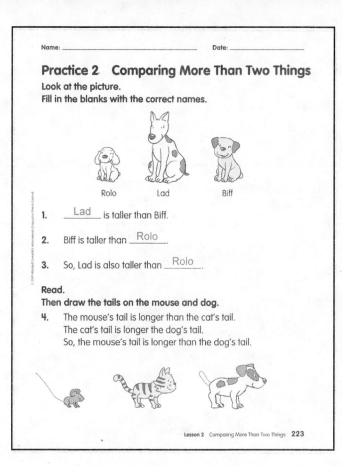

Rolo   Lad   Biff

1. ____Lad____ is taller than Biff.

2. Biff is taller than ____Rolo____.

3. So, Lad is also taller than ____Rolo____.

Read.
Then draw the tails on the mouse and dog.

4. The mouse's tail is longer than the cat's tail.
   The cat's tail is longer the dog's tail.
   So, the mouse's tail is longer than the dog's tail.

Lesson 2   Comparing More Than Two Things   **223**

Color.

┌─ Example ──────────────────────────┐
│ the longest string of beads   │
│   │
│   │
└─────────────────────────────────────┘

5. the shortest vegetable

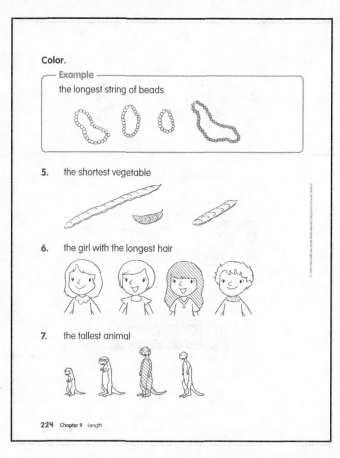

6. the girl with the longest hair

7. the tallest animal

224   Chapter 9   Length

Name: _____ Date: _____

Fill in the blanks with *taller, tallest, shorter,* or *shortest.*

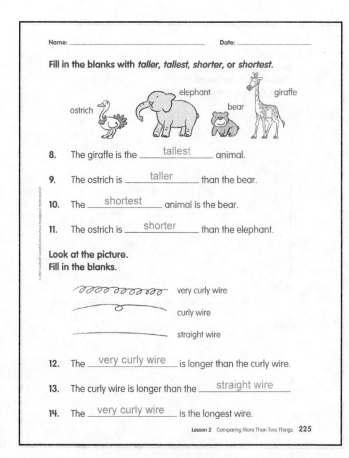

ostrich   elephant   bear   giraffe

8. The giraffe is the ____tallest____ animal.

9. The ostrich is ____taller____ than the bear.

10. The ____shortest____ animal is the bear.

11. The ostrich is ____shorter____ than the elephant.

Look at the picture.
Fill in the blanks.

very curly wire
curly wire
straight wire

12. The ____very curly wire____ is longer than the curly wire.

13. The curly wire is longer than the ____straight wire____.

14. The ____very curly wire____ is the longest wire.

Lesson 2   Comparing More Than Two Things   **225**

Math Journal

Help Jamie put his toys away. Read.
Then cut out the toys on page 227 and paste them on the shelf.

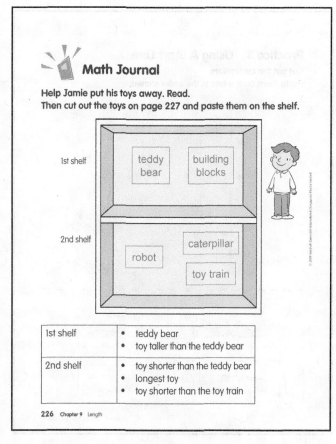

1st shelf

2nd shelf

1st shelf	• teddy bear • toy taller than the teddy bear
2nd shelf	• toy shorter than the teddy bear • longest toy • toy shorter than the toy train

226   Chapter 9   Length

Workbook Answers: Chapter 9
Math in Focus Homeschool Answer Key, Grade 1

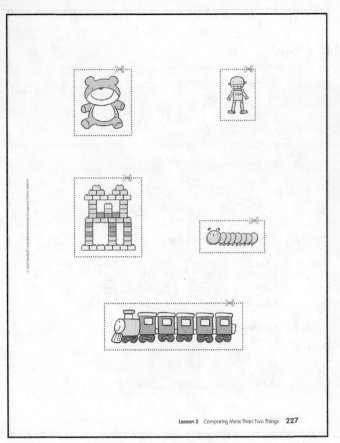

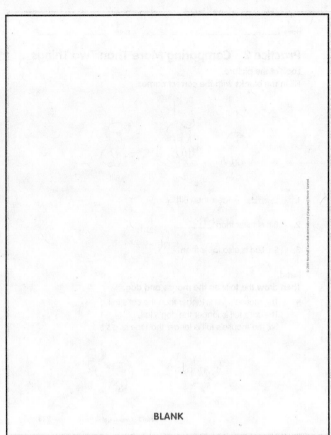

BLANK

Name: _____   Date: _____

Practice 3   Using A Start Line
Cut out the caterpillars.
Paste them on the box in the order shown.

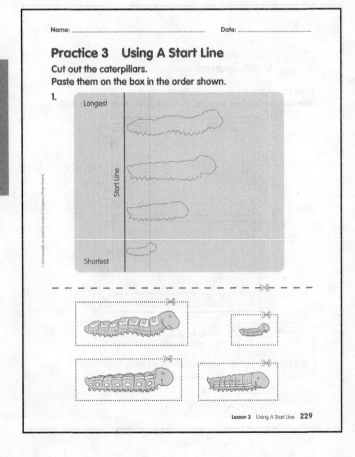

Draw 2 more pencils.
Color the longest pencil blue.
Color the shortest pencil green.

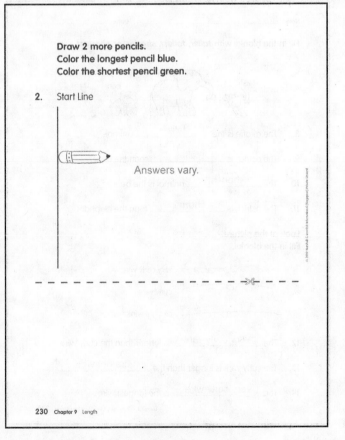

2.   Start Line

Answers vary.

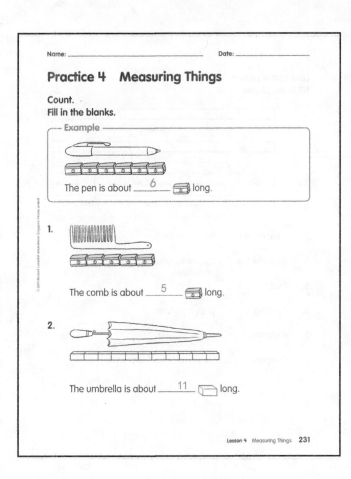

Practice 4   Measuring Things

Count.
Fill in the blanks.

Example

The pen is about __6__ 🔲 long.

1.

The comb is about __5__ 🔲 long.

2.

The umbrella is about __11__ 🔲 long.

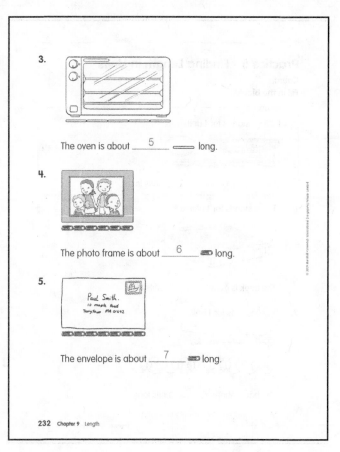

3.

The oven is about __5__ ▭ long.

4.

The photo frame is about __6__ ⬤ long.

5.

The envelope is about __7__ ⬤ long.

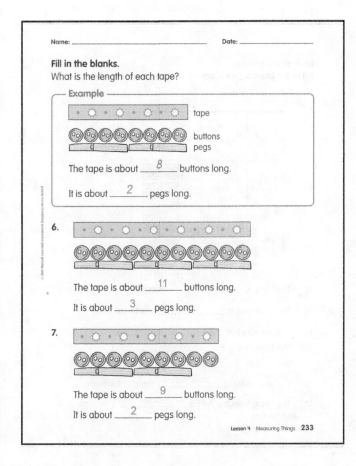

Fill in the blanks.
What is the length of each tape?

Example

tape

buttons
pegs

The tape is about __8__ buttons long.

It is about __2__ pegs long.

6.

The tape is about __11__ buttons long.

It is about __3__ pegs long.

7.

The tape is about __9__ buttons long.

It is about __2__ pegs long.

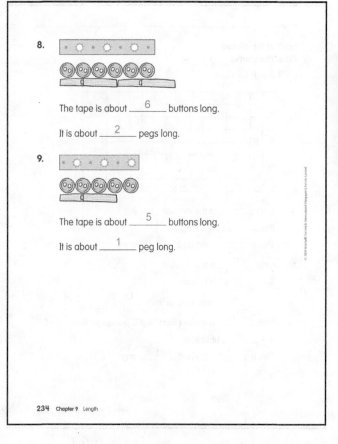

8.

The tape is about __6__ buttons long.

It is about __2__ pegs long.

9.

The tape is about __5__ buttons long.

It is about __1__ peg long.

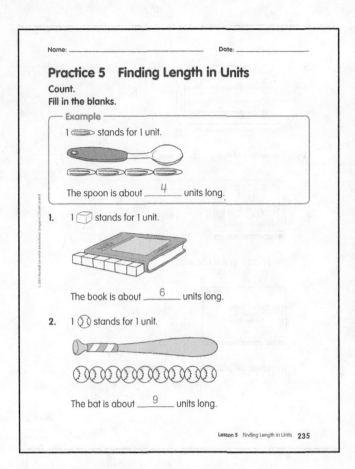

Practice 5 Finding Length in Units

Count.
Fill in the blanks.

Example

1 ⬭ stands for 1 unit.

The spoon is about __4__ units long.

1. 1 ⬜ stands for 1 unit.

The book is about __6__ units long.

2. 1 ⚾ stands for 1 unit.

The bat is about __9__ units long.

Lesson 5 Finding Length in Units **235**

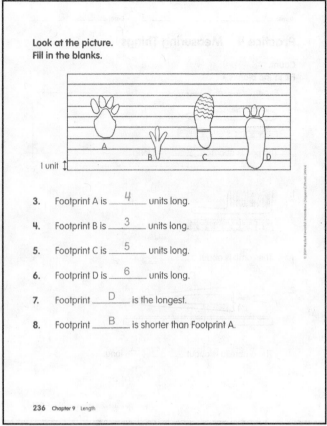

Look at the picture.
Fill in the blanks.

1 unit ↕

3. Footprint A is __4__ units long.

4. Footprint B is __3__ units long.

5. Footprint C is __5__ units long.

6. Footprint D is __6__ units long.

7. Footprint __D__ is the longest.

8. Footprint __B__ is shorter than Footprint A.

236 Chapter 9 Length

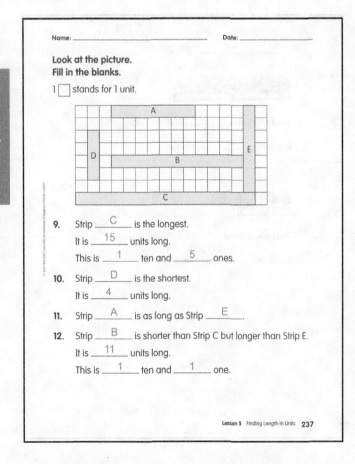

Name: _____ Date: _____

Look at the picture.
Fill in the blanks.

1 ⬜ stands for 1 unit.

9. Strip __C__ is the longest.
   It is __15__ units long.
   This is __1__ ten and __5__ ones.

10. Strip __D__ is the shortest.
    It is __4__ units long.

11. Strip __A__ is as long as Strip __E__.

12. Strip __B__ is shorter than Strip C but longer than Strip E.
    It is __11__ units long.
    This is __1__ ten and __1__ one.

Lesson 5 Finding Length in Units **237**

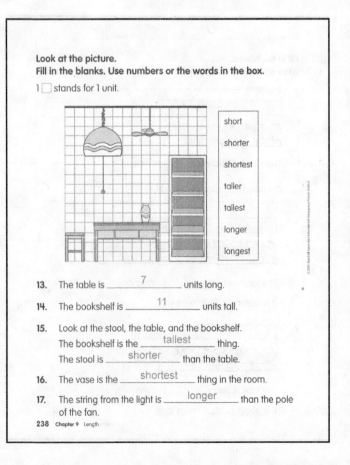

Look at the picture.
Fill in the blanks. Use numbers or the words in the box.

1 ⬜ stands for 1 unit.

short
shorter
shortest
taller
tallest
longer
longest

13. The table is __7__ units long.

14. The bookshelf is __11__ units tall.

15. Look at the stool, the table, and the bookshelf.
    The bookshelf is the __tallest__ thing.
    The stool is __shorter__ than the table.

16. The vase is the __shortest__ thing in the room.

17. The string from the light is __longer__ than the pole of the fan.

238 Chapter 9 Length

---

www.harcourtschoolsupply.com

204

Workbook Answers: Chapter 9
Math in Focus Homeschool Answer Key, Grade 1

Name: _____ Date: _____

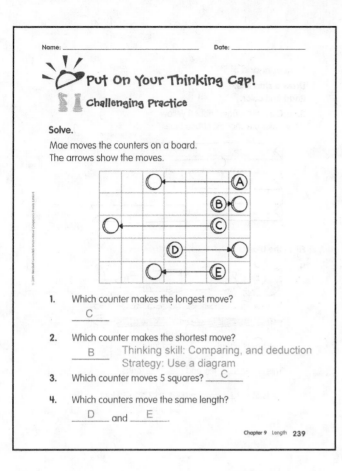

Put On Your Thinking Cap!
Challenging Practice

Solve.
Mae moves the counters on a board.
The arrows show the moves.

1. Which counter makes the longest move?
   __C__

2. Which counter makes the shortest move?
   __B__

3. Which counter moves 5 squares? __C__

4. Which counters move the same length?
   __D__ and __E__

Thinking skill: Comparing, and deduction
Strategy: Use a diagram

Chapter 9 Length **239**

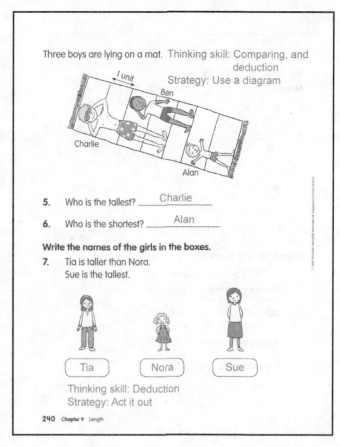

Three boys are lying on a mat. Thinking skill: Comparing, and deduction
Strategy: Use a diagram

5. Who is the tallest? ___Charlie___

6. Who is the shortest? ___Alan___

Write the names of the girls in the boxes.

7. Tia is taller than Nora.
   Sue is the tallest.

Tia   Nora   Sue

Thinking skill: Deduction
Strategy: Act it out

240 Chapter 9 Length

Name: _____ Date: _____

Look at the picture and read.
Then draw.

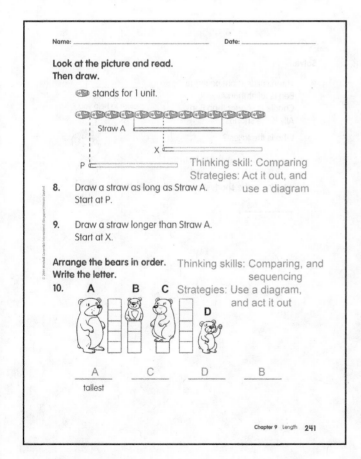

stands for 1 unit.

Straw A

Thinking skill: Comparing
Strategies: Act it out, and
use a diagram

8. Draw a straw as long as Straw A.
   Start at P.

9. Draw a straw longer than Straw A.
   Start at X.

Arrange the bears in order. Thinking skills: Comparing, and
Write the letter. sequencing

10.   **A**   **B**   **C**   Strategies: Use a diagram,
                            D   and act it out

   __A__   __C__   __D__   __B__
   tallest

Chapter 9 Length **241**

Put On Your Thinking Cap!
Problem Solving

Fill in the blanks.

1. Tim, Ella, Rosa, and Ling knit some scarves.
   Who does each scarf belong to?

   Scarf A _____ Rosa
   Scarf B _____ Ella
   Scarf C _____ Ling
   Scarf D _____ Tim

   Ella's scarf is longer than Ling's scarf.

   Rosa's scarf is the longest.

   Ling's scarf is longer than Tim's scarf.

Thinking skill: Deduction
Strategy: Guess and check

242 Chapter 9 Length

Chapter 9

Name: _____ **Date:** _____

Chapter Review/Test
Vocabulary
Match.

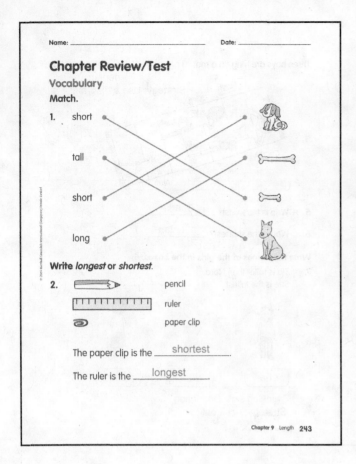

1. short
   tall
   short
   long

Write *longest* or *shortest*.

2.
   pencil
   ruler
   paper clip

   The paper clip is the ____shortest____

   The ruler is the ____longest____

Concepts and Skills
Draw a start line.
Read and color.

3. Color the longest ribbon yellow.
   Color the shortest ribbon blue.

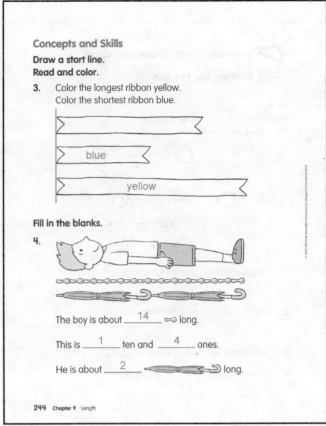

blue

yellow

Fill in the blanks.

4.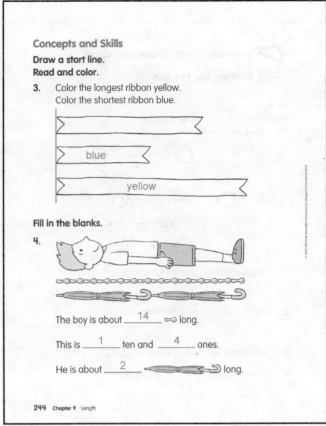

The boy is about ___14___ ⊸ long.

This is ___1___ ten and ___4___ ones.

He is about ___2___ ⟨⟨⟩⟩ long.

Name: _____ **Date:** _____

Problem Solving
Solve.

1 ☐ stands for 1 unit.

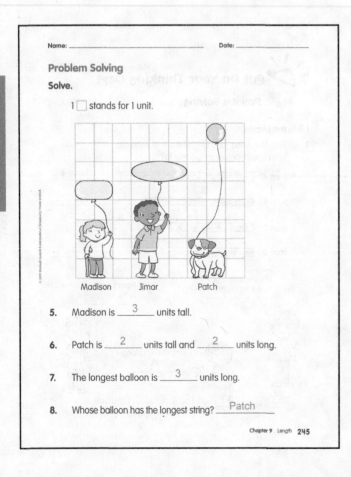

Madison   Jimar   Patch

5. Madison is ___3___ units tall.

6. Patch is ___2___ units tall and ___2___ units long.

7. The longest balloon is ___3___ units long.

8. Whose balloon has the longest string? ___Patch___

Solve.

9. Three children are on stage.
   Ben is taller than Ally.
   Charlie is shorter than Ben.
   Ally is the shortest.

   Who is the tallest?

   ___Ben___ is the tallest.

   Who is not the shortest and not the tallest?

   ___Charlie___

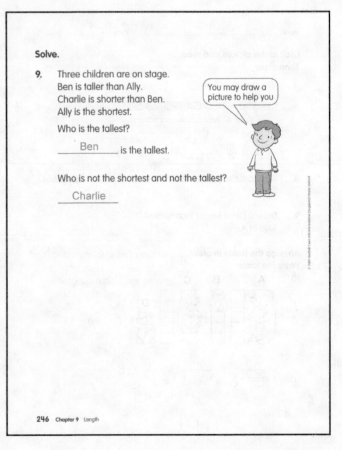

You may draw a picture to help you

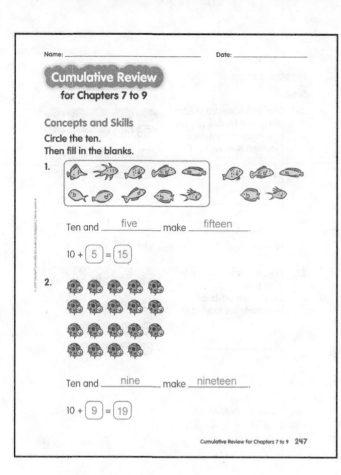

Cumulative Review
for Chapters 7 to 9

Concepts and Skills

Circle the ten.
Then fill in the blanks.

1.

Ten and ___five___ make ___fifteen___

10 + ⑤ = ⑮

2.

Ten and ___nine___ make ___nineteen___

10 + ⑨ = ⑲

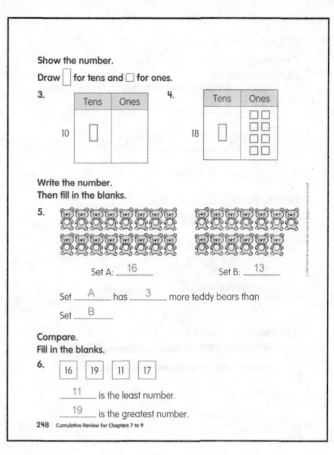

Show the number.
Draw ▭ for tens and □ for ones.

3.

Tens	Ones

10

4.

Tens	Ones

18

Write the number.
Then fill in the blanks.

5.

Set A: ___16___   Set B: ___13___

Set ___A___ has ___3___ more teddy bears than
Set ___B___.

Compare.
Fill in the blanks.

6.

| 16 | 19 | 11 | 17 |

___11___ is the least number.

___19___ is the greatest number.

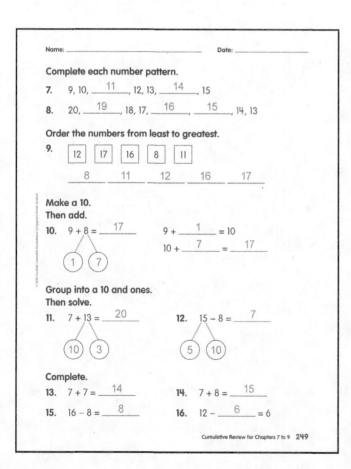

Complete each number pattern.

7.   9, 10, ___11___, 12, 13, ___14___, 15

8.   20, ___19___, 18, 17, ___16___, ___15___, 14, 13

Order the numbers from least to greatest.

9.

| 12 | 17 | 16 | 8 | 11 |

___8___ ___11___ ___12___ ___16___ ___17___

Make a 10.
Then add.

10.   9 + 8 = ___17___   9 + ___1___ = 10

   ① ⑦   10 + ___7___ = ___17___

Group into a 10 and ones.
Then solve.

11.   7 + 13 = ___20___   12.   15 − 8 = ___7___

   ⑩ ③   ⑤ ⑩

Complete.

13.   7 + 7 = ___14___   14.   7 + 8 = ___15___

15.   16 − 8 = ___8___   16.   12 − ___6___ = 6

Fill in the blanks.
Use the words in the box.

Trey   Rosa   Lauren

| shorter | shortest | longer | longest | taller | tallest |

17.   Rosa is ___taller___ than Lauren.

18.   Lauren is ___shorter___ than Rosa.

19.   Trey is ___taller___ than Rosa and Lauren.

   So, Trey is the ___tallest___

20.   The tail on the white dog is ___longer___ than the tail
   on the spotted dog.

21.   The tail on the black dog is ___longer___ than the tail
   on the white dog.

22.   The tail on the spotted dog is the ___shortest___

Workbook Answers: Chapters 7-9 Review
Math in Focus Homeschool Answer Key, Grade 1

Complete.

23. Draw a start line.
Then draw a strip that is longer than A and shorter than B.

A

B

Fill in the blanks.

24.

The dog collar is about ___4___ ▭ long.

It is about ___2___ 🦴 long.

25. 1 ▱ stands for 1 unit.

The leash is about ___12___ units long.

___12___ is 10 and ___2___ units.

Problem Solving

Solve.

26. Grandma bakes 20 muffins.
She gives 8 muffins to Emily.
How many muffins does
Grandma have left?

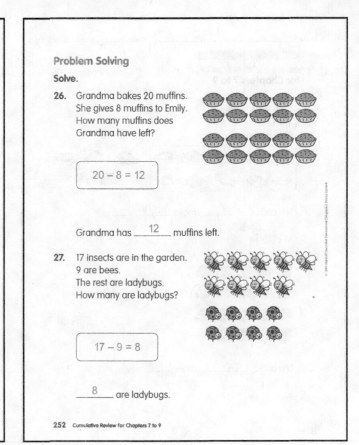

20 − 8 = 12

Grandma has ___12___ muffins left.

27. 17 insects are in the garden.
9 are bees.
The rest are ladybugs.
How many are ladybugs?

17 − 9 = 8

___8___ are ladybugs.

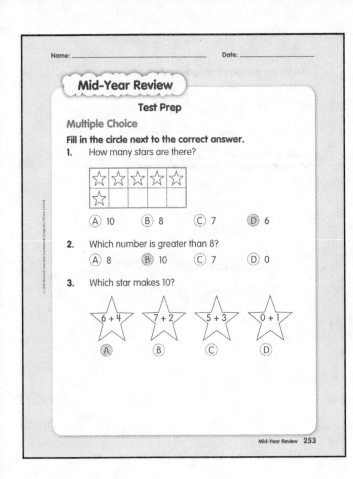

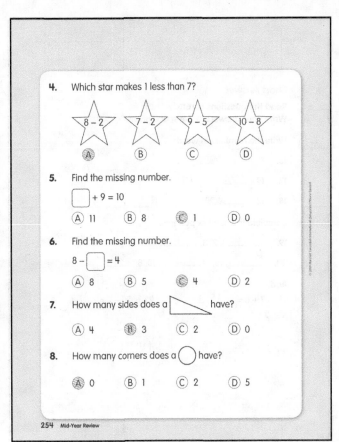

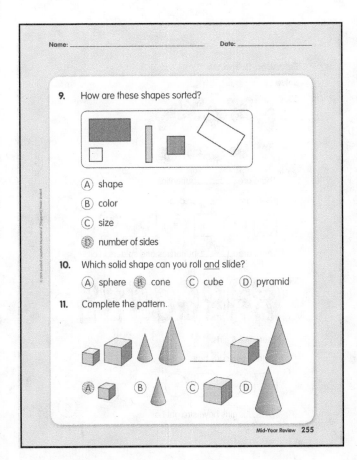

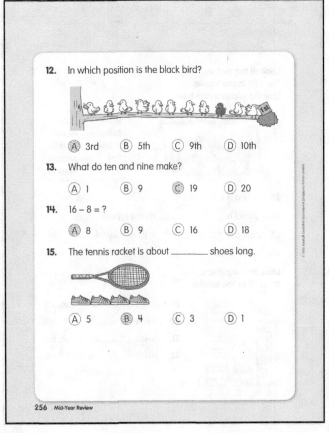

Mid-Year Review

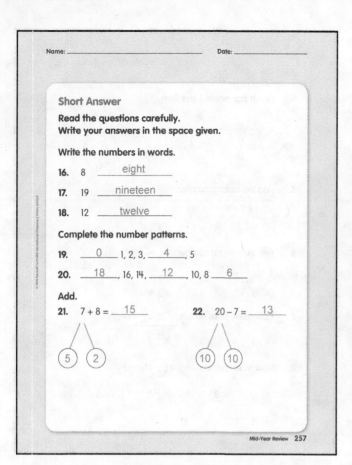

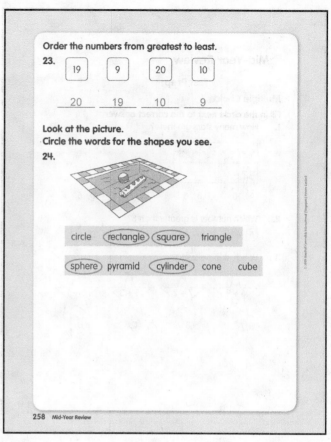

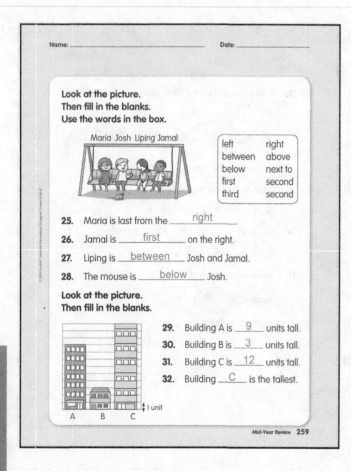

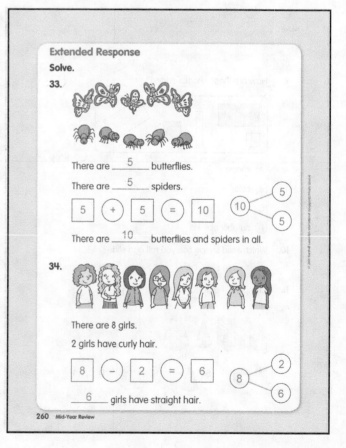

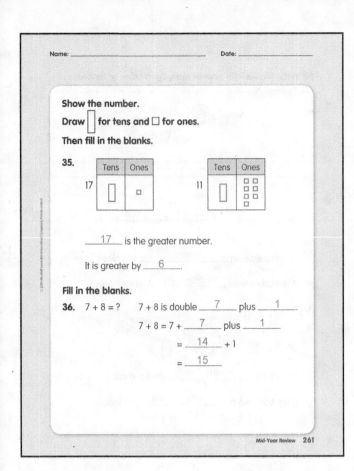

Show the number.
Draw ▯ for tens and □ for ones.
Then fill in the blanks.

35.

Tens	Ones
17 | ▯ | □ |

Tens	Ones
11 | ▯ | □ □ □ □ □ □ |

_____17_____ is the greater number.

It is greater by _____6_____.

Fill in the blanks.

36. 7 + 8 = ?   7 + 8 is double _____7_____ plus _____1_____.

7 + 8 = 7 + _____7_____ plus _____1_____

= _____14_____ + 1

= _____15_____

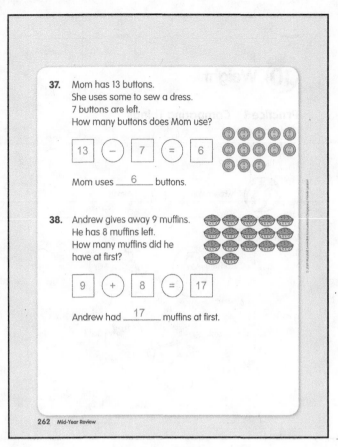

37. Mom has 13 buttons.
She uses some to sew a dress.
7 buttons are left.
How many buttons does Mom use?

[13] (−) [7] (=) (6)

Mom uses _____6_____ buttons.

38. Andrew gives away 9 muffins.
He has 8 muffins left.
How many muffins did he
have at first?

[9] (+) [8] (=) [17]

Andrew had _____17_____ muffins at first.

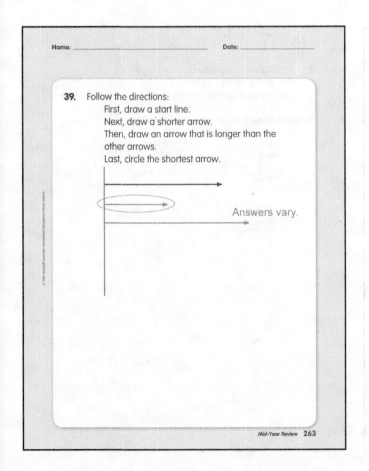

39. Follow the directions:
First, draw a start line.
Next, draw a shorter arrow.
Then, draw an arrow that is longer than the
other arrows.
Last, circle the shortest arrow.

Answers vary.

211

Workbook Answers: Mid-Year Review
Math in Focus Homeschool Answer Key, Grade 1

Name: _____ Date: _____

CHAPTER
(10) Weight

Practice 1 Comparing Things

Circle your answer.

┌─ Example ─────────────────────────────────┐
│ Which is lighter? │
│ 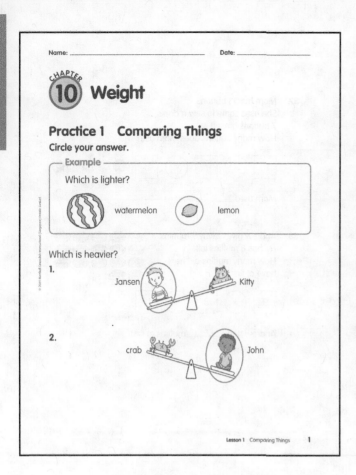 watermelon   lemon │
└───┘

Which is heavier?

1. Jansen   Kitty

2. crab   John

Fill in the blanks with *heavier than*, *lighter than* or *as heavy as*.

┌─ Example ─────────────────────────────────┐
│ muffin 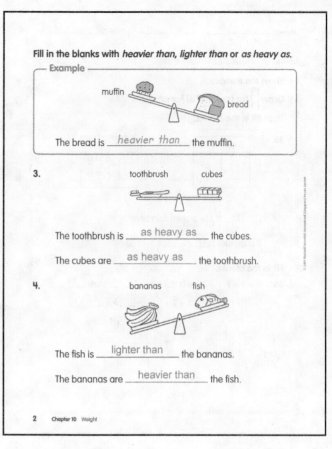 bread │
│ The bread is __*heavier than*__ the muffin. │
└───┘

3.   toothbrush   cubes

The toothbrush is __as heavy as__ the cubes.

The cubes are __as heavy as__ the toothbrush.

4.   bananas   fish

The fish is __lighter than__ the bananas.

The bananas are __heavier than__ the fish.

Name: _____ Date: _____

Fill in the blanks.

┌─ Example ─────────────────────────────────┐
│ cup 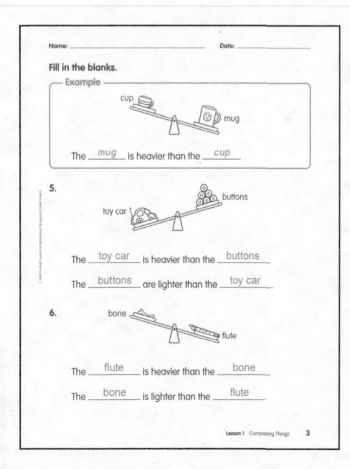 mug │
│ The __mug__ is heavier than the __cup__. │
└───┘

5.   toy car   buttons

The __toy car__ is heavier than the __buttons__.

The __buttons__ are lighter than the __toy car__.

6.   bone   flute

The __flute__ is heavier than the __bone__.

The __bone__ is lighter than the __flute__.

---

7. Mrs. Todd has an apple and an orange.
   She puts them on a balance.
   The orange is heavier than the apple.

Draw the apple and orange in the correct pans.

apple   orange

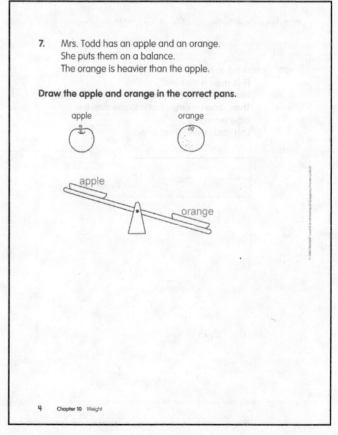

apple   orange

212

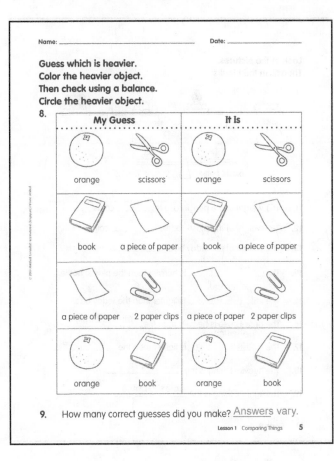

Name: _____   Date: _____

Guess which is heavier.
Color the heavier object.
Then check using a balance.
Circle the heavier object.

8.

My Guess	It Is
orange scissors	orange scissors
book a piece of paper	book a piece of paper
a piece of paper 2 paper clips	a piece of paper 2 paper clips
orange book	orange book

9. How many correct guesses did you make? __Answers__ vary.

Lesson 1   Comparing Things   5

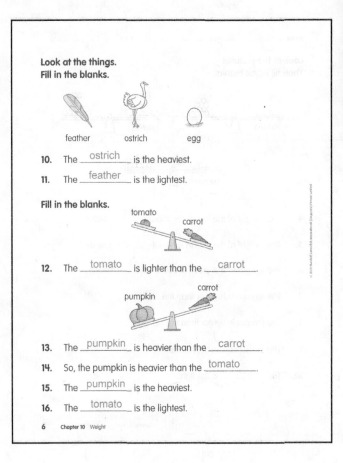

Look at the things.
Fill in the blanks.

feather   ostrich   egg

10. The ___ostrich___ is the heaviest.

11. The ___feather___ is the lightest.

Fill in the blanks.

tomato   carrot

12. The ___tomato___ is lighter than the ___carrot___.

pumpkin   carrot

13. The ___pumpkin___ is heavier than the ___carrot___.

14. So, the pumpkin is heavier than the ___tomato___

15. The ___pumpkin___ is the heaviest.

16. The ___tomato___ is the lightest.

6   Chapter 10   Weight

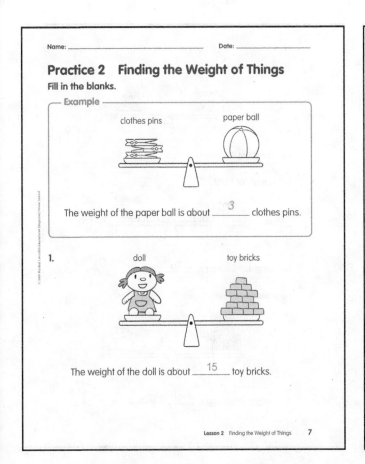

Name: _____   Date: _____

Practice 2   Finding the Weight of Things

Fill in the blanks.

Example

clothes pins   paper ball

The weight of the paper ball is about ___3___ clothes pins.

1.

doll   toy bricks

The weight of the doll is about ___15___ toy bricks.

Lesson 2   Finding the Weight of Things   7

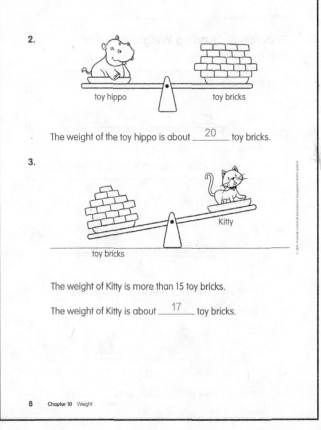

2.

toy hippo   toy bricks

The weight of the toy hippo is about ___20___ toy bricks.

3.

toy bricks   Kitty

The weight of Kitty is more than 15 toy bricks.

The weight of Kitty is about ___17___ toy bricks.

8   Chapter 10   Weight

Workbook Answers: Chapter 10
Math in Focus Homeschool Answer Key, Grade 1

Name: _____   Date: _____

Look at the pictures
Then fill in the blanks.

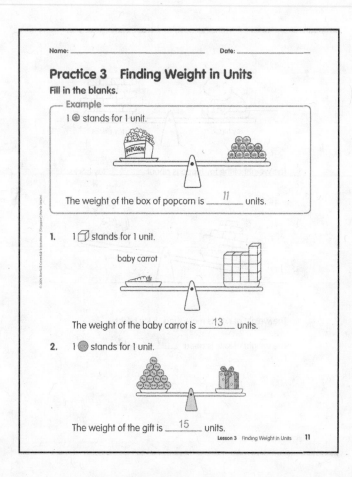

tomato   lemon

onion

4. The weight of the tomato is about ___15___ beads.

5. The weight of the lemon is about ___20___ beads.

6. The weight of the onion is about ___12___ beads.

7. The tomato is heavier than the ___onion___

8. The tomato is lighter than the ___lemon___

9. The ___lemon___ is the heaviest.

10. The ___onion___ is the lightest.

Lesson 2   Finding the Weight of Things   9

Name: _____   Date: _____

Look at the pictures.
Then fill in the blanks.

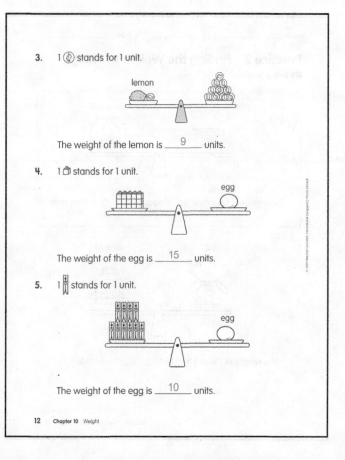

pencil case   coins   teddy bear

plastic bottle

11. The weight of the pencil case is ___10___ coins.

12. The weight of the plastic bottle is ___6___ coins.

13. The weight of the teddy bear is ___17___ coins.

14. The __pencil case/ teddy bear__ is heavier than the plastic bottle.

15. The __pencil case/ plastic bottle__ is lighter than the teddy bear.

16. The pencil case is heavier than the ___plastic bottle___

17. The __pencil case/ plastic bottle__ is lighter than the ___teddy bear___

18. The heaviest thing is the ___teddy bear___

19. The lightest thing is the ___plastic bottle___

10   Chapter 10   Weight

Name: _____   Date: _____

Practice 3   Finding Weight in Units

Fill in the blanks.

— Example —

1 ⊕ stands for 1 unit.

The weight of the box of popcorn is ___11___ units.

1. 1 ⬜ stands for 1 unit.

baby carrot

The weight of the baby carrot is ___13___ units.

2. 1 ⬤ stands for 1 unit.

The weight of the gift is ___15___ units.

Lesson 3   Finding Weight in Units   11

3. 1 ◯ stands for 1 unit.

lemon

The weight of the lemon is ___9___ units.

4. 1 ⬜ stands for 1 unit.

egg

The weight of the egg is ___15___ units.

5. 1 ▯ stands for 1 unit.

egg

The weight of the egg is ___10___ units.

12   Chapter 10   Weight

Fill in the blanks.
1 ☆ stands for 1 unit.

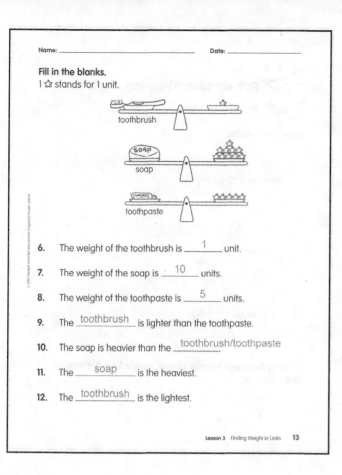

6. The weight of the toothbrush is ___1___ unit.

7. The weight of the soap is ___10___ units.

8. The weight of the toothpaste is ___5___ units.

9. The ___toothbrush___ is lighter than the toothpaste.

10. The soap is heavier than the ___toothbrush/toothpaste___

11. The ___soap___ is the heaviest.

12. The ___toothbrush___ is the lightest.

Fill in the blanks.
1 ⊙ stands for 1 unit.

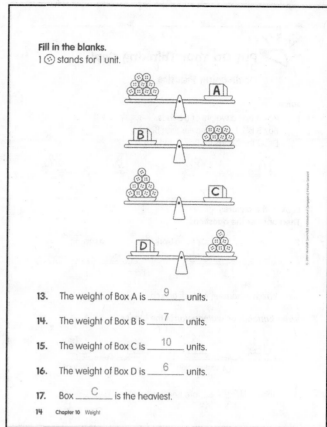

13. The weight of Box A is ___9___ units.

14. The weight of Box B is ___7___ units.

15. The weight of Box C is ___10___ units.

16. The weight of Box D is ___6___ units.

17. Box ___C___ is the heaviest.

Name: _____   Date: _____

18. Box ___D___ is the lightest.

19. Box ___A/B/C___ is heavier than Box D.

20. Box ___B/D___ is lighter than Box A.

21. Arrange the Boxes A to D in order from the heaviest to the lightest.

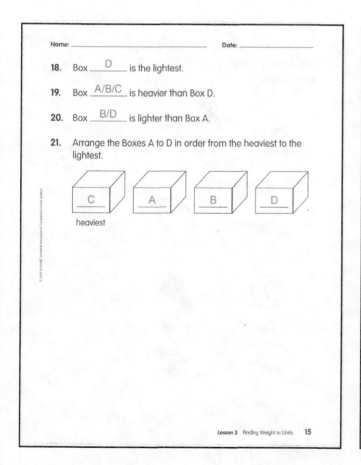

heaviest

Math Journal

Look at the pictures.
1 🖊 stands for 1 unit.

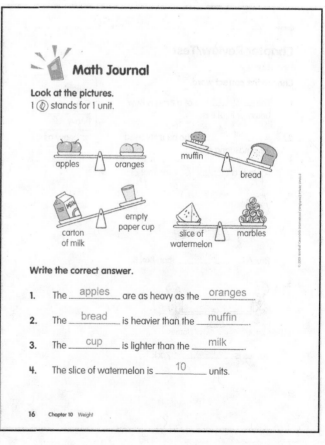

Write the correct answer.

1. The ___apples___ are as heavy as the ___oranges___

2. The ___bread___ is heavier than the ___muffin___.

3. The ___cup___ is lighter than the ___milk___.

4. The slice of watermelon is ___10___ units.

215

Workbook Answers: Chapter 10
Math in Focus Homeschool Answer Key, Grade 1

Name: _____ Date: _____

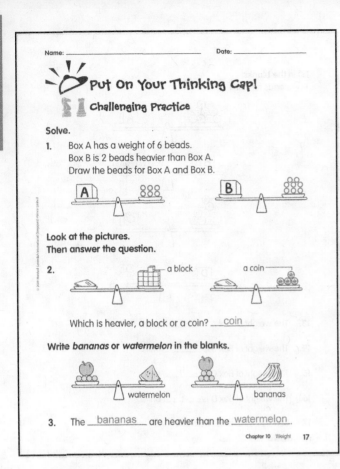

Put On Your Thinking Cap!
Challenging Practice

Solve.

1. Box A has a weight of 6 beads.
   Box B is 2 beads heavier than Box A.
   Draw the beads for Box A and Box B.

Look at the pictures.
Then answer the question.

2.

   Which is heavier, a block or a coin? __coin__

Write bananas or watermelon in the blanks.

3. The __bananas__ are heavier than the __watermelon__

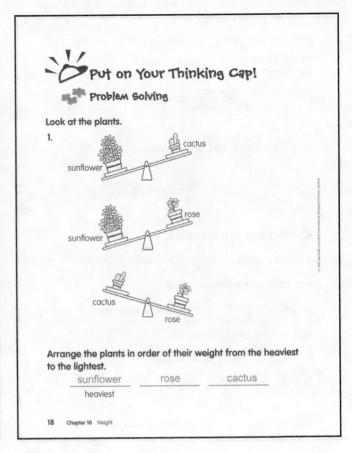

Put On Your Thinking Cap!
Problem Solving

Look at the plants.

1. sunflower — cactus

   sunflower — rose

   cactus — rose

Arrange the plants in order of their weight from the heaviest to the lightest.

__sunflower__   __rose__   __cactus__
heaviest

Name: _____ Date: _____

Chapter Review/Test
Vocabulary
Choose the correct word.

weight	
unit	
heavy	
as heavy as	
lighter	

1. The __weight__ of a thing is how heavy or light it is.

2. A __unit__ is the quantity used for measuring a thing.

3. A lion is a __heavy__ animal.

4.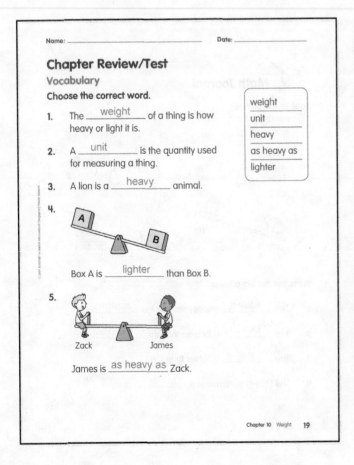

   Box A is __lighter__ than Box B.

5.

   Zack   James

   James is __as heavy as__ Zack.

Concepts and Skills
Fill in the blanks.

6.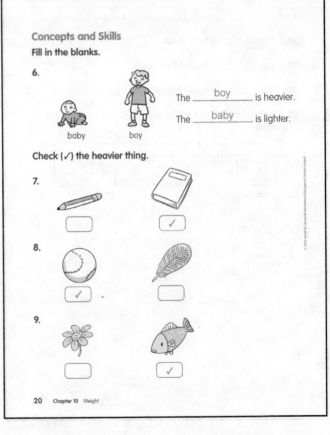

   baby   boy

   The __boy__ is heavier.
   The __baby__ is lighter.

Check (✓) the heavier thing.

7. [ ]   [✓]

8. [✓]   [ ]

9. [ ]   [✓]

216

Name: _____ Date: _____

10.

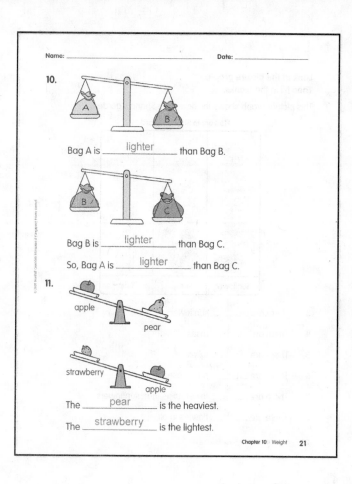

Bag A is ___lighter___ than Bag B.

Bag B is ___lighter___ than Bag C.

So, Bag A is ___lighter___ than Bag C.

11.

The ___pear___ is the heaviest.

The ___strawberry___ is the lightest.

---

1 ⬜ stands for 1 unit.

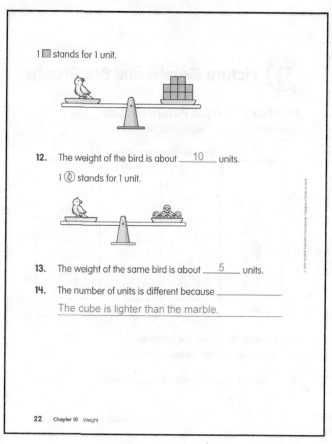

12. The weight of the bird is about ___10___ units.

1 ⓠ stands for 1 unit.

13. The weight of the same bird is about ___5___ units.

14. The number of units is different because _____

The cube is lighter than the marble.

Name: _____ Date: _____

Problem Solving
Solve.

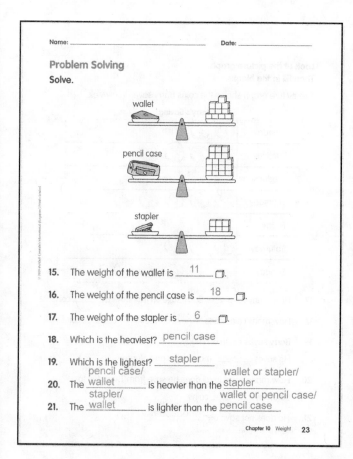

15. The weight of the wallet is ___11___ 🔲.

16. The weight of the pencil case is ___18___ 🔲.

17. The weight of the stapler is ___6___ 🔲.

18. Which is the heaviest? ___pencil case___

19. Which is the lightest? ___stapler___

20. The ___wallet___ is heavier than the ___stapler___
pencil case/ .... wallet or stapler/

21. The ___wallet___ is lighter than the ___pencil case___
stapler/ .... wallet or pencil case/

---

1 ◉ stands for 1 unit.

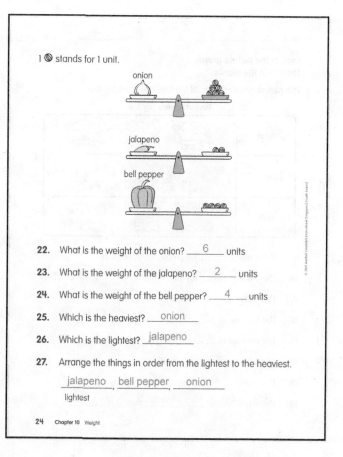

22. What is the weight of the onion? ___6___ units

23. What is the weight of the jalapeno? ___2___ units

24. What is the weight of the bell pepper? ___4___ units

25. Which is the heaviest? ___onion___

26. Which is the lightest? ___jalapeno___

27. Arrange the things in order from the lightest to the heaviest.

___jalapeno___, ___bell pepper___, ___onion___
lightest

Name: _____   Date: _____

CHAPTER 11 Picture Graphs and Bar Graphs

Practice 1   Simple Picture Graphs

Daniel draws a picture graph of his friends' birth months.

Daniel's Friends' Birth Months

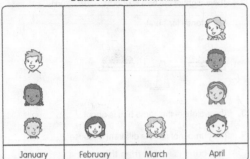

| January | February | March | April |

Use the graph to answer the questions.

1. How many friends are born in January?   3

2. In which month are most of his friends born?   April

**Look at the picture graph.
Then fill in the blanks.**

This picture graph shows the flowers in Shana's garden.

Flowers in Shana's Garden

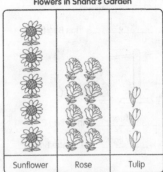

| Sunflower | Rose | Tulip |

3. There are ___5___ sunflowers.

4. There are ___8___ roses.

5. There are ___3___ tulips.

6. There are ___5___ more roses than tulips.

7. There are ___2___ fewer tulips than sunflowers.

8. There are ___16___ flowers in all.

Name: _____   Date: _____

**Look at the picture graph.
Then fill in the blanks.**

This picture graph shows all the toys in Annie's toy box.

Toys in Annie's Toy Box

Toy Plane	✈ ✈ ✈
Toy Car	🚗🚗🚗🚗🚗🚗🚗🚗🚗🚗
Toy Train	🚂🚂🚂🚂🚂🚂

9. There are ___3___ toy planes in Annie's box.

10. There are ___10___ toy cars.

11. There are ___6___ toy trains.

12. The number of __toy cars__ is the greatest.

13. The number of __toy planes__ is the least.

14. Annie has ___19___ toys in all.

15. There are ___4___ more toy cars than toy trains.

16. There are 7 fewer __toy planes__ than __toy cars__.

**Look at the picture graph.
Then fill in the blanks.**

This picture graph shows the coins Barry saves in a week.

Barry's Savings

Monday	🪙🪙
Tuesday	🪙🪙🪙🪙
Wednesday	
Thursday	🪙🪙🪙🪙
Friday	🪙
Saturday	🪙🪙🪙
Sunday	🪙🪙🪙🪙🪙

17. How many coins does Barry save on Monday?   ___2___ coins

18. How many coins does he save on Tuesday?   ___4___ coins

19. Barry saves 1 coin on Friday.
    He saves ___2___ more coins on Saturday.

20. How many coins in all does he save from Thursday to
    Saturday?   ___9___ coins

21. He does not save on __Wednesday__

Workbook Answers: Chapter 11
Math in Focus Homeschool Answer Key, Grade 1

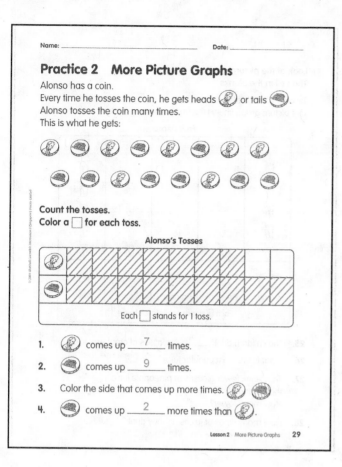

Practice 2   More Picture Graphs

Alonso has a coin.
Every time he tosses the coin, he gets heads or tails.
Alonso tosses the coin many times.
This is what he gets:

Count the tosses.
Color a ☐ for each toss.

Alonso's Tosses

Each ☐ stands for 1 toss.

1. comes up ___7___ times.
2. comes up ___9___ times.
3. Color the side that comes up more times.
4. comes up ___2___ more times than .

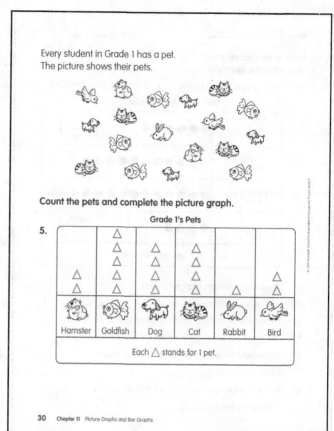

Every student in Grade 1 has a pet.
The picture shows their pets.

Count the pets and complete the picture graph.

5.

Grade 1's Pets

Hamster	Goldfish	Dog	Cat	Rabbit	Bird

Each △ stands for 1 pet.

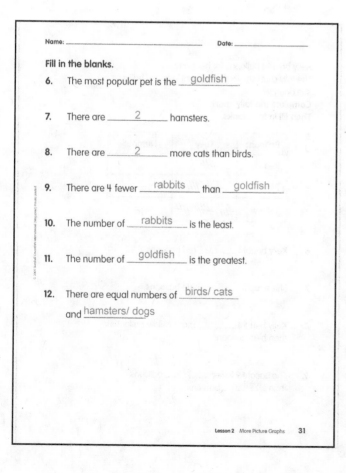

Fill in the blanks.

6. The most popular pet is the ___goldfish___.

7. There are ___2___ hamsters.

8. There are ___2___ more cats than birds.

9. There are 4 fewer ___rabbits___ than ___goldfish___.

10. The number of ___rabbits___ is the least.

11. The number of ___goldfish___ is the greatest.

12. There are equal numbers of ___birds/ cats___ and ___hamsters/ dogs___

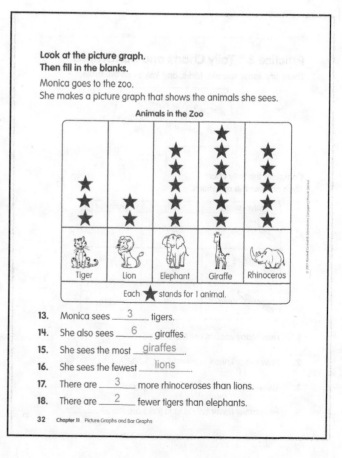

Look at the picture graph.
Then fill in the blanks.

Monica goes to the zoo.
She makes a picture graph that shows the animals she sees.

Animals in the Zoo

Tiger	Lion	Elephant	Giraffe	Rhinoceros

Each ★ stands for 1 animal.

13. Monica sees ___3___ tigers.
14. She also sees ___6___ giraffes.
15. She sees the most ___giraffes___.
16. She sees the fewest ___lions___.
17. There are ___3___ more rhinoceroses than lions.
18. There are ___2___ fewer tigers than elephants.

Name: _____ Date: _____

Look at the picture graph.
Then fill in the blanks.

This picture graph shows how a group of children goes to school.

Ways of Going to School

🚶 Walk	● ● ● ● ● ●
🚗 Car	● ● ● ● ● ● ● ● ● ● ●
🚌 Bus	● ● ● ● ● ● ● ● ● ● ● ● ● ●
🚲 Bicycle	● ● ● ●

Each ● stands for 1 child.

19. How many children walk to school? ___6___
20. How many children go to school by bus? ___14___
21. How do most of the children go to school? ___by bus___
22. The fewest children go to school by ___bicycle___.
23. More children walk to school than ride a bicycle.
    How many more? ___2___
24. Fewer children go to school by car than by bus.
    How many fewer? ___3___

Lesson 2 More Picture Graphs   33

Look at the picture graph.
Then fill in the blanks.

Jason invites his friends to a party.
This picture graph shows the fruit juices they drink.

Fruit Juices

Each 🥤 stands for 1 glass of juice.

| Orange | Pineapple | Cranberry | Grape | Apple |

25. The children drink ___2___ glasses of cranberry juice.
26. What is the most popular juice? ___Apple juice___
27. They drink fewer glasses of pineapple juice
    than orange juice.
    How many fewer? ___4___
28. How many types of juices do they drink? ___5___

34   Chapter 11 Picture Graphs and Bar Graphs

Name: _____ Date: _____

Practice 3   Tally Charts and Bar Graphs

There are some spoons, forks, and knives on the table.

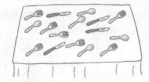

Complete the tally chart.
Then answer the questions.

Silverware	Tally	Number
🥄 Spoon	~~IIII~~	5
🍴 Fork	~~IIII~~ II	7
🔪 Knife	IIII	4

1. How many spoons are there? ___5___
2. How many knives are there? ___4___
3. There are 2 more ___forks___ than spoons.
4. How many fewer knives than forks are there? ___3___

Lesson 3 Tally Charts and Bar Graphs   35

Kelly bought balloons for her party.
The tally chart shows the different colors of balloons
she bought.
Complete the tally chart.
Then fill in the blanks.

5.

Balloons	Tally	Number
Red	~~IIII~~ I	6
Blue	~~IIII~~ IIII	9
Yellow	~~IIII~~ ~~IIII~~ ~~IIII~~	15

6. Kelly bought ___6___ red balloons.

7. She bought ___9___ blue balloons.

8. Kelly bought ___6___ more yellow balloons
   than blue balloons.

9. She bought 9 fewer ___red___ balloons
   than ___yellow___ balloons.

36   Chapter 11 Picture Graphs and Bar Graphs

Name: _____ Date: _____

Abby bought some seed packages.
The tally chart shows the different kinds of seeds she bought.
Complete the tally chart.

10.

Seed Packages	Tally	Number
Cucumber	✝✝✝ //	7
Pumpkin	///	3
Sunflower	✝✝✝	5

Make a bar graph.

11.

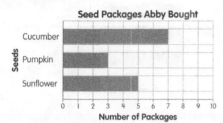

Seed Packages Abby Bought

Seeds: Cucumber, Pumpkin, Sunflower

Number of Packages: 0 1 2 3 4 5 6 7 8 9 10

Answer the questions.

12. How many packages of sunflower seeds did she buy? __5__

13. How many more packages of cucumber seeds than pumpkin seeds did she buy? __4__

14. How many packages of seeds did she buy in all? __15__

15. She bought 2 more packages of _cucumber_ seeds than sunflower seeds.

Lesson 3 Tally Charts and Bar Graphs 37

Math Journal

Keep a record of how many books you read this week.
Include the books you read in class and those your teacher or your family reads to you.
Draw 📖 to represent 1 book.

Number of Books I Read this Week

Sunday	Monday	Tuesday	Wednesday	Thursday	Friday	Saturday

Each 📖 stands for 1 book. Answers vary.

Look at your graph.
Write sentences about the number of books you have read.
You may use the words below.

[more than] [less than] [most] [fewest]

Answers vary.
_____
_____

38 Chapter 11 Picture Graphs and Bar Graphs

Name: _____ Date: _____

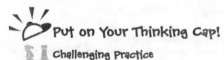**Put on Your Thinking Cap!**

Challenging Practice

Team A, Team B, and Team C play a game.
The graph shows the number of points each child on Team A scores.

Answer the questions.
Thinking skill: Comparing
Strategy: Draw a diagram (graph)

Points for Team A

Lila, Dan, Billy, Juanita

Each ● stands for 1 point.

1. How many points did Team A score in all? __17__

2. Team B scores 7 points fewer than Team A.
   How many points does Team B score? __10__

3. Team A scores 3 points fewer than Team C.
   How many points does Team C score? __20__

Chapter 11 Picture Graphs and Bar Graphs 39

Tina and her friends, Eva and Pedro, brought some crackers to school.
The tally chart shows the number of crackers each child brought.

Thinking skill: Comparing
Strategies: Drawing, Interpreting a graph

Complete the tally chart.

4.

Children	Tally	Number of Crackers
Tina	✝✝✝ //	7
Eva	///	3
Pedro	✝✝✝	5

Make a bar graph.

5.

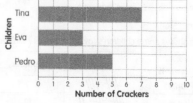

Crackers the Children Brought to School

Children: Tina, Eva, Pedro

Number of Crackers: 0 1 2 3 4 5 6 7 8 9 10

6. How many crackers did Pedro bring? __5__

7. How many more crackers did Tina bring than Eva? __4__

8. How many crackers did the children bring in all? __15__

9. Tina brought __2__ more crackers than Pedro.

40 Chapter 11 Picture Graphs and Bar Graphs

Workbook Answers: Chapter 11
Math in Focus Homeschool Answer Key, Grade 1

Name: _____ Date: _____

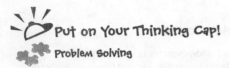
Put on Your Thinking Cap!
Problem Solving

The Art Club sold boxes of cards to three families along the same street.

Cards Sold by The Art Club

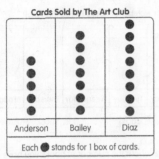

| Anderson | Bailey | Diaz |

Each ● stands for 1 box of cards.

Fill in the blanks.

1. The Bailey family bought ___7___ boxes of cards.

2. The __Anderson__ family bought the fewest boxes of cards.

3. The ___Diaz___ family bought the most boxes of cards.

Chapter 11 Picture Graphs and Bar Graphs **41**

---

4. The Anderson family bought ___2___ fewer boxes of cards fewer than the Bailey family.

5. The families bought ___20___ boxes of cards in all.

6. Make a bar graph.

Cards Sold by the Art Club

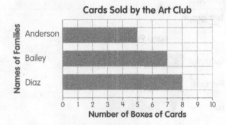

Thinking skill: Comparing
Strategy: Drawing a model (graph)

42 Chapter 11 Picture Graphs and Bar Graphs

Name: _____ Date: _____

Chapter Review/Test

Vocabulary
Choose the correct word.

| more |
| fewer |
| bar graph |

1. A __bar graph__ uses bars and a scale to show data.

Children at the Library

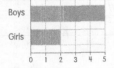

2. There are __fewer__ girls than boys.

3. There are __more__ boys than girls.

Concepts and Skills
The tally chart shows some children's favorite musical instruments.

Favorite Instruments	Tally	Number
Piano	ⵌ ////	9
Guitar	ⵌ ⵌ //	12
Drum	ⵌ /	6

4. __Guitar__ is the most popular musical instrument.

5. __Drum__ is the favorite musical instrument of the fewest children.

Chapter 11 Picture Graphs and Bar Graphs **43**

Problem Solving
A recycling project was carried out in a class.
Some children brought bottles for recycling.
The tally chart shows the number of bottles each child brought.

Complete the tally chart.

6.

Children	Tally	Number
Jay	ⵌ ⵌ	10
Madison	///	3
Kimberly	ⵌ //	7

Make a bar graph.

7.

Bottles for Recycling

Fill in the blanks.

8. How many bottles did Kimberly bring? ___7___

9. __Madison__ brought the fewest bottles.

44 Chapter 11 Picture Graphs and Bar Graphs

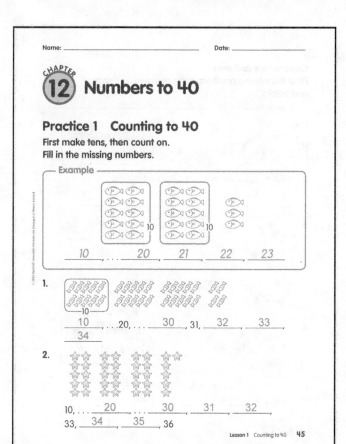

Name: _____ Date: _____

CHAPTER 12 Numbers to 40

Practice 1   Counting to 40

First make tens, then count on.
Fill in the missing numbers.

Example

10 ... 20   21   22 , 23

1.
10 ... 20 , 30   31 , 32 , 33
34

2.
10 , ... 20   30   31   32
33 , 34 , 35 , 36

Lesson 1   Counting to 40   45

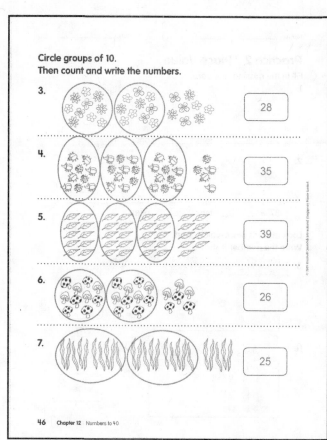

Circle groups of 10.
Then count and write the numbers.

3. 28

4. 35

5. 39

6. 26

7. 25

46   Chapter 12   Numbers to 40

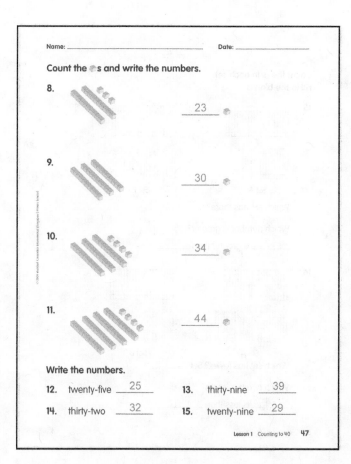

Name: _____ Date: _____

Count the ◼s and write the numbers.

8. 23

9. 30

10. 34

11. 44

Write the numbers.

12. twenty-five   25   13. thirty-nine   39

14. thirty-two   32   15. twenty-nine   29

Lesson 1   Counting to 40   47

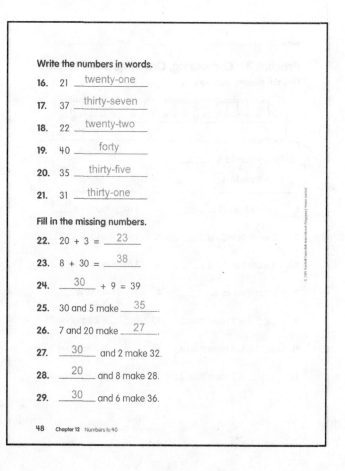

Write the numbers in words.

16. 21   twenty-one
17. 37   thirty-seven
18. 22   twenty-two
19. 40   forty
20. 35   thirty-five
21. 31   thirty-one

Fill in the missing numbers.

22. $20 + 3 =$ 23
23. $8 + 30 =$ 38
24. 30 $+ 9 = 39$
25. 30 and 5 make 35 .
26. 7 and 20 make 27 .
27. 30 and 2 make 32.
28. 20 and 8 make 28.
29. 30 and 6 make 36.

48   Chapter 12   Numbers to 40

Workbook Answers: Chapter 12
Math in Focus Homeschool Answer Key, Grade 1

Name: _____ **Date:** _____

Practice 2   Place Value

Fill in the missing numbers.

1.

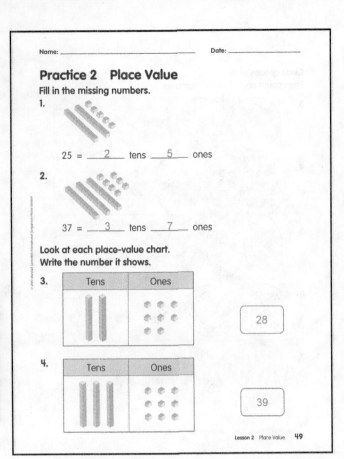

25 = __2__ tens __5__ ones

2.

37 = __3__ tens __7__ ones

Look at each place-value chart.
Write the number it shows.

3.

Tens	Ones
‖ ‖	⬡⬡⬡ ⬡⬡⬡⬡⬡

28

4.

Tens	Ones
‖‖‖	⬡⬡⬡ ⬡⬡⬡ ⬡⬡⬡

39

Count in tens and ones.
Fill in the missing numbers in the place-value charts
and blanks.

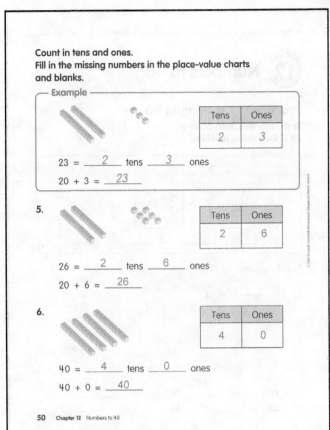

┌─ Example ────────────────────────────┐

Tens	Ones
2	3

23 = __2__ tens __3__ ones

20 + 3 = __23__

└──────────────────────────────────────┘

5.

Tens	Ones
2	6

26 = __2__ tens __6__ ones

20 + 6 = __26__

6.

Tens	Ones
4	0

40 = __4__ tens __0__ ones

40 + 0 = __40__

Name: _____ **Date:** _____

Practice 3   Comparing, Ordering, and Patterns

Find the missing numbers.

23 24 25 26 27 28 29 30 31 32 33 34 35 36 37 38 39 40

┌─ Example ────────────────────────────┐

1 more than 23 is __24__

1 less than 35 is __34__

└──────────────────────────────────────┘

1. 1 more than 29 is __30__   2. 2 more than 19 is __21__

3. 2 more than 26 is __28__   4. 2 less than 31 is __29__

5. 3 more than 27 is __30__   6. 3 more than 36 is __39__

7. 3 less than 25 is __22__   8. 3 less than 40 is __37__

9. __29__ is 2 more than 27.   10. __24__ is 2 less than 26.

11. __33__ is 3 more than 30.   12. __27__ is 3 less than 30.

13. __37__ is 2 more than 35.   14. __33__ is 2 less than 35.

Count the |s in each set.
Fill in the blanks.

15.

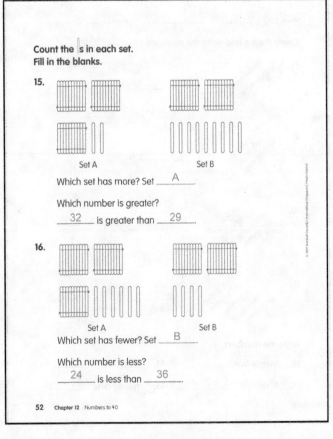

Set A   Set B

Which set has more? Set __A__.

Which number is greater?

__32__ is greater than __29__.

16.

Set A   Set B

Which set has fewer? Set __B__.

Which number is less?

__24__ is less than __36__.

Page 1 (Lesson 3, p.53)

Name: _____ Date: _____

Circle the greater number.

17. (32) or 23   18. 37 or (39)

19. 19 or (21)   20. 15 or (25)

Circle the number that is less.

21. 32 or (28)   22. (38) or 40

Compare the numbers.
Then fill in the blanks.

△34   △39   △37

23. ___34___ is the least.

24. ___39___ is the greatest.

Order the numbers from least to greatest.

25. △36   △24   △32

___24___, ___32___, ___36___
least

Lesson 3   Comparing, Ordering, and Patterns   53

Page 2 (Chapter 12, p.54)

Compare the numbers.
Then fill in the blanks.

(23)   (38)   (35)   (27)

26. ___23___ is less than 27.

27. ___38___ is greater than 35.

28. 35 is greater than ___23___ and ___27___ but

less than ___38___.

29. The least number is ___23___.

30. The greatest number is ___38___.

Compare the numbers.
Then fill in the blanks.

(40)   (24)   (39)   (26)

31. ___26___ is 2 more than 24.

32. ___39___ is 1 less than 40.

33. ___26___ is less than 39 but greater than 24.

34. The least number is ___24___.

35. The greatest number is ___40___.

54   Chapter 12   Numbers to 40

Page 3 (Lesson 3, p.55)

Name: _____ Date: _____

Complete each number pattern.

36. 18, 19, ___20___, 21, ___22___, 23, ___24___

37. 30, 31, 32, ___33___, ___34___, 35, ___36___

38. ___28___, ___29___, 30, 31, ___32___ 33, 34

39. 33, ___32___, 31, ___30___, ___29___, 28, 27

40. 30, 32, ___34___, ___36___, 38, ___40___

41. 27, ___25___, ___23___, ___21___, 19, 17, 15

42. ___20___, 23, 26, 29, ___32___, 35

43. 33, ___30___, ___27___, 24, 21, ___18___

44. ___0___, 10, ___20___, 30, 40

Lesson 3   Comparing, Ordering, and Patterns   55

Page 4 (Chapter 12, p.56)

Solve.

45. Kim's ball falls into a number machine.
Which ball is it?
Write the missing number in the ◯.

56   Chapter 12   Numbers to 40

Workbook Answers: Chapter 12
Math in Focus Homeschool Answer Key, Grade 1

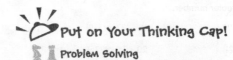

Put on Your Thinking Cap!
Challenging Practice

Fill in the blanks.

Wayne has four cards.
Each card has a number on it.

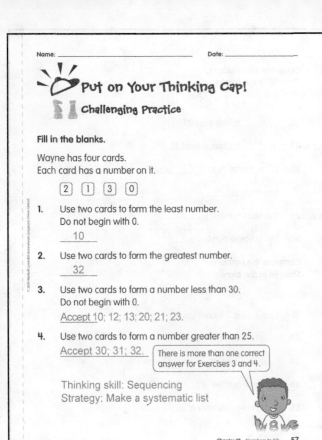

2   1   3   0

1. Use two cards to form the least number.
    Do not begin with 0.
    ___10___

2. Use two cards to form the greatest number.
    ___32___

3. Use two cards to form a number less than 30.
    Do not begin with 0.
    Accept 10; 12; 13; 20; 21; 23.

4. Use two cards to form a number greater than 25.
    Accept 30; 31; 32.

    There is more than one correct answer for Exercises 3 and 4.

Thinking skill: Sequencing
Strategy: Make a systematic list

Chapter 12 Numbers to 40 **57**

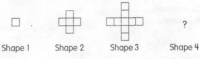

Put on Your Thinking Cap!
Problem Solving

Fill in the blanks.

Jan uses tiles to make shapes that form a pattern.

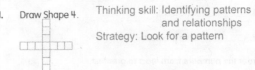

Shape 1   Shape 2   Shape 3   Shape 4

1. Draw Shape 4.

    Thinking skill: Identifying patterns
    and relationships
    Strategy: Look for a pattern

2. Jan needs ___4___ more tiles to make Shape 4.

3. Complete the table.

Shape Number	1	2	3	4	5
Number of Tiles	1	5	9	13	17

4. Complete the number pattern.
    1, 5, 9, ___13___, ___17___, ___21___

58 Chapter 12 Numbers to 40

Name: _____   Date: _____

Chapter Review/Test
Vocabulary
Match.

1. 27 ——— twenty-seven
    36 ——— forty
    24 ——— thirty-eight
    38 ——— twenty-four
    40 ——— thirty-six

Concepts and Skills
Count to find how many.

2. [drawing] 24

3. [drawing] 36

Write the numbers.

4. twenty-four   ___24___
5. thirty   ___30___

Write the number that is greater.

6. (25) (17)   ___25___
7. (26) (29)   ___29___

Chapter 12 Numbers to 40 **59**

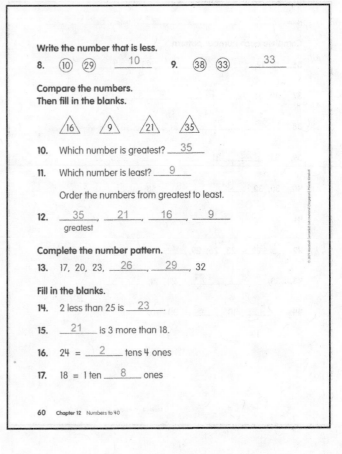

Write the number that is less.

8. (10) (29)   ___10___
9. (38) (33)   ___33___

Compare the numbers.
Then fill in the blanks.

[16] [9] [21] [35]

10. Which number is greatest? ___35___

11. Which number is least? ___9___

    Order the numbers from greatest to least.

12. ___35___, ___21___, ___16___, ___9___
    greatest

Complete the number pattern.

13. 17, 20, 23, ___26___, ___29___, 32

Fill in the blanks.

14. 2 less than 25 is ___23___.

15. ___21___ is 3 more than 18.

16. 24 = ___2___ tens 4 ones

17. 18 = 1 ten ___8___ ones

60 Chapter 12 Numbers to 40

CHAPTER 13 — Addition and Subtraction to 40

Name: _____   **Date:** _____

Practice 1 Addition Without Regrouping
Add by counting on.

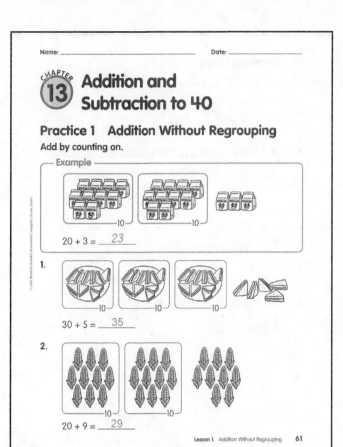

┌─ Example ─────────────────────────┐

20 + 3 = _23_

└───────────────────────────────────┘

1.

30 + 5 = _35_

2.

20 + 9 = _29_

3.

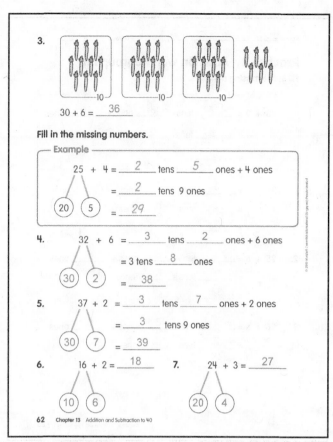

30 + 6 = _36_

Fill in the missing numbers.

┌─ Example ──────────────────────────────────┐

25 + 4 = _2_ tens _5_ ones + 4 ones

= _2_ tens 9 ones

(20) (5)   = _29_

└──┘

4.   32 + 6 = _3_ tens _2_ ones + 6 ones

= 3 tens _8_ ones

(30) (2)   = _38_

5.   37 + 2 = _3_ tens _7_ ones + 2 ones

= _3_ tens 9 ones

(30) (7)   = _39_

6.   16 + 2 = _18_   **7.**   24 + 3 = _27_

(10) (6)   (20) (4)

Name: _____   **Date:** _____

Complete each place-value chart.
Then add.

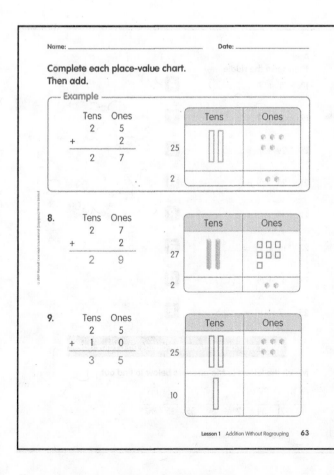

┌─ Example ─────────────────────────────┐

	Tens	Ones
	2	5
+		2
	2	7

└───────────────────────────────────────┘

8.

	Tens	Ones
	2	7
+		2
	2	9

9.

	Tens	Ones
	2	5
+	1	0
	3	5

Complete the place-value chart.
Then add.

10.

	Tens	Ones
	1	4
+	2	3
	3	7

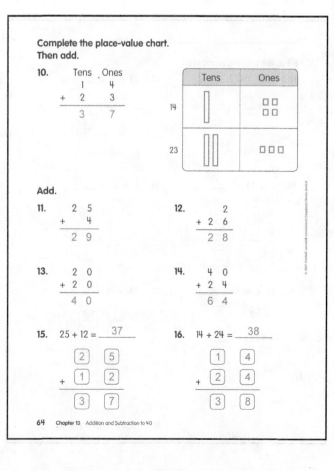

Add.

11.

	Tens	Ones
	2	5
+		4
	2	9

12.

	2
+	2 6
	2 8

13.

	2 0
+	2 0
	4 0

14.

	4 0
+	2 4
	6 4

15.   25 + 12 = _37_

[2] [5]
+ [1] [2]
[3] [7]

16.   14 + 24 = _38_

[1] [4]
+ [2] [4]
[3] [8]

Chapter 13

Practice 2   Addition with Regrouping
Fill in the missing numbers.

Name: _____ Date: _____

Example

$23 + 9 =$ __2__ tens __3__ ones + __9__ ones

$=$ __2__ tens __12__ ones

$=$ __32__

1. $37 + 3 =$ __3__ tens __7__ ones + __3__ ones

$=$ __3__ tens __10__ ones

$=$ __40__

2. $25 + 8 =$ __2__ tens __5__ ones + __8__ ones

$=$ __2__ tens __13__ ones

$=$ __33__

3. $26 + 6 =$ __2__ tens __6__ ones + __6__ ones

$=$ __2__ tens __12__ ones

$=$ __32__

Fill in the missing numbers.

4. $5 + 29 =$ __5__ ones + __2__ tens __9__ ones

$=$ __2__ tens __14__ ones

$=$ __34__

5. $19 + 21 =$ __1__ ten __9__ ones + __2__ tens __1__ one

$=$ __3__ tens __10__ ones

$=$ __40__

Add.

6.
```
   1 8
 +   5
 ─────
   2 3
```

7.
```
   2 4
 +   9
 ─────
   3 3
```

8.
```
     5
 + 2 6
 ─────
   3 1
```

9.
```
   1 6
 +   7
 ─────
   2 3
```

10.
```
   1 6
 + 1 4
 ─────
   3 0
```

11.
```
   2 5
 + 1 5
 ─────
   4 0
```

Name: _____ Date: _____

Fill in the missing numbers.

12. $18 + 7 =$ __25__
```
  [1] [8]
+ [ ] [7]
─────────
  [2] [5]
```

13. $21 + 9 =$ __30__
```
  [2] [1]
+ [ ] [9]
─────────
  [3] [0]
```

14. $6 + 15 =$ __21__
```
  [ ] [6]
+ [1] [5]
─────────
  [2] [1]
```

15. $8 + 32 =$ __40__
```
  [ ] [8]
+ [3] [2]
─────────
  [4] [0]
```

16. $17 + 16 =$ __33__
```
  [1] [7]
+ [1] [6]
─────────
  [3] [3]
```

17. $13 + 19 =$ __32__
```
  [1] [3]
+ [1] [9]
─────────
  [3] [2]
```

Add.
Then solve the riddle.

18. $14 + 7 =$ __21__   **A**

19. $26 + 8 =$ __34__   **I**

20. $29 + 6 =$ __35__   **E**

21. $23 + 9 =$ __32__   **N**

22. $33 + 7 =$ __40__   **R**

23. $18 + 22 =$ __40__   **R**

24. $6 + 24 =$ __30__   **D**

25. $17 + 18 =$ __35__   **E**

What animal falls from the clouds on a rainy day?

Match the letters to the answers below to find out.

R A I N - D E E R
40 21 34 32   30 35 35 40

Name: _____ Date: _____

Practice 3 Subtraction Without Regrouping
Subtract by counting back.

Example

24, 23, 22

24 – 2 = __22__

1. 27 – 6 = __21__   2. 35 – 4 = __31__

3. 38 – 8 = __30__   4. 24 – 3 = __21__

5. 39 – 4 = __35__   6. 39 – 9 = __30__

Fill in the missing numbers.

Example

37 – 4 = __3__ tens 7 ones – __4__ ones

= __3__ tens 3 ones

= __33__

7. 38 – 3 = __3__ tens __8__ ones – 3 ones

= 3 tens __5__ ones

= __35__

Fill in the missing numbers.

8. 26 – 4 = __2__ tens 6 ones – __4__ ones

= __2__ tens 2 ones

= __22__

Subtract.

9.
Tens	Ones
1	6
–	2
1	4

10.
Tens	Ones
2	8
–	4
2	4

11.
Tens	Ones
3	5
–	2
3	3

12.
Tens	Ones
3	6
–	6
3	0

13.
Tens	Ones
4	0
– 2	0
2	0

14.
Tens	Ones
2	3
– 1	0
1	3

15.
Tens	Ones
3	6
– 1	1
2	5

16.
Tens	Ones
3	4
– 1	4
2	0

Name: _____ Date: _____

Fill in the missing numbers.

17. 29 – 26 = __3__

Tens	Ones
2	9
– 2	6
	3

18. 38 – 10 = __28__

Tens	Ones
3	8
– 1	0
2	8

19. 31 – 20 = __11__

Tens	Ones
3	1
– 2	0
1	1

20. 27 – 17 = __10__

Tens	Ones
2	7
– 1	7
1	0

21. 36 – 5 = __31__

Tens	Ones
3	6
–	5
3	1

22. 38 – 8 = __30__

Tens	Ones
3	8
–	8
3	0

---

23. Joel puts a ball into a number machine.
Which ball is it?
Write the correct number in the ⬤.

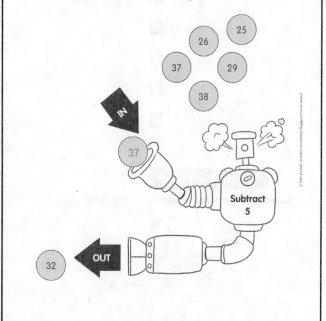

229

Chapter 13

Practice 4 Subtraction with Regrouping

Regroup.

1. 27 = 1 ten _____17_____ ones

2. 15 = 0 tens _____15_____ ones

3. 30 = 2 tens _____10_____ ones

Subtract.

4.
```
   2 3
 -   6
 -----
   1 7
```

5.
```
   2 4
 -   8
 -----
   1 6
```

6.
```
   3 3
 -   5
 -----
   2 8
```

7.
```
   3 6
 -   9
 -----
   2 7
```

8.
```
   2 5
 - 1 6
 -----
     9
```

9.
```
   2 0
 - 1 8
 -----
     2
```

Fill in the missing numbers.

10. 21 − 5 = _____16_____
```
   2   1
 -     5
 -----
   1   6
```

11. 36 − 7 = _____29_____
```
   3   6
 -     7
 -----
   2   9
```

12. 25 − 18 = _____7_____
```
   2   5
 - 1   8
 -----
       7
```

13. 31 − 18 = _____13_____
```
   3   1
 - 1   8
 -----
   1   3
```

14. 32 − 14 = _____18_____
```
   3   2
 - 1   4
 -----
   1   8
```

15. 30 − 17 = _____13_____
```
   3   0
 - 1   7
 -----
   1   3
```

Subtract.
Then solve the riddle.

16. 38 − 9 = _____29_____ **W**

17. 30 − 18 = _____12_____ **E**

18. 32 − 5 = _____27_____ **S**

19. 35 − 8 = _____27_____ **S**

20. 27 − 7 = _____20_____ **A**

21. 34 − 19 = _____15_____ **A**

How do you cut the sea?

Match the letters to the answers below to find out.

WITH A S E A - S A W
        27 12 20   27 15 29

Natasha drops a ball into each number machine.
Write the missing numbers in the blanks to show what happens to each ball.

22.

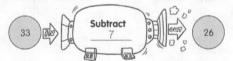

33 IN Subtract _____7_____ OUT 26

23.

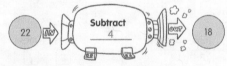

22 IN Subtract _____4_____ OUT 18

Practice 5   Adding Three Numbers

Add.

1.

$4 + 5 + 6 =$ ___15___

2.

$8 + 7 + 7 =$ ___22___

3.

$6 + 9 + 8 =$ ___23___

4.

$5 + 4 + 8 =$ ___17___

Make ten.
Then add.

Example

$6 + 3 + 7 =$ ___16___

$6 + 10 = 16$

(10)

5. $5 + 8 + 5 =$ ___18___

$10 + 8 = 18$

Make 10 first.

6. $8 + 9 + 2 =$ ___19___

$10 + 9 = 19$

7. $9 + 7 + 2 =$ ___18___

8. $9 + 4 + 4 =$ ___17___

9. $2 + 9 + 5 =$ ___16___

Practice 6   Real-World Problems: Addition and Subtraction

Solve.

1. Lynn has 12 trophies.
    Geeta has 5 more trophies than Lynn.
    How many trophies does Geeta have?

$12 + 5 = 17$

Geeta has ___17___ trophies.

2. Rima buys 15 stickers.
    Susie buys 7 fewer stickers than Rima.
    How many stickers does Susie buy?

$15 - 7 = 8$

Susie buys ___8___ stickers.

Solve.

3. Tara has 14 toy cars.
    She has 9 more toy cars than Carlos.
    How many toy cars does Carlos have?

$14 - 9 = 5$

Carlos has ___5___ toy cars.

4. Aaron makes 6 friendship bracelets.
    He makes 5 fewer friendship bracelets than Kate.
    How many friendship bracelets does Kate make?

$6 + 5 = 11$

Kate makes ___11___ friendship bracelets.

Name: _____ Date: _____

Solve.

5. Michelle has 18 snowballs.
   Miguel has 14 snowballs.
   How many more snowballs does Michelle have?

   $18 - 14 = 4$

   Michelle has ___4___ more snowballs.

6. Rose buys 17 hairclips.
   Sarah buys 13 more hairclips than Rose.
   How many hairclips does Sarah buy?

   $17 + 13 = 30$

   Sarah buys ___30___ hairclips.

7. Tess has 22 walnuts.
   She has 13 more walnuts than Chris.
   How many walnuts does Chris have?

   $22 - 13 = 9$

   Chris has ___9___ walnuts.

8. Ashley makes 36 muffins.
   Janice makes 17 muffins.
   How many more muffins does Ashley make?

   $36 - 17 = 19$

   Ashley makes ___19___ more muffins.

Name: _____ Date: _____

Put on Your Thinking Cap!

Challenging Practice

Fill in the circles with numbers.

1. Each ○—○—○ must make 8.

   1
   4   2
   3   0   5

   Thinking skill:
   Identifying relationships,
   Sequencing

   Strategy:
   Listing,
   Guess and check

2. Each ○—○—○ must make 10.

   1
   6   4
   3   2   5

3. Luis places a ball into the number machine below.
   What happens to the number on the ball?

   Fill in the missing numbers.

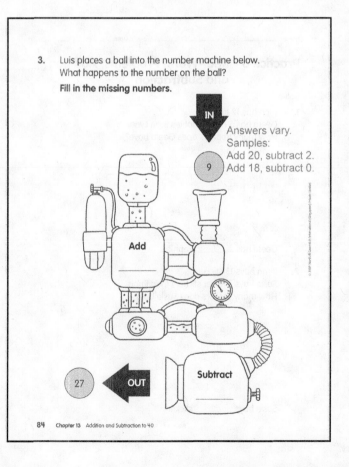

   IN
   9

   Answers vary.
   Samples:
   Add 20, subtract 2.
   Add 18, subtract 0.

   Add _____

   Subtract _____

   27   OUT

Name: _____ Date: _____

4. Luis places another ball into the number machine below. What happens to the number on the ball?

Fill in the missing numbers.

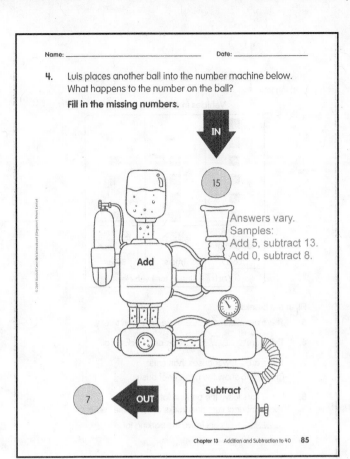

Answers vary.
Samples:
Add 5, subtract 13.
Add 0, subtract 8.

Chapter 13 Addition and Subtraction to 40 **85**

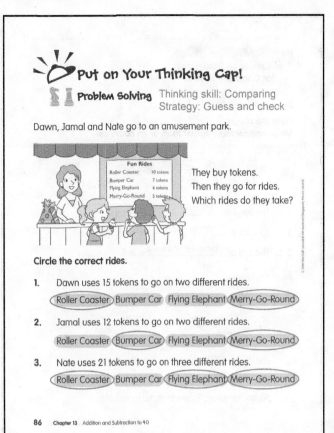

Put on Your Thinking Cap!

Problem Solving Thinking skill: Comparing
Strategy: Guess and check

Dawn, Jamal and Nate go to an amusement park.

They buy tokens.
Then they go for rides.
Which rides do they take?

Circle the correct rides.

1. Dawn uses 15 tokens to go on two different rides.
   (Roller Coaster) Bumper Car Flying Elephant (Merry-Go-Round)

2. Jamal uses 12 tokens to go on two different rides.
   Roller Coaster (Bumper Car) Flying Elephant (Merry-Go-Round)

3. Nate uses 21 tokens to go on three different rides.
   (Roller Coaster) Bumper Car (Flying Elephant) (Merry-Go-Round)

86 Chapter 13 Addition and Subtraction to 40

Name: _____ Date: _____

Chapter Review/Test
Vocabulary
Choose the correct word.

1. You __count back__ from the greater number when you subtract.

2. You can __regroup__ 13 ones into 1 ten 3 ones.

3. You can add two numbers using the __counting on__ method.

4. A __place-value chart__ can be used to add numbers.

| regroup |
| counting on |
| count back |
| place-value chart |

Concepts and Skills
Add or subtract.

5. 32 + 7 = __39__

6. 18 + 19 = __37__

7. 27 − 3 = __24__

8. 36 − 18 = __18__

9. 4 + 8 + 6 = __18__

10. 9 + 8 + 5 = __22__

Chapter 13 Addition and Subtraction to 40 **87**

Problem Solving
Solve.

11. Nicole blows up 30 balloons for a class party. Michael blows up 4 fewer balloons than Nicole. How many balloons does Michael blow up?

    30 − 4 = 26

    Michael blows up __26__ balloons.

12. Ryan has 23 bookmarks. He has 5 fewer bookmarks than Ivy. How many bookmarks does Ivy have?

    23 + 5 = 28

    Ivy has __28__ bookmarks.

88 Chapter 13 Addition and Subtraction to 40

---

www.harcourtschoolsupply.com

233

Workbook Answers: Chapter 13
Math in Focus Homeschool Answer Key, Grade 1

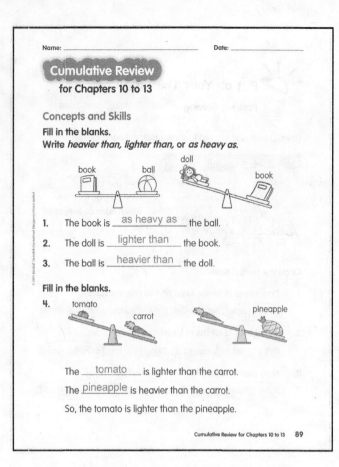

Cumulative Review
for Chapters 10 to 13

Concepts and Skills

Fill in the blanks.
Write *heavier than, lighter than,* or *as heavy as.*

1. The book is ___as heavy as___ the ball.
2. The doll is ___lighter than___ the book.
3. The ball is ___heavier than___ the doll.

Fill in the blanks.

4. tomato   carrot   pineapple

The ___tomato___ is lighter than the carrot.

The ___pineapple___ is heavier than the carrot.

So, the tomato is lighter than the pineapple.

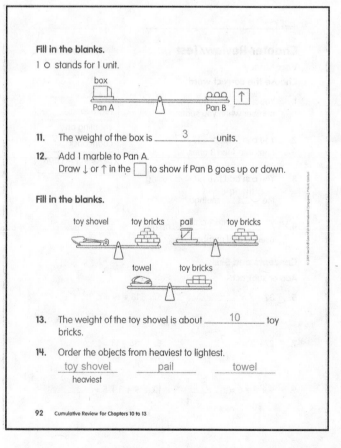

The picture graph shows the number of cars and trucks in a parking lot.

Vehicles in a Parking Lot

Cars   Trucks   Buses

Each ▪ stands for 1 vehicle.

Fill in the blanks.

5. There are ___2___ more cars than trucks.
6. There are ___10___ cars and trucks in all.
7. There are 2 fewer buses than cars.
   Draw ▪ to show the number of buses.
8. Some cars leave the parking lot.
   The number of cars and trucks are now the same.
   ___2___ cars leave the parking lot.

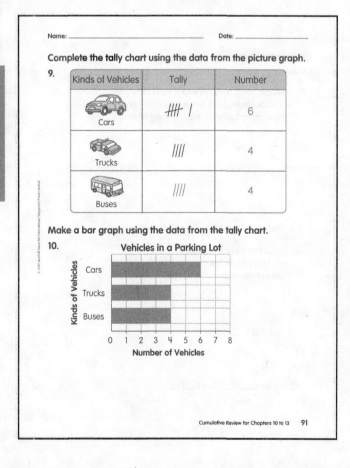

Complete the tally chart using the data from the picture graph.

9.

Kinds of Vehicles	Tally	Number
Cars	⊬⊬ l	6
Trucks	llll	4
Buses	llll	4

Make a bar graph using the data from the tally chart.

10.
Vehicles in a Parking Lot

Fill in the blanks.
1 ○ stands for 1 unit.

box
Pan A   Pan B   ↑

11. The weight of the box is ___3___ units.
12. Add 1 marble to Pan A.
    Draw ↓ or ↑ in the ☐ to show if Pan B goes up or down.

Fill in the blanks.

toy shovel   toy bricks   pail   toy bricks

towel   toy bricks

13. The weight of the toy shovel is about ___10___ toy bricks.
14. Order the objects from heaviest to lightest.
    ___toy shovel___   ___pail___   ___towel___
    heaviest

234

Name: _____ Date: _____

First make tens.
Then count on.
Fill in the missing numbers.

15.   `24`

16. 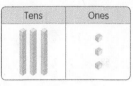   `37`

Write the number.

17. twenty-five ___25___

18. thirty ___30___

Write the number in words.

19. 37 _thirty-seven_

20. 40 ___forty___

Fill in the missing numbers.

21. 7 + 20 = ___27___

22. ___26___ + 10 = 36

Find the missing numbers.

23.

38 = ___3___ tens ___8___ ones

Look at the place-value chart.
Write the number it shows.

24.

Tens	Ones

`27`

25.

Tens	Ones

`33`

Name: _____ Date: _____

Circle the greater number.

26. (25) or 17   27. 26 or (29)

Circle the number that is less.

28. (10) or 29   29. 38 or (33)

Compare the numbers.
Then fill in the blanks.

16   9   21   35

30. ___9___ is the least.

31. ___35___ is the greatest.

32. ___21___ is less than 35 but greater than 16.

33. Order the numbers from the least to greatest.

___9___, ___16___, ___21___, ___35___
least

Complete each number pattern.

34. 17, 20, 23, ___26___, ___29___, 32

35. 28, ___32___, 36, 40

Fill in the blanks.

36. 2 less than 25 is ___23___

37. ___21___ is 3 more than 18.

38. 24 = ___2___ tens 4 ones

39. 18 = 1 ten ___8___ ones

Add or subtract.

40. 21 + 7 = ___28___

41. 24 + 10 = ___34___

42. 27 − 3 = ___24___

43. 38 − 15 = ___23___

44. 6 + 3 + 7 = ___16___

45. 9 + 8 + 5 = ___22___

Workbook Answers: Chapters 10-13 Review
Math in Focus Homeschool Answer Key, Grade 1

46.
```
   2 3
 + 1 6
 -----
   3 9
```

47.
```
   2 9
 + 1 1
 -----
   4 0
```

48.
```
   1 4
 + 1 7
 -----
   3 1
```

49.
```
   1 8
 + 1 7
 -----
   3 5
```

50.
```
   3 6
 - 2 4
 -----
   1 2
```

51.
```
   3 6
 - 1 8
 -----
   1 8
```

52.
```
   2 1
 - 1 7
 -----
     4
```

53.
```
   3 2
 - 1 5
 -----
   1 7
```

Problem Solving

Solve.

54. Jamal has 20 stamps.
Michelle has 4 fewer stamps than Jamal.
How many stamps does Michelle have?

$$20 - 4 = 16$$

Michelle has ___16___ stamps.

55. Nate blows up 30 balloons for his birthday party.
Nate blows up 6 fewer balloons than Miguel.
How many balloons does Miguel blow up?

$$30 + 6 = 36$$

Miguel blows up ___36___ balloons.

Name: _____ Date: _____

14 Mental Math Strategies

Practice 1 Mental Addition

Add mentally.
First add the ones.
Then add the ones to the tens.

┌─ Example ─────────────────────────────┐
│   14 + 3 = ___17___   │
│   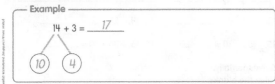   │
│   (10)   (4)   │
└───────────────────────────────────────┘

1. 15 + 2 = ___17___   2. 12 + 4 = ___16___

3. 35 + 1 = ___36___   4. 23 + 5 = ___28___

5. 22 + 7 = ___29___   6. 31 + 8 = ___39___

7. 6 + 32 = ___38___   8. 5 + 34 = ___39___

Add mentally.
First add the tens.
Then add the tens to the ones.

┌─ Example ─────────────────────────────┐
│   13 + 10 = ___23___   │
│   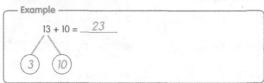   │
│   (3)   (10)   │
└───────────────────────────────────────┘

9. 18 + 10 = ___28___   10. 11 + 20 = ___31___

11. 12 + 10 = ___22___   12. 14 + 20 = ___34___

13. 16 + 10 = ___26___   14. 20 + 19 = ___39___

15. 10 + 17 = ___27___   16. 20 + 13 = ___33___

17. 10 + 14 = ___24___   18. 20 + 16 = ___36___

Name: _____ Date: _____

Add mentally.
Use doubles facts.

┌─ Example ─────────────────────────────┐
│   6 + 7 = ___13___   ┌──────────┐   │
│   │ 6 + 7 is double│
│   │ 6 plus 1.│   │
│   └──────────┘   │
│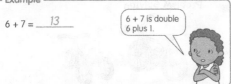
└───────────────────────────────────────┘

19. 4 + 5 = ___9___   20. 7 + 8 = ___15___

21. 5 + 6 = ___11___   22. 8 + 9 = ___17___

Solve mentally.
Fill in the blanks.

23. ┌──────────────────┐ Emily
    │ I have 24 stickers.│
    │ I want 5 more.   │
    └──────────────────┘
    Book Shop

How many stickers will Emily have?   ___29___

Solve mentally.
Fill in the blanks.

24.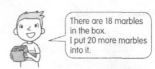
    ┌──────────────────────┐
    │ There are 18 marbles │
    │ in the box.   │
    │ I put 20 more marbles │
    │ into it.   │
    └──────────────────────┘

How many marbles are there in the box now?   ___38___

25. ┌──────────────────────┐
    │ I bake 11 pecan muffins│
    │ and 6 oat muffins.   │
    └──────────────────────┘
                              Baker Ross

How many muffins does Baker Ross bake in all?   ___17___

237

Chapter 14

Practice 2 Mental Subtraction

Subtract mentally.
Think of addition.

1. $8 - 5 =$ ___3___
2. $9 - 6 =$ ___3___
3. $11 - 3 =$ ___8___
4. $13 - 7 =$ ___6___
5. $15 - 6 =$ ___9___
6. $12 - 8 =$ ___4___

Subtract mentally.
First subtract the ones.
Then add the ones to the tens.

Example

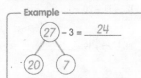

$27 - 3 =$ ___24___

7. $28 - 4 =$ ___24___
8. $29 - 5 =$ ___24___
9. $27 - 6 =$ ___21___
10. $37 - 2 =$ ___35___
11. $38 - 8 =$ ___30___
12. $36 - 6 =$ ___30___

Subtract mentally.
First subtract the tens.
Then add the tens to the ones.

Example

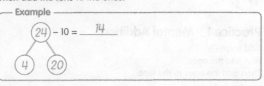

$24 - 10 =$ ___14___

13. $22 - 10 =$ ___12___
14. $23 - 20 =$ ___3___
15. $35 - 30 =$ ___5___
16. $36 - 20 =$ ___16___

Solve mentally.
Fill in the blanks.

17.

I have 16 fish. 9 of them swim away.

How many fish are left? ___7___

18.

There are 29 apples and 10 pears in the basket.

How many more apples than pears are there? ___19___

Put On Your Thinking Cap!

Challenging Practice

Thinking skill: Comparing
Strategy: Use guess and check

You can use a telephone dial to find the value of a word.

Example

$YES = 9 + 3 + 7 = 19$

1. Name a three-letter word with a value of 14.
    Samples: PAL; DAY; HAT; FIR; LAP; PIE
    Answers vary.

2. Find a word that has the same value as BOAT.
    Samples: HOLE; HOT; COAT; COIN

3. Think of a four-letter word.
    Find its value.
    Ask your friend to guess the word.

    Answers vary.

My word has a value of 20. Guess the word.

Put On Your Thinking Cap!

Problem Solving

There are 6 bicycles and tricycles at Sunshine Day Care Center. There are 16 wheels in all. How many bicycles are there?
Thinking skill: Comparing Strategies: Use a diagram, Use guess and check, Make a systematic list

Draw a picture to help you.

Method 1

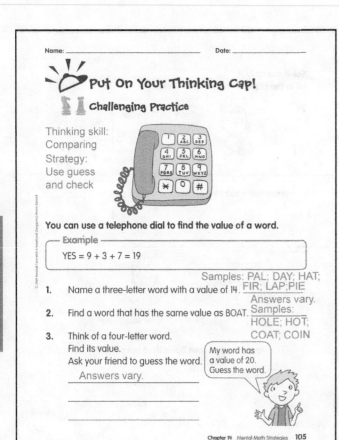

Method 2

Bicycles	Tricycles	Wheels in all
1	5	2 + 15 = 17
2	4	4 + 12 = 16

There are 2 bicycles and 4 tricycles.

Name: _____ Date: _____

Chapter Review/Test

Vocabulary

Choose the correct word.

1. To help you subtract __mentally__, think of addition.

2. 4 + 4 = 8 is a __doubles fact__

> doubles fact
> mentally

Concepts and Skills

Add mentally.

3. 25 + 4 = __29__   4. 33 + 4 = __37__

5. 10 + 28 = __38__   6. 15 + 20 = __35__

7. 6 + 7 = __13__   8. 4 + 7 = __11__

Subtract mentally.
Think of addition.

9. 8 – 6 = __2__   10. 9 – 7 = __2__

11. 16 – 7 = __9__   12. 18 – 9 = __9__

13. 15 – 8 = __7__   14. 14 – 7 = __7__

Subtract mentally.

15. 15 – 4 = __11__   16. 38 – 6 = __32__

17. 21 – 10 = __11__   18. 37 – 20 = __17__

Problem Solving

Fill in the blanks.

19.

There were 27 stamps. I lost 4 of them.

How many stamps are left? ____23____

20. 13 children are on a school bus.
6 more children get on the bus.
How many children are on the bus? ____19____

239

Chapter 14

Name: _____ Date: _____

CHAPTER 15 Calendar and Time

Practice 1 Using a Calendar

Fill in the blanks.

1. How many days are in one week?

    __7__

Write the days of the week.

2. The first day is ___Sunday___

3. The third day is ___Tuesday___

4. The fifth day is ___Thursday___

5. The last day is ___Saturday___

6. Which is your favorite day of the week?

    ___Answers vary.___

Every week begins on a Sunday.

Color or circle.

Example

Color the third month of the year gray.

January	February	March
April	May	June
July	August	September
October	November	December

7. Color the month that it is now red. Answers vary.

8. Color the month of your birthday yellow. Answers vary.

9. Color the ninth month of the year green.

10. Circle the month that has 28 days using blue.

11. Circle the months that have only 30 days using purple.

blue circle

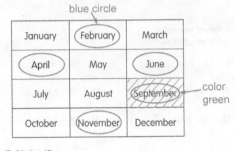

January	February	March
April	May	June
July	August	September
October	November	December

color green

Name: _____ Date: _____

2010

OCTOBER						
Sunday	Monday	Tuesday	Wednesday	Thursday	Friday	Saturday
					1	2
3	4	5	6	7	8	9
10	11	12	13	14	15	16
17	18	19	20	21	22	23
24	25	26	27	28	29	30
31						

Fill in the blanks.
Use the calendar to help you.

12. The name of the month is ___October___

13. ___Tuesday___ is the day just before Wednesday.

14. There are ___31___ days in this month.

15. ___Thursday___ is the day between Wednesday and Friday.

16. The date of the second Monday is ___October 11, 2010___

17. The day of the week just after October 22, 2010 is
    ___Saturday___

Match the picture to the season.

18.

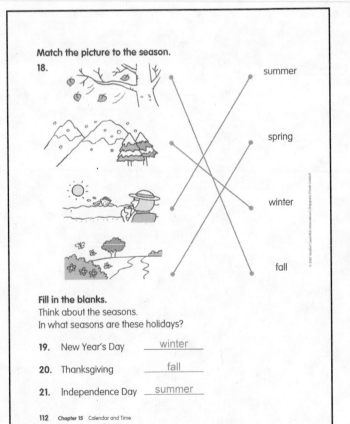

- summer
- spring
- winter
- fall

Fill in the blanks.
Think about the seasons.
In what seasons are these holidays?

19. New Year's Day ___winter___

20. Thanksgiving ___fall___

21. Independence Day ___summer___

Practice 2   Telling Time to the Hour

Match the clock to the time.

1.

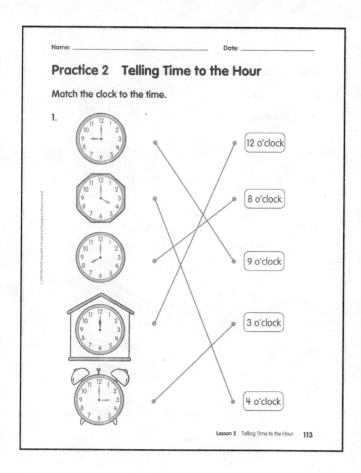

12 o'clock

8 o'clock

9 o'clock

3 o'clock

4 o'clock

Fill in the blanks.
This is what Roberta does on Monday.

Example

She brushes her teeth at ___7 o'clock___

2.

Her math class starts at ___9 o'clock___

3.

She has lunch at ___12 o'clock___

4.

She plays with her friends at ___4 o'clock___

5.

Roberta practices piano at ___5 o'clock___

6.

She has her dinner at ___6 o'clock___

7.

She does her homework at ___7 o'clock___

8.

She goes to bed at ___8 o'clock___

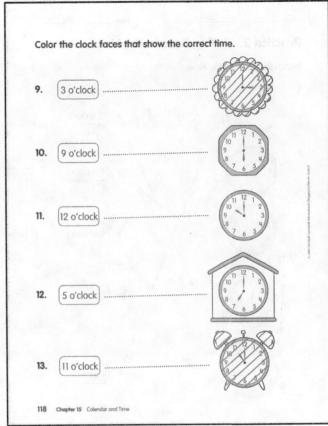

Color the clock faces that show the correct time.

9. 3 o'clock ....

10. 9 o'clock ....

11. 12 o'clock ....

12. 5 o'clock ....

13. 11 o'clock ....

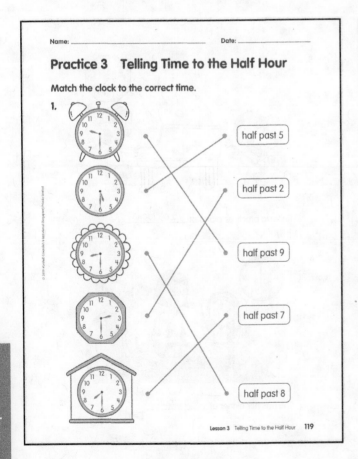

Practice 3 Telling Time to the Half Hour

Match the clock to the correct time.

1.

half past 5

half past 2

half past 9

half past 7

half past 8

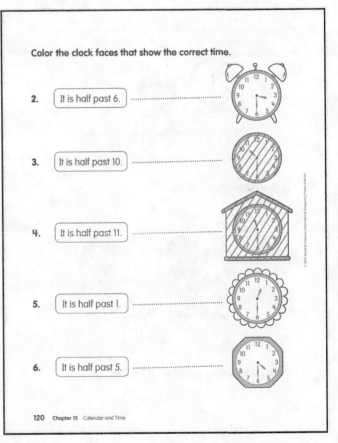

Color the clock faces that show the correct time.

2. It is half past 6. ....

3. It is half past 10. ....

4. It is half past 11. ....

5. It is half past 1. ....

6. It is half past 5. ....

Name: _____   Date: _____

The children go to the zoo with their parents.
Look at the pictures.
Write the correct times.

7. They visit the butterflies and birdlife enclosure at 10 o'clock

8. They look at the bears at half past 11

The pictures show what each child does on a Sunday.
Look at the pictures.
Then fill in the blanks.

— Example —

Jamal rides the bike with his Dad at *half past 9*

9. At half past 12 , Ashley enjoys lunch with her mother.

Name: _____   Date: _____

10. Pedro goes to the bowling alley with his Grandpa at 3 o'clock

11. John walks his dog at half past 5

Math Journal

Look at each clock.
Then write about an activity you do at that time.
Use **o'clock** or **half past** in your sentences.   Answers vary.

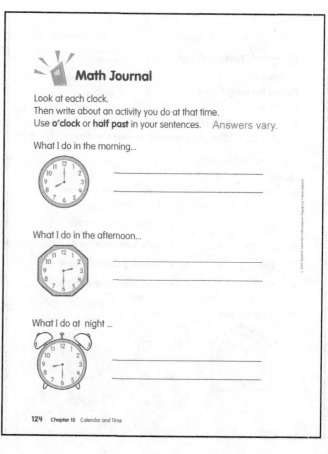

What I do in the morning...

_____
_____

What I do in the afternoon...

_____
_____

What I do at night ...

_____
_____

Put On Your Thinking Cap!
Challenging Practice

Thinking skill: Interpret data
Strategy: Apply data

Use the calendar to find the answer.

September						
Sun.	Mon.	Tue.	Wed.	Thu.	Fri.	Sat.
		1	2	3	4	5
6	7	8	9	10	11	12
13	14	15	16	17	18	19
20	21	22	23	24	25	26
27	28	29	30			

1. What is the date of the second Monday? September 14
2. How many Wednesdays are there? 5
3. What is the date of the third Thursday? September 17
4. What day of the week is September 25? Friday
5. a. Which day of the week will the next month begin on?
   Thursday
   b. What will be the date? October 1
6. a. Which day of the week did the last month end on?
   Monday
   b. What was the date? August 31

Chapter 15 Calendar and Time 125

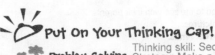

Put On Your Thinking Cap!
Problem Solving

Thinking skill: Sequencing
Strategy: Make a systematic list

Aunt Betsy is baking some muffins for Lori.
Look at the pictures.
Write 1, 2, 3, and 4 to show the correct order.

2

4

3

1

126 Chapter 15 Calendar and Time

Chapter Review/Test
Vocabulary
Choose the correct word.

week	days
months	year
calendar	

1. There are 7 days in one week
2. There are 12 months in one year
3. The calendar orders time into days, weeks, and months.

Concepts and Skills
Match.

4. October — is the season that comes before winter.
5. February — comes before Saturday.
6. Sunday — is the tenth month of the year.
7. Friday — is the first day of the week.
8. Fall — is the only month with 28 or 29 days.

9. Write the time.

11 o'clock   half past 3   5 o'clock

Chapter 15 Calendar and Time 127

Fill in the blanks.

10. School starts at _____ half past 8 _____
11. School is over at _____ 3 o'clock _____
12. Name your favorite season. Explain your answer.
    Answers vary.
    _____

Problem Solving
Solve.

13. Today is May 12, 2010.
    What will the date be in one week?
    May 19, 2010

14. Leon's birthday is on March 15.
    Angelina's is one week after Leon's.
    When is Angelina's birthday?
    March 22

128 Chapter 15 Calendar and Time

Chapter 15

Name: _____ Date: _____

Cumulative Review
for Chapters 14 and 15

Concepts and Skills

Add.
Use doubles facts or doubles plus one facts.

1. $6 + 6 =$ ___12___

2. $8 + 7 =$ ___15___

Add mentally.

3. $12 + 5 =$ ___17___

4. $24 + 3 =$ ___27___

5. $21 + 8 =$ ___29___

6. $32 + 4 =$ ___36___

Add mentally.

7. $10 + 23 =$ ___33___

8. $18 + 10 =$ ___28___

Subtract mentally.

9. $11 - 5 =$ ___6___

10. $18 - 9 =$ ___9___

11. $23 - 2 =$ ___21___

12. $27 - 2 =$ ___25___

Cumulative Review for Chapters 14 and 15   129

Subtract mentally.

13. $26 - 10 =$ ___16___

14. $35 - 10 =$ ___25___

15. $30 - 20 =$ ___10___

16. $27 - 20 =$ ___7___

Fill in the blanks.

17. There are ___12___ months in one year.

18. ___June___ is the sixth month of the year.

19. ___November___ is the month that comes before December.

20. ___7___ months have 31 days.

21. The four seasons are spring, ___summer___, ___fall___, and ___winter___.

130   Cumulative Review for Chapters 14 and 15

Name: _____ Date: _____

Match.

22.

23.

24.

25.

half past 10

7 o'clock

6 o'clock

half past 2

Cumulative Review for Chapters 14 and 15   131

Ethan does some activities on a Sunday.
Write the time for each activity.

26. Ethan eats his breakfast at ___8 o'clock___

27. Ethan swims at ___half past 3___

28. Ethan reads his book at ___half past 8___

Which clock shows the correct time?
Put a ✓ in the ▢.

29. 10 o'clock ▢

30. half past 4 ✓

132   Cumulative Review for Chapters 14 and 15

Workbook Answers: Chapters 14-15 Review
Math in Focus Homeschool Answer Key, Grade 1

Name: _____ Date: _____

Problem Solving

SEPTEMBER						
Sunday	Monday	Tuesday	Wednesday	Thursday	Friday	Saturday
			1	2	3	4	5
6	7	8	9	10	11	12
13	14	15	16	17	18	19
20	21	22	23	24	25	26
27	28	29	30			

Fill in the blanks.
Use the calendar to help you.

31. The third day of the month falls on a ___Thursday___.

32. There are ___30___ days in this month.

33. The date of the third Thursday of the month is
    ___September 17___

34. The day of the week after September 15 is ___Wednesday___

35. The first day of September is on a ___Tuesday___.

    So, the last day of August was on a ___Monday___

Use the calendar on pg 133.

SEPTEMBER						
Sunday	Monday	Tuesday	Wednesday	Thursday	Friday	Saturday
		1	2	3	4	5
6	7	8	9	10	11	12
13	14	15	16	17	18	19
20	21	22	23	24	25	26
27	28	29	30			

36. Fill in the blanks with the dates for all the Fridays.
    ___4___, ___11___, ___18___, ___25___

Fill in the blanks. Use your answers in Exercise 36 to help you.

37. The date for each Friday is ___7___ more than the date for
    the Friday before.

38. This is because there are ___7___ days in a week.

Problem Solving
Solve.
Show your work.

39. Laila ice skates for three weeks.
    She ice skates only from Monday to Thursday for each week.
    How many days does she ice skate in all?

    $4 + 4 + 4 = 12$

    She ice skates for ___12___ days.

246

Name: _____ Date: _____

16 Numbers to 100

Practice 1 Counting to 100

Count in tens and ones.
Fill in the blanks.

Example

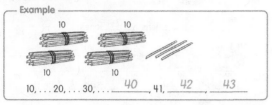

10, . . . 20, . . . 30, . . . _40_, 41, _42_, _43_

1.

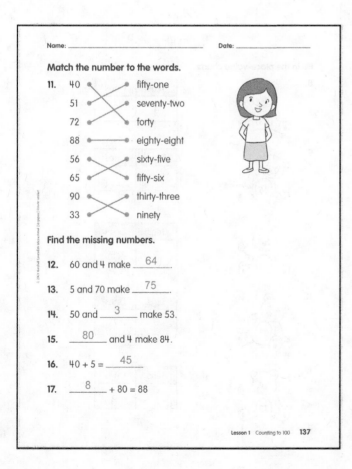

10, . . . 20, . . . 30, . . . 40, . . . _50_ _51_ _52_

2.

10, . . . 20, . . . 30, . . . 40, . . . 50, . . . 60, _61_, _62_ _63_

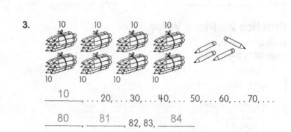

Lesson 1 Counting to 100 **135**

3.

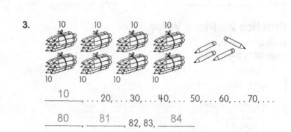

_10_, . . . 20, . . . 30, . . . 40, . . . 50, . . . 60, . . . 70, . . .

_80_ _81_, 82, 83, _84_

Write the number.

4. forty-nine _49_

5. sixty-eight _68_

6. ninety-five _95_

7. eighty-seven _87_

8. fifty-six _56_

9. seventy-three _73_

10. ninety-two _92_

136 Chapter 16 Numbers to 100

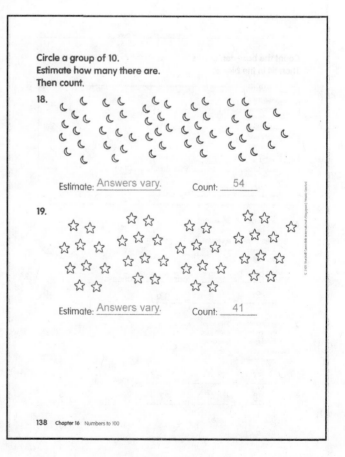

Name: _____ Date: _____

Match the number to the words.

11.
40 — forty
51 — fifty-one
72 — seventy-two
88 — eighty-eight
56 — sixty-five
65 — fifty-six
90 — thirty-three
33 — ninety

Find the missing numbers.

12. 60 and 4 make _64_

13. 5 and 70 make _75_

14. 50 and _3_ make 53.

15. _80_ and 4 make 84.

16. 40 + 5 = _45_

17. _8_ + 80 = 88

Lesson 1 Counting to 100 **137**

Circle a group of 10.
Estimate how many there are.
Then count.

18.

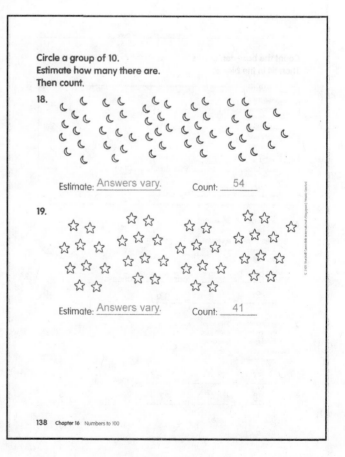

Estimate: _Answers vary._   Count: _54_

19.

Estimate: _Answers vary._   Count: _41_

138 Chapter 16 Numbers to 100

Practice 2 Place Value

Look at the pictures.
Then fill in the blanks.

Example

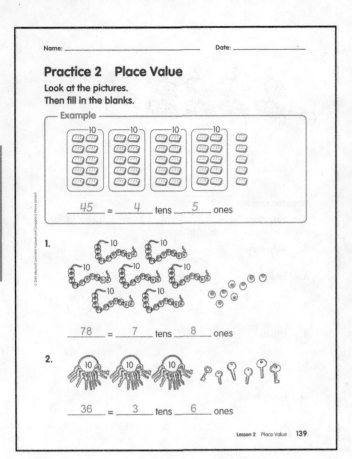

___45___ = ___4___ tens ___5___ ones

1.

___78___ = ___7___ tens ___8___ ones

2.

___36___ = ___3___ tens ___6___ ones

Lesson 2 Place Value   **139**

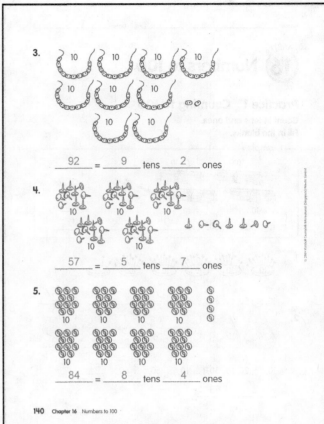

3.

___92___ = ___9___ tens ___2___ ones

4.

___57___ = ___5___ tens ___7___ ones

5.

___84___ = ___8___ tens ___4___ ones

140 Chapter 16 Numbers to 100

Count the base-ten blocks.
Then fill in the blanks.

Example

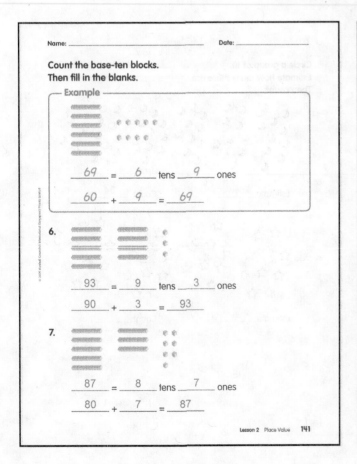

___69___ = ___6___ tens ___9___ ones

___60___ + ___9___ = ___69___

6.

___93___ = ___9___ tens ___3___ ones

___90___ + ___3___ = ___93___

7.

___87___ = ___8___ tens ___7___ ones

___80___ + ___7___ = ___87___

Lesson 2 Place Value   **141**

Fill in the place-value charts.

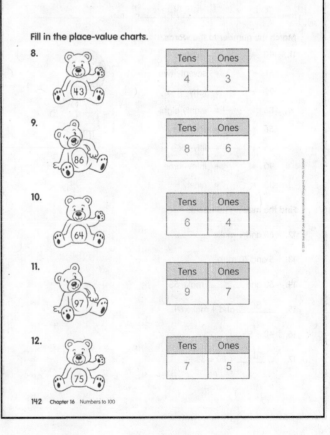

8.

Tens	Ones
4	3

9.

Tens	Ones
8	6

10.

Tens	Ones
6	4

11.

Tens	Ones
9	7

12.

Tens	Ones
7	5

142 Chapter 16 Numbers to 100

Workbook Answers: Chapter 16
Math in Focus Homeschool Answer Key, Grade 1

Practice 3 Comparing, Ordering, and Patterns

Find the missing numbers.

Example
2 more than 50 is __52__
2 less than 66 is __64__

1. 2 more than 54 is __56__
2. __68__ is 2 more than 66.
3. 2 less than 78 is __76__
4. __72__ is 2 less than 74.

45 50 55 60 65 70 75 80 85 90 95 100

5. 5 more than 50 is __55__
6. 10 more than 85 is __95__
7. 5 less than 65 is __60__
8. __90__ is 10 less than 100.
9. __80__ is 5 more than 75.
10. __70__ is 5 less than 75.

Circle the greater number.

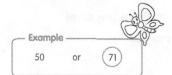

Example
50 or (71)

11. 72 or (87)
12. (92) or 69
13. (54) or 45
14. 67 or (76)
15. (86) or 83
16. 94 or (98)

Color the number that is less.

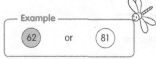

Example
(62) or (81)

17. ⊘ or △71
18. ⊘ or △93
19. ⊘ or □97
20. □84 or ⊘
21. ⊘ or ○67
22. ○96 or ⊘

Compare the numbers.
Then fill in the blanks.

23.

65   72   49

The least number is __49__
The greatest number is __72__

24.
73   69   90

The least number is __69__
The greatest number is __90__

25. Order the numbers from greatest to least.

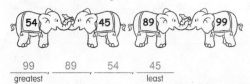
54   45   89   99

__99__   __89__   __54__   __45__
greatest   least

Use the numbers to fill in the blanks.

67   84   46   92   73   100

26. The greatest number is __100__
27. The least number is __46__
28. __46__, __67__, and __73__ are less than 84.
29. __92__ and __100__ are greater than 84.
30. 67 is greater than __46__ but less than 100.
31. 92 is less than __100__ but greater than 84.

Complete each number pattern.

32. 50, 51, 52, __53__, 54, 55, __56__, __57__, 58
33. 73, 72, 71, __70__, 69, 68, __67__
34. __85__, 87, 89, __91__, 93, __95__
35. 99, __97__, 95, 93, __91__, __89__
36. 50, 60, __70__, 80, __90__, __100__
37. 93, 83, 73, __63__, __53__, 43, __33__

Put on Your Thinking Cap!

Challenging Practice

Read each clue.
Cross out the numbers that are incorrect.
Fill in the blanks.

1.

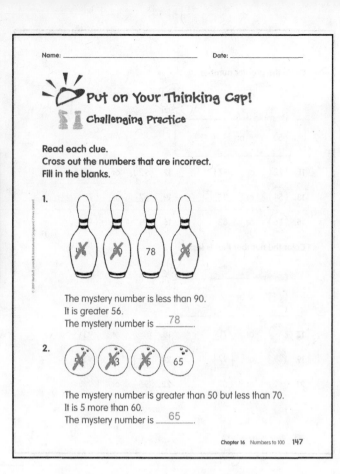

The mystery number is less than 90.
It is greater 56.
The mystery number is __78__

2.

The mystery number is greater than 50 but less than 70.
It is 5 more than 60.
The mystery number is __65__

Chapter 16 Numbers to 100 **147**

3.

The mystery number is less than 90 but greater than 63.
It is 1 less than 80.
The mystery number is __79__

148 Chapter 16 Numbers to 100

Put on Your Thinking Cap!

Problem Solving

Use the chart to complete the following number patterns.
Explain the rule for the number pattern.

1	2	3	4	5	6	7	8	9	10
11	12	13	14	15	16	17	18	19	20
21	22	23	24	25	26	27	28	29	30
31	32	33	34	35	36	37	38	39	40
41	42	43	44	45	46	47	48	49	50
51	52	53	54	55	56	57	58	59	60
61	62	63	64	65	66	67	68	69	70
71	72	73	74	75	76	77	78	79	80
81	82	83	84	85	86	87	88	89	90
91	92	93	94	95	96	97	98	99	100

Example

22, 25, 28, 31, __34__, __37__, __40__

Rule: _Counting on in steps of 3 from the_
number before it.

Or _Adding 3 to the number before it_

Chapter 16 Numbers to 100 **149**

---

1. 41, 46, 51, 56, __61__, __66__, __71__

   Rule: Counting on in steps of 5 from the number before it.

2. 30, 36, 42, 48, __54__, __60__, __66__

   Rule: Adding 6 to the number before it.

3. 10, 20, 30, 40, __50__, __60__, __70__

   Rule: Counting on in steps of 10.

4. 81, 78, 75, 72, __69__, __66__, __63__

   Rule: Counting back in steps of 3.

5. 90, 85, 80, 75, __70__, __65__, __60__

   Rule: Counting back in steps of 5.

6. 80, 70, 60, 50, __40__, __30__, __20__

   Rule: Counting back in steps of 10.

150 Chapter 16 Numbers to 100

Name: _____ Date: _____

Chapter Review/Test
Vocabulary
Choose the correct word.

```
compare    estimate    number line
```

1. You __compare__ numbers by finding which number is greater than or less than the other.

2. When you do not need an exact number, you can __estimate__

3. A __number line__ is used to compare numbers.

Concepts and Skills
Fill in the blanks.

4. Write ninety-eight as a number. __98__

5. Write 74 in word form. __seventy-four__

6. 80 and 7 make __87__.

7. 64 = __6__ tens __4__ ones

8. __60__ is 6 more than 54.

Compare.

9. Circle the greatest number.

10. Circle the least number.

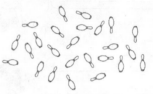

Estimate then count.

11. Estimate the number of bowling pins. Then count the exact number.

Estimate: __Answers vary.__

Count: __25__

CHAPTER 17 Addition and Subtraction to 100

Practice 1 Addition Without Regrouping

Add by counting on.

Example

73 + 4 = __77__

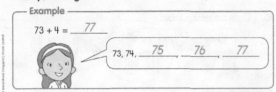

73, 74, __75__, __76__, __77__

1. 85 + 3 = __88__

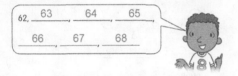

85, __86__, __87__, __88__

2. 62 + 6 = __68__

62, __63__, __64__, __65__, __66__, __67__, __68__

Lesson 1 Addition Without Regrouping **153**

Add.

3.
```
   5  3
+     4
-------
   5  7
```
4.
```
   9  2
+     7
-------
   9  9
```

5.
```
   8  3
+     5
-------
   8  8
```
6.
```
   4  4
+     5
-------
   4  9
```

7.
```
      2
+  6  3
-------
   6  5
```
8.
```
      4
+  7  3
-------
   7  7
```

Fill in the missing numbers.

9. 5 + 82 = __87__

10. 93 + 2 = __95__

```
   [ ]  [5]
+  [8]  [2]
----------
   [8]  [7]
```

```
   [9]  [3]
+  [ ]  [2]
----------
   [9]  [5]
```

154 Chapter 17 Addition and Subtraction to 100

Add.

11.
```
   2  0
+  5  0
-------
   7  0
```
12.
```
   6  0
+  2  3
-------
   8  3
```

13.
```
   3  7
+  4  0
-------
   7  7
```
14.
```
   5  3
+  4  5
-------
   9  8
```

15.
```
   6  3
+  2  4
-------
   8  7
```
16.
```
   4  7
+  1  2
-------
   5  9
```

Fill in the missing numbers.

17. 56 + 23 = __79__

18. 86 + 13 = __99__

```
   [5]  [6]
+  [2]  [3]
----------
   [7]  [9]
```

```
   [8]  [6]
+  [1]  [3]
----------
   [9]  [9]
```

Lesson 1 Addition Without Regrouping **155**

Match.

19.

89 ⎯⎯ 20 + 70

85 ⎯⎯ 0 + 42

77 ⎯⎯ 72 + 5

42 ⎯⎯ 54 + 31

90 ⎯⎯ 40 + 49

156 Chapter 17 Addition and Subtraction to 100

Chapter 17

Practice 2 Addition with Regrouping

Name: _____   Date: _____

Add.

1.
```
    4  8
 +     5
 _____
    5  3
```

2.
```
    5  7
 +     8
 _____
    6  5
```

3.
```
       7
 +  6  4
 _____
    7  1
```

4.
```
    5  9
 +     4
 _____
    6  3
```

5.
```
    7  3
 +     9
 _____
    8  2
```

6.
```
       5
 +  8  6
 _____
    9  1
```

Fill in the missing numbers.

7. 4 + 66 = __70__

```
   [ ]  [4]
 + [6]  [6]
 _____
   [7]  [0]
```

8. 89 + 8 = __97__

```
   [8]  [9]
 + [ ]  [8]
 _____
   [9]  [7]
```

9. Matt drops a ball into the number machine below.
    What happens to the number on the ball?
    Write the number in the ◯.

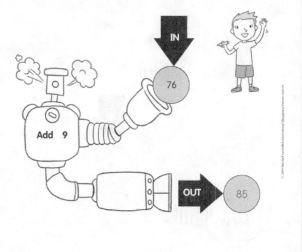

IN
76
Add 9
OUT 85

Name: _____   Date: _____

Add.

10.
```
    2  7
 +  2  8
 _____
    5  5
```

11.
```
    8  6
 +  1  4
 _____
   10  0
```

12.
```
    2  5
 +  3  7
 _____
    6  2
```

13.
```
    4  4
 +  3  7
 _____
    8  1
```

14.
```
    3  9
 +  2  1
 _____
    6  0
```

15.
```
    3  6
 +  5  4
 _____
    9  0
```

Fill in the missing numbers.

16. 19 + 14 = __33__

```
   [1]  [9]
 + [1]  [4]
 _____
   [3]  [3]
```

17. 58 + 36 = __94__

```
   [5]  [8]
 + [3]  [6]
 _____
   [9]  [4]
```

Add.
Then answer the question.

18. 52 + 19 = __71__ (Y)   19. 58 + 6 = __64__ (B)

20. 67 + 18 = __85__ (A)   21. 48 + 38 = __86__ (E)

22. 7 + 59 = __66__ (D)   23. 43 + 57 = __100__ (R)

24. 39 + 49 = __88__ (T)   25. 27 + 49 = __76__ (D)

26. 56 + 35 = __91__ (E)

What toy is named after President Theodore Roosevelt?

Match the letters to the answers below to find out.

```
[T] [E] [D] [D] [Y]      [B] [E] [A] [R]
 88  86  66  76  71       64  91  85  100
```

Lesson 2 Addition with Regrouping 157

158 Chapter 17 Addition and Subtraction to 100

Lesson 2 Addition with Regrouping 159

160 Chapter 17 Addition and Subtraction to 100

Chapter 17

Name: _____ Date: _____

27. Ron drops a ball into a number machine.
Which ball is it?

Write the number in the ◯.

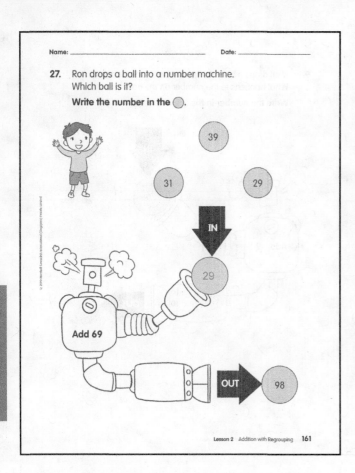

39

31   29

IN

29

Add 69

OUT → 98

Add.
Then solve the riddle.

28. 45 + 7 = __52__

29. 52 + 5 = __57__

30. 2 + 78 = __80__

31. 72 + 8 = __80__

32. 2 + 70 = __72__

33. 64 + 19 = __83__

34. 28 + 40 = __68__

35. 40 + 30 = __70__

36. 61 + 16 = __77__

37. 17 + 63 = __80__

T
A
S
N
R
I
H
D
F
S

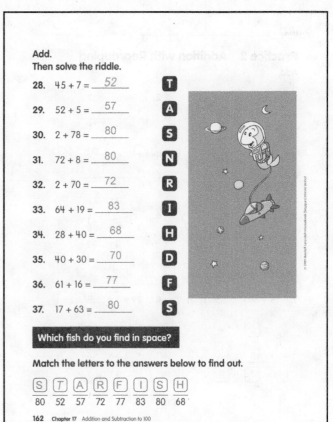

Which fish do you find in space?

Match the letters to the answers below to find out.

Ⓢ Ⓣ Ⓐ Ⓡ Ⓕ Ⓘ Ⓢ Ⓗ
80 52 57 72 77 83 80 68

Name: _____ Date: _____

Practice 3 Subtraction Without Regrouping

Count back to subtract.

┌─ Example ─
│ 67 − 4 = __63__
│
│ 67, 66, __65__, __64__, __63__

1. 95 − 3 = __92__

95, 94, __93__, __92__

2. 88 − 5 = __83__

88, 87, __86__, __85__
__84__, __83__

3. 79 − 6 = __73__

79, 78, __77__ __76__
__75__, __74__, __73__

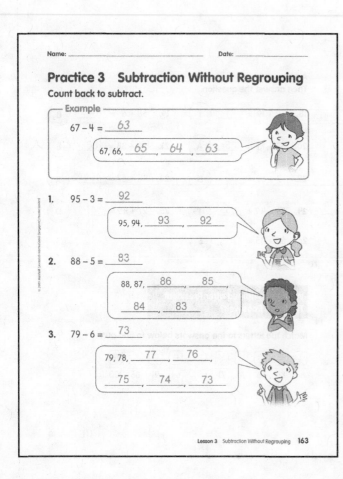

Subtract.

4.   5 8
       −   3
       ─────
         5 5

5.   6 9
       −   4
       ─────
         6 5

6.   7 4
       −   3
       ─────
         7 1

7.   6 7
       −   5
       ─────
         6 2

8.   9 6
       −   3
       ─────
         9 3

9.   8 8
       −   7
       ─────
         8 1

Fill in the missing numbers.

10. 79 − 6 = __73__

 [7] [9]
−[ ] [6]
 [7] [3]

11. 99 − 5 = __94__

 [9] [9]
−[ ] [5]
 [9] [4]

Name: _____ **Date:** _____

Subtract.

12.
```
    9  5
 -  2  0
 ------
    7  5
```

13.
```
    4  9
 -  3  0
 ------
    1  9
```

14.
```
    7  0
 -  2  0
 ------
    5  0
```

15.
```
    4  0
 -  2  0
 ------
    2  0
```

16.
```
    6  8
 -  3  2
 ------
    3  6
```

17.
```
    9  7
 -  5  4
 ------
    4  3
```

Fill in the missing numbers.

18. 56 − 23 = __33__

```
    5  6
 -  2  3
 ------
    3  3
```

19. 86 − 42 = __44__

```
    8  6
 -  4  2
 ------
    4  4
```

Match.

20.

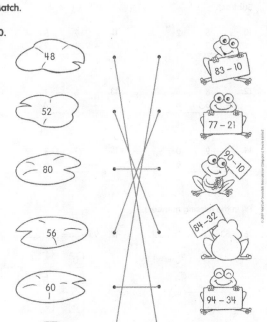

48 52 80 56 60 73

83 − 10
77 − 21
90 − 10
84 − 32
94 − 34
68 − 20

Name: _____ **Date:** _____

Practice 4   Subtraction with Regrouping

Subtract.

1.
```
    6  4
 -     8
 ------
    5  6
```

2.
```
    9  3
 -     5
 ------
    8  8
```

3.
```
    7  8
 -     9
 ------
    6  9
```

4.
```
    8  7
 -     8
 ------
    7  9
```

5.
```
    5  0
 -     2
 ------
    4  8
```

6.
```
    8  0
 -     6
 ------
    7  4
```

Fill in the missing numbers.

7. 72 − 9 = __63__

```
    7  2
 -     9
 ------
    6  3
```

8. 91 − 4 = __87__

```
    9  1
 -     4
 ------
    8  7
```

9. Kayla drops a ball into a number machine. Which ball is it?

Write the number in the ◯.

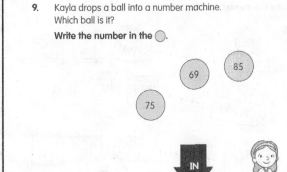

69 85 75

IN 85

Subtract 8

OUT 77

Name: _____   Date: _____

Subtract.

10.
```
    5  2
  - 3  8
  ─────
    1  4
```

11.
```
    7  6
  - 4  9
  ─────
    2  7
```

12.
```
    8  5
  - 3  8
  ─────
    4  7
```

13.
```
    5  3
  - 4  7
  ─────
       6
```

14.
```
    9  0
  - 5  6
  ─────
    3  4
```

15.
```
    7  3
  - 5  6
  ─────
    1  7
```

Fill in the missing numbers.

16. 83 − 26 = ___57___

```
    8   3
  - 2   6
  ───────
    5   7
```

17. 95 − 38 = ___57___

```
    9   5
  - 3   8
  ───────
    5   7
```

Lesson 4 Subtraction with Regrouping **169**

---

18. Ken drops a ball into a number machine.
Which ball is it?

Write the number in the ◯.

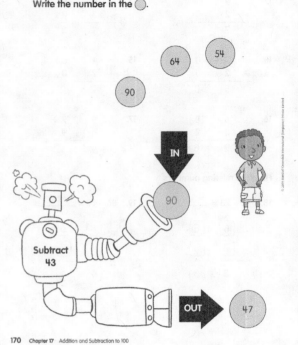

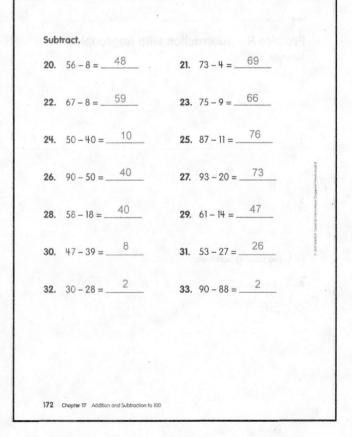

170 Chapter 17 Addition and Subtraction to 100

Name: _____   Date: _____

Color the correct answer.

19.

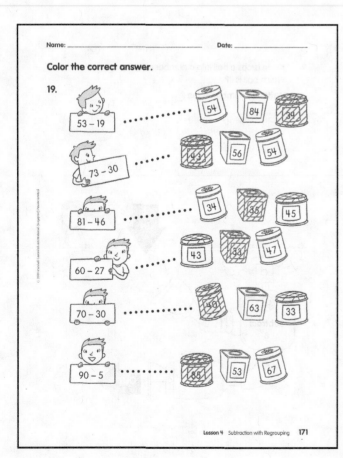

53 − 19

73 − 30

81 − 46

60 − 27

70 − 30

90 − 5

Lesson 4 Subtraction with Regrouping **171**

Subtract.

20. 56 − 8 = ___48___

21. 73 − 4 = ___69___

22. 67 − 8 = ___59___

23. 75 − 9 = ___66___

24. 50 − 40 = ___10___

25. 87 − 11 = ___76___

26. 90 − 50 = ___40___

27. 93 − 20 = ___73___

28. 58 − 18 = ___40___

29. 61 − 14 = ___47___

30. 47 − 39 = ___8___

31. 53 − 27 = ___26___

32. 30 − 28 = ___2___

33. 90 − 88 = ___2___

172 Chapter 17 Addition and Subtraction to 100

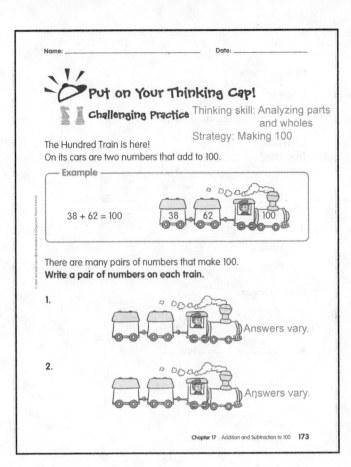

Name: _____ Date: _____

Put on Your Thinking Cap!

Challenging Practice Thinking skill: Analyzing parts and wholes
Strategy: Making 100

The Hundred Train is here!
On its cars are two numbers that add to 100.

— Example —

$38 + 62 = 100$

38 62 100

There are many pairs of numbers that make 100.
Write a pair of numbers on each train.

1.

Answers vary.

2.

Answers vary.

Chapter 17 Addition and Subtraction to 100 **173**

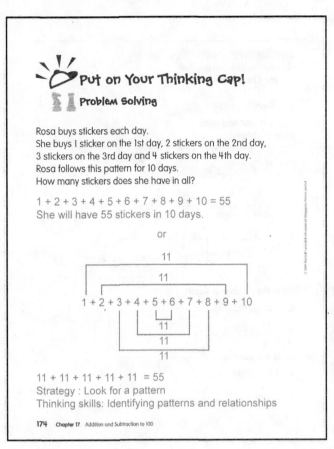

Put on Your Thinking Cap!

Problem Solving

Rosa buys stickers each day.
She buys 1 sticker on the 1st day, 2 stickers on the 2nd day,
3 stickers on the 3rd day and 4 stickers on the 4th day.
Rosa follows this pattern for 10 days.
How many stickers does she have in all?

$1 + 2 + 3 + 4 + 5 + 6 + 7 + 8 + 9 + 10 = 55$
She will have 55 stickers in 10 days.

or

11
11
$1 + 2 + 3 + 4 + 5 + 6 + 7 + 8 + 9 + 10$
11
11
11

$11 + 11 + 11 + 11 + 11 = 55$
Strategy : Look for a pattern
Thinking skills: Identifying patterns and relationships

174 Chapter 17 Addition and Subtraction to 100

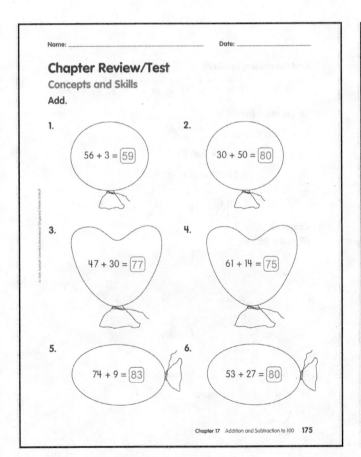

Name: _____ Date: _____

Chapter Review/Test
Concepts and Skills
Add.

1.
$56 + 3 = 59$

2.
$30 + 50 = 80$

3.
$47 + 30 = 77$

4.
$61 + 14 = 75$

5.
$74 + 9 = 83$

6.
$53 + 27 = 80$

Chapter 17 Addition and Subtraction to 100 **175**

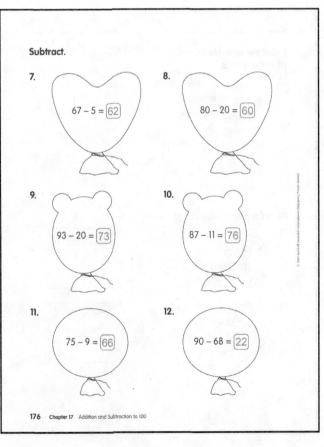

Subtract.

7.
$67 - 5 = 62$

8.
$80 - 20 = 60$

9.
$93 - 20 = 73$

10.
$87 - 11 = 76$

11.
$75 - 9 = 66$

12.
$90 - 68 = 22$

176 Chapter 17 Addition and Subtraction to 100

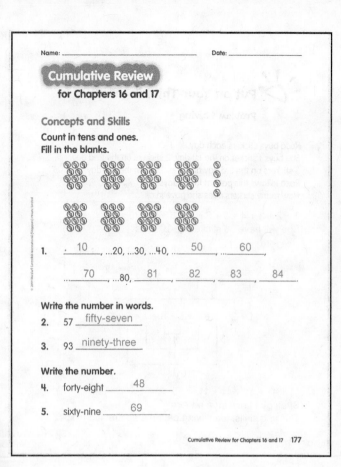

Name: _____ Date: _____

Cumulative Review
for Chapters 16 and 17

Concepts and Skills

Count in tens and ones.
Fill in the blanks.

1. __10__, ...20, ...30, ...40, __50__, __60__

...__70__, ...80, __81__, __82__, __83__, __84__

Write the number in words.

2. 57 __fifty-seven__

3. 93 __ninety-three__

Write the number.

4. forty-eight __48__

5. sixty-nine __69__

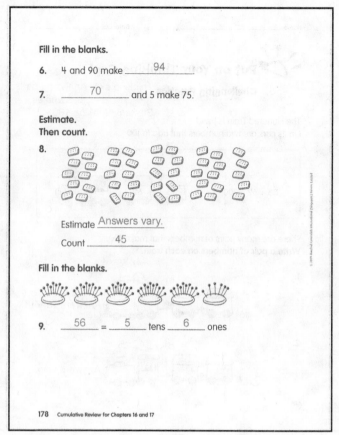

Fill in the blanks.

6. 4 and 90 make __94__

7. __70__ and 5 make 75.

Estimate.
Then count.

8.

Estimate __Answers vary.__

Count __45__

Fill in the blanks.

9. __56__ = __5__ tens __6__ ones

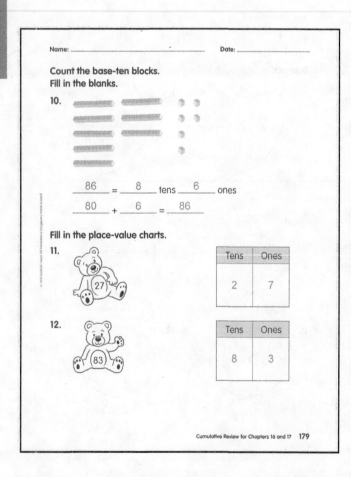

Name: _____ Date: _____

Count the base-ten blocks.
Fill in the blanks.

10.

__86__ = __8__ tens __6__ ones

__80__ + __6__ = __86__

Fill in the place-value charts.

11. (27)

Tens	Ones
2	7

12. (83)

Tens	Ones
8	3

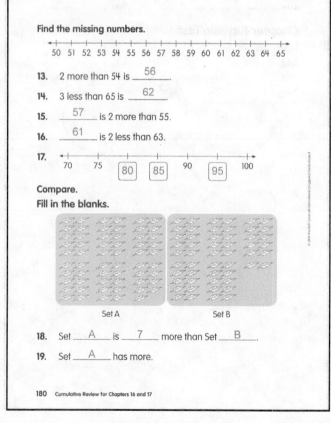

Find the missing numbers.

50 51 52 53 54 55 56 57 58 59 60 61 62 63 64 65

13. 2 more than 54 is __56__.

14. 3 less than 65 is __62__.

15. __57__ is 2 more than 55.

16. __61__ is 2 less than 63.

17. 70   75   [80]   [85]   90   [95]   100

Compare.
Fill in the blanks.

Set A   Set B

18. Set __A__ is __7__ more than Set __B__.

19. Set __A__ has more.

258

Page 1 (181)

Name: _____ Date: _____

Color the greater number.

20. (71) or (**80**) 21. (45) or (**54**)

Color the number that is less.

22. △(35) or △(51) 23. △(91) or △(89)

Fill in the blanks.

24.

| 15 | | 41 |
| | 36 | |

The least number is __15__.

The greatest number is __41__.

Order the numbers from least to greatest.

25. (76) (50) (67)

__50__, __67__, __76__
least

Complete each number pattern.

26. 73, 72, 71, __70__, __69__, 68, __67__

27. 50, 60, __70__, 80, __90__, __100__

Add by counting on.

28. 82 + 7 = __89__   29. 50 + 40 = __90__

Cumulative Review for Chapters 16 and 17   181

Page 2 (182)

Add.

30.
```
  7 6
+   7
─────
[8][3]
```

31.
```
  2 6
+ 3 8
─────
[6][4]
```

Fill in the missing numbers.

32. 8 + 33 = __41__
```
[ ][8]
+[3][3]
──────
[4][1]
```

33. 64 + 19 = __83__
```
[6][4]
+[1][9]
──────
[8][3]
```

Count back to subtract.

34. 97 − 6 = __91__   35. 50 − 30 = __20__

Subtract.

36.
```
  6 3
−   7
─────
[5][6]
```

37.
```
  9 0
−   6
─────
[8][4]
```

Fill in the missing numbers.

38. 45 − 6 = __39__
```
[4][5]
−[ ][6]
──────
[3][9]
```

39. 73 − 58 = __15__
```
[7][3]
−[5][8]
──────
[1][5]
```

182   Cumulative Review for Chapters 16 and 17

Page 3 (183)

Name: _____ Date: _____

Problem Solving

Solve.

40. A number is less than 30 but greater than 10.
It has 6 in the ones place.
What are the possible numbers? 26, 16

41. A number is 65 when you subtract 6 then add 7.
What is the number?
Circle the number.

(58) (**64**) (71) (52)

Cumulative Review for Chapters 16 and 17   183

Page 4 (184)

42. Write an addition sentence to make 100.
One of the numbers must have 3 in the ones place.

_____ + _____ = 100

Answers vary.
Sample:
33 + 67 = 100

There is more than one correct answer.

Fill in the blank.
Choose a number in the box.

43. | 63 40 36 88 |

62 − __36__ = 26

184   Cumulative Review for Chapters 16 and 17

Workbook Answers: Chapters 16-17 Review
Math in Focus Homeschool Answer Key, Grade 1

Chapters 16-17 Review

CHAPTER 18 Multiplication and Division

Practice 1 Adding the Same Number

Count the number of groups.
Then count the number of bugs in each group.
Write the numbers in the blanks.

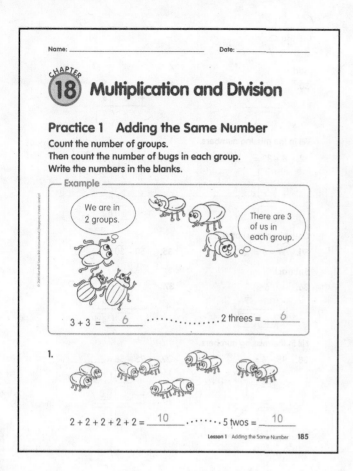

Example

We are in 2 groups.

There are 3 of us in each group.

3 + 3 = __6__ · · · · · · · · 2 threes = __6__

1.

2 + 2 + 2 + 2 + 2 = __10__ · · · · · · 5 twos = __10__

Count the number of groups.
Then count the number of bugs in each group.
Write the numbers in the blanks.

2.

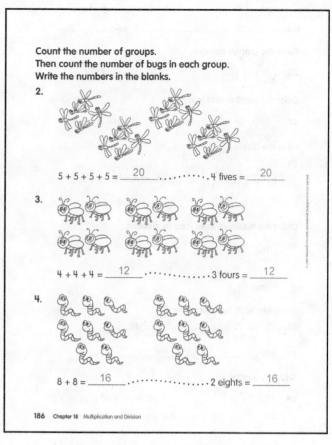

5 + 5 + 5 + 5 = __20__ · · · · · · · · 4 fives = __20__

3.

4 + 4 + 4 = __12__ · · · · · · · · · · 3 fours = __12__

4.

8 + 8 = __16__ · · · · · · · · · · 2 eights = __16__

Look at the pictures.
Then fill in the blanks.

5.

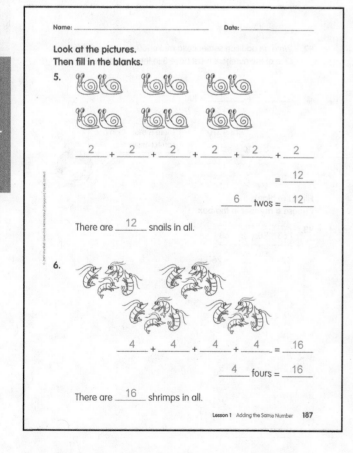

__2__ + __2__ + __2__ + __2__ + __2__ + __2__

= __12__

__6__ twos = __12__

There are __12__ snails in all.

6.

__4__ + __4__ + __4__ + __4__ = __16__

__4__ fours = __16__

There are __16__ shrimps in all.

Look at the pictures.
Then fill in the blanks.

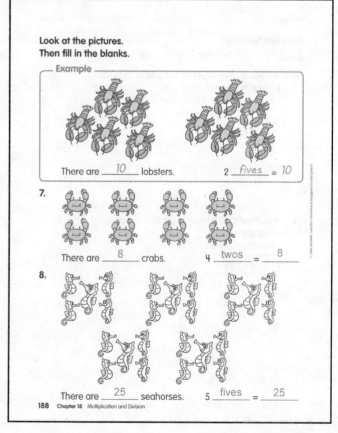

Example

There are __10__ lobsters.   2 __fives__ = __10__

7.

There are __8__ crabs.   4 __twos__ = __8__

8.

There are __25__ seahorses.   5 __fives__ = __25__

Chapter 18

Worksheet 9-11 (top left)

Name: _____   Date: _____

**Look at the picture.
Then fill in the blanks.**

9. A starfish has __5__ arms.

    6 _fives_ = __30__

    6 starfishes have __30__ arms.

10. Each dress has 5 buttons.

    3 _fives_ = __15__

    3 dresses have __15__ buttons.

11. One flower has __6__ petals.

    6 _sixes_ = __36__

    6 flowers have __36__ petals.

Worksheet 12-13 (top right)

**Look at the picture.
Then fill in the blanks.**

12. Each plant has __4__ leaves.

    5 _fours_ = __20__

    5 plants have __20__ leaves.

13. An octopus has __8__ arms.

    4 _eights_ = __32__

    4 octopuses have __32__ arms.

Worksheet Practice 2 (bottom left)

Name: _____   Date: _____

Practice 2   Sharing Equally

**Look at the pack of fish crackers.
Then fill in the blanks.**

1.

    There are __6__ fish crackers in all.

    How many fish crackers are in each pack? __2__

2. There are __12__ fish crackers in all.

    How many fish crackers are in each pack? __4__

Worksheet 3-4 (bottom right)

**Look at the pictures.
Then fill in the blanks.**

3. There are __4__ mice in all.

    There are __2__ tubs.

    There are __2__ mice in each tub.

4.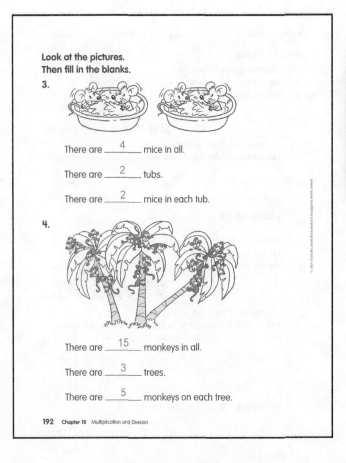

    There are __15__ monkeys in all.

    There are __3__ trees.

    There are __5__ monkeys on each tree.

Chapter 18

Top-left panel

Name: _____   Date: _____

Look at the pictures.
Then fill in the blanks.

5.

There are ___4___ dogs in all.

There are ___4___ dog houses.

There is ___1___ dog in each dog house.

6.

There are ___12___ cats in all.

There are ___3___ baskets.

There are ___4___ cats in each basket.

Top-right panel

Fill in the blanks.

Dylan is cleaning the shoe rack.
He has to put 8 shoes equally into 4 groups.

He puts 1 shoe in each group.

Then he puts 1 more in each group.

— Example —
Each group has ___2___ shoes.

Bottom-left panel

Name: _____   Date: _____

Fill in the blanks.

7. Martin is in the garden.
He has to put 10 flowers
equally into 2 groups.

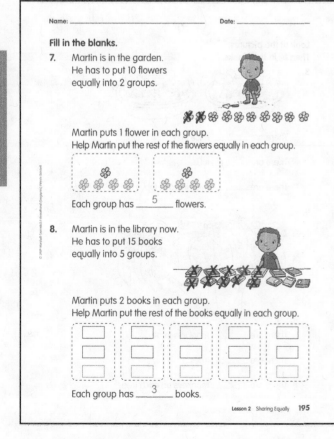

Martin puts 1 flower in each group.
Help Martin put the rest of the flowers equally in each group.

Each group has ___5___ flowers.

8. Martin is in the library now.
He has to put 15 books
equally into 5 groups.

Martin puts 2 books in each group.
Help Martin put the rest of the books equally in each group.

Each group has ___3___ books.

Bottom-right panel

Draw.
Then fill in the blanks.

9. There are 12 peanuts.
Draw an equal number of peanuts in each bag.

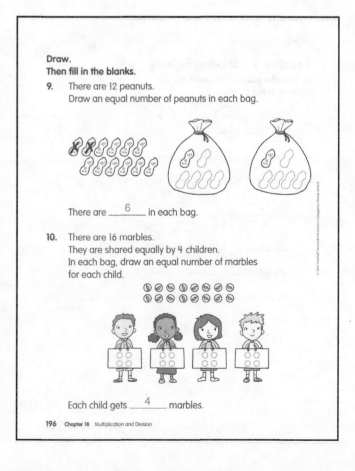

There are ___6___ in each bag.

10. There are 16 marbles.
They are shared equally by 4 children.
In each bag, draw an equal number of marbles
for each child.

Each child gets ___4___ marbles.

Name: _____   Date: _____

Fill in the blanks.

11. There are 10 toys.
Suki packs them into 5 boxes equally.
How many toys are in each box?

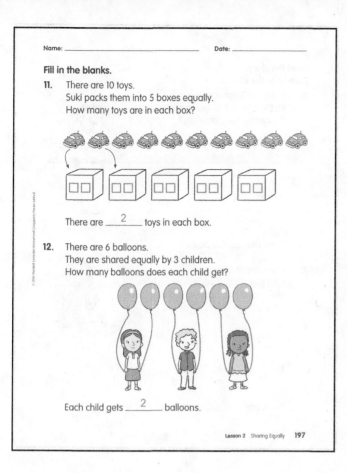

There are _____2_____ toys in each box.

12. There are 6 balloons.
They are shared equally by 3 children.
How many balloons does each child get?

Each child gets _____2_____ balloons.

Fill in the blanks.

13. Put 18 coins into 3 equal groups.

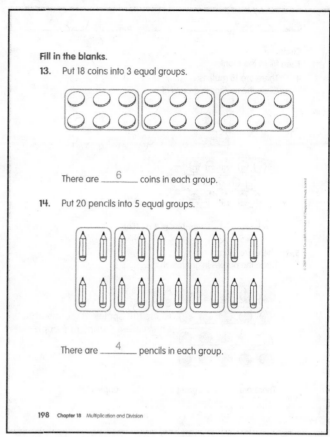

There are _____6_____ coins in each group.

14. Put 20 pencils into 5 equal groups.

There are _____4_____ pencils in each group.

Name: _____   Date: _____

Practice 3   Finding the Number of Groups
Circle.
Then fill in the blanks.

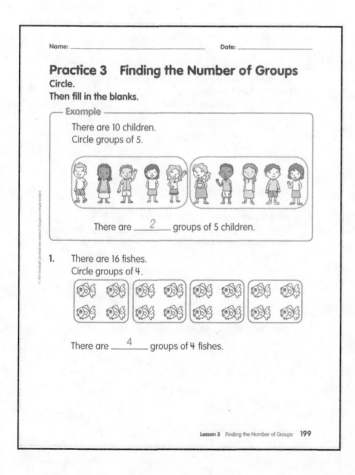

— Example —

There are 10 children.
Circle groups of 5.

There are _____2_____ groups of 5 children.

1. There are 16 fishes.
Circle groups of 4.

There are _____4_____ groups of 4 fishes.

Circle.
Then fill in the blanks.

2. There are 15 oranges.
Circle groups of 3.

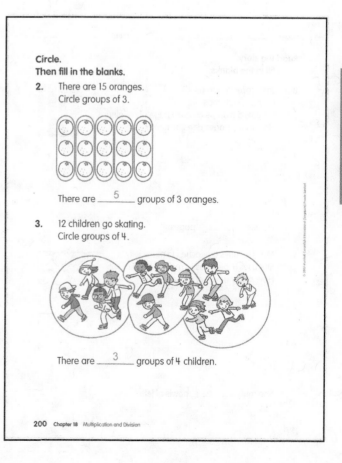

There are _____5_____ groups of 3 oranges.

3. 12 children go skating.
Circle groups of 4.

There are _____3_____ groups of 4 children.

Name: _____ Date: _____

Circle.
Then fill in the blanks.

4. There are 18 muffins.
    Circle the muffins in groups of 3.

    There are ___6___ groups of 3 muffins.

5. There are 20 apples.
    Circle the apples in groups of _____.

    Answers vary.
    Sample:
    Circle the apples in groups of 5.
    There are 4 groups of 5 apples.

    There are _____ groups of _____ apples.

Read the story.
Then fill in the blanks.

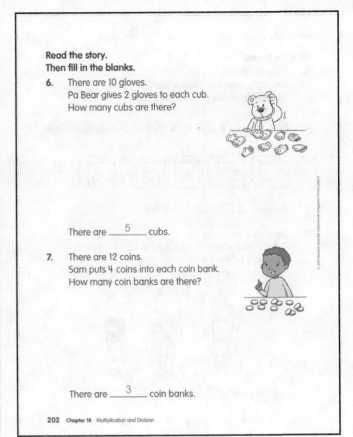

6. There are 10 gloves.
    Pa Bear gives 2 gloves to each cub.
    How many cubs are there?

    There are ___5___ cubs.

7. There are 12 coins.
    Sam puts 4 coins into each coin bank.
    How many coin banks are there?

    There are ___3___ coin banks.

Name: _____ Date: _____

Read the story.
Then fill in the blanks.

8. Josh collects stamps.
    He has 20 stamps.
    He puts 5 stamps on each page of his album.
    How many pages does he need?

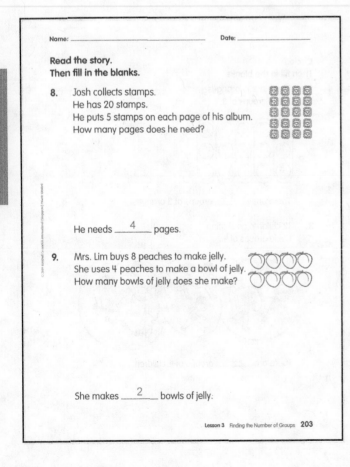

    He needs ___4___ pages.

9. Mrs. Lim buys 8 peaches to make jelly.
    She uses 4 peaches to make a bowl of jelly.
    How many bowls of jelly does she make?

    She makes ___2___ bowls of jelly.

---

10. Mary buys 15 oranges.
    She divides them equally into a few boxes.
    Each box has 5 oranges.
    How many boxes does she use?

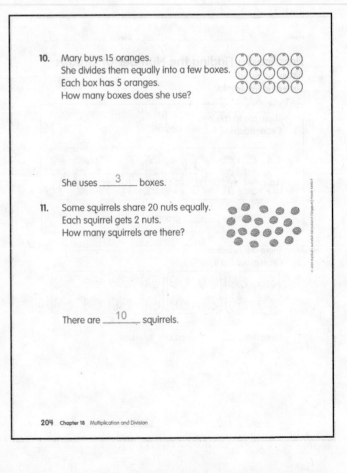

    She uses ___3___ boxes.

11. Some squirrels share 20 nuts equally.
    Each squirrel gets 2 nuts.
    How many squirrels are there?

    There are ___10___ squirrels.

Put On Your Thinking Cap!

Challenging Practice

Lena collects erasers.
Look at the picture.
Then fill in the blanks.

1. Lena has ___20___ erasers.

2. She puts the erasers equally into 5 boxes.
   How many erasers are in each box? ___4___

3. She puts the erasers equally into 4 boxes.
   How many erasers are in each box? ___5___

4. She puts 10 erasers into each box.
   How many boxes does she need? ___2___

5. She puts 4 erasers into each box.
   How many boxes does she need? ___5___

Chapter 18 Multiplication and Division **205**

Put On Your Thinking Cap!

Problem Solving

Solve.

There are 8 squares and 12 triangles.
Put an equal number of each shape into each group.

1. Put them into 2 groups.

There are ___4___ ☐ in each group.
There are ___6___ △ in each group.
There are ___10___ shapes in each group.

2. Put them into 4 groups.   Thinking skill: Classifying
                              Strategy: Act it out

There are ___2___ ☐ in each group.
There are ___3___ △ in each group.
There are ___5___ shapes in each group.

206 Chapter 18 Multiplication and Division

Chapter Review/Test

Vocabulary

Choose the correct word.

same
groups

1. ⭐⭐⭐ ⭐⭐⭐ ⭐⭐⭐

   The picture shows equal ___groups___.

2. By adding the ___same___ number, you will have 9 ⭐ in all.

Concepts and Skills

Fill in the blanks.

3. 2 + 2 + 2 = ___6___
   3 twos = ___6___

4. 5 + 5 + 5 + 5 = ___20___
   4 fives = ___20___

Match.

5. 5 threes   4 fours
   4 + 4 + 4 + 4   3 + 3 + 3 + 3 + 3
   7 + 7 + 7   7 threes
   3 + 3 + 3 + 3 + 3 + 3 + 3   3 sevens
   7 twos   14

Chapter 18 Multiplication and Division **207**

6. A farmer has 16 chickens.
   He puts 8 chickens in a coop.
   How many coops does he need?

He needs ___2___ coops.

7. There are 20 seeds.
   Put an equal number of seeds in each pot.

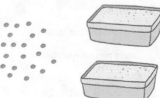

There are ___10___ seeds in each pot.

208 Chapter 18 Multiplication and Division

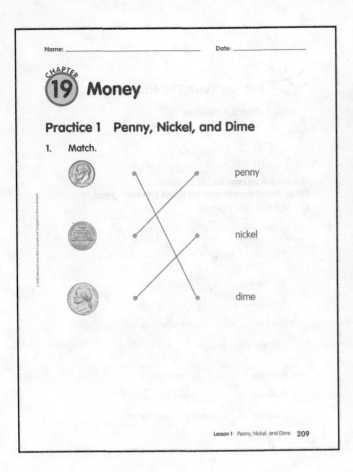

Name: _____ Date: _____

CHAPTER 19 Money

Practice 1 Penny, Nickel, and Dime

1. Match.

penny

nickel

dime

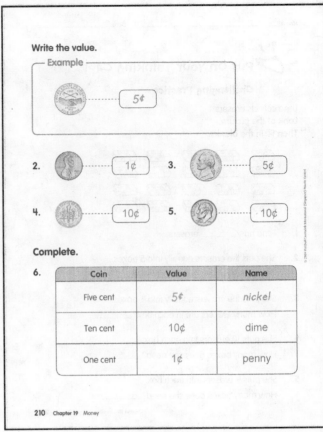

Write the value.

Example

5¢

2. 1¢   3. 5¢

4. 10¢   5. 10¢

Complete.

6.

Coin	Value	Name
Five cent	5¢	nickel
Ten cent	10¢	dime
One cent	1¢	penny

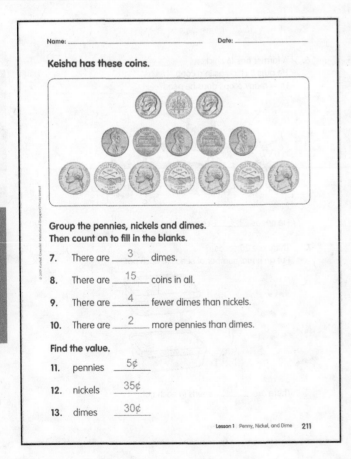

Name: _____ Date: _____

Keisha has these coins.

Group the pennies, nickels and dimes. Then count on to fill in the blanks.

7. There are ___3___ dimes.

8. There are ___15___ coins in all.

9. There are ___4___ fewer dimes than nickels.

10. There are ___2___ more pennies than dimes.

Find the value.

11. pennies ___5¢___

12. nickels ___35¢___

13. dimes ___30¢___

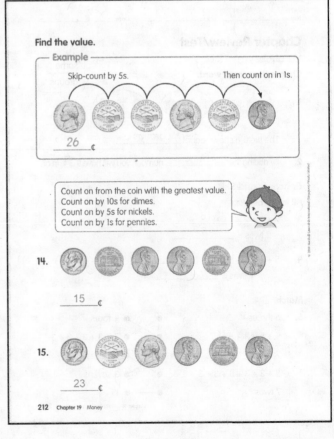

Find the value.

Example

Skip-count by 5s.   Then count on in 1s.

___26___ ¢

Count on from the coin with the greatest value.
Count on by 10s for dimes.
Count on by 5s for nickels.
Count on by 1s for pennies.

14. ___15___ ¢

15. ___23___ ¢

Solve the riddle.
Circle the correct coin.

--- Example ---

You need 10 of me
to make a dime.
What am I?

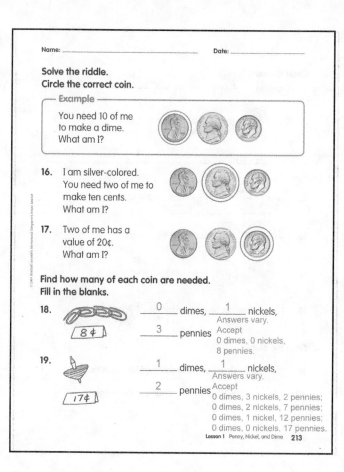

16. I am silver-colored.
You need two of me to
make ten cents.
What am I?

17. Two of me has a
value of 20¢.
What am I?

Find how many of each coin are needed.
Fill in the blanks.

18.
8¢
_0_ dimes, _1_ nickels,
_3_ pennies
Answers vary.
Accept
0 dimes, 0 nickels,
8 pennies.

19.
17¢
_1_ dimes, _1_ nickels,
_2_ pennies
Answers vary.
Accept
0 dimes, 3 nickels, 2 pennies;
0 dimes, 2 nickels, 7 pennies;
0 dimes, 1 nickel, 12 pennies;
0 dimes, 0 nickels, 17 pennies.

Lesson 1 Penny, Nickel, and Dime **213**

Find how many of each coin are needed.
Fill in the blanks.

Answers vary.
Accept

20.
22¢
_2_ dimes, _0_ nickels,
_2_ pennies

1 dime, 2 nickels, 2 pennies;
0 dimes, 4 nickels, 2 pennies;
0 dimes, 3 nickels, 7 pennies;
0 dimes, 2 nickels, 12 pennies;
0 dimes, 1 nickel, 17 pennies;
0 dimes, 0 nickels, 22 pennies.

Draw the coins to buy each thing.
Use pennies (1¢), nickels (5¢) and dimes (10¢).

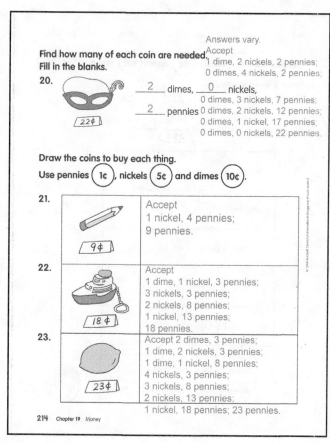

21. **9¢**	Accept 1 nickel, 4 pennies; 9 pennies.
22. **18¢**	Accept 1 dime, 1 nickel, 3 pennies; 3 nickels, 3 pennies; 2 nickels, 8 pennies; 1 nickel, 13 pennies; 18 pennies.
23. **23¢**	Accept 2 dimes, 3 pennies; 1 dime, 2 nickels, 3 pennies; 1 dime, 1 nickel, 8 pennies; 4 nickels, 3 pennies; 3 nickels, 8 pennies; 2 nickels, 13 pennies; 1 nickel, 18 pennies; 23 pennies.

214 Chapter 19 Money

Practice 2   Quarter
Fill in the blanks.

1.
This is a _quarter_.

Its value is _25_ ¢.

Complete.

2. Exchange 1 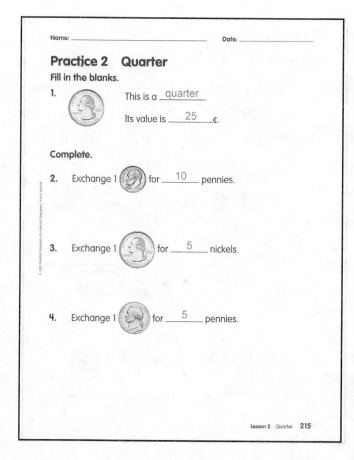 for _10_ pennies.

3. Exchange 1 for _5_ nickels.

4. Exchange 1 for _5_ pennies.

Lesson 2 Quarter **215**

Circle the coins to show the same value.

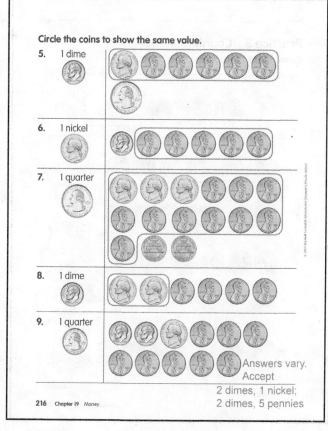

5. 1 dime

6. 1 nickel

7. 1 quarter

8. 1 dime

9. 1 quarter

Answers vary.
Accept
2 dimes, 1 nickel;
2 dimes, 5 pennies

216 Chapter 19 Money

Chapter 19

267

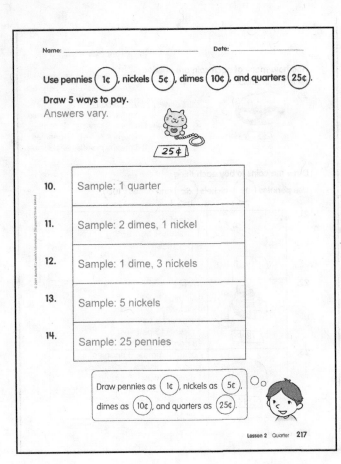

Name: _____ Date: _____

Use pennies (1¢), nickels (5¢), dimes (10¢), and quarters (25¢).
Draw 5 ways to pay.
Answers vary.

10.	Sample: 1 quarter
11.	Sample: 2 dimes, 1 nickel
12.	Sample: 1 dime, 3 nickels
13.	Sample: 5 nickels
14.	Sample: 25 pennies

Draw pennies as (1¢), nickels as (5¢),
dimes as (10¢), and quarters as (25¢).

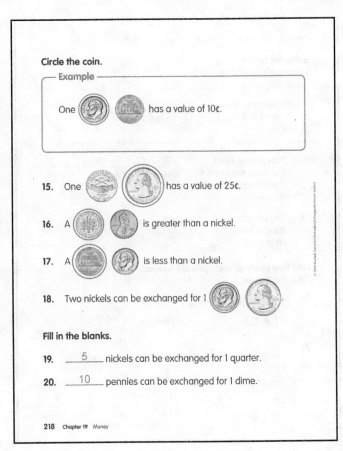

Circle the coin.

— Example —
One [dime] has a value of 10¢.

15. One [nickel] [quarter] has a value of 25¢.

16. A [dime] [penny] is greater than a nickel.

17. A [penny] [dime] is less than a nickel.

18. Two nickels can be exchanged for 1 [dime] [quarter]

Fill in the blanks.

19. ___5___ nickels can be exchanged for 1 quarter.

20. ___10___ pennies can be exchanged for 1 dime.

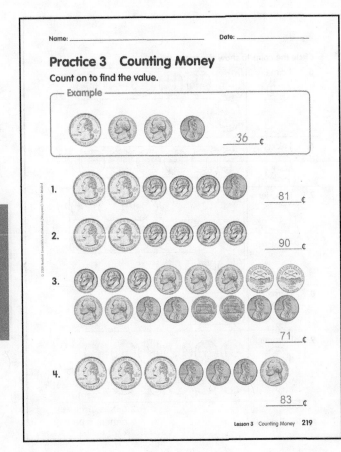

Name: _____ Date: _____

Practice 3   Counting Money

Count on to find the value.

— Example —
[coins] ___36___ ¢

1. [coins] ___81___ ¢

2. [coins] ___90___ ¢

3. [coins] ___71___ ¢

4. [coins] ___83___ ¢

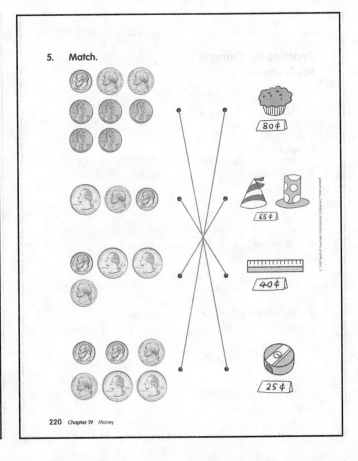

5. Match.

[muffin] 80¢

[party hat] 65¢

[ruler] 40¢

[pie] 25¢

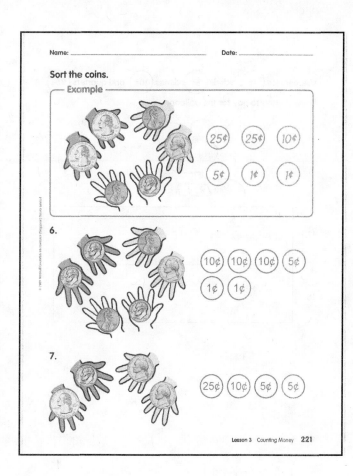

Name: _____   Date: _____

Sort the coins.

Example

25¢   25¢   10¢
5¢   1¢   1¢

6.

10¢ 10¢ 10¢ 5¢
1¢   1¢

7.

25¢ 10¢ 5¢ 5¢

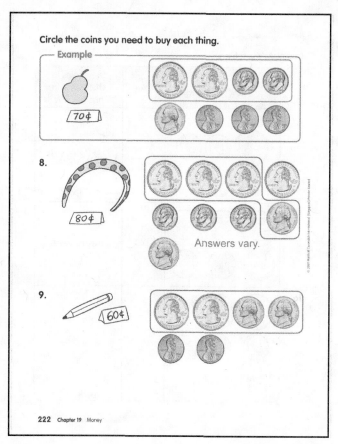

Circle the coins you need to buy each thing.

Example

70¢

8.

80¢

Answers vary.

9.

60¢

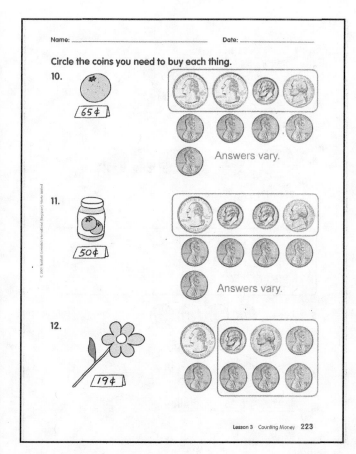

Name: _____   Date: _____

Circle the coins you need to buy each thing.

10.

65¢

Answers vary.

11.

50¢

Answers vary.

12.

19¢

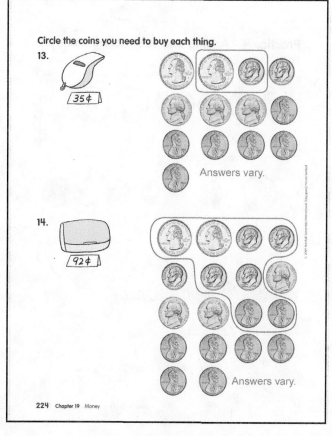

Circle the coins you need to buy each thing.

13.

35¢

Answers vary.

14.

92¢

Answers vary.

Chapter 19

269

Name: _____ **Date:** _____

Complete the table.

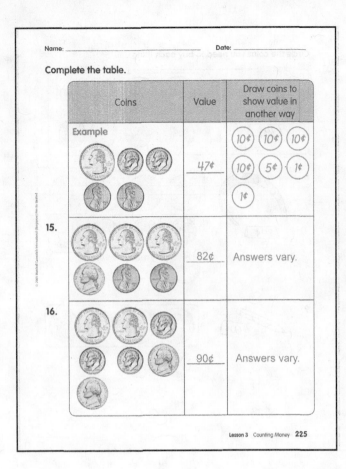

Coins	Value	Draw coins to show value in another way
Example	47¢	10¢ 10¢ 10¢ / 10¢ 5¢ 1¢ / 1¢
15.	82¢	Answers vary.
16.	90¢	Answers vary.

Lesson 3   Counting Money   **225**

Use pennies ①¢ , nickels ⑤¢ , dimes ⑩¢ , and quarters ㉕¢ .
Draw 2 ways to pay for the balloon.

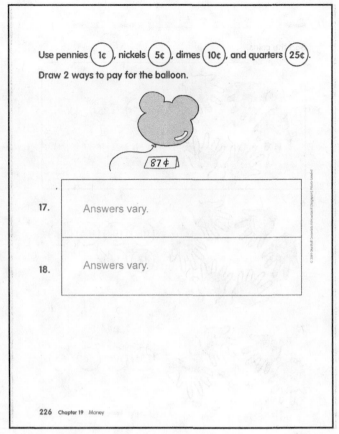

87¢

17. Answers vary.

18. Answers vary.

226   Chapter 19   Money

Name: _____ **Date:** _____

Practice 4   Adding and Subtracting Money

Add.

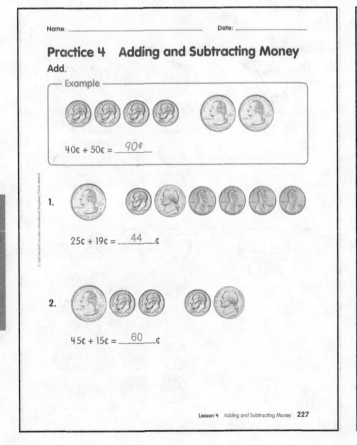

Example

40¢ + 50¢ = __90¢__

1. 25¢ + 19¢ = __44__ ¢

2. 45¢ + 15¢ = __60__ ¢

Lesson 4   Adding and Subtracting Money   **227**

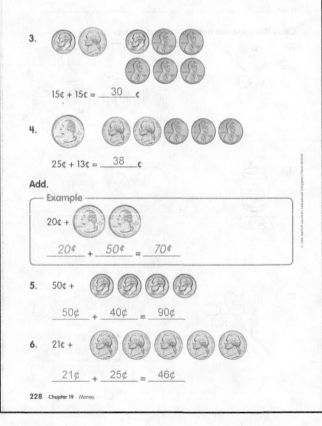

3. 15¢ + 15¢ = __30__ ¢

4. 25¢ + 13¢ = __38__ ¢

Add.

Example

20¢ +

__20¢__ + __50¢__ = __70¢__

5. 50¢ +

__50¢__ + __40¢__ = __90¢__

6. 21¢ +

__21¢__ + __25¢__ = __46¢__

228   Chapter 19   Money

---

www.harcourtschoolsupply.com

270

Workbook Answers: Chapter 19
Math in Focus Homeschool Answer Key, Grade 1

Name: _____ Date: _____

Add.

7. 8¢ +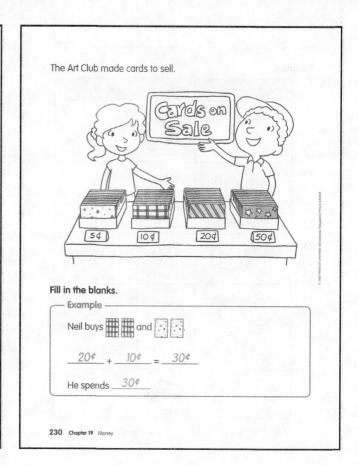

___8¢___ + ___30¢___ = ___38¢___

8. 17¢ +

___17¢___ + ___44¢___ = ___61¢___

9. 13¢ +

___13¢___ + ___51¢___ = ___64¢___

10. 6¢ +

___6¢___ + ___81¢___ = ___87¢___

11. 38¢ +

___38¢___ + ___40¢___ = ___78¢___

The Art Club made cards to sell.

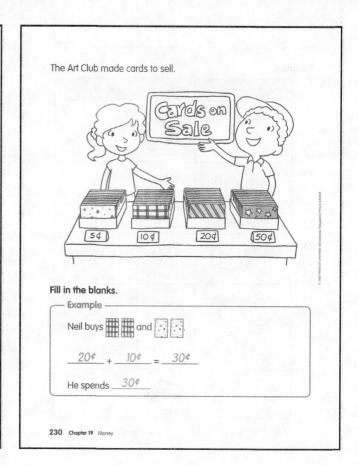

Fill in the blanks.

— Example —

Neil buys ▦▦ and ⠿⠿

___20¢___ + ___10¢___ = ___30¢___

He spends ___30¢___

Name: _____ Date: _____

12. Zack buys ▨ and ▦.

___20¢___ + ___10¢___ = ___30¢___

He spends ___30¢___.

13. Tara buys ▦, ⠿ ⠿, and ▨ ▨.

___10¢___ + ___10¢___ + ___40¢___ = ___60¢___

She spends ___60¢___.

14. Kerrie buys ⠿ ▦, and ⠿.

___50¢___ + ___10¢___ + ___5¢___ = ___65¢___

She spends ___65¢___.

15. How much do Zack and Neil spend in all?

___30¢___ + ___30¢___ = ___60¢___

They spend ___60¢___ in all.

Subtract.

16. 55¢ – 20¢ = ___35¢___   17. 45¢ – 15¢ = ___30¢___

18. 60¢ – 5¢ = ___55¢___   19. 99¢ – 35¢ = ___64¢___

Subtract.

— Example —

50¢ from 60¢

___60¢___ – ___50¢___ = ___10¢___

20. 35¢ from 50¢

___50¢___ – ___35¢___ = ___15¢___

21. 25¢ from 70¢

___70¢___ – ___25¢___ = ___45¢___

22. 60¢ from 90¢

___90¢___ – ___60¢___ = ___30¢___

23. 35¢ from 95¢

___95¢___ – ___35¢___ = ___60¢___

Chapter 19

Complete.

You Have	You Buy	Your Change
Example 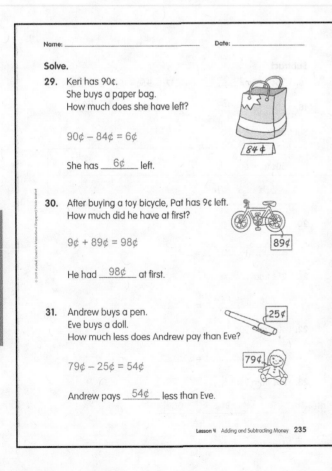	stamp 5¢	25¢ - 5¢ = 20¢
24.	muffin 50¢	55¢ − 50¢ = 5¢
25.	toy scooter 30¢	50¢ − 30¢ = 20¢
26.	kite 80¢	85¢ − 80¢ = 5¢
27.	whistle 45¢	50¢ − 45¢ = 5¢

Solve.

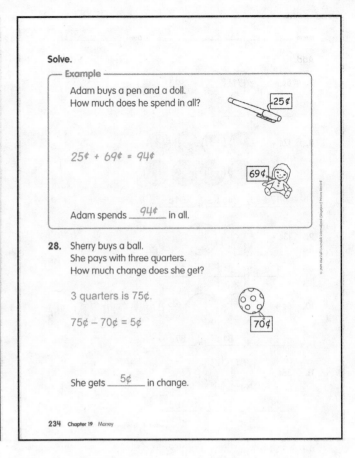

Example

Adam buys a pen and a doll.
How much does he spend in all?

25¢

69¢

25¢ + 69¢ = 94¢

Adam spends ___94¢___ in all.

28. Sherry buys a ball.
She pays with three quarters.
How much change does she get?

3 quarters is 75¢.

75¢ − 70¢ = 5¢

70¢

She gets ___5¢___ in change.

Solve.

29. Keri has 90¢.
She buys a paper bag.
How much does she have left?

84¢

90¢ − 84¢ = 6¢

She has ___6¢___ left.

30. After buying a toy bicycle, Pat has 9¢ left.
How much did he have at first?

9¢ + 89¢ = 98¢

89¢

He had ___98¢___ at first.

31. Andrew buys a pen.
Eve buys a doll.
How much less does Andrew pay than Eve?

25¢

79¢

79¢ − 25¢ = 54¢

Andrew pays ___54¢___ less than Eve.

Solve.

32. Derrick has 32¢.
He wants to buy a toy bicycle.
How much more does he need?

89¢

89¢ − 32¢ = 57¢

Derrick needs ___57¢___ more.

33. How much more is the pencil than the eraser?

60¢ − 25¢ = 35¢

60¢

25¢

The pencil is ___35¢___ more
than the eraser.

34. Brad spends 99¢ during break time.
What does he buy?

65¢ + 34¢ = 99¢

drink sandwich apple
55¢   65¢   34¢

He buys the ___sandwich___ and the ___apple___

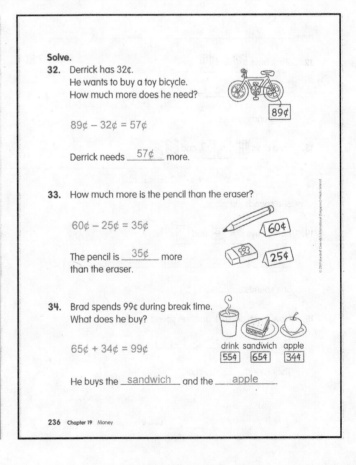

Chapter 19

Name: _____ Date: _____

Gary and Fina are at the cafeteria.

orange	crackers	cereal	muffin
30¢	20¢	50¢	65¢

Fill in the blanks.

35. Gary buys a bowl of cereal and crackers.
    How much does he spend in all? __70¢__

36. Gary uses 50¢ to buy an orange.
    How much change does he get? __20¢__

37. Fina uses two quarters to buy an orange.
    How much change does she get? __20¢__

38. Gary buys a muffin and has 25¢ left.
    How much did he have at first? __90¢__

39. Fina has 3 dimes.
    She buys her food and has 10¢ left.
    What does she buy? __crackers__

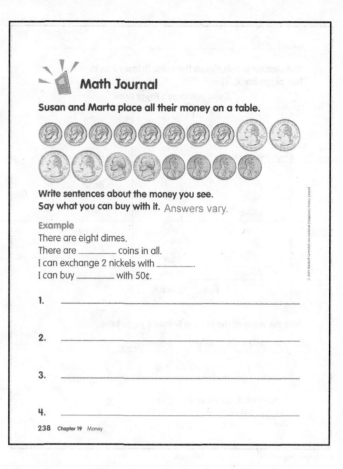

Math Journal

Susan and Marta place all their money on a table.

Write sentences about the money you see.
Say what you can buy with it. Answers vary.

Example
There are eight dimes.
There are _____ coins in all.
I can exchange 2 nickels with _____.
I can buy _____ with 50¢.

1. _____

2. _____

3. _____

4. _____

Name: _____ Date: _____

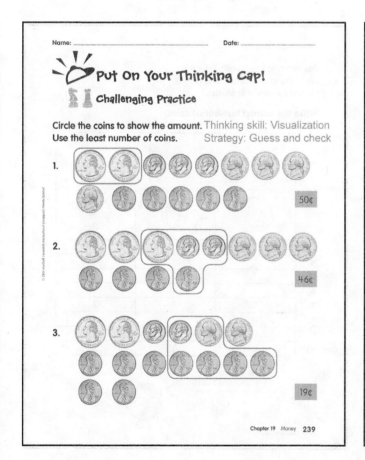

Put On Your Thinking Cap!

Challenging Practice

Circle the coins to show the amount. Thinking skill: Visualization
Use the least number of coins. Strategy: Guess and check

1. `50¢`

2. `46¢`

3. `19¢`

Thinking skill: Comparing
Strategy: Act it out

Solve.
Does Jordan have enough money?

Example	
Jordon	☐ Yes. He will get change.
	☑ No. He needs __30¢__ more.

4. ☑ Yes. He will get change.
   ☐ No. He needs _____ more.

5. ☑ Yes. He will get change.
   ☐ No. He needs _____ more.

6. ☐ Yes. He will get change.
   ☑ No. He needs __24¢__ more.

Chapter 19

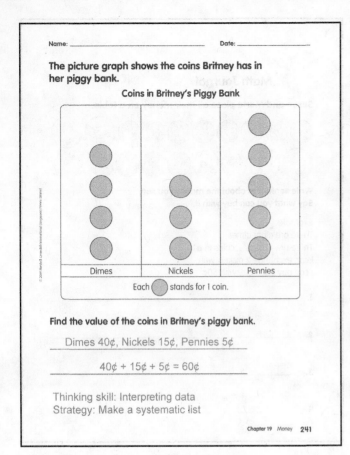

Name: _____ Date: _____

The picture graph shows the coins Britney has in her piggy bank.

Coins in Britney's Piggy Bank

| Dimes | Nickels | Pennies |

Each ⬤ stands for 1 coin.

Find the value of the coins in Britney's piggy bank.

Dimes 40¢, Nickels 15¢, Pennies 5¢

40¢ + 15¢ + 5¢ = 60¢

Thinking skill: Interpreting data
Strategy: Make a systematic list

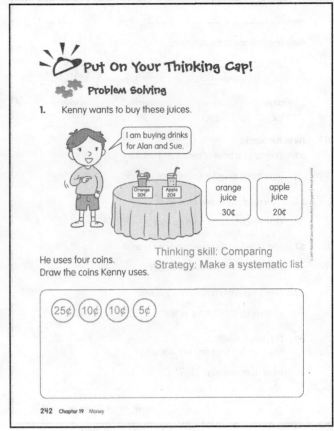

Put On Your Thinking Cap!

Problem Solving

1. Kenny wants to buy these juices.

I am buying drinks for Alan and Sue.

Orange 30¢ Apple 20¢

| orange juice 30¢ | apple juice 20¢ |

He uses four coins.
Draw the coins Kenny uses.

Thinking skill: Comparing
Strategy: Make a systematic list

25¢ 10¢ 10¢ 5¢

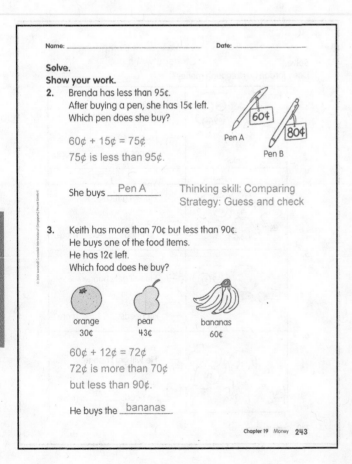

Name: _____ Date: _____

Solve.
Show your work.

2. Brenda has less than 95¢.
After buying a pen, she has 15¢ left.
Which pen does she buy?

Pen A 60¢
Pen B 80¢

60¢ + 15¢ = 75¢

75¢ is less than 95¢.

She buys ___Pen A___

Thinking skill: Comparing
Strategy: Guess and check

3. Keith has more than 70¢ but less than 90¢.
He buys one of the food items.
He has 12¢ left.
Which food does he buy?

orange 30¢   pear 43¢   bananas 60¢

60¢ + 12¢ = 72¢

72¢ is more than 70¢
but less than 90¢.

He buys the ___bananas___

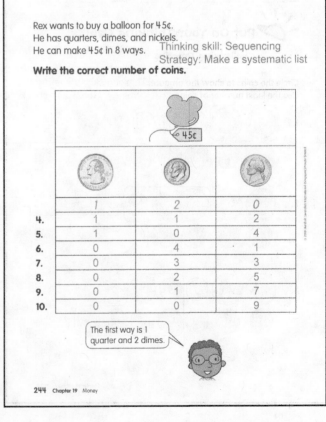

Rex wants to buy a balloon for 45¢.
He has quarters, dimes, and nickels.
He can make 45¢ in 8 ways.

Thinking skill: Sequencing
Strategy: Make a systematic list

Write the correct number of coins.

45¢

	quarter	dime	nickel
	1	2	0
4.	1	1	2
5.	1	0	4
6.	0	4	1
7.	0	3	3
8.	0	2	5
9.	0	1	7
10.	0	0	9

The first way is 1 quarter and 2 dimes.

Chapter Review/Test

Vocabulary

Choose the correct word.

quarter
less
penny
dime
nickels

1. A <u>dime</u> has a value of 10¢.

2. A <u>quarter</u> has a value of 25¢.

3. A dime is <u>less</u> than a quarter.

4. A nickel is greater than a <u>penny</u>.

5. 2 <u>nickels</u> have a value of 10¢.

Concepts and Skills

Identify each coin.

6. <u>dime</u>

7. <u>nickel</u>

8. <u>penny</u>

9. <u>quarter</u>

Fill in the blanks. Answers vary.

Exchange	Accept	For
10. 1 quarter	1 dime, 3 nickels; 0 dimes, 5 nickels. <u>2</u> dimes, <u>1</u> nickel
11. 1 dime	<u>2</u> nickels, <u>0</u> pennies Accept 1 nickel, 5 pennies; 0 nickels, 10 pennies.

Count the money.

12. is <u>55</u> ¢.

13. is <u>58</u> ¢.

Add or subtract.

14. 80¢ + 15¢ = <u>95¢</u>

15. 38¢ − 19¢ = <u>19¢</u>

Problem Solving

Solve.

16. Zack has 64¢. He buys a pencil for 25¢. How much does he have left?

   64¢ − 25¢ = 39¢

   He has <u>39¢</u> left.

17. Wendy wants to buy a notebook for 52¢, a bun for 19¢, and a drink for 23¢. How much does she spend?

   52¢ + 19¢ + 23¢ = 94¢

   She spends <u>94¢</u>.

Name: _____ Date: _____

Cumulative Review
for Chapters 18 and 19

Concepts and Skills

Count the number of groups.
Count the number in each group.
Then fill in the blanks.

1.

$6 + 6 + 6 + 6 =$ ___24___

4 sixes = ___24___

There are ___24___ starfishes in all.

2.

$4 + 4 + 4 + 4 =$ ___16___

4 fours = ___16___

There are ___16___ shrimps in all.

Look at the pictures.
Then fill in the blanks.

3.
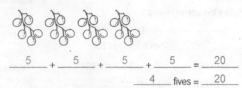

___5___ + ___5___ + ___5___ + ___5___ = ___20___

___4___ fives = ___20___

4.

There are ___18___ pineapple cubes in all.

There are ___6___ sticks.

There are ___3___ pineapple cubes in each stick.

Solve.

5. There are 12 sandwiches.
They are shared equally by 3 children.

Each child gets ___4___ sandwiches.

Name: _____ Date: _____

Solve.

6. There are 16 toy soldiers.
Jamal packs them equally into 4 boxes.

There are ___4___ toy soldiers in each box.

7. Timmy puts 6 pillows equally into 3 groups.

Each group has ___2___ pillows.

8. There are 9 oranges.
Circle groups of 3.

There are ___3___ groups of 3.

Look at the pictures.
Then fill in the blanks.

Maria has 12 flowers.

9. She puts the flowers equally into 3 vases.

There are ___4___ flowers in each vase.

10. She puts 2 flowers in each vase.

She needs ___6___ vases.

11. She puts 4 flowers in each vase.

She needs ___3___ vases.

Write the value.

12.

5 ¢

13.

3 ¢

276

Chapters 18-19 Review

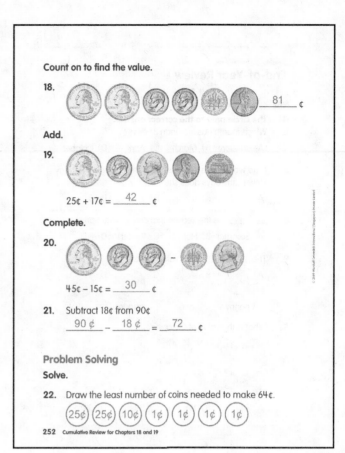

Name: _____ **Date:** _____

Fill in the blanks.

14. Find how many of each coin are needed.

    _1_ dimes _1_ nickels

    _2_ pennies

    [17¢]

15. 1 quarter = _5_ nickels

Circle the coins to show the same value.

16. 1 quarter

    or 2 dimes and 5 pennies

Circle the coins that are *not* dimes.

17.

Count on to find the value.

18. _81_ ¢

Add.

19.

    25¢ + 17¢ = _42_ ¢

Complete.

20.

    45¢ − 15¢ = _30_ ¢

21. Subtract 18¢ from 90¢

    _90_ ¢ − _18_ ¢ = _72_ ¢

Problem Solving

Solve.

22. Draw the least number of coins needed to make 64¢.

    (25¢) (25¢) (10¢) (1¢) (1¢) (1¢) (1¢)

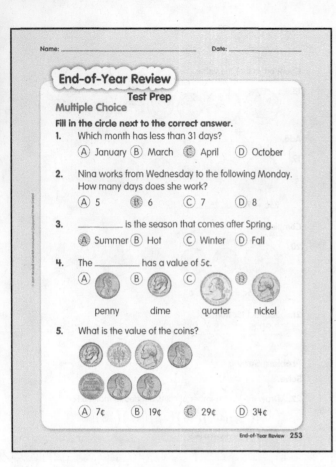

End-of-Year Review
Test Prep
Multiple Choice
Fill in the circle next to the correct answer.

1. Which month has less than 31 days?
   (A) January (B) March (C) April (D) October

2. Nina works from Wednesday to the following Monday. How many days does she work?
   (A) 5 (B) 6 (C) 7 (D) 8

3. _____ is the season that comes after Spring.
   (A) Summer (B) Hot (C) Winter (D) Fall

4. The _____ has a value of 5¢.
   (A) penny (B) dime (C) quarter (D) nickel

5. What is the value of the coins?
   (A) 7¢ (B) 19¢ (C) 29¢ (D) 34¢

End-of-Year Review 253

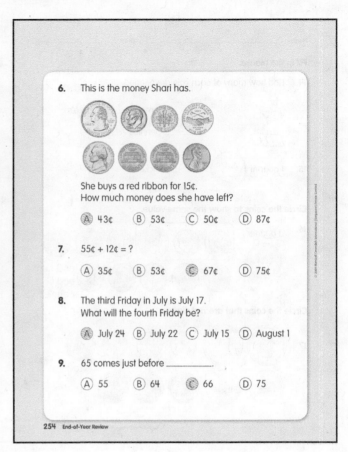

6. This is the money Shari has.

   She buys a red ribbon for 15¢.
   How much money does she have left?
   (A) 43¢ (B) 53¢ (C) 50¢ (D) 87¢

7. 55¢ + 12¢ = ?
   (A) 35¢ (B) 53¢ (C) 67¢ (D) 75¢

8. The third Friday in July is July 17. What will the fourth Friday be?
   (A) July 24 (B) July 22 (C) July 15 (D) August 1

9. 65 comes just before _____.
   (A) 55 (B) 64 (C) 66 (D) 75

254 End-of-Year Review

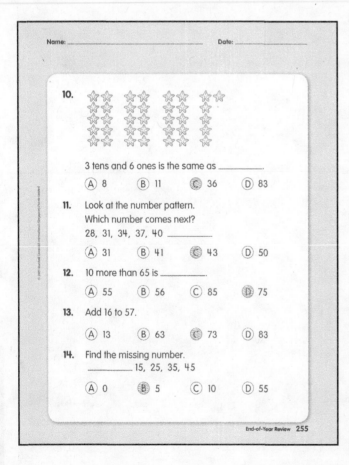

10. 3 tens and 6 ones is the same as _____.
    (A) 8 (B) 11 (C) 36 (D) 83

11. Look at the number pattern. Which number comes next?
    28, 31, 34, 37, 40 _____
    (A) 31 (B) 41 (C) 43 (D) 50

12. 10 more than 65 is _____.
    (A) 55 (B) 56 (C) 85 (D) 75

13. Add 16 to 57.
    (A) 13 (B) 63 (C) 73 (D) 83

14. Find the missing number.
    _____ 15, 25, 35, 45
    (A) 0 (B) 5 (C) 10 (D) 55

End-of-Year Review 255

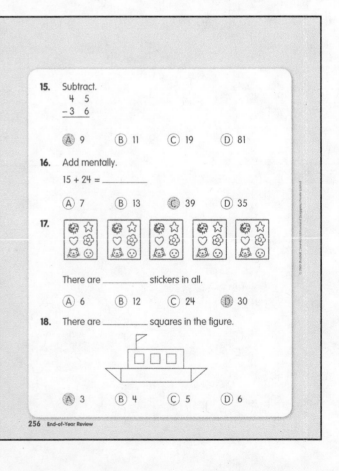

15. Subtract.
    $\begin{array}{r} 4\ 5 \\ -\ 3\ 6 \\ \hline \end{array}$
    (A) 9 (B) 11 (C) 19 (D) 81

16. Add mentally.
    15 + 24 = _____
    (A) 7 (B) 13 (C) 39 (D) 35

17. There are _____ stickers in all.
    (A) 6 (B) 12 (C) 24 (D) 30

18. There are _____ squares in the figure.
    (A) 3 (B) 4 (C) 5 (D) 6

256 End-of-Year Review

278

Name: _____ Date: _____

19.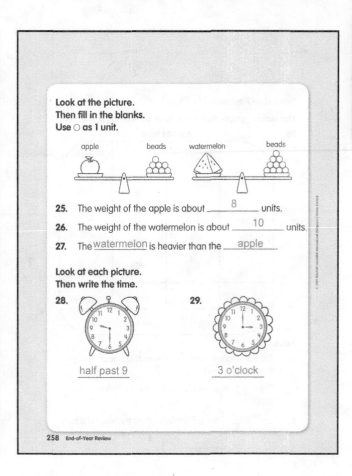

The pencil is about _____ —○ long.

(A) 8   (B) 2   (C) 6   (D) 4

Short Answer

Write the number in words.

20. 11 _____eleven_____   **21.** 87 _____eighty-seven_____

Write the number.

22. fifty-four _____54_____

23. twenty-six _____26_____

Look at the pictures.
Then fill in the blanks.

24. Order the bags from lightest to heaviest.

_____Bag B_____   _____Bag C_____   _____Bag A_____
lightest

End-of-Year Review 257

Look at the picture.
Then fill in the blanks.
Use ○ as 1 unit.

apple   beads   watermelon   beads

25. The weight of the apple is about _____8_____ units.

26. The weight of the watermelon is about _____10_____ units.

27. The _____watermelon_____ is heavier than the _____apple_____.

Look at each picture.
Then write the time.

28. _____half past 9_____   **29.** _____3 o'clock_____

258 End-of-Year Review

Name: _____ Date: _____

30. Look at the picture.
Then write the number in words.

_____fifty-seven_____

31. Order the numbers from greatest to least.

| 75 | 41 | 18 | 29 |

_____75_____ , _____41_____ , _____29_____ , _____18_____
greatest

Circle the two numbers that add up to 4 tens and 4 ones.

32. 24   (27)   51   30   (17)

Add the 2nd and 5th numbers.

33.

37	20	19	62	45	83	51
1st						

_____65_____

34. Subtract 6 tens 4 ones
from 8 tens 2 ones.

_____18_____

End-of-Year Review 259

Name the shape that is shaded.

35.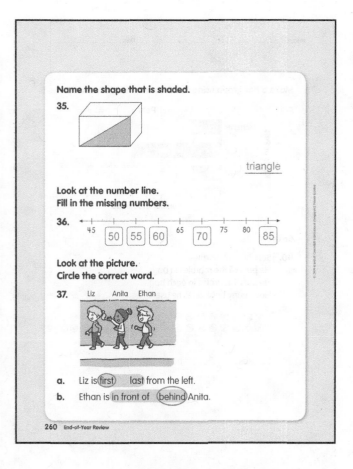

_____triangle_____

Look at the number line.
Fill in the missing numbers.

36.

45 [50] [55] [60] 65 [70] 75 80 [85]

Look at the picture.
Circle the correct word.

37. Liz   Anita   Ethan

a. Liz is (first)   last from the left.

b. Ethan is in front of   (behind) Anita.

260 End-of-Year Review

Workbook Answers: End-of-Year Review
Math in Focus Homeschool Answer Key, Grade 1

Name: _____ Date: _____

Extended Response

The picture graph shows the favorite food of 12 children.

38.

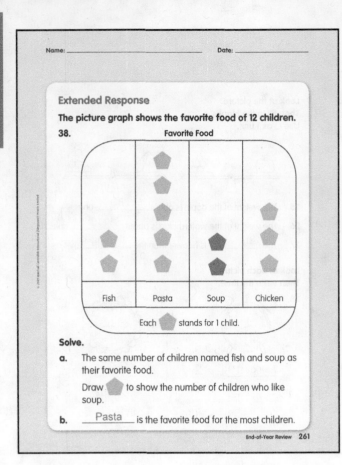

Favorite Food

Fish | Pasta | Soup | Chicken

Each ⬠ stands for 1 child.

Solve.

a. The same number of children named fish and soup as their favorite food.

Draw ⬠ to show the number of children who like soup.

b. ____Pasta____ is the favorite food for the most children.

Ten families live on the same street.
Every family has one pet.
The picture shows their pets.

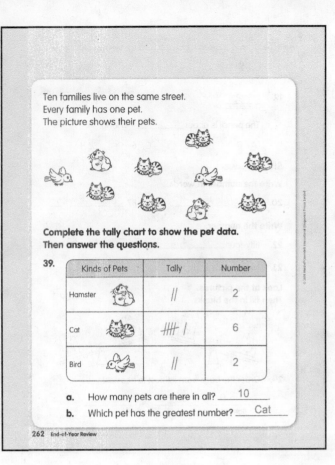

Complete the tally chart to show the pet data.
Then answer the questions.

39.

Kinds of Pets		Tally	Number
Hamster		//	2
Cat		⊬⊬ /	6
Bird		//	2

a. How many pets are there in all? ____10____

b. Which pet has the greatest number? ____Cat____

Name: _____ Date: _____

Make a bar graph using the data from the tally chart.

c.

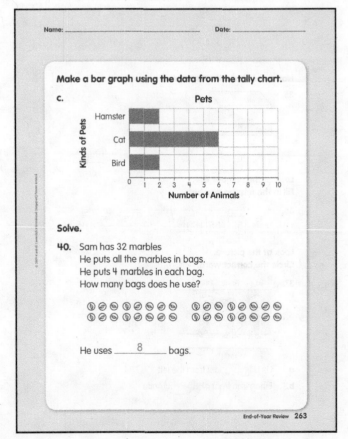

Pets

Kinds of Pets — Hamster, Cat, Bird
Number of Animals — 0 1 2 3 4 5 6 7 8 9 10

Solve.

40. Sam has 32 marbles
He puts all the marbles in bags.
He puts 4 marbles in each bag.
How many bags does he use?

He uses ____8____ bags.